WRITE AND WRITE AGAIN

WRITE AND WRITE AGAIN

A Worktext
with Readings

Jane Paznik-Bondarin

Milton Baxter

Borough of Manhattan Community College, CUNY

Macmillan Publishing Company

New York

Macmillan Publishing Company
866 Third Avenue, New York, New York 10022

Collier Macmillan Canada, Inc.

Library of Congress Cataloging-in-Publication Data

Paznik-Bondarin, Jane.
  Write and write again.

  Includes index.
  1. English language—Rhetoric. 2. English
language—Grammar—   . 3. College readers.
I. Baxter, Milton. II. Title
PE1408.P34 1987   808′.042   86–23909
ISBN 0–02–393220–1

Printing: 2 3 4 5 6 7 8   Year: 8 9 0 1 2 3 4 5

ISBN 0-02-393220-1

ACKNOWLEDGMENTS

The authors gratefully acknowledge permission to reprint the following copyrighted material:

Angoff, Charles, "Alte Bobbe," from *When I Was a Boy in Boston*. Copyright © 1974 by Mrs. Charles Angoff.

"A Kitchen" by James Baldwin from *Go Tell It on the Mountain*. Copyright © 1952, 1953 by James Baldwin. Reprinted by permission of Doubleday & Company, Inc.

Dell, Floyd, "When I Discovered I Was Poor," from *The Homecoming*. Copyright © 1933, Holt, Rinehart & Winston, Inc.

"A Mexican House," from *Barrio Boy* by Ernesto Galarza © 1971 by University of Notre Dame Press. Reprinted by permission.

Hanson, Elizabeth, "Blessings of Emptiness." Reprinted by permission of *The National Observer*, © Dow Jones & Company, Inc. 1975. All Rights Reserved.

"Salvation" from *The Big Sea* by Langston Hughes. Copyright 1940 by Langston Hughes. Copyright renewed © 1968 by Arna Bontemps and George Houston Bass. Reprinted by permission of Hill and Wang, a division of Farrar, Straus and Giroux, Inc.

Random House College Dictionary, selected definitions and list of consultants. Reprinted by permission from *The Random House College Dictionary*, Revised Edition, Copyright © 1984 by Random House, Inc.

Safire, William, "Genovese to Goetz," from *The New York Times*, April 8, 1985. Copyright © 1985 by The New York Times Company. Reprinted by permission.

Syfres, Judy, "Why I Want a Wife," from *Ms*, December 1971.

Thurber, James, "The Bear Who Let It Alone," from *Fables for Our Time*. Copyright © 1964, Mrs. James Thurber. Published by Harper & Row Publishing Co., New York, 1954.

Van den Haag, Ernest, "Smokers Have Rights, Too," from *The New York Times*, April 9, 1985. Copyright © 1985 by The New York Times Company. Reprinted by permission.

Jim Villas's "Fried Chicken" first appeared in *Esquire*, December 1975. Copyright © 1975 by James Villas. Reprinted by permission of the Robin Straus Agency, Inc.

Webster's New World Dictionary entries: *Webster's New World Dictionary*, 2nd College Edition. Copyright © 1970, 1972, 1974, 1976, 1978, 1980, 1982 by Simon & Schuster. Reprinted by permission of Simon & Schuster, Inc.

X, Malcolm, and Haley, Alex, "Language," from *The Autobiography of Malcolm X*. Copyright © 1965 by Random House, Inc. Published by Random House, Inc., 1965.

Zinsser, William, "The Transaction," from *On Writing Well*, Third Edition. Published by Harper & Row Publishing Co., 1985. Copyright © 1976, 1980, and 1985 by William K. Zinsser. Reprinted by permission of the author.

This book is dedicated to the loving memory of my grandmother, Ethel Baxter, my mother, Josephine Baxter, and my father, William Baxter.

M.B.

And to Devorah Abigail, Arley, and the Pazniks, Philmuses, Levines, and Bondarins.

J.P.-B.

PREFACE

For years we looked for a book we wanted to teach from. We wanted a book that treated our students like the intelligent adults they are. We wanted a book that made our students more aware of the language they used and wanted to use. We wanted a book that demonstrated the writing process professional writers use and that supplied within one set of covers interesting things to read and instruction about the sticky points of standard English grammar. Never having found that book, we wrote one ourselves, hoping it would do what we think is most important.

Write and Write Again: A Worktext with Readings is a book for basic writers. In it we use the process approach to writing that professional writers use. That is, we help students reach into their own experience to find ideas they want to set down on paper; we help students rethink their pieces based on their audience and purpose, and we propose systematic guidance for rewriting; we also review aspects of standard English grammar and sentence structure that will help students proofread their work.

Writers, of course, do all three things at once: set down ideas, rewrite, and proofread. They are always going back and forth—inserting a new idea here, moving a thought from one place to another, polishing a phrase there. Writing is a chaotic process. For teaching purposes we have tried to simplify it and talk about the writing process in three stages: setting down ideas, rewriting ideas, proofreading. Our students have found this method helpful, even though it is clear from their drafts that, once they get the hang of it, they, too, are constantly moving back and forth from one part of the process to another. Each chapter of *Write and Write Again* "walks" a student through the creation and polishing of an essay.

Basic writers often do not trust their understanding of their own language or reading. We attempt to build on students' intuitions about spoken language to increase understanding of the demands and possibilities of written language.

Each chapter of *Write and Write Again* contains many opportunities for students to read and write. Each chapter begins with a short, interesting passage. We follow each of the ten reading passages with questions and information that enhance students' abilities to read "on the line," "between the lines," and "beyond the lines." The early questions build confidence in literal understanding; the later ones ask students to stretch their minds and relate their own lives to the text. A vocabulary section helps students integrate new words into their own writing and points out interesting features of the language.

Because the writing process is the heart of the book, each chapter guides the students through the stages of writing an essay, including exercises and strategies that focus their rewriting. Each chapter also contains instruction and exercises in grammar, spelling, and punctuation to help students with the proofreading stage of the writing process.

Chapter 1, "Learning the Writing Process," introduces students to the stages in the writing process and asks them to compose an essay by working through the steps of the process. We introduce students to free writing and focused writing as ways of producing a first draft. Chapter 2, "Choosing Your Writing Voice," helps students to distinguish between written and oral language by using the dictionary to discuss language variation. Chapter 3, "Writing a Narrative: Telling What Happened," shows students how to read and write narratives with effective detail and order. Chapter 4, "Writing a Narrative: Making a Point," adds a discussion of theme and topic sentence to the discussion of narratives. In Chapter 5, "Describing a Place: Showing Versus Telling," students learn about descriptive words that "show" rather than "tell" and work on various strategies involving spatial order for organizing their ideas. In Chapter 6, "Describing a Person: Making a Point," students learn to organize their details around a dominant impression or theme.

In Chapter 7, "Giving Directions," we introduce expository writing. Students read and write process papers and become more aware of using explicit details and of sequencing ideas. Chapter 8, "Defining," illustrates how to clarify by extended definition. Chapter 9, "Comparing, Contrasting, and Giving Examples," presents strategies to help students organize and develop their ideas by examining and explicating similarities and differences. In Chapter 10, "Taking a Stand," students learn to develop an "arguable thesis" and to support it.

An Instructor's Manual for the text is also available. The manual offers practical suggestions for teaching with the text, strategies for using the text in different courses, and answers to selected exercises.

Throughout our years of teaching, we have learned a great deal from our students. We hope we have helped them become better writers; we know they have helped us and continue to help us become better and more sensitive teachers.

Besides our students, we are grateful for the continuing encouragement of our colleagues in the English Department and the Writing Center at Borough of Manhattan Community College, whose commitment to finding new ways to teach writing is very strong. We are indebted to our editors, Paul O'Connell, Jennifer Crewe, Barbara Heinssen and Eben Ludlow. We gratefully acknowledge our debt to Ron Harris, our production editor, and to Judith Longo (Ocean County College) and Audrey J. Roth (Miami-Dade Community College), who reviewed the manuscript. Our friend and colleague Georgia S. Dunbar gave us invaluable assistance on the manuscript and thoughtful suggestions for alternative ways of using the book.

Most of all, we thank our families—Arley and Devorah; Maxine, Eric, and Gerard—who have allowed us time to work and supported us throughout. We're grateful that Arley Bondarin, Kathy Sloane, and Barbara Smith have allowed their photographs to be shown in the text.

More than any other person, we thank Arley Bondarin for his prodigious efforts on our behalf. In every phase of the writing, rewriting, and production, his professional judgment and good sense were invaluable aids to reworking our ideas and words.

J. P.-B.
M. B.

CONTENTS

3 WRITING A NARRATIVE: TELLING WHAT HAPPENED 87

4 WRITING A NARRATIVE: MAKING A POINT 127

5 DESCRIBING A PLACE: SHOWING VERSUS TELLING   175

Learning the Writing Process

1

READING

Pre means "before" and *view* means "look." The preview questions point out certain words or phrases that will help you focus on the ideas in the essay that follows. They also ask you to look at the way in which the essay is written.

As you read "The Transaction" by William Zinsser, look for information that answers these questions:

1. What does Dr. Brock think about writing?
2. What does Zinsser think about writing?
3. Do all writers work in the same way?
4. What makes writing good?
5. Did you like reading about Zinsser's experience? Was the essay more interesting because it was about something that happened to the author?
6. Do you like to read the exact words someone uses? Is the use of "direct quotations" effective?

Notes

E. B. White (1899–1985). American writer of essays and poetry. He also wrote children's books, among them *Charlotte's Web.*

James Thurber (1894–1961). American writer and humorist; one of his essays, "The Bear Who Let It Alone," appears in this book.

Walden Pond. A place in Concord, Massachusetts, where philosopher Henry David Thoreau composed *Walden,* an essay about simplifying life.

The Transaction
William Zinsser

William Zinsser is an American writer, teacher, editor, and critic. He has written for the New York Times *and taught at Yale University. This essay is from his book* On Writing Well.

(1) Five or six years ago a school in Connecticut held "a day devoted to the arts," and I was asked if I would come and talk about writing as a

vocation. When I arrived I found that a second speaker had been invited—Dr. Brock (as I'll call him), a surgeon who had recently begun to write and had sold some stories to national magazines. He was going to talk about writing as an avocation. That made us a panel, and we sat down to face a crowd of student newspaper editors and reporters, English teachers and parents, all eager to learn the secrets of our glamorous work.

(2) Dr. Brock was dressed in a bright red jacket, looking vaguely Bohemian, as authors are supposed to look, and the first question went to him. What is it like to be a writer?

(3) He said it was tremendous fun. Coming home from an arduous day at the hospital, he would go straight to his yellow pad and write his tensions away. The words just flowed. It was easy.

(4) I then said that writing wasn't easy and it wasn't fun. It was hard and lonely, and the words seldom just flowed.

(5) Next Dr. Brock was asked if it was important to rewrite. Absolutely not, he said. "Let it all hang out," and whatever form the sentences take will reflect the writer at his most natural.

(6) I then said that rewriting is the essence of writing. I pointed out that professional writers rewrite their sentences repeatedly and they rewrite what they have rewritten. I mentioned that E. B. White and James Thurber were known to rewrite their pieces eight or nine times.

(7) "What do you do on days when it isn't going well?" Dr. Brock was asked. He said he just stopped writing and put the work aside for a day when it would go better.

(8) I then said that the professional writer must establish a daily schedule and stick to it. I said that writing is a craft, not an art, and that the man who runs away from his craft because he lacks inspiration is fooling himself. He is also going broke.

(9) "What if you're feeling depressed or unhappy?" a student asked. "Won't that affect your writing?"

(10) Probably it will, Dr. Brock replied. Go fishing. Take a walk.

(11) Probably it won't, I said. If your job is to write everyday, you learn to do it like any other job.

(12) A student asked if we found it useful to circulate in the literary world. Dr. Brock said that he was greatly enjoying his new life as a man of letters, and he told several lavish stories of being taken to lunch by his publisher and his agent at Manhattan restaurants where writers and editors gather. I said that professional writers are solitary drudges who seldom see other writers.

(13) "Do you put symbolism in your writing?" a student asked me.

(14) "Not if I can help it," I replied. I have an unbroken record of missing the deeper meaning in any story, play or movie, and as for dance and mime, I have never had even a remote notion of what is being conveyed.

(15) "I *love* symbols!" Dr. Brock exclaimed, and he described with gusto the joys of weaving them through his work.

(16) So the morning went, and it was a revelation to all of us. At the end Dr. Brock told me he was enormously interested in my answers—it had

never occurred to him that writing could be hard. I told him I was just as interested in *his* answers—it had never occurred to me that writing could be easy. (Maybe I should take up surgery on the side.)

(17) As for the students, anyone might think that we left them bewildered, but in fact we probably gave them a broader glimpse of the writing process than if only one of us had talked. For of course there isn't any "right" way to do such intensely personal work. There are all kinds of writers and all kinds of methods, and any method that helps somebody to say what he wants to say is the right method for him.

(18) Some people write by day, others by night. Some people need silence, others turn on the radio. Some write by hand, some by typewriters, some by talking into a tape recorder. Some people write their first draft in one long burst and then revise; others can't write the second paragraph until they have fiddled endlessly with the first.

(19) But all of them are vulnerable and all of them are tense. They are driven by a compulsion to put some part of themselves on paper, and yet they don't just write what comes naturally. They sit down to commit an act of literature, and the self who emerges on paper is a far stiffer person than the one who sat down. The problem is to find the real man or woman behind all the tension.

(20) For ultimately the product that any writer has to sell is not his subject, but who he is. I often find myself reading with interest about a topic that I never thought would interest me—some unusual scientific quest, for instance. What holds me is the enthusiasm of the writer for his field. How was he drawn into it? What emotional baggage did he bring along? How did it change his life? It is not necessary to want to spend a year alone at Walden Pond to become deeply involved with a man who did.

(21) This is the personal transaction that is at the heart of good nonfiction writing. Out of it come two of the most important qualities that this book will go in search of: humanity and warmth. Good writing has an aliveness that keeps the reader reading from one paragraph to the next, and it's not a question of gimmicks to "personalize" the author. It's a question of using the English language in a way that will achieve the greatest strength and the least clutter.

(22) Can such principles be taught? Maybe not. But most of them can be learned.

QUESTIONS OF CONTENT

These questions will help you understand what is in the essay:

Circle the letter of the best answer to each question.

1. Why were Zinsser and Dr. Brock invited to speak at the school?
   a. to discuss glamour.
   b. to talk about writing.
   c. to work.
   d. to face a crowd of students.

2. Brock said that writers don't need to rewrite but should "let it all hang out." What did Zinsser say that writers should do?
   a. let it all hang out, too.
   b. sit alone in a room.
   c. write and rewrite.
   d. stop writing when they don't feel creative.

3. According to Zinsser, why are writers tense?
   a. They really don't want to write.
   b. They want to write literature.
   c. They have to revise.
   d. Their writing reveals something about themselves.

4. Why does Zinsser often find himself reading about a topic that he didn't think would interest him?
   a. He knows the author.
   b. He wants to learn about the topic.
   c. The writer conveys his enthusiasm for his topic.
   d. It changes the writer's life.

5. According to Zinsser, what does good writing do?
   a. It reveals something about the author's life.
   b. It tells something about the topic.
   c. It says something about humanity.
   d. It keeps the reader interested.

Answer these questions in full sentences.

1. Dr. Brock said that a person should write when he feels like it. Why did

Zinsser say that a writer must make a schedule and stick to it? _____

_____

_____

2. How are all writers different from one another, and how are they alike?

_____

_____

3. What holds a reader's attention to a piece of writing? _____

_____

4. What is the best way to use the English language? _____

_____

5. In your own words, restate Brock's and Zinsser's ideas about writing.

_____

_____

_____

_____

Match each statement from the text (first column) with a similar statement written in a different way (second column).

1. I said that writing is a craft, not an art, and that the man who runs away from his craft because he lacks inspiration is fooling himself.

2. I told him I was just as interested in his answers—it had never occurred to me that writing could be easy. (Maybe I should take up surgery on the side.)

3. But all of them are vulnerable and all of them are tense. They are driven by a compulsion to put some part of themselves on paper, and yet they don't just write what comes naturally.

4. It is not necessary to spend a year at Walden Pond to become deeply involved with a man who did.

a. Writers feel nervous and open to criticism because they need to express themselves in a personal way, and yet writing is so hard.

b. You don't have to have experienced something to be interested in reading about it.

c. His answers were based on the fact that he was not a full-time writer, but someone who wrote as a hobby.

d. Writing is a job, and you can't avoid doing your job because you aren't in the mood.

QUESTIONS OF INFERENCE

Inferences are the ideas, opinions, and judgments that are logically drawn, or concluded, from information.

Look back at the text to answer these questions. Answer in full sentences.

1. How might Dr. Brock's attitude toward writing change if he had to make

his living at it? _____

_____

_____

2. Why did the students find the panel session a "revelation"? _____

_____

_____

3. What is odd about Zinsser's suggesting that he might take up surgery as

a hobby? _____

_____

4. Why isn't it just as odd that Dr. Brock should have writing as a hobby?

_____

_____

5. What is the main point of this essay?
  a. Writers can't be doctors, but doctors can be writers.
  b. All writers work differently.
  c. Writing is a difficult job that requires effort and personal commitment.
  d. If you don't like associating with writers, you shouldn't be one.

QUESTIONS OF CRITICAL THINKING

Critical thinking means putting your mind to work to explore, analyze, critique, and personalize ideas.

Answer each question in a short paragraph. You may want to use your own paper.

1. Why does writing improve as the writer rewrites? _____

_____

_____

_____

2. Why is writing better when it's personal? _____

_____

_____

_____

3. Look back at paragraph 18 of the essay. When, where, and how do you write? Describe your own writing process as clearly as possible. _____

_____

_____

_____

4. What have you read and enjoyed that you didn't expect at first to find interesting? Why do you think you became interested? _____

_____

_____

_____

5. Jot down any questions you would like to ask Zinsser about writing:

    a. _____

    b. _____

    c. _____

VOCABULARY

These words from Zinsser's "The Transaction" may be unfamiliar to you. These exercises will help you learn the meanings of these words and how to use them in sentences.

panel	(1)	craft	(8)	revelation	(16)
vocation	(1)	art	(8)	glimpse	(17)
avocation	(1)	inspiration	(8)	bewildered	(17)
vaguely	(2)	literary	(12)	vulnerable	(19)
Bohemian	(2)	lavish	(12)	ultimately	(20)
arduous	(2)	drudge	(12)	transaction	(21)
essence	(6)	symbolism	(13)	gimmicks	(22)

Word Meanings

Words often have more than one meaning and can be used as more than one part of speech. It's important to know which meaning of a word a writer has in mind and how the word is used in a particular sentence. In Chapter 2 we'll discuss how to find word meanings in the dictionary. Meanwhile, the following are some definitions of words in "The Transaction." Underline the meaning of the word as Zinsser uses it.

Sometimes *panel* means *a section of a wall, BUT it also means <u>a group of people selected for a specific purpose.</u>*

Sometimes *vocation* means *a call or summons to do something, BUT it can also mean a job or profession.*

Sometimes *essence* means *the nature of something, BUT it can also mean flavor or fragrance.*

Sometimes *art* means *the ability to make things, BUT it can also mean creative work or creating things that are beautiful.*

Use each of the words in its underlined meaning in a sentence of your own. Make sure you use it in the same way as Zinsser did.

panel *The panel of landlords discussed the rent increases.*

vocation _____

essence _____

craft _____

art _____

Word Clues

It's annoying to look up words in the dictionary while you're reading. But sometimes you don't have to. Many words are made up of recognizable parts called *prefixes* (beginnings), *roots* (middles), and *suffixes* (endings). These parts can often give you a good "working definition" you can use as you are reading or until you have a chance to look up the word in the dictionary.

Humanity

Look at it carefully.   humanity
Divide it.   human   ity
Think about it.

Human means being a person; the suffix (ending) *ity* means the "quality, state, or degree" of being something. Thus *humanity* means the "quality of being human."

Below is a list of some of the most common prefixes and suffixes that can be attached to roots. They can help you figure out the meanings of words that, up to now, you thought you didn't know.

PREFIXES THAT RELATE TO TIME

Prefix	Meaning	Example	Your example
ante	before	antedate	*anteroom*
post	after, later than	postdate	_____
		postwar	_____
pre	before	preview	_____
re	again, anew	redo, retell, recall	_____
retro	back	retroactive	_____

PREFIXES THAT RELATE TO NEGATIVES

a (an)	not, without	amoral	*atypical*
ab	from, way, off	abnormal	_____
anti	opposite, opposed	antiwar	_____
contra	against, contrary	contraception	_____
de	do the opposite,	devitalize	_____
	remove	delouse	_____
dis	opposite of,	disrobe	_____
	not,	disagreeable	_____
	exclude	disbar	_____

il[1]	not	illogical	_____
im[2]	not	impractical	_____
in[3]	not	inconclusive	_____
ir[4]	not	irrelevant	_____
mal	bad,	malpractice	_____
	abnormal	malformed	_____
mis	badly, wrongly	misjudge	_____
non	not	noncombatant	_____

PREFIXES THAT RELATE TO NUMBERS

bi	two,	bicycle	*biweekly*
	in two parts,	bisect	_____
	every two	bimonthly	_____
hyper	excessive,	hypertension	_____
	existing in more than three dimensions	hyperspace	_____
mono	single	monoplane	_____
multi	many,	multicolored	_____
	many times over	multimillionaire	_____
poly	many, several, much	polysyllabic	_____

[1] With words that begin with *l*.
[2] Words that begin with *b*, *m*, and *p*.
[3] Words that begin with all letters not mentioned.
[4] Words that begin with *r*.

semi	half,	semicircle	_____
	partly	semiconscious	_____
tri	three,	tricycle	_____
	in three parts,	trisect	_____
	every third	triannual	

PREFIXES THAT RELATE TO LOCATION

circum	around	circumnavigate	*circumference*
co	with,	coauthor	_____
	together,	coexist	_____
	to the same extent	coextensive	_____
col[5]	with, together, joint	collinear	_____
com[6]	with, together, joint	commingle	_____
con[7]	with, together, joint	concurrent	_____
hypo	under	hypodermic	_____
inter	between, among,	interstellar	_____
	shared by	interfaith	_____
intra	within	intraoffice	_____
trans	across	transatlantic	_____

[5] With words that begin with *l.*
[6] With words that begin with *b, p,* and *m.*
[7] With all other letters.

12

SUFFIXES

Suffix	Meaning	Example	Your example
ary	of, relating to	literary	_____
ence	action, process,	reference	_____
	quality, state	despondence	_____
hood	state, condition,	boyhood	_____
	specified quality	falsehood	_____
ion	act or process,	validation	_____
	result of process,	regulation	_____
	state or condition	hydration	_____
ism	act, practice, process	criticism	_____
	state, condition	barbarianism	_____
ity	quality, state, degree,	alkalinity	_____
ly	in a specific manner,	slowly	_____
	in the manner of,	partly	_____
	from a specific point of view	particularly	_____
ment	action, process,	enlargement	_____
	state, condition,	amazement	_____
	place of action	encampment	_____
ness	condition, quality	kindness	_____
ship	state, condition,	censorship	_____
	profession	clerkship	_____

Look carefully at each of the words below. Try to see them as the sum of their parts. Consult the preceding list of prefixes and suffixes, and then write a "working definition" for each.

inspiration *Inspire + ation - the act of inspiring; being inspiring.*

ultimately _____

transaction _____

humanity _____

vaguely _____

symbolism _____

literary _____

revelation[8] _____

Seeing Words in Context

These words appear in "The Transaction." You may find clues to the meaning of each in the words or phrases near it—that is, in the word's *context*. As you reread, circle the words or phrases that form the context for each word. Then write (1) your working definition, (2) the dictionary definition that's right for the context, and (3) an original sentence using the word. If you have difficulty figuring out the meaning of the word from the context of "The Transaction," you may find it helpful to read the following story, in which the words appear in italics:

1. word: *arduous*

    a. working definition ___*hard*_____

    b. dictionary definition ___*difficult to do - adj.*_____

    c. your sentence ___*Cleaning the house is arduous work.*___

2. word: *drudge*

    a. working definition _____

    b. dictionary definition _____

---

[8] The root of *revelation* is *reveal,* not *revel.*

c. your sentence _____

3. word: *bewilder*(ed)

  a. working definition _____

  b. dictionary definition _____

  c. your sentence _____

4. word: *gimmick*(s)

  a. working definition _____

  b. dictionary definition _____

  c. your sentence _____

5. word: *glimpse*

  a. working definition _____

  b. dictionary definition _____

  c. your sentence _____

6. word: *vulnerable*

  a. working definition _____

  b. dictionary definition _____

  c. your sentence _____

7. word: *avocation*

  a. working definition _____

  b. dictionary definition _____

  c. your sentence _____

8. word: *lavish*

  a. working definition _____

  b. dictionary definition _____

  c. your sentence _____

THE PENCIL MAN

John worked all day as a pencil sharpener. He sat near an industrial-sized electric pencil sharpener and waited for the other employees of his company to bring him their spent pencils. Then he stuck the pencils into the machine and returned them, sharpened, to his colleagues. It was not an *arduous* task; it was easy and mechanical. In fact, John was the office *drudge* because his work was so routine. John's coworkers were confused and *bewildered* that he could sit all day doing nothing but sharpening pencils. They could not understand why he created no schemes or *gimmicks* to keep himself from dying of boredom. They would sometimes sneak by him to catch a *glimpse* of him just sitting peacefully near the sharpener.

What they did not know was that John did not want a more complicated job that might make him *vulnerable* or open to criticism by his employers. He wanted to concentrate on his other life. Disco dancing was his *avocation*, which he indulged in every night after work. He was known as the "king" of the Starlight Disco, where he gyrated the night away to wild applause. In fact, as he sat at the pencil sharpener, he dreamt up the outrageous and *lavish* costume he would wear each night.

Using Words in Context

One way to make new words part of your vocabulary is to use them in your writing. Write a paragraph about some problem you have had with writing. Begin with the sentence:

I have always had trouble with (1) spelling, (2) grammar, (3) writing (choose one).

Make sure to use at least five of the words from "The Transaction" listed in the Vocabulary section. When you proofread your paragraph, underline the words you used.

_____

_____

_____

_____

_____

_____

_____

WRITING AND REWRITING

We'd all like to produce the "good writing" Zinsser describes. Whether we are telling the story of something that happened to us or arguing passionately for one side of an issue, we want our audience—friends, classmates, teachers— to know exactly what we mean, to feel what we feel, and to finish the essay and say "wow!" How can we write well? First, we've got to have something to write about—a topic—and that's where many students have trouble. Every student complains, "I don't have anything to write about." But that's almost never true. More often, "I don't have anything to write about" really means

"I'm afraid to write."
"I don't like to write."
"This assignment bores me."
"I have plenty to say, but the teacher won't like it."
"I don't want to write about personal things for a stranger."
"Every time I write something, my teachers just criticize my spelling and don't even comment on what I mean."

Check the statements above that are true for you, and add some of your own:

_____

_____

_____

Any or all of these statements are true at some time. The point is that you've got plenty to write about. Your mind is always working, and so you always have some ideas. When you say, "I don't have anything to write about," you may *feel* that you have no ideas, but you probably do, only they are hidden and don't come into your conscious mind and on to paper. One way to become conscious of them is called *free writing*.

FREE WRITING ▬▬▬▬▬▬

Take out a piece of paper and a pen or pencil. Write today's date at the top. Now relax for a moment. Close your eyes, Breathe deeply. Now open your eyes. At the signal, start writing, and do not stop for ten minutes. Write anything that comes into your head, in any order. Just let the ideas flow and—most important—keep your pen moving no matter how odd it feels. DO NOT pause if you are unsure about spelling, punctuation, or grammar. DO NOT stop to look up words in the dictionary. If you get stuck momentarily with nothing in your mind, write the word *stuck* until your next idea comes. Okay, begin. (If you're in class, your teacher will time you. If you're at home, use a kitchen timer or a large-faced clock.) After ten minutes, stop.

Which of these statements best describes your thoughts about free writing?

_____ **1.** I loved it.

_____ **2.** I hated it.

_____ **3.** I got tired of writing, and my hand hurt.

_____ **4.** I started to wish the ten minutes would end so I could stop.

_____ **5.** I got stuck a lot.

_____ **6.** I felt free to write whatever I wanted to.

_____ **7.** It was fun not to be careful as I wrote.

_____ **8.** I had trouble at the beginning, but as I wrote, it got easier.

_____ **9.** I couldn't write because I was worried about spelling and organization.

_____**10.** I couldn't write without a dictionary.

_____**11.** _____

(Free writing is difficult at first, so don't worry if you had some negative feelings. What's important is that you can write for ten minutes and get some ideas down on paper.)

Read some of the pieces of free writing done by other members of your class. Which ones did you enjoy the most? Why? Which ones sounded the "freest"? Why?

Reread your own free writing. Are there any ideas you were not aware of thinking before you began to write? Jot them down.

1. _____

2. _____

3. _____

If there were no revelations, don't worry. Look for a new idea in your next free writing. But keep your free writing, because it contains ideas you may want to develop later in the chapter.

Read these student samples of first-time free writing:

FREE WRITING 1

At this moment I'm feeling rather depressed and this free writing isn't helping me to feel better. As a matter of fact I think I hate it, I feel I'm wasting my time and paper.

This room is so small and crummy, the wall is falling apart so is the ceiling. The floor is filthy, so is the blackboard. There is math on the board, a subject which I detest.

Mentioning math I've been place in Math 011. I mean gosh! that class is boring. I know for sure I'll be sleeping everyday in class. The work the professor gives my little sister would make fun of me if she know that's what I was doing. Believe me it's kid stuff and I aint dumb. I'm not fooling. I'm bad but I ain't that bad.

Everyone here seems pretty contented with what they are doing. What makes me so different. Sometimes I wonder if I really know what I want out of life. So Miss _____ is looking my way I wonder why. Oh! I see, what I'm saying, naturally. I can tell her one thing. I ain't saying much.

Probably if she knew my feelings she wouldn't be too pleased

FREE WRITING 2

The room is warm, but outside is kind of chilly. Everybody is writing about nothing in particular. I would like to close the door of the classroom because noises outside disturbe me. There is a man talking, maybe teaching a class and someone working on a typewriter. I keep listening to that man and it bothers me. Some people in this class write really fast. They turned the page already. That man is getting on my nerve. It is not him only, now I hear two voices. Somebody just scream and everybody laugh. A telephone rang, it was not for me. I can not write too fast, but I would like to. I do not know what else to write and I cannot stop writing until the teacher says stop. Stuck. Stuck. Stuck. She just said it.

Pick out some of the ideas in the two samples of free writing and jot them down.

Free Writing 1	*Free Writing 2*
1. _____	1. _____
2. _____	2. _____
3. _____	3. _____
4. _____	4. _____

Which sample sounds "freer"? What makes it sound that way?

Free writing invites you to listen to your own mind, to hear what you are thinking. Perhaps the student who wrote the first essay didn't know that she cared about how different she seemed from the other students. Sometimes thoughts roll around in your mind and are difficult to sort out. You've got something in mind, but you can't quite get it in focus. Writing is a good way to focus your thinking.

FOCUSED WRITING

Take out a piece of paper and a pen or pencil. Write today's date on the top. Now relax for a moment. Close your eyes. Breathe deeply. As the room begins to quiet, think about *hamburger* or *sleep*. Now open your eyes. At the signal, start writing and do not stop for ten minutes. Focus on either *hamburger* or *sleep*, and write what comes into your head, in any order. Just let the ideas flow and—most important—keep your pen moving, no matter how odd it feels. DO NOT pause when you are unsure about spelling, punctuation, or grammar. DO NOT stop to look up words in the dictionary. If you get stuck momentarily with nothing in your mind, write the word *stuck*, or keep repeating the last word you wrote until your next idea comes. Okay, begin. After ten minutes, stop. Look back at the statements at the beginning of the Writing and Rewriting section. Do you feel differently about *focused writing* than you do about free writing? Why or why not? Jot down some thoughts about the two kinds of writing:

_____

_____

_____

_____

Keep your focused writing, as you may want to consider it the first draft of an essay you will write later in the chapter.

THE STAGES OF THE WRITING PROCESS

What Is the
Difference
Between Free
Writing and
Focused
Writing?

Free writing helps you become aware of the ideas in your mind, and focused writing helps you sort out your ideas on one topic. How can you use these two techniques? They are the first stage of the three-stage writing process we shall develop in this book. The process of moving from your ideas to an essay that you can present to your teacher or another audience can be divided into three stages, although you may often find it necessary to repeat some of the stages at different points of the process:

1. Getting started: free writing, focused writing (writing a first draft).
2. Rewriting: taking a second look at your ideas, getting organized, adding details, rearranging, changing paragraphs and sentences (shaping your ideas into a second draft).
3. Proofreading: cleaning up (creating a final draft).

What Are the Stages of the Writing Process?

1. *Free writing and focused writing.* When you write, you can start in one of two ways. If you think your mind is blank or you're "stuck," *free write.* Do it the way we did it here: Take out a piece of paper, start to write, and don't stop for ten minutes.

What Do You Do in the First Stage?

You may discover one idea from the many in your free writing that you will want to develop into an essay (such as the ideas you noted from the student samples). Or you may already have something in mind but need to focus it. Once you have an idea, do focused writing. Write down all of your ideas about your subject, in any order. You probably will find that you know more about it than you thought you did. You may have had some experience that gives you certain feelings about or special knowledge of what you're writing about. Write it all down, without worrying about how it looks.

What you will have when you're finished with your focused writing is called a *first draft* or a *rough draft* (*first* because you've collected your ideas on this topic for the first time and *rough* because the ideas are spilled out on the page in no particular order. Only you can understand what's there).

What Is a First (or Rough) Draft?

2. *Rewriting.* Once you have your ideas on paper where you can see them, you can start to shape them into an essay. The free writing and focused writing were to help you make your ideas clear to *yourself,* whereas revising helps you make your ideas clear to *someone else.*

Rewriting is the heart of the writing process. It is where you

What Do You Do in the Second Stage?

a. Take a second look (or relook) at what you've written and get a new vision of your ideas.
b. Add new thoughts or information or remove information that no longer serves your purpose; that is, you rewrite so the reader can better understand you and your topic.

Why Do You Need to Revise?

When you rewrite, you should think of several things. First, what are you writing about? What's your topic? Second, who are you writing for? Who is your audience? And third, why are your writing this? It could be

What Should You Think of When You Rewrite?

a story of a memorable event in your life.
a discussion of the causes of the French Revolution.
a comparison of automobile travel versus bus travel.

Your essay could be read by

a friend.
a teacher.
the readers of the school newspaper.

And your purpose could be to

confide in someone.

convince.

explain.

You also will need to think about *details.* Have you said all you need to say? Maybe you left certain details out of your focused writing. You may not consider them important, but someone else might need to know them. Or you may want to add an idea that you didn't have at first but that you decide is a good one when you reread your essay.

You also want to present your ideas in a particular *order.* If it's a story, you may want to tell your readers how it all came about, to set the stage. Or, for example, you may want to express your preference for one kind of travel over another.

Finally, you will want to think about the words you've used. Is your *language* appropriate to what you're saying and to whom it's written? Do you want to use the word *automobile* or the word *car?* Each word leaves a slightly different impression on the audience, and so you should think carefully about your choice.

Sometimes you can do all the rewriting in one draft, sometimes not. Later in the book we introduce the term *middle drafts* so you will feel free to write more than one if you need to.

What Do You Do in the Third Stage?

3. *Proofreading.* By this third stage, you are almost finished. You have everything down on paper, in just the way you want it. Should you send the letter or hand in the essay to the teacher? Not yet. Read it one more time. This time, check for standard English conventions: sentence structure, grammar, spelling, and manuscript form. All along, you may have been aware that you aren't sure how to spell a certain word, like *receive.* This is the time to look it up. You may be unsure whether or not there is a *d* at the end of the phrase "I am divorce*d.*" This is your chance to add it if it is not already there. Should you indent for a new paragraph? Decide now.

Sometimes it is necessary to recopy an essay after you have proofread it, sometimes not. Recopying depends on the number and extent of the corrections you make.

Why Is Proofreading Left to the End?

We leave proofreading for the end because—important as it is to present a paper that is technically correct—it is really separate from writing and rewriting. If you try to correct and be creative at the same time, your creativity often will suffer. But if you separate the two activities, you can get the best out of both.

Thus far in this chapter, you have done some free writing and focused writing. Consider your focused writing as the first draft of an essay, and put it aside. (If you don't like your focused writing, read your free writing. Find one idea you like and use it as the basis of a new focused writing.)

Do These Exercises Before You Revise Your First Draft.

1. Look at the first draft of a student paper below:

DRAFT 1

One of the saddest moments of my life was when my brother decided to leave and join the Air force. My brother is two years older than myself and we were very close. I knew everything that happened to him and vice versa. Before he told our parents we talked it over, and decided that he could get the training that he wanted. My parents were disappointed because they knew he would be going away. The day he left we were very sad but since that day he has come home about three times. He was last shipped to Korea where he has been for a year we get a letter every so often and we call from time to time. He'll be out next year but he doesn't want to live in N.Y. I guess I have to save my money because neither one of us write a lot and I'll have to spend alot of time calling with all my problems.

a. What is this paper about? _____

_____

b. Why do you think the student may be writing this? _____

_____

c. Whom do you think the student may be writing for? _____

_____

2. Read the second draft of this essay:

DRAFT 2

One of the saddest moments in my life was when my brother, Ronald decided to leave home and join the Air Force. This took place in the spring 1978. My brother is two years older than myself and he was just getting out of high school. The two of us were closer with one another than with our sister. Because we used to go to the same school we had alot of secrets between us. I was the first one he told about his decision because he wanted to know what I thought. After I told him what I thought he went and told our parents they were kind of sad because he would be going away. We were all sad when he went and glad it was only for a short period of time. He has come home about three times since he left. The last time we saw him was June 1980 just because he had to go to Korea for two years. He's not much of a writer so we don't receive letters often, we got to call him one and found out he was going fine. He'll be finished his service next year and I'll be very glad to see him but until then just keep on writing.

a. What, if any, information did the student add that was not in the

first draft? _____

_____

_____

b. Has the student deleted anything that was in the first draft? Why

do you think she took it out? _____

_____

_____

_____

c. Has the student changed the order of any of the ideas in the essay?

If so, what and why? _____

_____

_____

d. Do you think the second draft is better than the first? Why or

why not?_____

_____

_____

e. What questions do you still have about the topic? What do you want

to know more about?_____

_____

_____

3. Read the third draft of this student essay, and compare it with the second draft.

DRAFT 3

One of the saddest moments of my life was when my brother, Ronald, decided to leave home and join the Air Force. This took place in the spring of 1978. My brother is two years older than myself, and he was just getting out of high school. The two of us were closer with one another than with our sister. Because we used to go to the same schools, we had a lot of secrets between us. I was the first one he told about his decision because he wanted to know what I thought. After I told him what I thought, he went and told our parents. We were all sad when he went and glad it was only for a short period of time.

He has come home about three times since he left. The last time we saw him was June, 1980, just before he had to go to Korea for two years. He's not much of a writer, so we don't receive letters often. We got to call him once and found out he was doing fine. He'll be finished his service next year, and I'll be glad to see him, but until then I just keep on writing.

a. Write down the differences in spelling, punctuation, and paragraphs in the two drafts:

Draft 2

(1) _____

(2) _____

(3) _____

(4) _____

Draft 3

(1) _____

(2) _____

(3) _____

(4) _____

b. Do you think the student made appropriate changes in the manuscript?

_____

c. What other changes, if any, would you make? _____

_____

_____

REWRITING: A SECOND DRAFT

Now you are ready to turn your focused writing into a second draft. Read it carefully, aloud, and, if you can, to a friend or classmate. Try to get a new vision of your subject. As you revise, think about

1. *Topic, audience, and purpose.* What do you want to tell about, to whom, and why?
2. *Detail.* Have you said all you want to say, or now that you have reread your essay, can you think of new ideas to add? Add them now. Have you named people and described places? Some details are whole new ideas, and some are just single words.
3. *Order.* Will your audience get your point?
4. *Language.* Are you happy with the words you've used? If not, you can always change them.

After you've written your second draft, go on to the Proofreading section, where you'll get some help on the proofreading stage of your writing.

PROOFREADING

Proofreading is the final stage of the writing process, but it's important because it determines how your essay will appear in finished form. Proofreading means taking another look at your work and making changes.

If you read your essay carefully, you will probably see places where you want to change spelling, punctuation, or grammar. You may not know exactly why you want to make a change; maybe it just "sounds better" to you. That's fine.

Why Is Proofreading Difficult?

It's a good idea to read aloud, slowly, and to concentrate on the parts of your paper you have not yet read. Proofreading is hard. You may be tempted to read quickly and skip over the exact words or punctuation because you already know what you have written. But your readers won't know what you have written until they read it, and this is all they will ever see. They may be so distracted by incorrect spelling, punctuation, and grammar problems that they may never get the point you are trying to convey.

Many people proofread well without ever being aware of the rules of spelling, punctuation, and grammar. So why do we teach them? You are in a class to improve your writing. The issues, rules, and conventions we shall discuss will make you aware of how you use words when you speak and write; they will teach you what to look for when you proofread and give you and your teacher a common vocabulary for talking about the technical aspects of your writing.

The proofreading section of each chapter concentrates on particular aspects of proofreading:

1. *Conventions:* how the essay should look on a page—what words to capitalize, when and how to hyphenate, how to write words that are sometimes written as one word and sometimes as two, and how to handle spelling problems.
2. *Punctuation:* how to use periods, commas, semicolons, and quotation marks correctly.
3. *Grammar:* what nouns, pronouns, verbs, adverbs, and adjectives are and how they function in standard English sentences. Standard English is the English commonly found in printed materials—newspapers, magazines, and books. However, if you compare the language used in each of these, you will find a range of standard English usage, from informal to formal. Textbooks sometimes use an informal style. We shall not try to cover every aspect of these issues but shall examine what seems to cause the most trouble for students.

What Three Things Will the Proofreading Section of Each Chapter Cover?

PARTS OF SPEECH

What are some of the grammatical terms that you will need to know in order to proofread effectively and to discuss your writing with your teacher? What follows is an overview of some of what you'll find later in this book: basic sentence structure, common word functions ("parts of speech"), and spelling.

Let us begin by finding out what you know about how words are used in sentences:

1. Old down dark the walked street the haltingly woman.
2. The old woman walked haltingly down the dark street.

What Does the Position of a Word in a Sentence Tell Us?

You know that sentence 1 does not make sense because the words are jumbled. To make sense, the words in a sentence must be in their correct positions. A word's position helps us determine how the word *functions* in a sentence. That is, the function of a word is often related to its position. Two important functions of words are stating the topic of the sentence (in the subject) and making a claim about the topic (in the predicate).

The old woman walked haltingly down the dark street.

The *subject* tells you who or what performs the action in the sentence. It is often a noun, phrase, or pronoun.

What Is the Subject of a Sentence?

*The old **woman** walked haltingly down the dark street.*

The *predicate* makes a statement about the subject. In this sentence, it tells you what the subject (woman) did. To find the predicate of a sentence, look for the main verb and then the words that go with it, its *complements.*

What Is the Predicate of a Sentence?

*The old woman **walked haltingly down the dark street.***

Subjects and predicates are the two main elements of a sentence. We should also look at the other parts of the sentence:

article adjective noun verb adverb preposition article adjective noun

The old woman walked haltingly down the dark street.

What Are Nouns?

Nouns name a person, place, or thing. *Woman* names a kind of person. *Street* names a thing. Proper nouns are the actual names of persons, places, and things: the old woman could really be the famous actress Katherine Hepburn; the street, Sniffen Court. Sometimes pronouns are substitutes for nouns.

What Are Pronouns?

Pronouns take the place of nouns. For example, we could rewrite the preceding sentence as

She walked haltingly down the dark street.

Pronouns also refer back to their *antecedents:*

*The old woman walked haltingly down the dark street leaning on **her** cane.*

What Are Adjectives?

Adjectives describe the nouns near them. For example, *old* describes *woman,* and *dark* describes *street.*

What Are Verbs?

Verbs often show action. *Walked* is an action word. But verbs have other functions as well. They can link the subject with some characteristic it possesses: For example,

The old woman is gray haired.
The old woman is blind.

These verbs do not show action, but they do point out some of the characteristics of the old woman.

What Are Adverbs?

Adverbs describe something about verbs, adjectives, or other adverbs. *Haltingly* tells us something about the verb *walk.* Adverbs answer questions like how? when? and where? and they frequently end in *ly.* How did the old woman walk? Haltingly.

What Are Prepositions?

Prepositions often help clarify relationships between words in a sentence. *Down* clarifies the relationship between *walked* and the phrase *the dark street.* What are the differences in meaning in these expressions?

1. The old woman walked down the dark street.
2. The old woman walked across the dark street.
3. The old woman walked to the dark street.

Articles help specify nouns. It can be a definite article like *the* in the phrase *the dark street*. *The* is considered to be definite because we have a particular street in mind. An article can also be indefinite (*a* or *an*). That is, we use *a* in the phrase *a dark street* when we don't have a particular street in mind.

What Are Articles?

Another important part of speech is the conjunction. *Conjunctions* link ideas in sentences. Some are called *coordinating conjunctions* (*and, but, or, nor, for, so, yet*):

What Are Conjunctions?

The old woman walked haltingly down the street, **and** *she stooped to look in garbage pails, foraging for food. She looked,* **but** *she didn't touch.*

Some are called *subordinating conjunctions* (*when, while, as, because,* and so on):

As the old woman walked haltingly down the street, she spied a bench.

She sat down to rest **because** *she was exhausted.*

SPELLING: MAKING YOUR OWN LIST

Spelling is something else to consider when you proofread. English spelling is complicated and often illogical. Many English words have been borrowed from other languages. Many words sound alike or nearly alike, and many words are pronounced differently from the way that they are spelled. In other words, learning to spell correctly is difficult.

Why Is Spelling Difficult?

In each chapter, we'll focus on some aspect of spelling that causes trouble for writers. In this chapter, we'll start by showing you how to pay attention to the words you spell incorrectly.

1. Take out the writing exercises you've done so far for this class and any papers you have written for other classes. List any words you think you may have spelled incorrectly. You may want to sit with a group and find misspelled words together.

_____   _____   _____

_____   _____   _____

_____   _____   _____

_____   _____   _____

2. Group these words into the columns according to type of error. You may want to list the words in more than one column.

A (words missing an s or an ed ending)	B (words you always seem to spell wrong)	C (words you guessed at and spelled wrong)
_____	_____	_____
_____	_____	_____
_____	_____	_____
_____	_____	_____
_____	_____	_____

3. Look at the words in the three columns.
   a. The words in Column A may or may not have spelling errors. Most likely they are problems with verbs or nouns, which we shall discuss in Chapters 7, 8, 9, and 10.
   b. The words in Column B do have spelling errors. Some are probably errors with "spelling demons," words that many people have trouble with. We shall talk about spelling demons in Chapter 10. Other errors may be homonym (words that sound alike) problems, which we shall cover in Chapters 2, 3, and 4.
   c. The words in Column C also have spelling errors that may have to do with certain rules for spelling or with educated guesses that people can learn to make. They may also have to do with finding your own "hints" for good spelling.

4. Even before you start to study spelling, it is a good idea to concentrate on the words you spell incorrectly. Use the following Spelling List: Each time your teacher returns a paper to you, check for any misspelled words and write them in the left-hand column *just the way they appear in your paper.* In the middle column write the word correctly. And in the right-hand column, write the correct syllabification of the word. Look in a dictionary to find out how to break the word into syllables. (We shall discuss syllables in the next chapter.)

It's important to learn your own pattern for misspelling, if you have one. Figure out which words you spell wrong often and why. Then you can study the areas of spelling you need to work on.

SPELLING LIST

A *(incorrect spelling)*	B *(correct spelling)*	C *(correct syllabification)*

Now you are ready to proofread the second draft of the essay you began earlier in this chapter. Read your essay again slowly and aloud. Make sure that all your sentences make sense, that all the words are in the right order, that you haven't left out any words, and that you are saying exactly what you want to say. Check your spelling. Change anything you think needs changing. Write a clean copy if you make more than one or two changes.

ADDITIONAL WRITING ASSIGNMENTS

A good source of ideas for essays is a *writer's journal.* You can start one as soon as you have a thin notebook (easy to carry around), preferably one with the pages sewn in so you won't rip any out.

If you carry it with you, you can jot down your thoughts about things you see, things that happen to you, or ideas that occur to you. You don't have to worry about spelling, punctuation, and grammar. Your writer's journal is an informal book of ideas for *you,* not for an audience.

1. At least three times a week, take ten to twenty minutes to sit down and free write. Use the same procedure we've outlined here. Write the day's date on top, and begin to write. Set a kitchen timer if you need to, and keep your pen moving for the entire session.
2. Try some focused writing as well. Choose your own focus. Write the word on the top of the page, and use the same technique as for free writing.
3. You may want to consider these ideas for focused writing.

a. socks	**k.** fire
b. coffee	**l.** shells
c. hamburgers	**m.** snowflake
d. sleep	**n.** baby
e. freedom	**o.** yawn
f. love	**p.** cult
g. writing	**q.** racism
h. soccer	**r.** window
i. hate	**s.** money
j. staplers	**t.** cigarette

Choosing Your Writing Voice

2

Photo by
Kathy Sloane

As you read "Language" by Malcolm X, look for information that answers these questions:

1. Where was Malcolm X in the story he recounts?
2. Why does he begin to write letters?
3. What does he find out about himself?
4. How does the dictionary help him?
5. Before Malcolm X talks about his becoming involved with the dictionary, he relates some of his life history. How does knowing this add to your interest in what he did?
6. Malcolm X's use of slang make the story easier or harder to read and more or less enjoyable?

Notes

Harlem and **Roxbury.** Two large black communities in the Northeast.
wires. Slang for gossip or rumor.
stir. Slang for prison.
hype. Slang for special trick.

Language
Malcolm X

Malcolm X was a leader of the Black Muslims and was assassinated in 1965 at the age of thirty-nine. As a young man, he was poor and uneducated and began a life of crime. But in prison, he converted to Islam and began to educate himself. This essay is an excerpt from The Autobiography of Malcolm X, *written with Alex Haley, who later wrote* Roots.

(1) I've never been one for inaction. Everything I've ever felt strongly about, I've done something about. I guess that's why, unable to do anything

else, I soon began writing to people I had known in the hustling world, such as Sammy the Pimp, John Hughes, the gambling house owner, the thief Jumpsteady, and several dope peddlers. I wrote them all about Allah and Islam and Mr. Elijah Muhammad. I had no idea where most of them lived. I addressed their letters in care of the Harlem or Roxbury bars and clubs where I'd known them.

(2) I never got a single reply. The average hustler and criminal was too uneducated to write a letter. I have known many slick, sharp-looking hustlers, who would have you think they had an interest in Wall Street; privately, they would get someone else to read a letter if they received one. Besides, neither would I have replied to anyone writing me something as wild as "the white man is the devil."

(3) What certainly went on the Harlem and Roxbury wires was that Detroit Red was going crazy in stir, or else he was trying some hype to shake up the warden's office.

(4) During the years I stayed in the Norfolk Prison Colony, never did any official directly say anything to me about those letters, although, of course, they all passed through the prison censorship. I'm sure, however, they monitored what I wrote to add to the files which every state and federal prison keeps on the conversion of Negro inmates by the teachings of Mr. Elijah Muhammad.

(5) But at that time, I felt that the real reason was that the white man knew that he was the devil.

(6) Later on, I even wrote to the Mayor of Boston, the Governor of Massachusetts, and to Harry S. Truman. They never answered; they probably never even saw my letters. I handscratched to them how the white man's society was responsible for the black man's condition in this wilderness of North America.

(7) It was because of my letters that I happened to stumble upon starting to acquire some kind of homemade education.

(8) I became increasingly frustrated at not being able to express what I wanted to convey in letters that I wrote, especially those to Mr. Elijah Muhammad. In the street, I had been the most articulate hustler out there—I had commanded attention when I said something. But now, trying to write simple English, I not only wasn't articulate, I wasn't even functional. How would I sound writing in slang, the way I would *say* it, something such as "Look, daddy, let me pull your coat about a cat, Elijah Muhammad."

(9) Many who today hear me somewhere in person, or on television, or those who read something I've said, will think I went to school far beyond the eighth grade. This impression is due entirely to my prison studies.

(10) It had really begun on the Charlestown Prison, when Bimbi first made me feel envy of his stock of knowledge. Bimbi had always taken charge of any conversation he was in, and I had tried to emulate him. But every book I picked up had few sentences which didn't contain anywhere from one to nearly all of the words that might as well have been in Chinese. When

I just skipped those words, of course I really ended up with little idea of what the book said. So I had come to the Norfolk Prison Colony still going through only book-reading motions. Pretty soon, I would have quit even these motions, unless I had received the motivations that I did.

(11) I saw that the best thing I could do was get hold of a dictionary—to study, to learn some words. I was lucky enough to reason also that I would try to improve my penmanship. It was sad. I couldn't even write in a straight line. It was both ideas together that moved me to request a dictionary along with some tablets and pencils from the Norfolk Prison Colony School.

(12) I spent two days just riffling uncertainly through the dictionary's pages. I'd never realized so many words existed! I didn't know *which* words I needed to learn. Finally, just to start some kind of action, I began copying.

(13) In my slow, painstaking, ragged handwriting, I copied into my tablet everything printed on that first page, down to the punctuation marks.

(14) I believe it took me a day. Then, aloud, I read back, to myself, everything I'd written on the tablet. Over and over, to myself, I read my own handwriting.

(15) I woke up the next morning, thinking about those words—immensely proud to realize that not only had I written so much at one time, but I'd written words that I never knew were in the world. Moreover, with a little effort, I also could remember what many of these words meant. I reviewed the words whose meanings I didn't remember. Funny thing, from the dictionary first page right now, that "aardvark" springs to my mind. The dictionary had a picture of it, a long-tailed, long-eared burrowing African mammal, which lives off termites caught by sticking out its tongue as an anteater does for ants.

(16) I was so fascinated I went on—I copied the dictionary's next page. And the same experience came when I studied that. With every succeeding page, I also learned of people and places and events from history. Actually the dictionary is like a miniature encyclopedia. Finally the dictionary's A section had filled a whole tablet—and I went into the B's. That was the way I started copying what eventually became the entire dictionary. It went a lot faster after so much practice helped me to pick up handwriting speed. Between what I wrote in my tablet, and writing letters, during the rest of my time in prison I would guess I wrote a million words.

(17) I suppose it was inevitable that as my word-base broadened, I could for the first time pick up a book and read and now begin to understand what the book was saying. Anyone who has read a great deal can imagine the new world that opened. Let me tell you something: from then until I left that prison, in every free moment I had, if I was not reading in the library, I was reading on my own bunk. You couldn't have gotten me out of books with a wedge. Between Mr. Muhammad's teachings, my correspondence, my visitors . . . and my reading of books, months passed without my even thinking about being imprisoned. In fact, up to then, I had never been so truly free in my life.

QUESTIONS OF CONTENT

Circle the letter of the best answer to each question:

1. What did Malcolm X write letters about?
   a. Allah, Islam, and Mr. Elijah Muhammad.
   b. Sammy the Pimp and John Hughes.
   c. Detroit Red.
   d. life in prison.
2. Why didn't Malcolm X get any replies to his letters?
   a. His letters were never received.
   b. His friends were too uneducated to write.
   c. His friends were in jail.
   d. He neglected to write his return address on the envelopes.
3. Malcolm X's hustling name was
   a. Bimbi.
   c. Malcolm.
   d. Detroit Red.
   e. Allah.
4. Malcolm X became increasingly frustrated by his letters because
   a. They were too long.
   b. They didn't express what he wanted to say.
   c. He received no replies.
   d. The letters were never mailed.
5. Which two things caused Malcolm X to get a dictionary?
   a. his concern about people.
   b. his poor penmanship.
   c. free time.
   d. his need to learn new words.

Answer these questions in full sentences:

1. How did Bimbi influence Malcolm X? _____

   _____

2. Why was Malcolm X going through "only book-reading motions" in the

   Norfolk Prison Colony? _____

   _____

3. Why did Malcolm X start copying words from the dictionary? And why

   was he proud of these words? _____

   _____

4. Why did Malcolm X's reading improve? _____

_____

5. Summarize the events that led Malcolm X to want to be a better reader

and writer. Then summarize the steps he took to achieve his goal. _____

_____

_____

_____

Match each statement from the text (first column) with a similar statement written in a different way (second column):

1. I have known many slick, sharp-looking hustlers, who would have you think they had an interest in Wall Street; privately, they would get someone else to read a letter if they received one.

2. I handscratched to them how the white man's society was responsible for the black man's condition in this wilderness of North America.

3. But now, trying to write simple English, I not only wasn't articulate, I wasn't even functional.

4. But every book I picked up had few sentences which didn't contain anywhere from one to nearly all of the words that might as well have been in Chinese.

a. I couldn't understand the words in the sentences of the books I read.

b. Many hustlers look as if they are rich, but in truth they cannot even read.

c. I wrote about how whites were to blame for what happened to blacks in the United States.

d. I couldn't write a simple letter.

QUESTIONS OF INFERENCE

Look back at the text to answer these questions. Answer in full sentences.

1. Why didn't Malcolm X want to use slang in his letters? _____

_____

2. In what way was Malcolm X a self-educated person? _____

_____

3. How did Malcolm X's prison studies change people's impression of him?

_____

_____

4. Although in prison, why did Malcolm X consider himself "truly free"? ____

_____

_____

5. What is the main point of Malcolm X's essay?
   a. There is nothing to do in prison but read.
   b. Learning to copy improves your penmanship.
   c. Reading opens your mind to important things.
   d. The dictionary is a worthwhile book to own.

QUESTIONS OF CRITICAL THINKING

**Answer each question in a short paragraph. You may want to use your
own paper.**

1. Why did Malcolm X write about his use of the dictionary? _____

_____

_____

_____

2. Why do you think some people talk better than they write? What, if any,
difference do you find between your own reading and writing? Which do

you prefer, and why? _____

_____

_____

_____

3. How has the dictionary helped you? _____

_____

_____

4. What was a time in your life when you felt "truly free"? _____

_____

_____

_____

5. What is life like for a person in this society who cannot read? _____

_____

_____

_____

6. Jot down any questions you would like to ask Malcolm X about his experiences in prison:

   a. _____

   b. _____

   c. _____

   d. _____

   e. _____

VOCABULARY

These words from Malcolm X's "Language" may be unfamiliar to you. The exercises will help you learn the meanings of these words and how to use them in sentences.

censorship (4)	convey (8)	riffling (12)
monitored (4)	emulate (8)	painstaking (13)
conversion (4)	penmanship (10)	succeeding (16)
articulate (8)	tablet (11)	inevitable (17)
frustrated (8)		

Word Meanings

Words often have more than one meaning and can be used as more than one part of speech. It's important to know which meaning of a word a writer has in mind and how the word is used in a particular sentence. Later in this chapter we shall talk about how to find word meanings in the dictionary. Meanwhile, the following are some definitions of words in "Language." Underline the meaning of the word as Malcolm X uses it.

Sometimes *articulate* means able to speak or express thoughts clearly and effectively, BUT sometimes it means to speak clearly.

Sometimes *succeeding* means getting or achieving a goal, BUT it can also mean to follow in sequence or immediately.

Sometimes *convey* means to carry, BUT it can also mean to communicate.

Sometimes *conversion* means an experience associated with the adoption of a religion, BUT sometimes it means a change from one thing to another, AND sometimes it means the scoring of an extra point in a football game after a touchdown.

Sometimes *tablet* means a thin piece of stone, wood, or metal shaped for a specific purpose, BUT sometimes it means a pad of paper with sheets fastened together at one edge, AND sometimes it means a solid, round dosage of medicine.

Put each word, using the underlined meaning, in a sentence. Make sure that you use the word in the same way in your sentence as Malcolm X used it in his essay.

articulate _____

succeeding _____

convey _____

conversion _____

tablet _____

Word Clues

Look carefully at each of the words below. Try to see them as the sum of their parts. Consult the list of prefixes and suffixes in Chapter 1, and write a "working definition" for each.

correspondence _____

censorship _____

Write a working definition for this word after you've thought about its parts:

penmanship _____

Seeing Words in Context

The words below appear in "Language." You may find clues to the meanings of each word from its context. As you reread, circle the words or phrases that form the context for each word. Then write (1) your working definition, (2) the dictionary definition that's right for the context, and (3) an original sentence using the word. If you have difficulty figuring out the meaning of the word from the context of "Language," you may find it helpful to read the following story, in which the words appear in italics:

1. word: *emulate*

   a. working definition _____

   b. dictionary definition _____

   c. your sentence _____

2. word: *monitored*

   a. working definition _____

b. dictionary definition _____

c. your sentence _____

3. word: *riffling*
   a. working definition _____

   b. dictionary definition _____

   c. your sentence _____

4. word: *inevitable*
   a. working definition _____

   b. dictionary definition _____

   c. your sentence _____

5. word: *frustrated*
   a. working definition _____

   b. dictionary definition _____

   c. your sentence _____

TWO-YEAR-OLDS

Young children are never satisfied with being young. They want to be adults. They want to *emulate* everything adults do. One day I noticed my two-year-old daughter watching me intently. She *monitored* everything I did as I sat reading the newspaper. She then picked up a section of the paper I had dropped on the floor and began turning the pages, *riffling* through them as I was doing. Her hands were so much smaller than mine that she could not quite get the pages to turn easily. I knew it would happen; it was *inevitable* that some of them ripped. She became so *frustrated* and angry that she started to scream.

Using Words in Context

One way to make new words part of your vocabulary is to use them in your writing. Malcolm X's essay deals with words. Write a paragraph about a time when you wanted to say something but felt you didn't have the right words to express yourself or a time when you said what you wanted to say, even though you were terrified. Begin with

Once I _____

Make sure to use at least five of the words from those in this chapter's Vocabulary section. When you proofread your paragraph, underline the words you used.

_____

_____

_____

_____

_____

_____

_____

_____

_____

_____

_____

WRITING AND REWRITING

What Did Malcolm X Want to Change?

Malcolm X wanted to be as articulate in his writing as he was in his speaking, and he felt he had to increase his vocabulary and change his way of expressing himself to suit the letters he was writing and the people to whom he addressed his letters. In other words, he wanted to adjust his *voice* to fit his topic and audience.

What Does Voice Mean?

We all possess a speaking voice, the way we make ourselves understood when we talk. We also possess a writing voice, produced by the words we choose and the way we put them together. We "speak" when we write in the same way we speak when we talk.

Can Two People Have the Same Voice?

Just as each person has a unique speaking voice, so too we each have a unique writing voice, and like a signature or fingerprint, that voice cannot be duplicated exactly. No two people sound exactly alike when they talk, and no two people sound exactly alike when they write, even when they are writing about the same topic.

It's important to recognize your writing voice so that you know what you sound like and if and when you must adjust your voice. You can use the dictionary, as Malcolm X did, as a valuable resource book and as a way of becoming conscious of your writing voice. Changing your vocabulary can also change your writing voice.

WRITING: A FIRST DRAFT

Take out a piece of paper and a pen or pencil. Write today's date at the top. Now relax for a moment. Close your eyes, breathe deeply. As the room starts to quiet, concentrate on your five senses: taste, touch, sight, smell, and hearing. Perhaps not all of your senses will be stimulated by this exercise, but some will. Tune your senses to this room. What can you hear? What can you feel, smell, taste? Now open your eyes. What can you see? How do you react to what your senses take in? At the signal, start writing, and do not stop for ten minutes. Write anything that comes into your head, in any order. Just let the ideas flow and—most important—keep your pen moving no matter how odd it feels. DO NOT attempt to write a story, and DO NOT pause if you are unsure about spelling, punctuation, or grammar. DO NOT stop to look up words in the dictionary. If you get stuck momentarily with nothing in your mind, write the word *stuck* until your next idea comes. Okay, begin. After ten minutes, stop.

Listen to some of your classmates read their focused writing. As you listen, write down what they saw and heard.

saw   *heard*

_____   _____

_____   _____

_____   _____

_____   _____

Which ideas are similar to the ideas in your focused writing?

_____

_____

_____

Which ideas are different?

_____

_____

_____

Focus on the ideas that were the same. Did the other writers express themselves in the same way that you did? Did they choose the same or different words to describe the same item? What words or phrases did the other writers use? Jot them down.

_____

_____

_____

What words or phrases did you use to describe the same item?

_____

_____

_____

These differences are part of what constitutes your voice and the voices of your classmates. Before you think about a second draft of your focused writing, let's consider how a dictionary can help you understand your voice.

Consider your focused writing as the first draft of an essay. Put it aside for now. We'll come back to it later in the chapter.

WHAT MAKES WRITING GOOD?
VOICE/DICTIONARY

Let's take a good look at the dictionary. If you own one, start bringing it to class. If you don't own one, start with the Webster's *New World* pocket dictionary.

What Is a Dictionary?

A dictionary is a book containing words, alphabetically arranged, and information about those words. People use a dictionary for many reasons.

1. Why do you use your dictionary? List five reasons:

_____

_____

_____

_____

2. For what reasons do your classmates use the dictionary?

_____

_____

Most people use the dictionary to find the meaning of a word. We call a word listed in the dictionary an *entry,* and we call the meaning or meanings for each word its *definitions.* Examine the cover of your pocket dictionary.

What Is an Entry?

What Is a Definition?

3. How many entries does your dictionary contain? _____

4. How many definitions? _____

Compare your pocket dictionary with those of your classmates.

5. Write down the number of entries and definitions:

Name of Dictionary	*Number of Entries*	*Number of Definitions*
_____	_____	_____
_____	_____	_____
_____	_____	_____

6. Why do you think the number of definitions is a selling point for a

dictionary? _____

7. If this information is not advertised on the cover, how can you get some

idea of how complete your dictionary is? _____

_____

Different Types of Dictionaries

Why Should We Look at Other Dictionaries?

What Are the Three Other Kinds of Dictionaries?

Pocket dictionaries are the most convenient to carry to class, but other types of dictionaries may be more helpful in other situations. You can find other dictionaries in your school library. Take your pocket dictionary for comparison. Ask the librarian to show you (1) a "college," "collegiate," or "desk" dictionary and (2) an unabridged dictionary.

1. How is a pocket dictionary different from a "collegiate" dictionary?

_____

_____

2. What is an unabridged dictionary? _____

_____

3. How does it differ from the pocket and collegiate dictionaries? _____

_____

Ask the librarian to show you any "specialized" dictionary.

4. What is the dictionary's title? _____

5. How does it differ from the other three you've been examining? _____

_____

6. Find three entries in the specialized dictionary that are *not* in the other dictionaries.

Entry   *Definition*

_____   _____

_____   _____

_____   _____

7. Why are these words in the specialized dictionary but not in the others?

_____

8. List the names of five specialized dictionaries in your library's collection. Check the names of those you think you might consult during your college career.

_____

_____

_____

_____

_____

9. Why do you think you might use these dictionaries? _____

_____

Who Writes Dictionaries?

Compiling a dictionary requires the participation of many people. A *lexicographer*, a specialist in compiling dictionaries, heads the team. The editorial and consultant staff are linguists and others who have special knowledge about language. *Linguists* study different aspects of language. Just as in medicine, in which people specialize in only one area, linguists specialize in *semantics*, the study of word meanings; *phonetics*, the study of sounds; or *etymology*, the study of the origins of words. The list on page 50 displays part of the consultant staff of the *Random House College Dictionary*. Consult it when you answer the following questions:

Who Is on the Staff of a Dictionary?

Who Are Some of the Language Specialists?

1. List five people on the consultant staff whom you would expect to help compile a dictionary.

Name	*Title*
_____	_____
_____	_____
_____	_____
_____	_____
_____	_____

CONSULTANT STAFF

Robert W. Abbett, Partner, Tippetts-Abbett-McCathy-Stratton, Consulting Engineers.

Loraine Alterman, Contemporary Music Critic.

American Telephone and Telegraph Company, Staff.

Frank C. Andrews, Professor of Chemistry, Merrill College, University of California, Santa Cruz.

Edmund C. Arnold, Professor and Chairman, Graphic Arts Department, Syracuse University.

J. G. Aston, Professor of Chemistry and Director, Cryogenic Laboratory, Pennsylvania State University.

Walter S. Avis, Professor of English, Royal Military College of Canada.

John A. Bailey, Director, The Transportation Center, Northwestern University.

Robert H. Ball, Professor of English, Queens College of the City University of New York; formerly, Curator, William Seymour Theatre Collection, Princeton University.

Stanley S. Ballard, Professor of Physics and Chairman, Department of Physics and Astronomy, University of Florida.

Theodore X. Barber, Director of Psychological Research, Medfield Foundation, Medfield State Hospital, Medfield, Mass.

Philip Bard, Professor and Director, Department of Physiology, School of Medicine, Johns Hopkins University.

Duncan Barnes, Writer-Reporter, *Sports Illustrated.*

Roy P. Basler, Director, Reference Department, Library of Congress.

Virgini: \. Basler, Editorial Researcher.

Caroline Bates, Senior Editor, *Gourmet Magazine.*

Ned D. Bayley, Assistant Director, Animal Husbandry Research Division, U.S. Department of Agriculture.

W.C. Benzer, Metallurgical Engineer, American Iron and Steel Institute.

Peter L. Bernstein, President, Peter L. Bernstein, Inc.; Visiting Professor of Economics, Graduate Faculty, The New School.

Theodore M. Bernstein, Assistant Managing Editor, *The New York Times.*

Raymond C. Binder, Professor of Mechanical Engineering, University of Southern California.

Max Birnbaum, Educational Consultant; Training Associate, Human Relations Center, Boston University.

Cyril E. Black, Professor of History, Princeton University.

Max Black, Professor, Sage School of Philosophy, Cornell University.

A. Harold Blatt, Professor and Chairman, Department of Chemistry, Queens College of the City University of New York.

Herbert Blumer, Professor of Sociology and Director, Institute of Social Sciences, University of California.

Ralph Philip Boas, Jr., Professor and Chairman, Department of Mathematics, Northwestern University.

Philip K. Bock, Professor of Anthropology, The University of New Mexico.

Winthrop S. Boggs, H. R. Harmer, Inc. International Philatelic Auctioneers; formerly, Director, Philatelic Foundation.

J. T. Bonner, Professor of Biology, Princeton University.

Alfred Bornemann, Professor of Metallurgy, Stevens Institute of Technology.

B. A. Botkin, formerly, President, American Folklore Society; Associate Professor of English, University of Oklahoma; Chief, Archive of Folk Song, and Fellow in Folklore, Library of Congress.

Jerald C. Brauer, Professor and Dean, Divinity School, University of Chicago.

Theodore M. Brody, Professor of Pharmacology, University of Michigan.

Arthur J. Bronstein, Professor of Speech, Queens College of the City University of New York.

Dirk Brouwer, Professor and Chairman, Department of Astronomy, Yale University; Director, Yale University Observatory.

Dorsey W. Bruner, Professor and Chairman, Department of Veterinary Microbiology, New York State Veterinary College, Cornell University.

Ralph Buchsbaum, Professor of Biology, University of Pittsburgh.

Arthur H. Burr, Sibley Professor of Mechanical Engineering and Head, Department of Machine Design, College of Engineering, Cornell University.

Meredith F. Burrill, Director, Office of Geography, U.S. Department of the Interior.

Meribeth E. Cameron, Professor of History and Dean, Mount Holyoke College.

William Card, Professor of English, Illinois Teachers College: Chicago —South.

James Cass, Associate Education Editor, *Saturday Review.*

Elliott E. Cheatham, Frank C. Rand Professor of Law, Vanderbilt University; Charles Evans Hughes Professor Emeritus of Law, Columbia University.

John E. Chrisinger, Major USAF, retired; formerly, Associate Professor of Aeronautics, U.S. Air Force Academy.

Anatole Chujoy, Editor and Publisher, *Dance News.*

Craig Claiborne, Food Editor, *The New York Times.*

Gerson D. Cohen, Chancellor, Jewish Theological Seminary of America.

Henry Steele Commager, Professor of American History, Amherst College.

Edward U. Condon, Professor of Physics and Fellow of the Joint Institute for Laboratory Astrophysics, University of Colorado.

Carleton S. Coon, Professor of Anthropology, retired, and Research Curator of Ethnology, University Museum, University of Pennsylvania.

Edward M. Crane, Jr., President, Pitman Publishing Corporation.

Charles R. Dahlberg, Associate Professor and Chairman, Department of English, Queens College of the City University of New York.

Russell E. Davis, Assistant Chief, Beef Cattle Research Branch, U.S. Department of Agriculture.

John P. Dawson, Professor of Law, Harvard University.

Arthur Gerard DeVoe, M.D.; Professor of Ophthalmology, Medical School, Columbia University.

Emery M. Dieffenbach, Assistant to Chief, Crop Production Engineering Research Branch, U.S. Department of Agriculture.

David Diringer, Professor, University of Florence, Italy; Lecturer, University of Cambridge, England.

Mario Einaudi, Walter Carpenter Professor of International and Comparative Politics, Cornell University.

Maximilian Ellenbogen, Professor of Classical and Oriental Languages, Queens College of the City University of New York.

John R. Elting, Colonel, USA; Deputy Chief of Staff for Intelligence, Military District of Washington; formerly, Acting Professor of Military Art and Engineering, U.S. Military Academy.

Erik H. Erikson, Professor of Human Development Emeritus, Harvard University.

Vincent J. Esposito, Brigadier General, USA; Head, Department of Military Art and Engineering, U.S. Military Academy.

Thomas H. Everett, Assistant Director (Horticulture) and Senior Curator of Education, New York Botanical Garden.

William L. Everitt, Professor and Dean, College of Engineering, University of Illinois.

Dorothy Fey, Executive Director, The United States Trademark Association.

Andreas Feininger, Photographer.

Donald Finkel, Poet-in-Residence, Washington University.

Louis Finkelstein, Professor and Chancellor, Jewish Theological Seminary of America.

Sydney N. Fisher, Professor of History, Ohio State University.

Georges Florovsky, Professor Emeritus of Eastern Church History, Divinity School, Harvard University; Visiting Professor of History, Princeton University.

Food and Nutrition Service, U.S. Department of Agriculture.

Henry B. Fried, Technical Director, American Watchmakers Institute; Teacher, Watch and Clock Mechanics, George Westinghouse Vocational and Technical High School.

Clifford Frondel, Professor of Mineralogy, Harvard University.

Bil Gilbert, Writer.

Bruce Gilchrist, Director, Columbia University Center for Computing Activities.

Wilbur E. Gilman, Professor and Chairman, Department of Speech. Queens College of the City University of New York.

Cyrus H. Gordon, Professor and Chairman, Department of Mediterranean Studies, Brandeis University.

Charles M. Goren, Author-Lecturer.

Stephen V. Grancsay, Curator Emeritus of Arms and Armor, The Metropolitan Museum of Art.

Joseph H. Greenberg, Professor of Anthropology, Stanford University.

Charles H. Greene, Professor and Chairman, Department of Glass Science, Alfred University.

Konrad Gries, Professor and Chairman, Department of Classical and Oriental Languages, Queens College of the City University of New York.

Harold J. Grossman, Harold J. Grossman Associates; Consultant, American Hotel and Motel Association.

Harry G. Guthmann, Professor Emeritus of Finance, School of Business, Northwestern University.

Sherman P. Haight, Jr., Chairman of Advisory Committee, formerly President, U.S. Pony Clubs; Joint Master, Litchfield County Hounds.

Livingston Hall, Roscoe Pound Professor of Law, Harvard University.

2. List five people on the consultant staff whom you would *not* expect to help compile a dictionary.

Name   *Title*

_____   _____

_____   _____

_____   _____

_____   _____

_____   _____

3. What do you think these people can contribute to a dictionary? _____

_____

What Goes into the Dictionary?

No dictionary can be large enough or current enough to include an entry for every word in the language and every definition of that word, and so lexicographers must choose what to include. Compilers of English dictionaries must be sensitive to the many varieties of English spoken all over the world. In many places, English is a *native language*. That is, it is the inhabitant's first language. List all the countries you can think of where English is the native language:

What Is a Native Language?

_____

_____

_____

_____

In many other places, English is the *official language*, not the native language. That is, it is the language of school instruction and the language in which business and government are conducted. It is the second language for the people in these areas; most of the population also speak a native

What Is an Official Language?

language or languages. List all the countries you can think of where English is the official language:

_____

_____

Varieties of English

Most dictionaries published in the United States are of "American English," which is different from the English used in the United Kingdom. The vocabularies differ; for example, sometimes the words that are used in the United States are not used in England and sometimes the same word has a different meaning.

1. Look up these words in your dictionary and write down their definitions:

queue _____

fortnight _____

2. Do you ordinarily use these words? Why or why not?

_____

_____

What Is a Usage Label?

In American dictionaries, words used mainly in the United Kingdom carry a *usage label* that indicates they are "chiefly British." Similarly, in British dictionaries, American words carry a usage label. These labels may help you decide whether you will want to use a particular word.

3. Does your dictionary give you information about where *queue* and *fortnight* are most commonly used? _____ Where? _____

_____

4. What do these italicized words mean? Write down the meaning in the space.
a. Last week we had to *sit* for two exams.

Sit means _____ in this sentence.

b. Last year we took a *holiday* for two weeks.

Holiday means _____ in this sentence.

5. Do you use these words in this way? Why or why not? _____

_____

6. Rewrite these sentences using your own words.

   a. _____

   b. _____

7. Use *sit* and *holiday* in sentences that sound natural to you:

   a. _____

   b. _____

8. Check your dictionary for the definitions of *sit* and *holiday*. Write down two definitions for each word. Try to use definitions that fit the two ways in which the words have been used. Check the definitions that match the example sentences, and double-check the definitions that match the sentences you wrote.[1]

Sit   *Holiday*

a. _____   **a.** _____

   _____   _____

b. _____   **b.** _____

   _____   _____

   Spelling also differs from country to country. For example:

         labour   cheque
         defence   centre

9. Are these words spelled correctly? Why or why not? _____

_____

10. How do you spell these words? _____

_____

[1] If one definition of the word has a usage label attached, put the usage label in parentheses next to the definition.

11. What information does your dictionary give you about the spelling of

these words? _____

_____

     Pronunciation also differs from place to place where people speak English. For example:

               lieutenant   laboratory   secretary

12. How are these words pronounced in England?

13. Which pronunciation is correct, the American or the British? _____

Varieties of American English

How Does English in Each Region of the Country Differ?

What Difference Does It Make Where You Were Raised?

Even if lexicographers decide to use American English, they still must choose which variety of American English to use. Pronunciation, vocabulary, and usage differ from region to region of the country, and lexicographers must decide how many and which of these *regionalisms* to include.

     We recognize differences in pronunciation (or accent) most easily. We are aware that people from the South (e.g., former President Jimmy Carter) speak differently from people in New England (e.g., former President John F. Kennedy). Where we were raised has a strong effect on the way in which we pronounce certain words. For example, people in the South may pronounce the word *for* without the final *r* sound: *fo'*. Some people in New England may pronounce the word *park* with a "broad" *a: pahk.*

  1. Which words do you use that are pronounced differently by others?

_____

_____

_____

_____

  2. How do you decide how to pronounce your words? _____

_____

  3. Whose pronunciation of these words is correct? Why? _____

_____

The meanings of words also differ from region to region in the United States. That is, people from different regions use different words to refer to the same thing. These words are called *synonyms*. For instance, each of these words refers to a sandwich made with a long roll:

    hero   hoagie   poor boy
    grinder   torpedo   submarine

4. Which one of these words is the "correct" word for the item? Why? ____

_____

5. How would you decide which word you'd use to order the sandwich?

_____

Some dictionaries include more regional varieties of language than others do. Check the regional varieties that your dictionary includes. Compare your findings with those of your classmates.

Sometimes words used in one region of the country are not used at all in another, or if they are used, their definitions are completely different. For each of these words or phrases, write a one- or two-word synonym:

snap beans _____   sack _____

butter beans _____   pop _____

ice potatoes _____   spigot _____

Frigidaire _____   dime store _____

Ask your classmates to define these words. If their definitions are different, note where the student comes from.

6. Define the italicized word in these sentences:

  a. We were not able to fry all the eggs in one *spider*.

  Spider means _____ in this sentence.

  b. The young couple finished drinking their *phosphate* and left the restaurant.

  Phosphate means _____ in this sentence.

7. Do you use these words in these ways? Why or why not? _____

_____

8. Rewrite the sentences using your own words:

a. _____

b. _____

9. Use the words *spider* and *phosphate* in sentences that sound natural to you.

a. _____

b. _____

10. Check your dictionary for the definitions of *spider* and *phosphate*. Write two definitions for each word. Try to use definitions that fit the two ways in which the words have been used. Check the definitions that match the example sentences, and double-check the definitions that match the sentences you wrote.[2]

Spider   *Phosphate*

a. _____   **a.** _____

_____   _____

b. _____   **b.** _____

_____   _____

Levels of Language

Where Do You Use Standard English?

What Is EAE?

Is NS as Correct as SE?

What Is Patois?

Some of the differences in the words that people use have nothing to do with where they come from but, rather, refer to the *level of language* they choose to use. In schools, in business, and in most writing, people are expected to use formal language, sometimes called *standard English* (SE). Because this language results from your editing and changing your writing, it is also called *edited American English* (EAE). EAE is important to know and use where and when appropriate. But it is only one variety of English.

Colloquial, informal, or *nonstandard* (NS) are other varieties. According to *Webster's New International Dictionary* (second edition), "Colloquial speech may be as correct as formal speech." Some people use NS or informal English almost all the time. Then we refer to it as a *dialect*. In many parts of the Caribbean, such dialects are called *patois* or *creole*.

How can colloquial English be as correct as EAE? It's a matter of appropri-

---

[2] If one definition of the word has a usage label attached, put the usage label in parentheses next to the definition.

ateness. Appropriateness in language is like appropriateness in dress. You would not ordinarily wear tennis shoes to a formal dance or a tuxedo to a football game—although it certainly is possible to do either. Rather, you dress for the occasion. Likewise, you would not ordinarily say "What's happening?" to your new boss or "Please communicate with me by telephone" to your best friend. You adjust your speech and writing to fit the situation.

Some people label SE as "proper" and NS as "broken" English.

1. Do you think there are such things as "proper" and "broken" English?

Why or why not? _____

_____

2. What constitutes "broken" English for you? _____

_____

Slang

Sometimes NS is called *slang*. Used by small groups of people, slang contains some of the newest expressions in the language. Not all people who use NS also use slang. Slang is a "private" language in which words have special meanings created to hide their messages from people outside the group. Often, however, words that start as private, in-group expressions become widely known and used—for instance, *dig* meaning "to understand" and *rap* meaning "to talk."

What Is Slang?

If you know the meaning of the italicized word in these sentences, write a synonym for it.

Those shoes are *hip.* _____

Those shoes are *groovy.* _____

Those shoes are *heavy.* _____

Those shoes are *the joint.* _____

Those shoes are *death.* _____

Those shoes are *what's happening.* _____

Those shoes are *to die.* _____

1. Look up each word in the dictionary, and note whether or not the dictionary has a definition similar to your synonym.

2. Why do you think some of these definitions are in the dictionary and some are not? _____

_____

The word most people think of when they think of NS is *ain't*.

3. Would you expect to find *ain't* in your dictionary? Why or why not? _____

_____

4. Look up *ain't* in your dictionary. If it is there, how does the dictionary indicate what kind of word it is? _____

_____

5. What situations does the dictionary list for the acceptable use of *ain't?* ___

_____

6. What situations do you find acceptable for using *ain't?* _____

_____

As you can see, usage labels also indicate at what level of language the lexicographers consider a word to be. Thus, they can guide you in using a new word in an appropriate situation. However, you may find that some NS words are not in the dictionary at all, because most dictionaries include formal English and only those NS words that are very widely used.

New Words and Old Words

What Is a Neologism?

Sometimes words are too new to be included in the dictionary; sometimes they are too old. *Neologisms* are new words. Some come and go in the language too quickly ever to be included in a dictionary, but some enter the language and stay.

1. What's your definition of *xerography?* _____

2. What is the "word clue" to its meaning? _____

3. How "old" do you think this word is? Why? _____

_____

4. Is *xerography* included in your dictionary? _____

5. In what year was your dictionary published? _____
What do you think the italicized words mean in these sentences?
 a. We *finalized* our discussion of the causes of the accident.
 b. All the students want to do is *party* every Friday night.
 c. How often will we have to *conversate* with her about the plans?
 d. Several sessions were held to *orientate* new students to the school.

6. Write your working definitions of these words:

finalized _____

party _____

conversate _____

orientate _____

7. Look up the preceding four words in the dictionary. Can they be used as verbs in a sentence? In what way(s) does your dictionary indicate

that they can be used? _____

_____

8. Which of these words is (are) not in your dictionary? _____

_____

9. Why do you think they have been omitted? _____

_____

10. Look up each word in these pairs:
 a. conversate—converse
 b. orientate—orient

11. Which word in each pair is newer? _____

12. How does your dictionary indicate this? _____

   Sometimes words that are no longer commonly used continue to appear in dictionaries. For example, consider the words *thy* and *thou*. Are these words in your dictionary? Why do lexicographers continue to

include them? _____

13. In what situations would these words be appropriate? _____

_____

14. Does your dictionary attach a usage label (like *archaic*) to them? _____

      Another old word, *wench*, has undergone a change in meaning. Look up the word in your dictionary, and write down the older definition:

_____

15. How do you know which meaning is older? _____

16. Are you familiar with the meanings of the following words?

      streak—"to make a quick dash nakedly in a public place."
      sputnik—"a Soviet satellite."

17. Look up these words in your dictionary. Check them if they appear. Do you think they will appear in the next edition of your dictionary? Why

or why not? _____

_____

18. Is a dictionary's date of publication important? Why or why not? _____

_____

19. How long should you keep a dictionary? Why? _____

_____

      Lexicographers do not include some words in the dictionary because the words are considered vulgar or offensive. These words are *obscenities* and *profanities.*

20. Do you think obscenities should be omitted from a dictionary? Why or

why not? _____

21. Why do certain words that you consider profane appear in the dictionary?

_____

22. Do you think obscenity has any place in the use of language? Why? ____

_____

How Is Information Presented in the Dictionary?

Let's look at the many ways in which a dictionary presents information about words, including the symbols and abbreviations used to code that information. Examine these entries for the word *abridge,* from two editions of *Webster's New World Dictionary:*

COLLEGE EDITION

a·bridge (ə brij′) *vt.* **a·bridged′, a·bridg′ing** [ME. *abregen* < OFr. *abregier* < LL. *abbreviare:* see ABBREVIATE] **1.** to reduce in scope, extent, etc.; shorten **2.** to shorten by using fewer words but keeping the main contents; condense **3.** to lessen or curtail (rights, authority, etc.) **4.** [Rare] to deprive (*of* rights, privileges, etc.) —*SYN.* see SHORTEN —**a·bridg′a·ble, a·bridge′a·ble** *adj.* —**a·bridg′er** *n.* **a·bridg·ment, a·bridge·ment** (ə brij′mənt) *n.* [ME.

POCKET EDITION

a·bridge (ə brij′) *vt.* **a·bridged′, a·bridg′ing** [see ABBREVIATE] **1.** to shorten, lessen, or curtail **2.** to shorten by using fewer words but keeping the substance —**a·bridg′ment, a·bridge′ment** *n.*

In what order do these items appear in the entry for *abridge* in the college edition? Number them from one to ten.

( ) origin   ( ) word ending, adjective
( ) definitions   ( ) pronunciation
( ) syllabification   ( ) synonym
( ) part of speech   ( ) spelling
( ) word ending, noun ( ) word ending, verb

1. Where do you find the correct spelling of the word? _____

2. Where do you find out how to divide *abridge* into syllables? _____

_____

3. How many syllables does *abridge* have? _____

4. What symbol is used to divide words into syllables? _____

5. Is this symbol the same as the one used in your dictionary? If not, what

symbol does your dictionary use? _____

6. Why is it helpful to know how words are divided into syllables? _____

_____

7. Where can you find the pronunciation of *abridge?* _____

8. Which symbols help you pronounce the word? _____

9. Are the same symbols used in your dictionary? If not, what symbols are

used in your dictionary? _____

10. Examine the following partial pronunciation key taken from *Webster's New World Dictionary* (college edition):

fat, āpe, cär; ten, ēven; is, bīte; gō, hôrn, tōōl, look; oil, out; up, fʉr; get; joy; yet; chin; she; thin, then; zh, leisure; ŋ, ring; ə for *a* in *ago*, *e* in *agent*, *i* in *sanity*, *o* in *comply*, *u* in *focus*; ' as in *able* (ā'b'l); Fr. bâl; ë, Fr. coeur; ö, Fr. feu; Fr. mon; ô, Fr. coq; ü, Fr. duc; r, Fr. cri; H, G. ich; kh, G. doch. See inside front cover. ☆ Americanism; ‡ foreign; *hypothetical; < derived from

11. Do you have a similar pronunciation key at the bottom of the pages of

your dictionary? If not, where is it? _____

12. (ə brij′) is given for the pronunciation of *abridge*. Use the pronunciation key to find the following information:

  a. "ə" is the sound of *a* in the word _____

  b. "i" is the sound of *i* in the word _____

  c. "j" is the sound of *j* in the word _____

13. What words does your dictionary give for each of these sounds?

  a. The word with the "ə" sound is _____

  b. The word with the "i" sound is _____

  c. The word with the "j" sound is _____

14. Are the sounds for these symbols in your dictionary the same as those

in the pronunciation key? If not, how are they different? _____

_____

15. What are some other sounds given in the pronunciation key for the

letter *a?* _____

16. What symbols are used to distinguish the different sounds for the

letter *a?* _____

17. Which syllable in *abridge* is stressed? _____

18. What symbol tells you this? _____

19. In each pair of words, what do the symbols tell you about the words? Think of sentences for each word.

> per′ mit   permit′
> tor′ ment   torment′
> sur′ vey   survey′
> im′ port   import′

20. What abbreviation does the dictionary use to indicate the part of speech

that *abridge* is? _____

21. Does your dictionary use the same symbol? If not, what symbol does it

use? _____

22. How many definitions for *abridge* are in the college edition's entry? How many are in the pocket edition's?

_____

23. According to the college edition, what is the origin of *abridge?* _____

_____

24. Look up the origin of *abbreviate* in your dictionary. How is it similar to

or different from the origin of *abridge?* _____

_____

25. How is the relationship between *abridge* and *abbreviate* indicated in the

entry for *abridge?* _____

26. Does your dictionary indicate this relationship between the two words?

27. List some of the word endings, suffixes, from the college edition's entry that can be added to *abridge:*

_____   _____

_____   _____

Which of these word endings change *abridge* into an adjective?

_____   _____

Which change it into a noun?

_____   _____

Which of these word endings do *not* change the part of speech?

_____   _____

Which of these word endings are included in the entry for *abridge* in your dictionary?

_____   _____

_____   _____

Why aren't all the word endings listed together in the entry?_____

_____

What are the different spellings for the adjective form of *abridge?*

_____   _____

Which spelling is preferred? _____

Practice Using the Dictionary

Look up each of the following words in your dictionary, and answer the questions:

1. *entrepreneur:*

    a. How is it divided into syllables? _____

    b. How is it pronounced? _____

    c. What part of speech is it? _____

    d. Which syllable has the primary stress? _____

    e. What is its origin? _____

    f. Write a sentence using it: _____

_____

2. *patois:*

    a. How is it divided into syllables? _____

    b. How is it pronounced? _____

    c. What part of speech is it? _____

    d. Which syllable has the primary stress? _____

    e. What is its origin? _____

    f. Write a sentence using it: _____

_____

3. *subtle:*

    a. How is it divided into syllables? _____

    b. How is it pronounced? _____

    c. What part of speech is it? _____

    d. Which syllable has the primary stress? _____

    e. What is its origin? _____

    f. Write a sentence using it: _____

_____

4. *euphoria:*

    a. How is it divided into syllables? _____

    b. How is it pronounced? _____

    c. What part of speech is it? _____

    d. Which syllable has the primary stress? _____

    e. What is its origin? _____

    f. Write a sentence using it: _____

5. *calliope:*

    a. How is it divided into syllables? _____

    b. How is it pronounced? _____

    c. What part of speech is it? _____

    d. Which syllable has the primary stress? _____

    e. What is its origin? _____

    f. Write a sentence using it: _____

    _____

6. *hegemony:*

    a. How is it divided into syllables? _____

    b. How is it pronounced? _____

    c. What part of speech is it? _____

    d. Which syllable has the primary stress? _____

    e. What is its origin? _____

    f. Write a sentence using it: _____

    _____

7. *posthumous:*

    a. How is it divided into syllables? _____

    b. How is it pronounced? _____

    c. What part of speech is it? _____

    d. Which syllable has the primary stress? _____

    e. What is its origin? _____

    f. Write a sentence using it: _____

    _____

8. *déjà vu:*

    a. How is it divided into syllables? ————————————

    b. How is it pronounced? ————————————

    c. What part of speech is it? ————————————

    d. Which syllable has the primary stress? ————————————

    e. What is its origin? ————————————

    f. Write a sentence using it: ————————————

    ————————————————————————

9. *malevolence:*

    a. How is it divided into syllables? ————————————

    b. How is it pronounced: ————————————

    c. What part of speech is it? ————————————

    d. Which syllable has the primary stress? ————————————

    e. What is its origin? ————————————

    f. Write a sentence using it: ————————————

    ————————————————————————

10. *neologism:*

    a. How is it divided into syllables? ————————————

    b. How is it pronounced: ————————————

    c. What part of speech is it? ————————————

    d. Which syllable has the primary stress? ————————————

    e. What is its origin? ————————————

    f. Write a sentence using it: ————————————

    ————————————————————————

Do These Exercises Before You Revise Your First Draft.

1. Look back at "Language" by Malcolm X.

    a. List some of the slang words he uses at the beginning of the essay:

Word   *Definition*

_____   _____

_____   _____

_____   _____

    b. Are these words listed in your dictionary?

    c. Are they defined as Malcolm X used them?

2. Do you agree or disagree that Malcolm X needed to change his writing voice? Why? _____

_____

_____

3. Describe a situation in your life when you felt the need to adjust your speaking or writing voice. _____

_____

_____

4. Read the following focused writing about a classroom. Read it twice. The first time, read it to understand what the writer is saying. The second time, underline the words or phrases you think the writer might want to change in order to make his voice more appropriate to an audience of college administrators.

THIS ROOM

    God, I hate this place. It's so grubby. Walls a yucky yellow, dirt mixed with paint. The linoleum is all chewed up and raggedy. The dark patches are filled with years of dirt. Somebody spilled a coke. My foot keeps getting stuck in the stinking slime. Stuck. Stuck. Hah. Hah. No windows. How can they make a classroom here. The jerks. Teacher says it usedta be a supply room. No air. I'm glad its February. In May we won't be able to breathe here. With the door open, too much noise. Telephones ringing, teachers talking, students hanging in the halls. Damn! Can't think.

Neon light buzzing in my brain. Coat rack with five coats—gray, brown, winter colors. Ah, a blue jacket. Not a mink in the bunch! Waste paper basket overflowing with crud. This ain't no place to learn. Wanna get outta here fast.

Everybody's writing. Stuck. The guy in front of me is cute. I like this class. The teacher's funny. She's kinda tall with dark hair. She says we'll learn to write alot. I hope so. Twenty-five students, all with heads down. Are they writing or watching that roach crawl across the wall. Say stop, lady, please. stuck.

Be prepared to discuss your choices with your classmates.

REWRITING: A SECOND DRAFT

Now you are ready to turn your focused writing into a second draft. Read it carefully, aloud, and, if you can, to a friend or classmate. Try to get a new vision of your subject. As you revise, think about

1. *Topic, audience, and purpose:* What do you want to tell about, to whom, and why?
2. *Details:* Have you said all you want to say, or now that you have reread your writing, have you thought of new ideas to add? Add them now. Have you named people and described places? Some details are whole new ideas, and some are just single words.
3. *Order:* Will your audience get your point?
4. *Language:* Are you happy with the words you used? Is your writing voice appropriate to your topic, audience, and purpose?

After you've written your second draft, go on to Proofreading, where you'll get some help on the proofreading stage of your writing.

PROOFREADING

CONVENTIONS

When you proofread, some of the "clean up" involves conventions. *Conventions* are the things we follow when writing that make the piece easier to read. Much like road signs that guide travelers on their way, conventions help readers progress through the writing. We shall look briefly at the conventions of *manuscript form, hyphenation, capitalization, abbreviations and numbers, apostrophes,* and *word boundaries.* You may already know much of this material. If so, review it quickly.

What Are Conventions?

Manuscript Form

1. Date each page of your work in the upper right-hand corner.
2. If your paper has a title, center it on the first line of the first page, and skip two lines between the title and first line of text.

3. Always use margins to guide you. Margins should be approximately one to one-and-one-half inches wide on all sides of the page. (Most often, you'll use composition paper on which the left-hand margin is drawn. You can see the right-hand margin through the paper. If there is no right-hand margin, you may pencil one in lightly.) Stay within the margins wherever reasonable, but remember that the right-hand margin is flexible. That is, you may go beyond the margin to finish a word, put in a comma, or use a hyhen.
4. Indent by five spaces the first word of each new paragraph.
5. Write on each line of the paper. Don't skip lines unless your teacher asks you to do so.
6. Begin one sentence immediately following the one before it. Don't begin the next sentence on a new line.
7. Begin a new paragraph on the next line of the page. Don't skip lines between paragraphs.
8. When a punctuation mark falls at the end of a line, put it *after* the word it follows—even if it goes beyond the margin. Never start a new line with a punctuation mark.

Sample 1: Manuscript Form

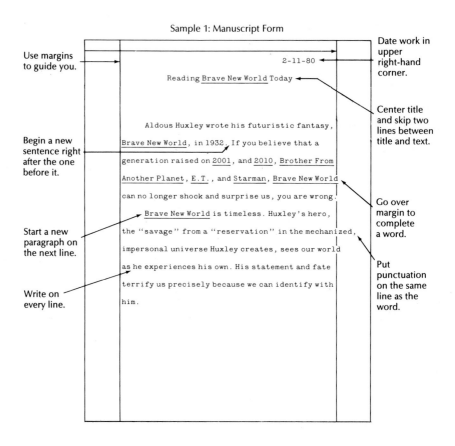

Use margins to guide you.

Date work in upper right-hand corner.

2-11-80

Reading Brave New World Today

Center title and skip two lines between title and text.

Begin a new sentence right after the one before it.

Aldous Huxley wrote his futuristic fantasy, Brave New World, in 1932. If you believe that a generation raised on 2001, and 2010, Brother From Another Planet, E.T., and Starman, Brave New World can no longer shock and surprise us, you are wrong.

Go over margin to complete a word.

Start a new paragraph on the next line.

Brave New World is timeless. Huxley's hero, the "savage" from a "reservation" in the mechanized, impersonal universe Huxley creates, sees our world

Put punctuation on the same line as the word.

Write on every line.

as he experiences his own. His statement and fate terrify us precisely because we can identify with him.

Hyphenation

A *hyphen* is a short line (-) that we use to signal that a word is being divided. When we hyphenate to divide a word at the end of a line, we use these conventions:

1. Divide words by syllables, as found in the dictionary.
2. Hyphenate only when you absolutely must. Remember that the right-hand margin is flexible; you can go beyond it to complete a word.
3. Never hyphenate one-syllable words: Write words like *huge, had, home,* and *all* on one line.
4. Never separate one letter from a word, even if it is a separate syllable. Write words like *enough* and *alone* on one line.
5. When you divide compound words *at the end of a line,* divide them by their recognizable parts. Write words like *bookkeeper, notebook,* and *birthday* as

book-	note-	birth-
keeper	book	day

We also use a hyphen to connect parts of certain compound words, like *mother-in-law.* Such compound words or put-together words are hyphenated (divided) even when they appear on one line:

1. Use a hyphen between words that are connected to form one word, like

    mother-in-law
    self-confidence

2. Use a hyphen between two-word numbers for 21 to 99 when they are spelled out.

    thirty-five
    seventy-two

3. Use a hyphen between two words used as a single adjective to describe a following noun.

    He drove a two-ton truck.

    The absence or presence of a hyphen sometimes can change the meaning of a sentence.

    I saw a man eating fish.
    I saw a man-eating fish.

    You can see that the hyphen makes a great deal of difference. In which one is the writer observing a frightening situation?

71

4. Use a hyphen between a prefix and a proper noun.

   un-American
   anti-Nixon

Sample 2: Hyphenation

Hyphenate certain compound words. → My sister-in-law, Carrie, is ex- ← Hyphenate according to syllables found in dictionary.

tremely helpful, but she never misses

an opportunity to proclaim her political

beliefs. When I gave a huge dinner party

Hyphenate the numbers between 21 and 99 when written out. → for my husband's thirty-third birth- ← Divide words by their parts.

day, she baked four cakes and the roast.

She brought the okra for me to steam — Do not divide words of one syllable.

and helped me with the salad. Then she

went upstairs, put on her expensive,

Hyphenate two words used as a single adjective. → light-blue dress and came to the party.

On the dress, she insisted on wearing a

Hyphenate a prefix connected to a proper noun. → pro-Republican button with the face of

some local politcian smiling at her ruffled

collar.

Practice with Manuscript Form and Hyphenation

Take out any paragraph you have written for this class. On a fresh piece of paper, draw margins that are one-half inch narrower than the original ones. Rewrite the paragraph within these new margins. Hyphenate any words that must be divided between lines. Remember that the right-hand margin is flexible. Use your own paper.

Capitalization

You probably know the conventions of capitalization, but you may not always use them.

Use a capital letter

1. At the beginning of each new sentence.

   The textbooks cost nearly a week's salary.

2. For the word *I:*

   "Everything I've ever felt strongly about, I've done something about."

3. For the first word of a direct quotation that is a complete sentence:

   The captain bellowed, "Let's all get aboard!"

4. For names of people, cities, countries, regions, and languages:

   Kemal Faruki *comes from* **Karachi, Pakistan,** *in* **Asia,** *where the population speaks* **Bengali.**

5. In titles and initials used with names of people:

   I met **Lord Peter Wimsey** *at the home of* E. X. Ferrars.

6. For days of the week, months, and holidays:

   We shall meet on the first **Tuesday** *of* **November,** *if it is not* **Veteran's Day.**

7. For trademarks and the names of companies, organizations, and institutions:

   After leaving the **United Nations,** *the delegate met with executives from* **General Foods** *to discuss the exportation of* **Cheerios** *to her country.*

8. For the first letter of a word formed from a proper noun:

   The vacation was the tourist's first exposure to **American** *culture.* (Amer-ican *comes from the proper noun* America.)

Sample 3: Capitalization

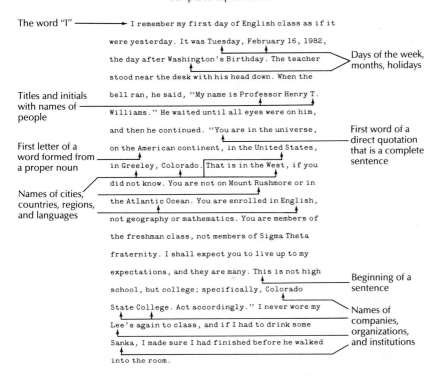

The word "I" ⟶ I remember my first day of English class as if it were yesterday. It was Tuesday, February 16, 1982, the day after Washington's Birthday. The teacher stood near the desk with his head down. When the bell rang, he said, "My name is Professor Henry T. Williams." He waited until all eyes were on him, and then he continued. "You are in the universe, on the American continent, in the United States, in Greeley, Colorado. That is in the West, if you did not know. You are not on Mount Rushmore or in the Atlantic Ocean. You are enrolled in English, not geography or mathematics. You are members of the freshman class, not members of Sigma Theta fraternity. I shall expect you to live up to my expectations, and they are many. This is not high school, but college; specifically, Colorado State College. Act accordingly." I never wore my Lee's again to class, and if I had to drink some Sanka, I made sure I had finished before he walked into the room.

Days of the week, months, holidays

Titles and initials with names of people

First letter of a word formed from a proper noun

Names of cities, countries, regions, and languages

First word of a direct quotation that is a complete sentence

Beginning of a sentence

Names of companies, organizations, and institutions

73

Do *not* use a capital letter for

1. The names of professions:

   I studied to be a doctor *but became a* teacher *instead.*

2. The seasons of the year:

   I like fall *best and* spring *second best.*

3. Most school subjects (when you are not referring to a specific or numbered course):

   We walked to nursing *from* physics.

4. Common nouns:

   The students *went straight from* high school *to college.*

Practice with Capitalization

1. Look back at "Language" by Malcolm X. Note each capital letter, and list the reason that each is capitalized.

   2. Read this story twice. The first time, read it to understand the content. The second time, proofread it, and put in capital letters where appropriate.

      amy adams was skinny. her mother, adele, told her so. her father told her too. her sisters, ann and amanda, just laughed. you think you can eat anything you want to because you're so thin, but you'll see. one day you'll be eating an ice cream sundae and you will see a stomach. just you wait."

      amy wasn't worried. in the fall she left akron for atlanta where she enrolled in college. she wanted to major in home economics. she wanted to teach cooking. on monday she went for an interview with the chairman of the department. professor c. s. allen took one look at her and said, "ah, amy, you are skinny. no one will want to learn cooking from someone who looks as if she never eats. maybe you ought to major in mathematics. you look like a number one."

amy started to cry. she cried all the way back to mountain view, the dormitory at the atlanta college for women. all night long she pondered her future and while she pondered, she ate. she considered majoring in english as she ate her way through a box of mallomars, but she didn't want to spend her life reading about fat people. she thought of history through a quart of howard johnson's vanilla but decided that history was the study of how people gained weight. "physics, no," she thought, through one cashew at a time and a bottle of ginger ale. she thought through the night and through four ham and cheese sandwiches, a chipwich, two dozen doughnuts, and a danny frozen yogurt.

by morning, she knew it was home ec. or bust. by morning her sisters' prophecy had come true. amy was the fattest person in the southeast. she went to allen. he looked at her and said, "now you look like a zero. you'll have to go on a diet. no one will want to learn cooking from someone who looks like she eats too much. go join muncher's repent." amy replied, "what are you saying? monday you told me to gain weight. tuesday you tell me to diet. i can't win."

Abbreviations and Numbers

Abbreviations and numbers are handy to use when you are taking notes or writing for yourself, but with certain exceptions, they have little place in formal writing. Use these conventions:

1. Write out the word *and.* Avoid the ampersand (&) and plus sign (+).

    Write: *My sister and I. . . .*
    rather than: *My sister & I. . . .*

2. Write out all numbers less than one hundred and the adjectives they form:

    Write: twenty-three miles   the twenty-third student
    rather than: 23 miles   the 23rd student

3. Use numerals for numbers of 100 or more.

    Write: 1987
    rather than: nineteen hundred eighty-seven

4. Never start a sentence with a numeral.

    Write: One hundred-fifty people jammed into the classroom.
    rather than: 150 people jammed into the classroom.

5. Avoid the "small letter" endings with dates.

    Write: January 23, 1946
    rather than: January 23rd 1946

6. Use numbers for percentages, decimals, and fractions.

    Write: 43 percent   6.5 or 6½
    rather than: forty-three percent six point five,
                                     six and one-half

7. Use abbreviations for titles before and after names.

    Write: Dr. Loretta Stone, Ph.D.
    rather than: Doctor Loretta Stone, Doctor of Philosophy

8. Use abbreviations after specific dates and times.

    Write: 10:30 P.M.   A.D. 1990
    rather than: 10:30 post meridian Anno Domini 1990

9. Write out the days of the week; measurements; weights; names of streets, cities, states, and countries; and school subjects.

Write:	Tuesday	*rather than:*	Tues.
	six feet tall		6 ft. tall
	120 pounds		120 lbs.
	Omaha, Nebraska		Omaha, Neb.
	mathematics		math

10. Use abbreviations for organizations that are nationally or internationally known by their acronyms (names made from the title's initial letters).

Write:	FBI	*rather than:*	Federal Bureau of Investigation
	UNESCO		United Nations Educational, Scientific and Cultural Organization
	OPEC		Organization of Petroleum Exporting Countries

Practice with Abbreviations and Numbers

Read this story twice. The first time, read it to understand the content. The second time, proofread it, and adjust the abbreviations and numbers where appropriate.

Barely 24 hrs. after the tragic explosion that blew apart the 10th Challenger space shuttle and killed its 7 crew members, including the first teacher in space, N.H. H.S. teacher, Christa McAuliffe, the Gallup Org. polled 533 adult Amers. by tel. for *Newsweek* mag. On Jan. 29th and 30th, 55% said putting civilians into space is important vs. 40% who said space flight is too dangerous and 5% who said they "don't know." The general public, reached in apts. and homes throughout the U.S. agreed with NASA and the Pres. of the U.S. that the space program should continue; 76% believed it should be maintained at its current level or increased (up from 69% in Feb. '84), whereas only 19% thought it should be decreased or ended (down from 28% in 2/84). Gallup claims its "margin of error" in these surveys is + or − 5%, giving them a fairly accurate sampling of Amer. pub. opinion.

The Apostrophe

The apostrophe is a punctuation mark that causes much trouble. It's used to indicate *contractions*, words that leave out one or more letters when they are joined. It's also used to indicate *possession* (see Chapter 7). Here we are interested in contraction.

Contractions are useful when taking notes because they shorten what you have to write. But contractions are not used in formal writing because they are too informal. Ask your teacher if he or she will accept contractions in your essays. (Note that we use them in this book.) If you do use contractions, follow these conventions:

1. Place the apostrophe so as to show exactly where the letter is left out.

   Write: didn't (for *did not*)
   rather than: did'nt

2. Leave out the letter that the apostrophe replaces.

   Write: I'm (for *I am*)
   rather than: I'am

3. Drop *all* of the letters that the apostrophe replaces, not just one.

   Write: can't (for *cannot*)
   rather than: cann't

4. Make sure you know what your contraction stands for.

   Could've *stands for* could have—*not*—could of.
   Should've *stands for* should have—*not*—should of.
   Would've *stands for* would have—*not*—would of.

(The confusion here is created by pronunciation.)

The most common contractions are formed as follows:

am	I am	I'm
is	he is	he's
	she is	she's
	it is	it's
	there is	there's
are	you are	you're
	they are	they're

not		
	are not	aren't
	is not	isn't
	was not	wasn't
	were not	weren't
	does not	doesn't
	did not	didn't
	has not	hasn't
	have not	haven't
	had not	hadn't
	could not	couldn't
	should not	shouldn't
	would not	wouldn't
have	could have	could've
	should have	should've
	would have	would've
will	you will	you'll
	they will	they'll
had	I had	I'd
would	she would	she'd

Practice with Contraction

1. Cross out the incorrect contractions.

a. don't   **f.** isn't
b. have'nt   **g.** its'
c. would've   **h.** cann't
d. didn't   **i.** could'of
e. I'am   **j.** werent

2. Ernest Hemingway's short story "Hills Like White Elephants" is mainly a dialogue between two people, and it contains many contractions. Change each to its uncontracted form.

The girl was looking off at the line of hills. They were white in the sun

and the country was brown and dry.

"They look like white elephants," she said.

"I've never seen one," the man drank his beer.

"No, you wouldn't have."

"I might have," the man said. "Just because you say I wouldn't have doesn't prove anything."

The girl looked at the bead curtain. "They've painted something on it," she said. "What does it say?"

"Anis del Toro. It's a drink."

. . . .

"Do you want it with water?"

"I don't know," the girl said. "Is it good with water?"

"It's all right."

"You want them with water?" asked the woman.

"Yes, with water."

"It tastes like licorice," the girl said and put the glass down.

"That's the way with everything."

"Yes," said the girl. "Everything tastes like licorice. Especially all the things you've waited so long for, like absinthe."

3. In the following we've changed Hemingway's contractions to their uncontracted forms. Change them back to the way Hemingway wrote them.

"Well, the main said, "if you ***do not*** want to you ***do not*** have to. I ***would not*** have you do it if you ***did not*** want to. But I know ***it is*** perfectly simple."

"And you really want to?"

"I think ***it is*** the best thing to do. But I ***do not*** want you to do it if you ***do not*** really want to."

"And if I do it ***you will*** be happy and things will be like they were and ***you will*** love me?"

Word Boundaries

Many writers are confused about whether some words should be written as one word or two.

1. These words are always written as one word:

another	mother-in-law	therefore
bathroom	nearby	whereabouts
cannot	nevertheless	wherewithal
however	notebook	whichever
inasmuch	roommate	within

2. These phrases are always written as two words:

a little	all right[3]	no one
a lot	in fact	

3. We often shorten these common words in everyday speech, but they are always written out in formal writing:

Write:		*rather than:*	
	because		cause
	until		til
	going to		gonna
	though (even though)		tho
	through		thru

Practice with Word Boundaries

Read this story twice. The first time, read it to understand the content. The second time, proofread it, and change any problems in word boundaries.

Edward Simpson found San Jose different from St. Louis. In fact, the two cities were so different that Edward felt lost. Til he arrived in San Jose, he'd always felt alright about himself, but now he didn't know if he was gonna make it thru the year. In St. Louis, he'd had a room mate and the wherewithal to support himself. All the stores were near by and he only had to use his car infrequently. He had been living a good life, but he wanted something different. "Maybe I'll go somewhere

[3] You may have expected to see *all right* written as *alright*. We don't use the second spelling because some dictionaries label it as a "disputed spelling."

where noone knows my name," he said to himself. "I'll go to California,

cause there's so much space."

But the move was not successful. Whereas in St. Louis Edwards

had worked, in San Jose he could not find a job. Because he was not

skilled in the computer business, nothing in the Silicon Valley suited him.

Edward felt he had failed. He was ready to return to the Midwest when

a nother unemployed gentleman suggested they join forces. Within a week

they had an apartment lined up and jobs as well. Edward began to find

San Jose quite wonderful.

SPELLING

Homonyms

Homonyms are words that sound alike but have different meanings and are spelled differently from one another. The following are nine of the most common homonyms:

1. here:[4] location.   I live *here.*
here: to be aware of sound.   I *hear* music.

*When I stand **here**, I can **hear** the noise.*

Write a sentence that uses both words. You try it:

_____

2. its: possessive pronoun.   The frog lay on *its* back.
it's: contraction of "it is,"   *It's* time to go.
        "it has."   *It's* been a long time.

***It's** been a long time since the school has had **its** own gymnasium.*

You try it: _____

3. passed: past tense of the verb *pass.*   I *passed* the corner yesterday.
past: elapsed time.   My *past* came back to haunt me.

[4] In some parts of the United States these words are pronounced slightly differently.

*I **passed** my driving test in the **past,** but I had to take a new one when I moved to this state.*

You try it: _____

4. peace: state of calm, absence of war. The nations lived in *peace.*
   piece: section or part of a whole. A *piece* of masonry fell from the roof.

*When we get some **peace** in the evening, I will put another **piece** in the puzzle.*

You try it: _____

5. to: direction, toward; also used with a verb. I walked *to* school every day. It's hard *to* learn *to* dive.
   too: also, excess. I drank coffee and ate cake, *too.* I ate *too* much.
   two: the number 2. I bought *two* pieces of fudge.

*The boy sharpened **two** pencils and returned **to** his desk before it was **too** late to take the exam.*

You try it: _____

6. there: location; also used as a "dummy" subject. We lived over *there.* *There* was a fight between them.
   their: possessive pronoun. *Their* books are on the table.
   they're: contraction of "they are." *They're* the nicest people I know.

*We live over **there,** and **their** flowers fall into our yard, which **they're** nice enough to pick up for us.*

You try it: _____

7. weather:[5] climate conditions. In winter, the *weather* is cold.
   whether: alternative. *Whether* or not you go, I'm going.

*I am going to the store **whether** or not the **weather** is good.*

You try it: _____

8. whose: possessive pronoun. The person *whose* book I borrowed wants it back.

[5] In some parts of the United States these words are pronounced slightly differently.

who's:	contraction of "who is" or "who has."	*Who's* that on the phone? *Who's* got my coat?

Who's *there? The girl* **whose** *car you dented last night.*

You try it: _____

9. your: possessive pronoun.   *Your* dishes need washing.
    you're: contraction of "you are."   *You're* the right person for the job.

You're *the only one who can know* **your** *own mind.*

You try it: _____

Practice with Homonyms

1. Fill in the blank spaces with the correct homonym.

I remember when my parents told me they were getting a divorce. I

was just returning from school. "I _____ my algebra test," I yelled, wav-
                                          passed/past

ing my paper in the air. My parents just stood _____.
                                                  their/there/they're

_____ faces were ashen. "That's nice, sweetheart, but we can't
Their/There/They're

discuss _____ you are doing well in school now. We have
          weather/whether

_____ talk about the future." _____ had been no
to/too/two   Their/There/They're

_____ in the house for a long time. Every night I would _____
peace/piece   hear/here

arguing from _____ room. "_____ welfare is most im-
                their/there/they're   Your/You're

portant _____, and so _____ the first to know," my father said.
          hear/here   your/you're

"Mother and I are getting a divorce." "_____ getting me?"
                                          Whose/Who's

I asked. "_____ not like that," my mother answered. "We love
           Its/It's

you _____ much_____ make you choose between us.
      to/too/two   to/too/two

_____ the person _____ most important to us. We will
Your/You're   whose/who's

84

live only _____ miles apart and share your custody. Believe me,
          to/too/two

the future will be better for all of us than the _____."
                                              passed/past

2. Read this paragraph twice. The first time, read it to understand the content. The second time, proofread it. Make sure you are using the proper homonym. Make any changes necessary. We've done the first one for you.

Peace among the people of the world is necessary for our future

                                              their
on this earth, but how can nations forget ~~there~~ past too live in harmony

when my neighbors can't and don't. There is so much tension between

these two people that sometimes I despair for the whole world. At 8 A.M.

every morning, when its time to leave for work, I can already here my

neighbors yelling at one another. "Who's trash is this?" one bellows, pointing

to a garbage can that the wind had overturned onto his lawn. "It's on

you're property," the can's owner laughs. They're arguments continue

regardless of the whether, and each morning I wonder whether or not

they will come to blows. Their nice people, but they're too hotheaded.

Its a shame. They make me wonder if all the people of the world can

share there earth when my two neighbors cannot share one small peace

of my block.

THE FINAL DRAFT

Now you are ready to proofread the second draft of the essay you began earlier in this chapter. Read your essay again slowly, and aloud. Remember what you learned about word order and sense in Chapter 1.

Make sure you can answer yes to these questions as you proofread your essay:

1. Did you use the appropriate manuscript form?
2. If you needed to hyphenate words, did you follow the rules and divide them into syllables, as found in the dictionary?
3. Did you capitalize only the first letter of the first word of a sentence and the first letter of the other kinds of words listed in the rules?

4. Did you correctly use abbreviations and numbers?
5. Did you correctly use apostrophes for contractions?
6. If you used any of the homonyms we studied, did you use the correct one?

Change anything that you think needs changing. Make a clean copy if you make more than one or two changes.

ADDITIONAL WRITING ASSIGNMENTS

Your writer's journal may have some ideas for you to develop into essays. Focus on things that change over time—yourself as well as others.

Other students have found the topics below to be stimulating. Remember to do focused writing first. Then read over your essay. You may want to review the Writing and Rewriting section of each chapter before you start a second draft. When you finish your second draft, proofread it, and write a clean copy.

Topic Suggestions

1. Just as Malcolm X did, many people find themselves inadequate in certain situations. Think of a time in your own life when you found you were ignorant of or just not up to a certain situation. Describe that situation for your classmates as completely as possible. Tell them what you did to remedy the problem.

2. Just as for some of the writers that William Zinsser described in "The Transaction," there was probably a time in your life when you thought you could not keep on, when there was no inspiration for you to continue what you were doing. Describe that time in your life, what situation you were in, and your reasons for your feelings. Tell your classmates what you did, whether you continued or made some radical change, and why.

3. Think of a time in your life when you realized that you were different from other people. Tell your classmates how you became aware of your difference.

4. Think of a time you really wanted to be like someone else. Tell your classmates what you were like, what the other person was like, and why you wanted to be like that person.

5. Tell a story in a nonstandard variety of English. It need be only a paragraph or two long. Then "translate" the story into standard English. When you are finished with both versions, write a paragraph explaining which version of the story you prefer, and why.

Writing a Narrative: Telling What Happened

3

**Photo by
Arley Bondarin**

These exercises will help you get started telling stories:

1. Take out a piece of paper and a pen or pencil to do some focused writing. Write today's date at the top. Relax for a moment. Close your eyes. Breathe deeply. As the room starts to quiet, think about something important that happened to you when you were young. It can be something funny, sad, silly, or serious, but it must be something that was important enough to you to remember as if it happened yesterday.

   Now open your eyes. At the signal, start writing, and don't stop for ten minutes. Tell your story, but DO NOT stop writing to think about where to put information. Just let the ideas flow. DO NOT attempt to make the story perfect, and DO NOT pause if you are unsure about spelling, punctuation, or grammar. DO NOT stop to look up words in the dictionary. If you get stuck momentarily with nothing in your mind, write the word *stuck* until your next idea comes.

2. Write the numbers 1 to 15 in a column at the left-hand margin of a blank sheet of paper. List, in order, the things that happened to you or things you did from the moment you awakened this morning until you arrived in class. Use your own paper.

3. As vividly as you can, describe your first day of classes at this school or your experiences at registration. Use your own paper.

4. A pantomime is a story told with gestures but without words. Choose *one* of the following topics for a pantomime you can act out for yourself in a mirror, for a partner in class, or for a small group:

   a. Breaking three eggs into a bowl.
   b. Trying to sleep next to someone who is snoring.
   c. Sneaking into class late.
   d. Trying to swat a mosquito that is disturbing your sleep.
   e. Sitting in the movies in front of someone who keeps kicking your seat or talking.
   f. Sitting in the movies behind someone who is very tall or wearing a hat.
   g. Trying to start your car on a cold winter morning.

   a. After you have acted out the pantomime, write down all the steps (or actions) you took, from beginning to end. Be as complete and detailed as possible.

   (1) First, I _____

   _____

   (2) Second, I _____

   _____

(3) Then, I _____

_____

(4) _____

_____

(5) _____

_____

(6) _____

_____

(7) _____

_____

(If you need more room, use your own paper.)

b. Fill in the following additional information about the character in the pantomime:

(1) Who am I? (age, sex, physical description, and any other relevant infor-

mation) _____

_____

_____

(2) What am I doing? _____

_____

_____

(3) Where am I? (exact location or locations; what it or they look like)

_____

_____

_____

(4) When am I doing this? (time of day, season of the year, and so on)

_____

_____

(5) How am I doing this? (skillfully, clumsily, or whatever)

_____

_____

(6) Why am I doing this? _____

_____

_____

(7) What mood am I in? _____

_____

_____

(8) What am I saying aloud to others or to myself? What, if anything, are other people saying to me? _____

_____

_____

(If you need more room, use your own paper.)

c. Put together all the information to write a story. Many stories begin with

Once upon a time. . . .
On a clear day. . . .
As I woke. . . .

If you need help getting started, use one of these lines. Don't spend much time on the beginning. Just get into the story. Try to use as much of the preceding information about your character as you can.

HINT

You use different words to report what someone said or to quote that person directly. For instance:

Report:	My mother said it was time for me to get a job.
	She said that I was old enough.
Quotation:	My mother said, "It's time for you to get a job."
	She said, "You're old enough."

Note: Quotations are introduced or followed by expressions like *he said, she said.*

Report:	He asked me if I could go.[1]
Quotation:	"Can you go?" he asked.

When you quote, you use the person's *exact words* instead of putting them into your own words. When you use direct quotations, as in the following dialogue between John and Mary, use these conventions:

1. Put quotation marks around *only* the exact words a person says, that is, at the opening and closing of the words, phrases, or sentences quoted. Quotation marks work in pairs: when you "open" quotations, you must "close" them when someone finishes speaking:

"Do you love me?" John asked.
Mary answered, "Yes, I do."

2. Put commas and periods inside the closing quotation marks:

"Let's get married," John suggested.

Put question marks and exclamation points inside the closing quotation marks when they are part of the sentence quoted:

Mary asked, "Should we really?"

3. When a phrase is used to identify the speaker (*he said, she said*), insert a comma to separate the phrase and the quotation:

"Yes, of course," John said.
"Okay! Sure!" Mary shouted.
"When?" John queried.

---

[1] See Appendix 1 for more discussion of direct and indirect questions.

4. A series of things spoken by the same person can be run together with no paragraph indentation:

"Well, how about next Tuesday," Mary replied. "I'm free that day, if it's a good day for you."

Reminder: Begin the sentences inside the quotation marks with a capital letter.

A change in the speaker is usually indicated by a new paragraph. Note that once you have indicated who is talking, you may stop identifying the speaker and simply begin a new paragraph when the speaker changes:

"That's fine with me," John added and laughed.
"What's so funny?" Mary asked.
"I don't know," John muttered. "I guess I didn't expect you to say yes."
"Do you want to change your mind?"
"Not on your life!"

Reminder: Try to use words besides *said* to introduce quotations. List the words used in this dialogue, and add any other words you think you might use.

_____ _____ _____ _____ _____

_____ _____ _____ _____ _____

_____ _____ _____ _____ _____

READING

PREVIEW QUESTIONS

As you read "Salvation" by Langston Hughes, look for information that answers these questions:

1. Why does Hughes go to church with his aunt?
2. How does he feel about the revival?
3. How was Hughes different from the other children?
4. Why was Hughes so upset about his lie?
5. How does Hughes indicate when a character in the story is speaking? What conventions does he use?
6. Why does Hughes's uses of direct quotation make the story more interesting to read?

Salvation

Langston Hughes

Langston Hughes wrote different types of work (fiction, humor, criticism, history, and poetry) over a period of more than fifty years. During part of that time, he was a leading member of the Harlem Renaissance. This story is from his first autobiography, The Big Sea.

(1) I was saved from sin when I was going on thirteen. But not really saved. It happened like this. There was a big revival at my Auntie Reed's church. Every night for weeks there had been much preaching, singing, praying, and shouting, and some very hardened sinners had been brought to Christ, and the membership of the church had grown by leaps and bounds. Then just before the revival ended, they held a special meeting for children, "to bring the young lambs to the fold." My aunt spoke of it for days ahead. That night I was escorted to the front row and placed on the mourners' bench with all the other young sinners, who had not yet been brought to Jesus.

(2) My aunt told me that when you were saved you saw a light, and something happened to you inside! And Jesus came into your life! And God was with you from then on! And she said you could see and hear and feel Jesus in your soul. I believed her. I had heard a great many old people say the same thing and it seemed to me they ought to know. So I sat calmly in the hot, crowded church, waiting for Jesus to come to me.

(3) The preacher preached a wonderful rhythmical sermon, all moans and shouts and lonely cries and dire pictures of hell, and then he sang a song about the ninety and nine safe in the fold, but one little lamb was left out in the cold. Then he said: "Won't you come? Won't you come to Jesus? Young lambs, won't you come?" And he held out his arms to all us young sinners there on the mourners' bench. And the little girls cried. And some of them jumped up and went to Jesus right away. But most of us just sat there.

(4) A great many old people came and knelt around us and prayed, old women with jet-black faces and braided hair, old men with work-gnarled hands. And the church sang a song about the lower lights are burning, some poor sinners to be saved. And the whole building rocked with prayer and song.

(5) Still I kept waiting to *see* Jesus.

(6) Finally all the young people had gone to the altar and were saved, but one boy and me. He was a rounder's son named Westley. Westley and I were surrounded by sisters and deacons praying. It was very hot in the church, and getting late now. Finally Westley said to me in a whisper: "God damn! I'm tired o' sitting here. Let's get up and be saved." So he got up and was saved.

(7) Then I was left all alone on the mourners' bench. My aunt came

and knelt at my knees and cried, while prayers and songs swirled all around me in the little church. The whole congregation prayed for me alone, in a mighty wail of moans and voices. And I kept waiting serenely for Jesus, waiting, waiting—but he didn't come. I wanted to see him, but nothing happened to me. Nothing! I wanted something to happen to me, but nothing happened.

(8) I heard the songs and the minister saying: "Why don't you come? My dear child, why don't you come to Jesus? Jesus is waiting for you. He wants you. Why don't you come? Sister Reed, what is this child's name?"

(9) "Langston," my aunt sobbed.

(10) "Langston, why don't you come? Why don't you come and be saved? Oh, Lamb of God! Why don't you come?"

(11) Now it was really getting late. I began to be ashamed of myself, holding everything up so long. I began to wonder what God thought about Westley, who certainly hadn't seen Jesus either, but who was now sitting proudly on the platform, swinging his knickerbockered legs and grinning down at me, surrounded by deacons and old women on their knees praying. God had not struck Westley dead for taking his name in vain or for lying in the temple. So I decided that maybe to save further trouble, I'd better lie, too, and say that Jesus had come, and get up and be saved.

(12) So I got up.

(13) Suddenly the whole room broke into a sea of shouting as they saw me rise. Waves of rejoicing swept the place. Women leaped in the air. My aunt threw her arms around me. The minister took me by the hand and led me to the platform.

(14) When things quieted down, in a hushed silence, punctuated by a few ecstatic "Amens," all the new young lambs were blessed in the name of God. Then joyous singing filled the room.

(15) That night, for the last time in my life but one—for I was a big boy twelve years old—I cried. I cried, in bed alone, and couldn't stop. I buried my head under the quilts, but my aunt heard me. She woke up and told my uncle I was crying because the Holy Ghost had come into my life, and because I had seen Jesus. But I was really crying because I couldn't bear to tell her that I had lied, that I had deceived everybody in the church, and I hadn't seen Jesus, and that now I didn't believe there was a Jesus anymore, since he didn't come to help me.

QUESTIONS OF CONTENT

Circle the letter of the best answer to each question.

1. What was the purpose of the church service?
   a. to sing and pray.
   b. to make the children members of the church.
   c. to meet everyone's children.
   d. to mourn for a dead child.

2. What did Hughes's aunt tell him?
   a. He would see and feel Jesus.
   b. He would be happy.
   c. The lights would come on.
   d. She wanted him to join the church.
3. Why did Westley get up?
   a. He saw Jesus.
   b. The other children had gotten up.
   c. He was tired of sitting on the bench.
   d. He was a rounder's son.
4. Why did Hughes get up?
   a. His aunt cried.
   b. He saw that God had not struck Westley dead.
   c. He thought his aunt would be ashamed of him.
   d. He didn't want any more trouble.
5. Why did he cry at night?
   a. The Holy Ghost had come into his life.
   b. He had lied about seeing Jesus.
   c. He was happy.
   d. He was lonely in his bed.

Answer these questions in full sentences:

1. Why did Hughes sit quietly on the mourners' bench? _____

_____

2. Why did he no longer believe in Jesus? _____

_____

3. What lie did Hughes tell? _____

_____

4. Why did Hughes's aunt think he was crying? _____

_____

5. In your own words, retell what happened to Hughes in his grandmother's

church and afterwards at home. _____

_____

_____

Match each statement from the text (first column) with a similar statement written in a different voice (second column).

1. I was saved from sin when I was going on thirteen.
2. . . . when you were saved you saw a light, and . . . you could see and hear and feel Jesus in your soul.
3. The preacher preached a wonderful rhythmical sermon, all moans and shouts and lonely cries and dire pictures of hell. . . .
4. Suddenly the whole room broke into a sea of shouting as they saw me rise.

a. The minister gave a very forceful talk.
b. I joined the church just before I became a teenager.
c. Everyone yelled when I got up.
d. You have a very different feeling when you believe in Jesus.

QUESTIONS OF INFERENCE

Look back at the text to answer these questions. Answer in full sentences.

1. What do you think Hughes's aunt meant when she said he would see a

   "light"? _____

   _____

2. Do you think the other children saw a light? _____

   _____

3. Why couldn't Hughes tell his aunt why he was crying? _____

   _____

4. What is the main point of the story?
   a. Things aren't what they seem.
   b. Children take everything literally and are apt to be disappointed.
   c. Children get tired in church.
   d. People have to conform to the expectations of others.

QUESTIONS OF CRITICAL THINKING

Answer each question in a short paragraph. You may want to use your own paper.

1. How do you think this experience might affect Hughes as he gets older?

_____

_____

2. Did Hughes have to do what he did? Why or why not? _____

_____

_____

_____

3. What decision would you have made if you had been Hughes? Why? ____

_____

_____

_____

4. Jot down any questions you would like to ask Hughes about his experience in the church:

a. _____

b. _____

c. _____

d. _____

VOCABULARY

These words from Hughes's "Salvation" may be unfamiliar to you. The exercises will help you learn the meanings of these words and how they function in sentences.

saved	(1)	rhythmical	(3)	congregation	(7)
revival	(1)	dire	(3)	serenely	(7)
hardened	(1)	gnarled	(4)	knickerbockered	(11)
fold	(1)	rounder	(6)	punctuated	(14)
mourner	(1)	swirled	(7)	ecstatic	(14)

Word Meanings

Words often have more than one meaning. When the dictionary lists more than one definition for a word, the most common definition appears first (for each part of speech), followed by the less common or specialized meanings. A good writer will sometimes use the more specialized meaning of a word to make a point. A good reader must learn to recognize when the specialized meanings are being used. One way to do this is to look for the *special context* in which the word is used. The special context is the setting or situation or topic of the whole selection. For instance, a church is the setting for "Salvation," and the specialized meanings of the words relate to religion.

Look at the dictionary entries for *save* and *mourner* from Webster's *New World Dictionary:*

save¹ (sāv) *vt.* **saved, sav′ing** [ME. *saven* < OFr. *sauver, salver* < L. *salvare* < *salvus*, SAFE] **1.** to rescue or preserve from harm, danger, injury, etc.; make or keep safe **2.** to keep in health and well-being: now only in certain formulas [God *save* the king!] **3.** to preserve for future use; lay by (often with *up*) **4.** to prevent or guard against loss or waste of [to *save* time, to *save* a game] **5.** to avoid, prevent, lessen, or guard against [to *save* wear and tear] **6.** to treat or use carefully in order to preserve, lessen wear, etc. **7.** *Theol.* to deliver from sin and punishment —*vi.* **1.** to avoid expense, loss, waste, etc.; be economical **2.** to keep something or someone from danger, harm, etc. **3.** to put by money or goods (often with *up*); hoard **4.** to keep; last **5.** *Theol.* to exercise power to redeem from evil and sin —*n. Sports* an action that keeps an opponent from scoring or winning —*SYN.* see RESCUE —**sav′a·ble, save′a·ble** *adj.* —**sav′er** *n.*
save² (sāv) *prep.* [ME. *sauf* < OFr., lit., SAFE: sense developed from use in absolute constructions, e.g., *sauf le droit*, right (being) safe] except; but —*conj.* **1.** except; but **2.** [Archaic] unless

mourn·er (môr′nər) *n.* **1.** *a*) a person who is in mourning *b*) any of the persons attending a funeral **2.** a person who makes a public profession of penitence at a revival meeting

1. Write down the more common, generalized meanings of these words:

save _____   mourner _____

_____   _____

2. Write down their more specialized meanings:

_____   _____

_____   _____

Many different types of settings form a special context for words. Sometimes the context is so special that the words have a completely different meaning or make no sense outside that context. For instance:

Person 1: Give me a combo, whiskey down, and an eighty-one.
Person 2: I thought you said a burn and a CB.
Person 1: Doesn't matter. He's an eighty-six anyway.

1. Where do you think these two people are? _____

2. What are they talking about? _____

If you don't know, you're not alone. This dialogue is in "restaurant language." The translation is

> Person 1: Give me a ham and Swiss cheese sandwich on rye toast and a glass of water.
> Person 2: I thought you said a chocolate malted and a cheeseburger.
> Person 1: It doesn't matter. This person won't leave a tip anyway.

1. What other places or situations form a special context for words? List as many as you can think of:

_____ _____

_____ _____

_____ _____

2. List as many words as you can for these special contexts:

_____ _____ _____ _____ _____

_____ _____ _____ _____ _____

_____ _____ _____ _____ _____

_____ _____ _____ _____

3. Write a short dialogue in the language of one of these special contexts:

_____

_____

_____

_____

_____

_____

_____

Look up each word in the dictionary and find the meaning closest to the one that Hughes used in "Salvation." Then use the word, with its specialized meaning, in a sentence of your own.

1. fold _____

2. punctuate(d) _____

3. rounder _____

Word Clues

Once you know the context or setting of a piece of writing, you may not have to look up a word in the dictionary. Sometimes you can decide on a good "working definition" just from seeing the word in its special context. Use your knowledge of the special context of "Salvation" to find the phrase that means the same thing as the italicized word. Then circle the letter of the correct answer, and underline the words or phrases that helped you find the meanings.

1. "I was *saved* from sin when I was going on thirteen."
   a. rescued from injury.
   b. put in the bank.
   c. stowed away.
   d. delivered from sin.
2. "There was a big *revival* at my Auntie Reed's church."
   a. a meeting to stimulate interest in an old movie.
   b. a meeting to renew religious faith.
   c. an attempt to regain consciousness.
3. "The whole *congregation* prayed for me alone, in a mighty wail of moans and voices."
   a. town meeting.
   b. church gathering.
   c. legislative body.
   d. any group.
4. "That night I was escorted to the front row and placed on the *mourners' bench* with all the other young sinners who had not yet been brought to Jesus."
   a. a place for people grieving for a lost loved one.
   b. a special seat for people waiting to be saved.
   c. a bench you sit on before noon.
5. "Every night for weeks there had been much preaching, singing, praying and shouting, and some very *hardened sinners* had been brought to Christ, and the membership of the church had grown by leaps and bounds."
   a. angry people.
   b. people who have turned to stone.

c. stubborn people.

d. people who love one another.

Look carefully at each of these words. Try to see them as the sum of their parts. Consult the list of prefixes and suffixes on pages 10–13, and write a "working definition" for each.

1. rhythmic(al) _____

2. knickerbocker _____

Seeing Words in Context

The words below appear in "Salvation." You may find clues to the meanings of each word from its context. Circle the words or phrases that form the context for each word. Then write (1) your working definition, (2) the dictionary definition that's right for the context, and (3) an original sentence using the word. If you have difficulty figuring out the meaning of the word from the context of "Salvation," you may find it helpful to read the following story, in which the words appear in italics:

1. word: *serene(ly)*

   a. working definition _____

   b. dictionary definition _____

   c. your sentence _____

2. word: *swirl(ed)*

   a. working definition _____

   b. dictionary definition _____

   c. your sentence _____

3. word: *gnarl(ed)*

   a. working definition _____

   b. dictionary definition _____

   c. your sentence _____

4. word: *dire*

   a. working definition _____

b. dictionary definition _____

c. your sentence _____

5. word: *ecstatic*

   a. working definition _____

   b. dictionary definition _____

   c. your sentence _____

EIGHTY-SECOND STREET AND BROADWAY

On the traffic island, the old woman sat peacefully, *serenely,* as the cars whipped past her. The pages of the newspapers that people had left behind on the benches or dropped in the streets *swirled* around and almost enveloped her. She was very old, and you could see that her life had not been easy. Her hands were rough and scarred; her knuckles were *gnarled* and stood out from her fingers like knots from a tree. Her few possessions lay in the shopping bags arrayed beside her. Her coat was threadbare, and her shoes were worn through the soles. Clearly, she lived in *dire* poverty. But she sat in the sun of the cold morning with her chin tilted toward the sky and looked very happy, *ecstatic,* and quite lovely.

Using Words in Context

One way to make new words part of your vocabulary is to use them in your writing. Write a paragraph about an experience you've had involving religion. The experience may have been positive or negative, serious or funny. Make sure to use at least five of the words listed in the Vocabulary section. When you proofread your paragraph, underline the words you used.

_____

_____

_____

_____

_____

_____

WRITING AND REWRITING

People love to tell stories and to read them. Stories let us share someone else's life and make us think about our own. For instance, "Salvation" tells of Langston Hughes's youthful experience in church. Many of us have had experiences with religion, God, or churches that the story reminds us of at the same time that we are sharing Hughes's experience with him. And we all have been the same age as Hughes was in the story, and so we can relate to the emotions he felt.

What Do Stories Do?

Stories often *focus* on one particular incident in the author's life. That focus gives the story a boundary, a place to begin and end. Incidents stand out in our minds because they are special: the time you received an award at graduation, the time you took your brother's best shirt and got paint on it. Sometimes it's difficult to decide exactly where a story begins and ends— your high school career lasted for four years, and your relationship with your brother even longer. But to focus the incident, you can pick some limiting devices: the graduation ceremony, the day you took the shirt.

What Does Focus Do?

You've already begun to write stories in the *Preliminary Exercises:* the story about an incident in your childhood and what happened to you during registration or the first day of class.

Let's try another story.

WRITING: A FIRST DRAFT

Choose one of these as the opening phrase of focused writing:

1. The silliest thing I ever did was . . .
2. Once a teacher . . .
3. _____was once the most important thing in my life, until . . .
4. The most embarrassing thing that ever happened to me was . . .
5. My childhood ended the day . . .
6. One of the happiest moments of my life was . . .
7. One of the saddest moments of my life was . . .
8. Once I saw the strangest . . .
9. My first crush was on _____
10. My sister (or brother) always . . .

Take out a piece of paper and a pen or pencil. Write today's date at the top. Now relax for a moment. Close your eyes. Breathe deeply. As the room begins to quiet, think about the phrase you have chosen. Carry yourself back to that time in your life. Try to see yourself as you were then, and feel the emotions you felt then. Now open your eyes. At the signal, start writing and don't stop for ten minutes. Tell your story, but don't stop to think about where to put information. Just let the ideas flow. DO NOT pause if you are unsure about spelling, punctuation, or grammar. DO NOT stop to look up words in the dictionary. If you get stuck momentarily with nothing in your mind, write the word *stuck* until your next idea comes. Okay, begin. After ten minutes stop.

WHAT MAKES WRITING GOOD? DETAILS AND ORDER

We've already begun to discuss four aspects of good writing: attention to (1) *topic, audience, and purpose;* (2) *details,* (3) *order;* and (4) *language.* In this chapter we'll emphasize *detail* and *order,* and in Chapter 4, we'll discuss the others. It's important to remember, however, that they all mix together when you rewrite.

Details

Why Are Details Important?

What Will Satisfy the Reader's Curiosity?

It is important to include enough details in your story to satisfy your audience's curiosity. Readers are curious people; they want to know everything—what people's names are, what they looked like, exactly what they said and did. We tend to overlook these details because we already know them. For instance, you were in the train station one day when you saw a tall, blond teenager named John Washington help an old man with a suitcase. You know the teenager; he's a "good kid." Thus, you may sum up the incident as "The boy was kind." That's fine for you, because you know all the details. The reader, however, would probably want to know that "John Washington bent down, took the old man's heavy suitcase, and carried it to the waiting train." These details of exactly what happened will satisfy the reader's curiosity.

The reader may want to know other details as well; for instance, what is the *setting?* What did the train station look like? You may not want to describe everything about the place, but it may be important to note that the train waited at the end of a long corridor. The old man therefore would have had trouble negotiating that distance to the train with a heavy suitcase in his hand. Perhaps it was a snowy day, and water from people's boots sat in puddles in the corridor. The old man's way would have been impeded even more, and John's kindness would have been all the more important. Thus, your sentence could read: "John Washington bent down, took the old man's heavy suitcase, and carried it down the long, slippery corridor to the waiting train."

You may also have overheard the conversation between John Washington and the old man. If the conversation reveals some important aspect of the situation or the participants' personalities, it is worth quoting:

John walked up to the old man. "I think you might need some help with that," he said, pointing to the suitcase.

"I don't want to trouble anyone," the old man replied.

"That's all right. I'm going that way anyway." John lied. He was on his way to work in the station cafeteria, but he knew it would make the old man feel better. John Washington bent down, took the old man's heavy suitcase, and carried it down the long, slippery corridor to the waiting train.

Order

Why Is Order Important?

It's also important to tell the story in the order in which the events occurred so that the reader can follow what happened. We often remember only the highlights of an experience and forget that incidents are made up of little events that follow one another in time, in the same way a movie is composed of countless still frames. For example, if you are writing about the time that you attempted to start your car on a frosty Monday morning, you may remember gunning the motor until you flooded it. Before that, however, you left your house (with or without a warm coat, hat, and gloves), opened the car door (was it locked or not?), sat down, and turned the key in the ignition. Some background may be necessary: There may have been someone waiting for you; you may have had an 8 A.M. class or been afraid to be late for work. These things may seem insignificant to you, compared with the trauma of actually getting the car started, but they are important to your audience because they enable them to follow the action.

Before we go any further, reread your focused writing. Have you told the whole story? If not, add anything you think may be important. Consider your focused writing as the first draft of an essay. Put it aside for now. We'll come back to it later in the chapter.

Do These Exercises Before You Revise Your First Draft.

Practice with Details

1. Revise these statements to give the reader more details. Sometimes you may need more than one sentence in order to include all the details you want or need. The first one has already been done.

   a. The man was nice. *The man stepped from the building, saw me struggling with my luggage to hail a taxi in the rain, and grasped the heaviest bag.*

b. I tripped and fell down. _____

_____

c. Drugs were important to me. _____

_____

d. I didn't get along with my sister. _____

_____

e. The day was nice. _____

_____

f. It's difficult for me to get to work. _____

_____

g. My car doesn't work well. _____

_____

h. The house is messy. _____

_____

i. On my day off, I like to have fun. _____

_____

j. My sister is a good kid. _____

_____

k. My head hurts. _____

_____

l. The husband and wife had a spat. _____

_____

2. Choose one of these situations:
• A couple arguing in the street.

- A teenager and a police officer meeting beside a parked car.
- A student confronting a professor.
- A "city slicker" visiting a shop in a small town.
- A person from outer space walking into a video store.

a. Describe the setting in which your encounter could take place.

_____

_____

_____

b. Name and describe the participants.

_____

_____

c. Write down some of the dialogue that might have been spoken during this encounter.

_____

_____

_____

Practice with Order

1. Each group of sentences tells a story, but the ideas are out of order. Decide on the best order, and renumber the sentences at the left, as follows:

      <u> 1 </u>**1.** The skunk crawled across the road.
      <u> 3 </u>**2.** I leaped in surprise.
      <u> 2 </u>**3.** I saw it out of the corner of my eye.

Your order may differ from your classmates'. Be prepared to defend it.

a. _____(1) I got out of the car.

    _____(2) As I turned the corner, I saw the other car.

    _____(3) I turned off the ignition.

    _____(4) Then I heard the crash.

_____(5) I felt the jolt.

_____(6) I looked away.

_____(7) I knew I was going too fast.

_____(8) I saw my bumper was crushed.

b. _____(1) I walked to the cafeteria.

_____(2) I entered the building.

_____(3) I stood in the hot, crowded line for ten minutes.

_____(4) I showed my ID card to the guard.

_____(5) I finally got a tray and silverware.

_____(6) I took the elevator to the right floor.

_____(7) The server said there was no more food.

_____(8) I read the menu.

c. _____(1) We drove down the highway toward the country.

_____(2) We got back into the car and drove to the motel.

_____(3) We stopped along the way for a picnic.

_____(4) We had packed all our belongings the night before.

_____(5) The children played ball in the park while the adults drank coffee.

_____(6) I piled everything into the back of my father's station wagon.

_____(7) Suddenly I realized I'd forgotten my toothbrush.

_____(8) We all climbed into the car.

2. Look back to the encounter you developed in the second part of "Practice with Detail." Put in order the events in the encounter, including the setting and dialogue. Use your own paper.

Practice with Details and Order

A *time line* is a good device to use to focus on the events in a story. The easiest time line to construct is a diagonal line from the upper left-hand corner to the lower right-hand corner of a piece of paper. You'll need your own paper for the following exercises:

1. Number from 1 to 10 on a piece of paper. List the events in "Salvation." (You may add more numbers if you need them.)
2. Draw a time line, and put the events along the line in the order in which they occurred.
3. Reread your time line. If you left out any details, rewrite what you have written to include them.
4. Reread your time line. Add any events you left out, putting them in the appropriate places.
5. Now list the events in your own story.
6. Draw a time line and put the events in your own story along it.
7. Reread your time line. If you left out any details, rewrite what you have written to include them.
8. Reread your time line. Add any events you left out, putting them in the appropriate places.

REWRITING: A SECOND DRAFT

Now you are ready to turn your focused writing into a second draft. Read it carefully, aloud, and, if you can, to a friend or classmate. Try to get a new vision of your subject. As you rewrite, think about

1. *Details.* Write enough details to keep your audience satisfied. Name and describe a character so the reader can see him or her in the same way you did. Make the setting clear, if it will help the story. Include the dialogue spoken by the people in your story. From reading "Salvation," you can see how interesting dialogue can be to the audience.
2. *Order.* Tell your story in the exact order in which the events occurred. Remember all the "insignificant" things that made up the event, and decide which of these the reader must know to understand it. If the reader needs some background information about you, someone else, or the situation, you should provide it. Make sure your story is focused on one incident and has a clear beginning and end.

After you've written your second draft, go on to Proofreading, where you'll get some help on the proofreading stage of your writing.

PROOFREADING

What Does Grammar "Do"?

Why Should We Know the Rules of Sentence Structure?

Clear sentences are an important part of formal writing. Whether or not you are conscious of them, you and your audience depend on grammar and punctuation to guide your understanding of what you read. You therefore should be familiar with some of the basic rules of sentence structure so that as you proofread, you can fix any problems you may find.

SUBJECTS AND VERBS

Read over any of your final drafts, and copy any eight sentences from them. Make sure the sentences differ in length; use some that contain commas and some that don't.

1. _____

2. _____

3. _____

4. _____

5. _____

6. _____

7. _____

8. _____

No matter how different these sentences may appear, they all have two things in common:

1. A *noun* or a *pronoun* that functions as the *subject* of the sentence.
2. A *verb* that functions as, or is part of, the *predicate* of the sentence.

110

What's a noun?

*A **noun** is a word that identifies a person, place, thing, or idea.*

HINT

Generally, a noun is also a word that can be plural, that is, something of which there can be more than one. But there are several exceptions, for example, *equipment, flour, cement, water,* and *sand.* See Chapter 9 for a discussion of some of these. When you are looking for a noun in a sentence, choose a number and insert it before the word you think is a noun. Then add *-s* or *-es* to the noun. If it sounds right, you probably have found a noun.
For example:

> *The girl brought the book to class for the teacher.*

Underline the word (or words) you think is a noun:

> *The <u>girl</u> brought the <u>book</u> to <u>class</u> for the <u>teacher</u>.*

Now pick a number, for example, three. Rewrite the sentence with the word *three* in front of the noun or nouns. Add *-s* or *-es* to the words you think are nouns:

> *The three <u>girls</u> brought the three <u>books</u> to the three <u>classes</u> for the three <u>teachers</u>.*

Girl, book, class, and *teacher* all are nouns.
Note: Although all four of these words are nouns, only one of them—*girl*—is the subject of the sentence. We'll explain that later.

What's a pronoun?

*A **pronoun** is a word that stands for or replaces a noun.*

HINT

Pronouns replace nouns that are in the same sentence or near it. For example,

> *The girl brought the book to class and gave <u>it</u> to the teacher.*

It replaces the noun *book* because it sounds better not to repeat *book* in the same sentence. Pronouns are sometimes tricky. We shall discuss them further in Chapter 7 and in Appendix 2.

Finding Subjects

What's a subject?

A **subject** *is what the sentence is about, the topic of the sentence.*[2] *The subject also answers the questions "Who?" or "What?"*

A subject is usually a noun or pronoun. Sometimes the subject is a phrase that is used as a noun. For example,

noun: The *Challenger* (space shuttle) exploded fifty-two seconds into lift-off.

pronoun: It disintegrated, and the pieces fell into the sea.

phrase: The families of the crew, along with a crowd of onlookers, watched in horror.

The subject, however, is not just any noun or pronoun in a sentence. It is the particular noun or pronoun that tells the reader who the main person is or what the main thing or idea is in the sentence.

List all the nouns (and some pronouns) you can think of that can function as the subject of a sentence. Start with those in the eight sentences you wrote in the Subjects and Verbs section.

___	___	___	___	___	___
___	___	___	___	___	___
___	___	___	___	___	___
___	___	___	___	___	___
___	___	___	___	___	

Practice Finding Subjects

1. Read this paragraph twice. The first time, read it to understand the content. The second time, circle the subject of each sentence. We've done the first one for you.

(Marge Piercy) wrote *Woman at the Edge of Time* in 1976. [2]It was

her fourth novel. [3]In it, Consuelo (Connie) Ramos is a Chicana living in

New York. [4]She was once beautiful and a college student, living with a

man she loved and raising her children. [5]After her lover is killed by the

---

[2] In sentences that contain passive constructions, the topic may not be the subject of the sentence.

police, she degenerates quickly into an angry, worn-out, welfare mother. [6]Her niece's fiancé attacks her, and she defends herself with a knife. [7]He has her arrested, and she's later confined against her will to a mental institution. [8]Connie is labeled "aggressive" when she tells her therapists the truth and "noncooperative" when she doesn't. [9]Finally, she volunteers for a dangerous neuroelectric experiment, during which she "time-travels" (or imagines) a new society. [10]In Mattapoisett, human life triumphs over everything else. [11]Children are nurtured by three parents—to prevent too much possessiveness—and then set free in the world without guilt. [12]Civility and kindness are the most important values of the culture.

2. Write a ten-sentence mystery story beginning with the following sentence. When you are finished writing, number your sentences and circle the subject of each one.

[1]Slowly (I) opened the door.

_____

_____

_____

_____

_____

_____

_____

_____

Finding Verbs

What's a verb?

*A **verb** is a word that tells what the subject (noun or pronoun) is or is doing.*

113

What's a predicate?

*A **predicate** is the part of the sentence that tells you something about the subject. It consists of a verb and sometimes its complement, that is, words that give you more information about the verb.*

   List all the verbs you can think of that could be the predicate (or part of it) in a sentence. Start with the verbs in the five sentences in the Subjects and Verbs section.

——— ——— ——— ——— ——— ———

——— ——— ——— ——— ——— ———

——— ——— ——— ——— ——— ———

——— ——— ——— ——— ——— ———

——— ——— ——— ——— ——— ———

Practice Finding Verbs

1. Read this paragraph twice. The first time, read it to understand the content. The second time, enclose the verb or verbs of each sentence in a box. We've done the first one for you.

[1]My grandfather $\boxed{\text{was}}$ a cantankerous but lovable man. [2]He grumbled all day long about almost everything. [3]The television blared too loudly, and the programs were too silly to watch. [4]The telephone rang too loudly, and my little sister tied up the line all evening. [5]My mother fixed dinner too early and wasn't as good a cook as my grandmother had been. [6]Nevertheless, we all adored him and did anything we could to make his old age comfortable. [7]I ran home from school every day just to sit with him and listen to stories about his life in the country. [8]He had worked on the railroad, and he had had eight children. [9]Every story touched me deeply. [10]To this day, years after grandpa died, I remember them word for word. [11]I hear my grandfather's voice telling each story, and I often cry when I think of him.

2. Write a ten-sentence love story beginning with the sentence below. When you're finished writing, number the sentences and draw a box around the verb in each one.

[1]Luke $\boxed{\text{stared}}$ deeply into Laura's eyes.

_____

_____

_____

_____

_____

_____

_____

_____

_____

Finding Subjects and Verbs

1. Find the subjects and verbs you have written in the preceding exercises in this proofreading section, and list them in the columns:

Subjects   *Verbs*

_____   _____

_____   _____

_____   _____

_____   _____

_____   _____

_____   _____

_____   _____

_____   _____

_____   _____

_____   _____

_____   _____

_____   _____

What words on the subject list can also be used as verbs?

_____   _____   _____

_____   _____   _____

_____   _____   _____

2. Write sentences using the words from your list, each first as a *subject* and then as a *verb*. Also check your classmates' lists. For example, if you had the word *love* on your list, you could make the two sentences:

subject: **Love** *makes the world go around.*

verb: I **love** *horseback riding and backpacking.*

word

_____   subject: _____

                            verb: _____

_____   subject: _____

                            verb: _____

_____   subject: _____

                            verb: _____

What words on the verb list can also be used as subjects?

_____   _____   _____

_____   _____   _____

3. Write sentences using words from your list or your classmates' lists. Use each first as a verb and then as a subject.

word

_____   subject: _____

                            verb: _____

_____   subject: _____

                            verb: _____

_____   subject: _____

                            verb: _____

117

4. Look up in your dictionary the words you have just used. According to the dictionary, what parts of speech are these words? What, if any, special endings are added to these words when they are used as different parts of speech?

word   *part of speech*   *endings*

_____   _____   _____

_____   _____   _____

_____   _____   _____

5. Look back at the subject and verb lists on page 116. Write as many two-word sentences as you can, using a subject and a verb from the lists. (You may change the ending of a verb if necessary, but do not add any words.)

a. _____   f. _____

b. _____   g. _____

c. _____   h. _____

d. _____   i. _____

e. _____   j. _____

Practice Finding Subjects and Verbs

1. Circle the subject and enclose the verb in the box for each of these two-word subject–verb combinations:

a. (Girls) [run].

b. Cards fall.

c. Men talk.

d. School helps.

e. I walk.

f. Sand blows.

g. Garters slip.

h. Babies toddle.

i. Smoking kills.

2. Write a ten-sentence horror story beginning with the sentence below. When you're finished writing, number the sentences, circle the subject, and draw a box around the verb.

¹ (Igor) [opened] the gate of the courtyard.

_____

_____

_____

_____

_____

_____

_____

_____

3. This paragraph begins with the word *yesterday,* and its verbs are in the past tense. After you have read through it, change the first word to *today,* and make all the necessary changes in the verbs.

Today   get
~~Yesterday~~, I ~~got~~ up late. I heard the birds singing outside my window.

I saw the sun peeking through my bedroom curtains. Then I slowly dropped

my legs over the side of the bed. My feet touched the floor, and the cold

startled me. I jumped up, looked at the clock, and dashed to the bathroom.

I turned on the shower, and the water warmed up as I brushed my teeth.

When I finished brushing, I got into the shower. "Oh, no!" I shouted as

the water ran all over me. It was still cold. What a way to start the day!

4. Write a paragraph beginning with the words *Today* or *Right now.*

_____

_____

_____

_____

_____

_____

_____

_____

_____

Change the first word to *Yesterday* or *Last week,* and change all the verbs accordingly.

SPELLING

More Homonyms

The following are eight more homonyms to work on:

1. capital: **a.** upper-case letter. Use a *capital* letter at the beginning of a sentence.

   b. seat of government. The *capital* of Idaho is Boise.

   c. accumulated wealth. The company used all its *capital* to expand its business.

   capitol: building that houses the U.S. Congress (first letter capitalized), or any statehouse. The *capitol* in Albany is an impressive building.

The government needed **capital** *to build a new* **capitol.**

Write a sentence that uses both of these words. You try it:

_____

2. know: to be aware of something.   I *know* all the spelling words.
no: negation.   There are *no* cookies in the jar.

Students who **know** *their work should get into* **no** *trouble on exams.*

You try it: _____

3. knew: past tense of *know*.   I *knew* all the answers.
new: fresh, recent.   I bought a *new* car.

I **knew** *the* **new** *job would be better than the old one.*

You try it: _____

4. principal: **a.** chief, leader.   The school *principal* worked hard.
          b. capital sum placed at   When he needed money, he withdrew
              interest.   the interest from the bank and left
                the *principal.*
          c. most important.   The *principal* thing one learns at
                school is how to think.
   principle: **a.** fundamental truth.   Religion teaches *principles* of creation.
          b. rule of action.   We live by certain *principles.*

It was my **principle** *to use the* **principal** *that was in the bank.*

You try it: _____

5. threw: past tense of *throw*.   Ted *threw* the ball to Eileen.
   through: **a.** passage from one
               boundary to another.   We drove *through* the tunnel.
          b. by means of.   I got my divorce *through* a lawyer.
          c. (colloq.) finished.   Nancy and Patty left the table when
                they were *through* eating.

Note: Often *thru* is used as an alternative spelling for *through*, especially on road signs where space is limited. But *thru* is a colloquial spelling and should not be used in formal writing.

The presidential candidate **threw** *her hat in the ring and then traveled* **through** *every state in the union.*

You try it: _____

121

The following homonyms are related in meaning and have similar origins.

6. assistance: help, aid, support.

I needed *assistance* crossing the street.

assistants: plural of *assistant,* that is, people who assist or give support.

The *assistants* worked with the doctor in the emergency room.

*The **assistants** to the president knew that their job was to give **assistance** to all newcomers to Washington.*

You try it: _____

7. dependence: reliance, trust, being dependent.

Dependence on drugs is dangerous.

dependents: plural of *dependent,* that is, people who depend on others.

The children were their parents' *dependents.*

*The woman's **dependents** showed great **dependence** on her financial support.*

You try it: _____

8. patience: ability to withstand pain without complaint.

I have *patience* with my child.

patients: plural of *patient,* that is, people who depend on others.

The *patients* sat in the doctor's waiting room.

*The **patients** needed more **patience** to wait for the results of the x-rays.*

You try it: _____

Practice with Homonyms

1. Write the correct homonym in the blank.

Drug rehabilitation programs are based on the _____ that
principal/principle

you must _____ the reasons for your addiction. Many counselors are former
know/no

addicts themselves and understand what addicts go _____ because
threw/through

of their _____ on drugs. They offer their
dependence/dependents

_____ on a twenty-four hour basis. But there are limits. They
assistance/assistants

have no _____ with the lies that some addicts tell just to
　　　　patience/patients

raise enough _____ to feed their habit. When they catch you in a
　　　　capital/capitol

lie, they'll say, "I _____ what you've been _____, but this
　　　　know/no　　　　　　　　　threw/through

behavior will not work here."

　　　　The _____ or clients in drug rehabilitation programs generally
　　　　patience/patients

respond well to this treatment. _____ program is perfect, but the people
　　　　Know/No

who run these treatment centers and their _____ seem
　　　　　　　　　　　　　　　　assistance/assistants

to _____ what they are doing.
　know/no

　　　　Last year, many representatives of drug rehabilitation programs went

to the _____ to plead for increased funding for their programs. They
　　　capital/capitol

were asked by some officials how many people they _____ out of
　　　　　　　　　　　　　　　　　　　threw/through

their programs, and they responded, "Very few." That answer brought them

increased _____ with which to operate.
　　　　capital/capitol

2. Proofread this paragraph and make any changes necessary in the spelling
　　or the homonyms we've studied. We've made the first change for you.

　　　　We all lived in fear of Mr. Crawford, the principal of Leighton High
　　　　　　　　　　　　　　　　　　　　　　　know
School. He was a sour, old man who didn't ~~no~~ or didn't remember what

it was like to be young. He drilled a hole threw the wall of his office so

he could spy on the students in the hallway. If he saw a student running,

he would send one of his trusted assistance to the student's homeroom

with a notice to appear in the principal's office that afternoon. There he

would deliver a lecture about our dependents on the generosity of the

state government in supplying capital to maintain our building and how

if we did not show proper respect for the premises, we would be suspended.

We had little patients with these lectures, but we knew we had to listen.

The man through students out of school as if they were stones in a flower

garden. He made people think it was only through his kind assistants

that anyone got out of high school with a diploma. He was the master of

Leighton High, and we were his dependents. I couldn't wait to graduate

so I would be threw with this treatment.

THE FINAL DRAFT

Now you are ready to proofread the second draft of the essay you began earlier in this chapter. Read your essay again slowly, and aloud. Remember what you learned about word order in Chapter 1 and about the conventions of writing in Chapter 2. You may need to look back at these chapters. Make sure you can answer yes to these questions:

1. Do all your sentences contain both a subject and a verb?
2. Do all your sentences begin with a capital letter and end with the proper punctuation (period, question mark, exclamation point)?

Also make sure that any homonyms you may have used are spelled correctly. Change anything you think needs changing. Write a clean copy if you make more than one or two changes.

ADDITIONAL WRITING ASSIGNMENTS

Your writer's journal may have some ideas for you to develop into essays. Focus on things that have happened to you and incidents that you have witnessed.

Other students have found the topics below to be stimulating. Remember to follow the writing process we are developing: Do focused writing first. Then look it over. You may want to review the Writing and Rewriting section of each chapter before you start a second draft. When you finish your second draft, proofread it, and write a clean copy.

Topic Suggestions

One of these topics may make a good subject for a story:

1. An event in your life that taught you something about yourself.
2. A confrontation with someone in authority.
3. An event that taught you something about human nature.

4. The dumbest thing you ever did.
5. A time when you suffered a big disappointment.

You may also want to interview the oldest member of your family or someone in your neighborhood who remembers the "good old days." Ask the person you interview to tell you a story about his or her life as a young person. Retell the events in this person's life in as much detail as possible. Then explain what the events tell you about how life was lived in that person's generation. Do you think you'd have liked to be a young person in those times? Note the differences from or similarities to life as you live it now.

Writing a Narrative: Making a Point

4

Photo by
Barbara Smith

Answer the questions following the story.

The Bear Who Let It Alone
James Thurber

In the woods of the Far West there once lived a brown bear who could take it or let it alone. He would go into a bar where they sold mead, a fermented drink made of honey, and he would have just two drinks. Then he would put some money on the bar and say, "See what the bears in the back room will have," and he would go home. But finally he took to drinking by himself most of the day. He would reel home at night, kick over the umbrella stand, knock down the bridge lamps, and ram his elbows through the windows. Then he would collapse on the floor and lie there until he went to sleep. His wife was greatly distressed and his children were very frightened.

At length the bear saw the error of his ways and began to reform. In the end he became a famous teetotaller and a persistent temperance lecturer. He would tell everyone that came to his house about the awful effects of drink, and he would boast about how strong and well he had become since he gave up touching the stuff. To demonstrate this, he would stand on his head and on his hands and he would turn cartwheels in the house, kicking over the umbrella stand, knocking down the bridge lamps, and ramming his elbows through the window. Then he would lie down on the floor, tired by this healthful exercise, and go to sleep. His wife was greatly distressed and his children were very frightened. Moral: You might as well fall flat on your face as lean over too far backward.

What does the bear do when he's drunk?_____

_____

What does he do when he's sober?_____

_____

Rewrite Thurber's moral in your own voice. _____

_____

Do you think the moral fits the story?_____

_____

Why does Thurber write about bears rather than people?_____

_____

Do you know anyone who acts like the bear in this story?_____

_____

What is the main point of the fable?_____

_____

_____

Is the main point clearly stated anywhere in the story? Explain. _____

_____

_____

How does the main point help you understand the story?_____

_____

READING

PREVIEW QUESTIONS

As you read "When I Discovered I Was Poor" by Floyd Dell, look for information that answers these questions:

1. Why are Dell's shoes a clue to his situation?
2. Why is the envelope another clue?
3. Why was Dell's father at home?
4. What kind of preparations did the family make for Christmas?
5. What did Dell find out at Christmas?
6. How does Dell handle quoting people directly and reporting what people said?

When I Discovered I Was Poor
Floyd Dell

Floyd Dell wrote novels, plays, and nonfiction. He was also involved in radical politics and the pacifist movement in the years between the two world wars. He was the editor of the radical journal The Masses *and, later,* The Liberator. *This essay is taken from his autobiography,* The Homecoming, *published in 1933.*

(1) That fall, before it was discovered that the soles of both my shoes were worn clear through, I still went to Sunday school. And one time the Sunday-school superintendent made a speech to all the classes. He said that these were hard times, and that many poor children weren't getting enough to eat. It was the first that I had heard about it. He asked everybody to bring some food for the poor children next Sunday. I felt very sorry for the poor children.

(2) Also, little envelopes were distributed to all the classes. Each little boy and girl was to bring money for the poor, next Sunday. The pretty Sunday-school teacher explained that we were to write our names, or have our parents write them, up in the left-hand corner of the little envelopes. . . . I told my mother all about it when I came home. And my mother gave me, the next Sunday, a small bag of potatoes to carry to Sunday school. I supposed the poor children's mothers would make potato soup out of them. . . . Potato soup was good. My father, who was a quite a joker, would always say, as if he were surprised, "Ah, I see we have some nourishing potato soup today!" It was so good that we had it every day. My father was at home all day long and every day, now; and I liked that, even if he was grumpy as he sat reading "Grant's Memoirs." I had my parents all to myself too; the others were away. My oldest brother was in Quincy, and memory does not reveal where the others were; perhaps with relatives in the country.

(3) Taking my small bag of potatoes to Sunday school, I looked around for the poor children; I was disappointed not to see them. I had heard about poor children in stories. But I was told just to put my contribution with the others on the big table in the side room.

(4) I had brought with me the little yellow envelope, with some money in it for the poor children. My mother had put the money in it and sealed it up. She wouldn't tell me how much money she had put in it, but it felt like several dimes. Only she wouldn't let me write my name on the envelope. I had learned to write my name, and I was proud of being able to do it. But my mother said firmly, no, I must not write my name on the envelope; she didn't tell me why. On the way to Sunday school I had pressed the envelope against the coins until I could tell what they were; they weren't dimes but pennies.

(5) When I handed in my envelope, my Sunday-school teacher noticed that my name wasn't on it, and she gave me a pencil; I could write my own name, she said. So I did. But I was confused because my mother had said not to; and when I came home, I confessed what I had done. She looked distressed. "I told you not to!" she said. But she didn't explain why. . . .

(6) I didn't go back to school that fall. My mother said it was because I was sick. I did have a cold the week school opened; I had been playing in the gutters and had got my feet wet, because there were holes in my shoes. My father cut insoles out of cardboard, and I wore those in my shoes. As long as I had to stay in the house anyway, they were all right.

(7) I stayed cooped up in the house, without any companionship. We didn't take a Sunday paper any more, but the Barry *Adage* came every week in the mails; and though I did not read small print, I could see the Santa Clauses and holly wreaths in the advertisements.

(8) There was a calendar in the kitchen. The red days were Sundays and holidays; and the red 25 was Christmas. (It was on a Monday, and the two red figures would come right together in 1893; but this represents research in the World Almanac, not memory.) I knew when Sunday was, because I could look out of the window and see the neighbor's children, all dressed up, going to Sunday school. I knew just when Christmas was going to be.

(9) But there was something queer! My father and mother didn't say a word about Christmas. And once, when I spoke of it, there was a strange, embarrassed silence; so I didn't say anything more about it. But I wondered, and was troubled. Why didn't they say anything about it? Was what I had said I wanted (memory refuses to supply that detail) too expensive?

(10) I wasn't arrogant and talkative now. I was silent and frightened. What was the matter? Why didn't my father and mother say anything about Christmas? As the day approached, my chest grew tighter with anxiety.

(11) Now it was the day before Christmas. I couldn't be mistaken. But not a word about it from my father and mother. I waited in painful bewilderment all day. I had supper with them, and was allowed to sit up for an hour. I was waiting for them to say something. "It's time for you to go to bed," my mother said gently. I had to say something.

(12) "This is Christmas Eve, isn't it?" I asked, as if I didn't know.

(13) My father and mother looked at one another. Then my mother looked away. Her face was pale and stony. My father cleared his throat, and his face took on a joking look. He pretended he hadn't known it was Christmas Eve, because he hadn't been reading the papers. He said he would go downtown and find out.

(14) My mother got up and walked out of the room. I didn't want my father to have to keep being funny about it, so I got up and went to bed. I went by myself without having a light. I undressed in the dark and crawled into bed.

(15) I was numb. As if I had been hit by something. It was hard to breathe. I ached all through. I was stunned—with finding out the truth.

(16) My body knew before my mind quite did. In a minute, when I

could think, my mind would know. And as the pain in my body ebbed, the pain in my mind began. I knew. I couldn't put it into words yet. But I knew why I had taken only a little bag of potatoes to Sunday school that fall. I knew why I hadn't gone to school that fall—why I hadn't any new shoes—why had been living on potato soup all winter. All these things, and others, many others, fitted themselves together in my mind, and meant something.

(17) Then the words came into my mind and I whispered them into the darkness:

(18) *"We're poor!"*

(19) That was it. I was one of those poor children I had been sorry for, when I heard about them in Sunday school. My mother hadn't told me. My father was out of work, and we hadn't any money. That was why there wasn't going to be any Christmas at our house.

(20) Then I remembered something that made me squirm with shame— a boast. (Memory will not yield this up. Had I said to some Nice little boy, "I'm going to be President of the United States" Or to a Nice little girl: "I'll marry you when I grow up"? It was some boast as horribly shameful to remember.)

(21) *"We're poor."* There in bed in the dark, I whispered it over and over to myself. I was making myself get used to it. (Or—just torturing myself, as one pressed the tongue against a sore tooth? No, memory says not like that—but to keep myself from ever being such a fool again: suffering now, to keep this awful thing from ever happening again. Memory is clear on that; it was more like pulling the tooth, to get it over with—never mind the pain, this will be the end!)

(22) It wasn't so bad, now that I knew. I just *hadn't known!* I had thought all sorts of foolish things: that I was going to Ann Arbor—going to be a lawyer— going to make speeches in the Square, going to be President. Now I knew better.

(23) I had wanted (something) for Christmas. I didn't want it, now. I didn't want anything.

(24) I lay there in the dark, feeling the cold emotion of renunciation. (The tendrils of desire unfold their clasp on the outer world of objects, with-draw, shrivel up. Wishes shrivel up, turn black, die. It is like that.)

(25) It hurt. But nothing would ever hurt again. I would never let myself want anything again.

(26) I lay there stretched out straight and stiff in the dark, my fists clenched hard upon nothing. . . .

(27) In the morning it had been like a nightmare that is not clearly remembered—that one wishes to forget. Though I hadn't hung up my stocking, there was one hanging at the foot of my bed. A bag of popcorn, and a lead pencil, for me. They had done the best they could, now they realized that I knew about Christmas. But they needn't have thought they had to. I didn't want anything.

QUESTIONS OF CONTENT ▬▬▬▬▬▬▬▬

Circle the letter of the best answer for each question.

1. Why were the children asked to bring food and money to school?
   a. to send them to poor children.
   b. to share them for Christmas.
   c. to give them to their teachers.
   d. to give them to the principal.
2. Why didn't Dell return to Sunday school in the fall?
   a. He was lonely for his siblings.
   b. He had to play indoors.
   c. He had no shoes.
   d. He had a very bad cold.
3. Why did Dell keep repeating, "We're poor!"?
   a. He wanted to keep his mind off his toothache.
   b. He wanted to make sure he understood what he had just realized.
   c. He liked hearing the sound of the words.
   d. He wanted to go to Ann Arbor.

Answer these questions in full sentences.

1. What did the Sunday-school superintendent tell the children? _____

_____

2. Why did Dell feel sorry for the poor children? _____

_____

3. Summarize the events that made Dell realize he was poor. _____

_____

_____

_____

Match each statement from the text (first column) with a similar statement written in a different voice (second column).

1. My father was at home all day long and every day, now; . . .
   a. The realization hit my body and then my mind.
2. As the day approached, my chest grew tighter with anxiety.
   b. When it got close to Christmas, I was very nervous.

3. My body knew before my mind quite did.

4. Wishes shrivel up, turn black, die.

c. My father was out of work.

d. When you don't get what you want, you stop wanting things at all.

QUESTIONS OF INFERENCE

Look back at the text to answer these questions. Answer in full sentences.

1. Why did Dell's mother ask him not to write his name on the envelope and then looked distressed when he confessed he had? _____

_____

_____

2. Why did Dell become "silent and frightened" as Christmas approached?

_____

_____

3. Why did Dell's mother look away from him when he asked if it were Christmas Eve? _____

_____

4. Why did Dell not want his father to have to continue joking about whether or not it was Christmas Eve?_____

_____

_____

5. Which statement best expresses the main point of the story?
   a. Parents should always tell their children about Christmas.
   b. Being poor is very difficult.
   c. Learning the truth about yourself can be very painful.
   d. Parents should talk honestly with their children about the family's financial condition.

QUESTIONS OF CRITICAL THINKING

Answer each question in a short paragraph. You may want to use your own paper.

1. At the end of the essay, Dell says, "I didn't want anything." What made him say that? Have you ever felt the same way? Under what circumstances?

_____

_____

_____

2. Why do you think Dell's parents handled the situation in the way that they did? How would you have handled it? _____

_____

_____

_____

3. Why did Dell believe that he had to give up his dream of becoming president of the United States? Was this renunciation appropriate? Why or why not?

_____

_____

_____

_____

4. Jot down any questions you would like to ask Dell about being poor:

a. _____

b. _____

c. _____

VOCABULARY

These words from Dell's "When I Discovered I Was Poor" may be unfamiliar to you. The exercises will help you learn the meanings of these words and how they function in sentences.

nourishing	(2)	research	(8)	ebbed	(16)
contribution	(3)	arrogant	(10)	squirm	(20)
gutters	(6)	anxiety	(10)	renunciation	(24)
cooped	(7)	bewilderment	(11)	tendrils	(24)
companionship	(7)	stony	(13)	shrivel	(24)

Word Meanings

Look up each word in the dictionary and write down its definition:

renunciation _____

tendrils _____

shrivel _____

HINT: METAPHORS

There is nothing especially difficult about finding the meanings of the words *renunciation, tendrils,* and *shrivel.* However, when you reread the paragraph in which they appear, you still may be uncertain what they mean because they are used in a special way. That is, they are used as *metaphors* or particular kinds of description. Let's look at a paragraph from "When I Discovered I Was Poor":

> *I lay there in the dark, feeling the cold emotion of renunciation. (The tendrils of desire unfold their clasp on the outer world of objects, withdraw, shrivel up. Wishes shrivel up, turn black, die. It is like that.)*

The paragraph comes almost at the end of Dell's story, but to understand the paragraph, we need to see it as part of the whole story. Dell has realized how poor his family is, and he thinks he knows what this poverty means: he will get no presents for Christmas and cannot be president of the United States someday. Thus he is renouncing or giving up all his dreams, and he calls this renunciation a "cold emotion." Emotions are feelings. Can they be "hot" or "cold"? List all the emotions you can think of, and next to the list, label each one as hot or cold.

emotion   hot/cold

_____   _____

_____   _____

_____   _____

_____   _____

_____   _____

Labeling an emotion as hot or cold is a use of metaphor. Emotions are not really hot or cold; they have no temperature. But we can use a word usually associated with one thing (cold weather) to help us describe another thing more vividly (cold emotion).

Dell uses metaphor again in the next sentence when he talks about the "tendrils of desire." We associate tendrils with plants, and Dell uses "tendrils" with "desire," or wanting things.

He uses metaphor once again when he says, "Wishes shrivel up, turn black, die." What can shrivel, turn black, or die? List the things in their appropriate columns:

shrivel	turn black	die
_____	_____	_____
_____	_____	_____
_____	_____	_____
_____	_____	_____
_____	_____	_____

Why do you think Dell associates *wishes* with these things? What do you think Dell wants to tell us about wishes? Can you think of any other nonliving things, like wishes, that might "shrivel, turn black, and die"?

Word Clues

Look carefully at each of these words. Try to see them as the sum of their parts. Consult the list of prefixes and suffixes on pages 10–13, and write a "working definition" for each.

nourishing _____

contribution _____

companionship _____

bewilderment[1] _____

stony _____

[1] *Bewilder* is the verb form of this word.

Seeing Words in Context

These words below appear in "When I Discovered I Was Poor." You can find clues to the meanings of each word from its context. As you reread, circle the words or phrases that form the context for each word. Then write (1) your working definition, (2) the dictionary definition that's right for the context, and (3) an original sentence using the word. If you have difficulty figuring out the meaning of the word from the context of "When I Discovered I Was Poor," you may find it helpful to read the following story, in which the words appear in italics:

1. word: *anxiety*

    a. working definition _____

    b. dictionary definition _____

    c. your sentence _____

2. word: *arrogant*

    a. working definition _____

    b. dictionary definition _____

    c. your sentence _____

3. word: *research*

    a. working definition _____

    b. dictionary definition _____

    c. your sentence _____

4. word: *cooped*

    a. working definition _____

    b. dictionary definition _____

    c. your sentence _____

5. word: *squirm*

    a. working definition _____

b. dictionary definition _____

c. your sentence _____

6. word: *gutters*

    a. working definition _____

    b. dictionary definition _____

    c. your sentence _____

7. word: *ebbed*

    a. working definition _____

    b. dictionary definition _____

    c. your sentence _____

A NIGHT IN THE LIBRARY

When I was a junior in high school, I was locked in the school library overnight. It all was a big accident, but I will never forget the nervousness and *anxiety* I felt that night.

For two weeks before the history midterm I laughed at all the other students who were studying so hard. I was *arrogant* and thought I knew it all and didn't need to study. Then the day before the exam I began to get nervous and decided to review my notes. I went to the library to look up the causes of World War I and do some *research* on the war. I sat in a corner of the library behind a pile of books, *cooped* up like a chicken in a pen. I became so engrossed in my reading that I didn't move or even *squirm* in my chair, as I usually do when I study.

I didn't realize that night had fallen and everyone had gone home. The librarian and the janitor had not noticed me, and so they had locked me in for the night. When it started to rain, I listened to the water running through the *gutters* that lined the roof. I had always wondered what purpose those concrete grooves fulfilled. Now I was thankful they carried the water away.

Eventually I saw the dawn. As the night *ebbed* and became day, I knew I'd get out of the library.

Using Words in Context

One way to make new words part of your vocabulary is to use them in your writing. Write a paragraph about a time you found out something you did not know before. The experience may have been positive or negative, serious or funny. Make sure to use at least five of the words listed in the Vocabulary section. As you proofread your paragraph, underline the words you used.

_____

_____

_____

_____

_____

WRITING AND REWRITING

Stories are our oldest form of literature. Every culture in the world has created stories that explain its history and ideas. The Bible is a collection of stories. And there are stories of all kinds, including fables like the Thurber story at the beginning of this chapter. Stories entertain us, stimulate our emotions, and teach us as well. We learn about growing and loving, living and dying, honor and treachery.

We enjoy and learn from a story when we move right into the situation in which the author has placed the characters, and we live with them through all the details of the plot to the conclusion. If the author provides enough *detail*, if it's believable and makes the characters interesting and if we can follow the *order* of the plot, we will likely enjoy the story.

WRITING: A FIRST DRAFT

Choose one of these topics and do focused writing:

1. A time when you got into trouble.
2. A time when you made the right decision.
3. A time when you saw something you wished you had not seen.
4. A time when work got to be "too much."
5. A time when you had a very pleasant day.
6. A day when the mail came too late.
7. A time when something you heard changed your life.
8. A time when you won a prize.

Take out a piece of paper and a pen or pencil. Write today's date at the top. Now relax for a moment. Close your eyes. Breathe deeply. As the room begins to quiet, think about the situation you have chosen. Carry yourself back to that time in your life. Try to see yourself as you were then and feel the emotions you felt then. Now open your eyes. At the signal, start writing and don't stop for ten minutes. Tell your story, but don't stop to think about where to put information. Just let the ideas flow. DO NOT pause if you are unsure about spelling, punctuation, or grammar. DO NOT stop to look up words in the dictionary. If you get stuck momentarily with nothing in your mind, write the word *stuck* until your next idea comes.

When the time is up, read what you've written. Did you tell the whole story? If not, finish telling it. Consider this focused writing as the first draft of an essay. Put it aside for now. We'll come back to it later in the chapter.

WHAT MAKES WRITING GOOD? MAIN POINT AND LANGUAGE

Topic, Audience, and Purpose

Your topic, what you are writing about, is made up of many details, told in a certain order. This is called the plot. But there's more to a story than the plot. The plot is the action, but the action usually is just part of the story's overall "meaning." For instance, you could make a time line of "When I Discovered I Was Poor":

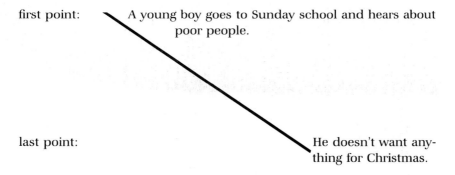

first point: A young boy goes to Sunday school and hears about poor people.

last point: He doesn't want anything for Christmas.

If you wanted to tell a friend about the topic of "When I Discovered I Was Poor," you could say, "It's about a little boy who discovers he's poor." And that's a good summary of the plot.

But what is the essay really about? It's about parents being honest with their children, about making the best of what little one has, and about how dreams are shattered. These are its *themes*—the meanings behind the action. Dell wanted us, his audience, to think about these things, perhaps to learn something from them. This was his *purpose*.

Main Point

What Does the
Moral Do?

Dell does not state his meaning, his *main point*, in the story. Some authors do and some don't. James Thurber attached a "moral" to his fable. "You might as well fall flat on your face as lean over too far backward." The moral expresses what the author learned, or what he wants us to learn, from the events in the story. Langston Hughes began "Salvation" with "I was saved from sin when I was going on thirteen." Of course, Hughes's line turns out to be *ironic*—we find out that exactly the opposite is true. But the statement, like all *main-point statements*, first introduces us to the context of the story and then tells us the topic of the story, what it will be about.

What Does the
Main-Point
Statement
Express?

The main-point statement should tell the audience (1) the topic, that is, what occurred, and (2) the purpose, that is, what the author wants the readers to know when they are finished reading. Writing a main-point statement (or *thesis statement*) will be easiest if you think of it as the completion of this sentence: "By the time I'm finished writing and my audience has finished reading, I want them to know/understand/feel/learn that

_____."

The part you filled in is all you need for a main-point statement. You may omit the beginning. Thus, if you wrote a story about your father dying of cancer when you were seven, you might write a main-point statement like:

"By the time I'm finished writing and my audience has finished reading, I want them to know/understand/feel/learn that when my father died of cancer when I was seven, I didn't understand that it wasn't my fault."

Main-point statements can help the reader "get into" the story. You may not want to use one for stories, but they are necessary for essays.

Language

What Kind of
Language
Should a Writer
Use?

Writers use language that fits the topic (what they are writing about), the audience (the people who will read or hear the story), and the setting (the place where the story takes place and where it will be read). Sometimes language that suits all three is hard to find, and writers must change their words.

When Do You
Change Your
Spoken Voice?

You alter your spoken language all the time. That is, you talk one way to your parents and another way to your friends, even about the same topic. You talk one way in school and another way at a party. How you talk in school may even change as the semester progresses: at the beginning you may use many big words to impress teachers and classmates, but as you become more relaxed, your language may become more informal.

When Do You
Change Your
Written Voice?

Your written voice can change in the same way. For instance, suppose that you were writing about an experience in prison. The language of prison is a "raw" language (containing slang and profanity), and so to fit the topic and setting, you would use that language. On the other hand, you would want to tell as broad an audience as possible about your prison experience. But part of the audience would be greatly offended by that raw language. Thus, you must decide how much of it to keep for the sake of truth and how much to alter for the sake of communication.

Do These Exercises Before You Revise Your First Draft.

Practice with Main-Point Statements

1. Read each of the short stories below. Choose the best main-point statement, and be prepared to defend your choices.

> On my thirteenth birthday, my father and I argued bitterly. I stormed out of the house and ran away. I took off down the street and didn't look back until I was several blocks away. I walked for hours. When my stomach started to rumble with hunger, I remembered my birthday party. My family had invited twelve of my friends, who were at that moment sitting in my living room eating my birthday cake as I roamed around the city alone.

By the time I'm finished writing and my audience has finished reading, I want them to know/understand/feel/learn that

   a. When I was thirteen I made a big mistake.
   b. Once I had a big fight with my father and ran away.
   c. When I got into a fight with my father on my birthday, I learned that sometimes anger doesn't pay.

> I stood in the back of the store for several minutes with the candles in my hand. I needed candles, but something kept me from buying them. I'm not sure what. I kept considering and reconsidering, the candles resting in my outstretched hand, while some thought lurked at the edges of my mind. Finally, I put them back into the bin and walked toward the front of the store empty-handed. The manager stepped into my path. "The candles, miss," he said, extending his hand.
> "I don't have any candles," I replied.
> "Oh, no?" he said, menacingly.
> "I took out some, but I put them back."
> "Well, we'll just have to see about that," he said, reaching for my purse.
> "If you touch me, you'll be sorry," I stated firmly and walked out of the store.

By the time I'm finished writing and my audience has finished reading, I want them to know/understand/feel/learn that

   a. The false accusations of a store manager taught me to assert myself when necessary.

b. Once a store manager embarrassed me so much I thought I'd die.

c. I once had a scary scene with a store manager.

"Joe Stevens, step up and receive the Sommerville High School Student Service Medal." The dean's voice rang out in the auditorium. Nervous and excited, I jumped from my seat and half walked, half ran to the stage. I climbed the stairs to the applause of the entire audience, advanced, and took the medal from the dean's hand. Then I grinned, waved to my parents, flashed the medal, and dashed back to my seat.

By the time I'm finished writing and my audience has finished reading, I want them to know/understand/feel/learn that

a. Getting awards is scary but fun.

b. My high school graduation ceremony was one of the proudest moments of my life.

c. At graduation, I won an award.

The lights went up as the movie ended, and I was immediately sorry they did. Two rows in front of me sat my older sister with a boy that my parents had forbidden her to go out with anymore. His arm caressed her back, and her head rested on his shoulder. He kissed her, and they stood up. I slumped down in my seat until they left the theater.

By the time I'm finished writing and my audience has finished reading, I want them to know/understand/feel/learn that

a. Sometimes at the movies you may see more than you bargained for.

b. When you see things you shouldn't, you are in an awkward position.

c. Once at the movies, I saw something I'd rather not have seen.

2. Read these short stories, and write a main-point statement for each:

I arrived at the office late and in a foul mood. The bus had stood in traffic for twenty minutes, and I had not been able to sleep well the night before. I barked at my coworkers, and they walked off without me for our coffee break. So I just sat at my desk muttering to myself. My supervisor, Mrs. Washington, marched across the room and leaned over my desk. "What do you want *now?*" I sneered. "Why don't you take the day off—without pay?" she replied.

By the time I'm finished writing and my audience has finished reading, I want them to know/understand/feel/learn that

_____

Up to that moment, the most important questions I'd asked myself were, "Will I see a movie this weekend?" and "Can I afford some new clothes?" Then the doctor said there was a problem with the blood test I'd taken as part of my yearly checkup. Too many white cells, he said. Everyone knew what that meant—leukemia.

The doctor ordered me back to his office for more tests, and here I was waiting for the results. "I'm sorry to have put you through this, Patrick," the doctor said. "The lab made a mistake labeling the blood tests. You're absolutely healthy." I was so happy, I ran out crying and laughing at the same time.

By the time I'm finished writing and my audience has finished reading, I want them to know/understand/feel/learn that

_____.

I awoke every morning at 4:30 A.M., made my bed, washed, dressed, and hiked for an hour with a twenty-pound pack on my back. After breakfast I suffered through hours of drills and training sessions. Everyone who outranked me—and that was everyone—had to be addressed as "sir" and otherwise treated with respect. They, in turn, treated me like an ant. Boot camp was one six-week hell.

By the time I'm finished writing and my audience has finished reading, I want them to know/understand/feel/learn that

_____.

The chair toppled back as I tried to avoid the man's fist. "Listen, man, we don't have to get physical," I said. "Can't we just talk this over calmly?"

"You took my seat," he slobbered, waving his hand in my direction. The bar was nearly deserted, and this drunk wanted the one bar stool I occupied.

"Listen, man," I tried again. "Take it easy. I'll move over here," I said. But clearly, nothing I said was going to satisfy him.

"You took my seat," he yelled, lunging at me with an imaginary bayonet in his hand.

I ducked, swerved behind him, grabbed the back of his jacket collar and escorted him into the alley.

By the time I'm finished writing and my audience has finished reading, I want them to know/understand/feel/learn that

_____.

3. Reread the focused writing you began earlier in this chapter. Write a main-point statement that could begin your story:

By the time I'm finished writing and my audience has finished reading, I want them to know/understand/feel/learn that

_____.

Practice with Language Appropriate to Topic, Audience, and Purpose

1. From the following list of words and phrases, indicate which are suitable for use in class (C), at home (H), or on the job (J). Use the appropriate letter in the space provided. Remember that the word or phrase may be appropriate in more than one setting.

_____ bogart   _____ gonna

_____ tardy   _____ anyhow

_____ jive   _____ like I said

_____ hi!   _____ relatively speaking

_____ uptight   _____ stuff it

_____ far out   _____ request notification

_____ balderdash   _____ later for you

_____ bogus   _____ May I help you?

_____ What's happening?   _____ Good morning

_____ hey, man   _____ Bye

2. Make up a list of words or phrases that you feel are suitable for

Home	*School*	*Job*
_____	_____	_____
_____	_____	_____
_____	_____	_____
_____	_____	_____
_____	_____	_____

Home	*School*	*Job*
_____	_____	_____
_____	_____	_____
_____	_____	_____
_____	_____	_____
_____	_____	_____

3. Look up in the dictionary five of the words or phrases you labeled "H" in Exercise 1 or put in the "home" column in Exercise 2. If they appear in the dictionary, note their usage label (if they have one):

Word/Phrase	*Usage Label*
_____	_____
_____	_____
_____	_____
_____	_____
_____	_____

4. Read each of the following letters twice. The first time, read them to understand the content. The second time, underline any words or phrases you think are not appropriate to the topic, audience, or setting. Write a second draft of each letter using language that you think is more appropriate. Jot down your reasons for the changes you make. The first one has already been done.

    a. topic: complaint about an RCA TV
       audience: Manager of Complaint Department
       setting: business office

FIRST DRAFT

Dear Sirs:
    I am very unhappy with the RCA TV I bought. You guys have a helluva lot of nerve selling TVs that don't work right. It really stinks. The

147

picture isn't clear; the color is <u>lousy</u>; and ! have to keep jumping up to fix the sound. Can't <u>you people</u> do anything right?

SECOND DRAFT

Dear Sirs:

I am very unhappy with the RCA television that I bought. Your company should be aware of the implications of selling televisions that do not work properly. The public will not buy them. The set has many problems. The picture is not clear; the color is hazy; and I have to keep adjusting the sound. I really expected more from RCA.

REASONS FOR CHANGES

1. language too informal.
2. profanity not necessary.
3. anger not necessary.

b. topic: application for a job
audience: potential employer
setting: personnel office

FIRST DRAFT

Hi! You have a job for an assistant buyer, and I know I'm the greatest for that position. I have tons of experience. I'm crazy for the business. And I work damn hard. Call me.

SECOND DRAFT

_____

_____

_____

_____

_____

_____

_____

_____

REASONS FOR CHANGES

1. _____

2. _____

3. _____

c. topic: a major disappointment
    audience: a friend
    setting: a letter to be read in a friend's home

FIRST DRAFT

Dear Yvonne:

God, I'm so unhappy. I didn't get the phone call from Hector last night. I desired that communication so badly. When I saw it was eleven o'clock and he hadn't called, I commenced to become hysterical and cried myself to sleep. Please do not inform any of our coacquaintances of this occurrence.

SECOND DRAFT

_____

_____

_____

_____

_____

REASONS FOR CHANGES

1. _____

2. _____

3. _____

d. topic: inflation
    audience: teachers and students
    setting: essay to be read in class

FIRST DRAFT

Inflation hits the poor harder than it does the rich. The rich can still hit the banks for loans, while the poor ain't got credit at all. The rich dig deeper into their assets, but the poor don't have a pot to you-know-what in.

SECOND DRAFT

_____

_____

_____

_____

_____

REASONS FOR CHANGES

1. _____

2. _____

3. _____

REWRITING: A SECOND DRAFT

Now you are ready to turn your focused writing into a second draft. Read it carefully, aloud, and, if you can, to a friend or classmate. Try to get a new vision of your subject. As you rewrite, think about detail and order, as discussed in Chapter 3. Also think about

1. Topic, *audience, and purpose.* Write a main-point statement that first introduces your audience to your topic and then tells them what you want them to know/feel/understand/experience by the time they are finished reading. Express your purpose for telling the story. Remember that your main-point statement is more than just a summary of the story's plot. It also expresses the underlying meaning of the story. That is, it should state the topic and the purpose.

2. *Language.* Read through the story, and change any words that are not suitable for your story's topic, audience, and setting. Use language that helps your audience understand and remember your story.

After you've written your second draft, go to Proofreading below, where you'll get some help on the proofreading stage of your writing.

PROOFREADING

MORE SUBJECTS AND VERBS

Write down your definitions of a sentence. A sentence is

1. _____

2. _____

3. _____

Your definitions may have contained some of these ideas about a sentence: A sentence is a *clause* (group of words), is *independent* (can stand by itself), or expresses a *complete thought*. These statements describe the elements of sentences, but they do not help you construct them. What you need is a good working, or functional, definition of a sentence.

Every sentence contains a subject and a verb. This means that the sentence has a topic (usually expressed by the subject), which is or is doing something (usually expressed by the verb). At its shortest, a sentence is a subject plus a verb.

But you can't say very much in just two or three words. To say more about the subject you must expand either the subject or the verb, or both. Look at this sentence from "When I Discovered I Was Poor":

"Also, little envelopes were distributed to all the classes."

This is an expansion of the subject–verb combination "envelopes were distributed." From the expanded subject we learn something about the envelopes—that they were little—and from the expanded verb, we learn where they were distributed.

The Fifty-Word Sentence

A group of students expanded the sentence *School helps* to fifty words:

When I was accepted into college, I began to understand that a good high school with dedicated teachers and up-to-date facilities helps students learn the subjects they need to know, like math and science and English, so they will get into a college and they can prepare themselves for the jobs they will hold in the future.

It is not necessary, and sometimes not advisable, to expand sentences to as many as fifty words, but it's helpful to know *how* to do it. Examine how the students expanded this two-word subject–verb combination.

School helps.

Each student was asked to add to the sentence. The word or words each student used to expand the original is enclosed in brackets.

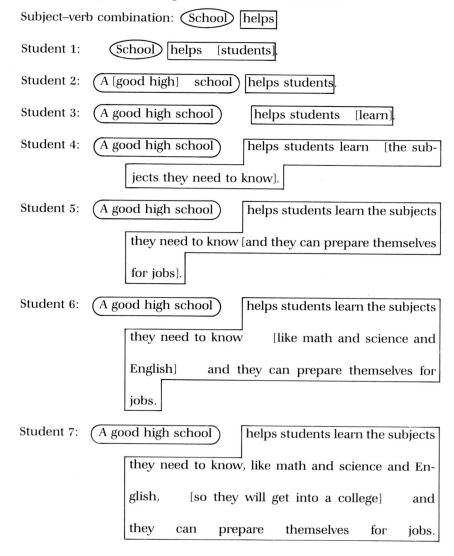

Subject–verb combination: (School) |helps|

Student 1:   (School) |helps   [students]|.

Student 2:   (A [good high]   school) |helps students|.

Student 3:   (A good high school) |helps students   [learn]|.

Student 4:   (A good high school) |helps students learn   [the subjects they need to know]|.

Student 5:   (A good high school) |helps students learn the subjects they need to know [and they can prepare themselves for jobs]|.

Student 6:   (A good high school) |helps students learn the subjects they need to know   [like math and science and English]   and they can prepare themselves for jobs|.

Student 7:   (A good high school) |helps students learn the subjects they need to know, like math and science and English,   [so they will get into a college]   and they   can   prepare   themselves   for   jobs|.

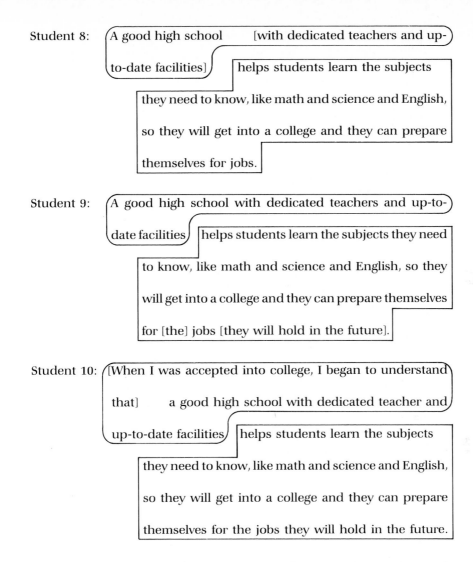

Student 8: (A good high school [with dedicated teachers and up-to-date facilities]) helps students learn the subjects they need to know, like math and science and English, so they will get into a college and they can prepare themselves for jobs.

Student 9: (A good high school with dedicated teachers and up-to-date facilities) helps students learn the subjects they need to know, like math and science and English, so they will get into a college and they can prepare themselves for [the] jobs [they will hold in the future].

Student 10: [When I was accepted into college, I began to understand that] (a good high school with dedicated teacher and up-to-date facilities) helps students learn the subjects they need to know, like math and science and English, so they will get into a college and they can prepare themselves for the jobs they will hold in the future.

Final sentence: When I was accepted into college, I began to understand that a good high school with good facilities and teachers helps students learn the subjects they need to know, like math and science and English, so they will get into a college and they can prepare themselves for the jobs they will hold in the future.

Below is a set of subject–verb combinations. Select one and expand it into a sentence of forty to fifty words. After you've finished, circle the expanded subject and enclose the expanded verb in a box. Add any words you want. But try to add words and phrases rather than merely another sentence.

1. Lions roar.
2. Puppies felt soft.
3. Women succeed.
4. Cars crash.
5. Machines were silent.
6. Headaches hurt.

_____

_____

_____

_____

_____

Practice Finding "Expanded Subjects" and "Expanded Verbs"

1. These sentences are from "When I Discovered I Was Poor," and the subject–verb combinations have been underlined. In the space below each sentence, explain how the expansions make the sentence clearer.

   a. I <u>waited</u> in painful bewilderment all day.

   _____

   _____

   b. I <u>had heard</u> about poor children in stories.

   _____

   _____

   c. And as the pain in my body ebbed, the <u>pain</u> in my mind <u>began</u>.

   _____

   _____

2. Read this story twice. The first time, read it to understand the content. The second time, circle the expanded subject, draw a box around the expanded verb. We've done the first one for you.

   ¹My half-brother, Richard, hoped to be hired as the permanent desk clerk in the Superior Hotel. ²The manager gave him a week's probation and started him at the desk from midnight to 8 A.M. ³Richard slept all

154

afternoon and then went to work. [4]Bright and cheerful, he fended off drunks who wanted to sleep in the hallways. [5]At least three times a night, he helped tipsy patrons to their rooms. [6]The manager liked Richard's work. [7]Then it happened. [8]One night, three armed and masked men ran in the front door. [9]They cleaned out the cash register and headed back outside. [10]One shouted, "Bye Richard," as he left. [11]My brother recognized the voice as that of an old high school acquaintance. [12]Richard told the manager he would go to the police to identify the robber. [13]But the manager wouldn't believe Richard had not had anything to do with the robbery. [14]And so because of guilt by association, Richard was fired from his job at the hotel.

Expanding Subjects

We expand the subject when we want to say more about the topic. For example,

(The man) [works].

We can expand the subject in the following ways:

1. (The man   in the factory) [works].

2. (The man   who is a member of the union) [works].

3. (The   intelligent, honest   man) [works].

4. (The man   and his coworkers) [work].

HINT

Expansion 4 tells you that the man was working with others, namely, his coworkers. To make this expansion you need the word *and*.

(The man and his coworkers) [work].

Notice that when you add to the number of people in the subject, your verb ending will change.

(The man) [works].

(The man and his coworkers) [work].

The expansions of the subject describe "the man" more fully as a person or describe his role as a worker. For instance, "The man in the factory works" tells you where the man is located. "The man, who is a member of the union, works" describes the man's labor affiliation.

Look at the sentence you wrote in The Fifty-Word Sentence section. Write the subject on the left and explain your expansion on the right. For example,

A good high school with dedicated teachers and up-to-date facilities

kind of school/
what school has

Add some of your classmates' expanded subjects.

1. _____

2. _____

3. _____

3. _____

4. _____

5. _____

Practice Expanding Subjects

1. In the subject–verb combinations below, circle the subject and enclose the verb in a box. Expand the subject and rewrite the sentence. We've done the first one for you.

   a. (Birds) [fly.]   (Most birds, even if they are old,) [fly.]

   b. Bandaids sting.   _____

   c. Typewriters skip.   _____

   d. Toddlers fall.   _____

   e. Sisters yell.   _____

   f. Cigarettes smell.   _____

   g. Disease kills.   _____

   h. Floors creak.   _____

156

i. Poverty hurts. _____

j. Maria tells. _____

k. Wind blows. _____

2. The following plot idea for a soap opera is written in short, choppy sentences, and as you'll see, they don't give you much information. We've started to expand the subject of the first sentence so as to provide more information. You do the rest. Use carets to indicate where you are inserting your expansions.

The heroine *who wants to get married*
Jonelle ∧ wishes. Murdock waits.

Jonelle plots the death. Murdock waits. Jonelle fails.

Murdock runs away.

3. The story below is written in very short sentences. Read it twice. The second time combine the sentences indicated by expanding the subject of one of them. Write the new story. We've combined the first set for you.

Combine

1, 2, 3
4, 5
6, 7
8, 9, 10
11, 12, 13
14, 15

[1]My sister took a trip to Jamaica. [2]My sister's name is Jessica. [3]Jessica is eighteen years old. [4]Her friend traveled with her. [5]Her friend's name is Denise. [6]Jessica loved the beach. [7]Denise loved the beach, too. [8]The sand was warm. [9]The sand was white. [10]The sand was lovely. [11]The water was not too cold. [12]It was calm. [13]It was blue. [14]Jessica swam for two weeks. [15]Denise swam for two weeks. [16]They ate and drank for two weeks. [17]They returned rested and happy.

(1, 2, 3) My eighteen-year-old sister Jessica took a trip to Jamaica.

_____

_____

_____

_____

_____

Expanding Verbs

Why Do We Expand Verbs? We expand the verb of a sentence when we want to say more about the subject or about what the subject is doing. For example,

And the verb expansions:

| plays against the best kids in the league |

| plays basketball as well as baseball |

| plays late at night |

| plays in the school yard near the fence |

| plays like a professional ball player |

| plays because he truly loves the game |

Expansions attempt to answer the questions who? what? when? where? how? and why? These questions are used in journalism courses to teach writers how to expand their stories; we used them in Chapter 3 to expand ideas in pantomime. Now we use them to help expand subject–verb combinations into fuller sentences. Which questions are answered in each of the example verb expansions?

Sometimes a sentence answers more than one question. Draw a box around the expanded verbs in the following sentences, which describe the plot of the novel *One Flew over the Cuckoo's Nest.* In the parentheses at the right, write the question or questions that the expanded verbs attempt to answer. We've done the first one for you.

1. *One Flew over the Cuckoo's Nest* was written by Ken Kesey and published in 1962. (who, what, when)
2. It has remained in print all these years because people see in it their own struggles against authority in its various forms.
   (   )
3. R. P. McMurphy, a freewheeling Irishman, feigns insanity to get away from a prison farm. (   )
4. He doesn't know that the "chronic" ward in the asylum is worse than anything he's yet experienced. (   )
5. Chronics are, according to McMurphy, "machines with flaws inside that can't be repaired, flaws born in, or flaws beat in over so many years of the guy running head-on into solid things that by the time

the hospital found him he was bleeding rust in some vacant lot."
(   )

6. The chronics are rendered hopelessly docile by the not-so-gentle hand of Big Nurse. (   )

7. Medication quiets most of the personality, and physical and psychological abuse does the rest. (   )

8. McMurphy tried to keep himself alive and to awaken the others.
(   )

9. The patients rally to him and begin their own reconstruction.
(   )

10. Big Nurse, however, has the backing of institutional power, and she uses it. (   )

Practice Expanding Verbs

1. Enclose each verb in a box. Expand the verb, rewrite the subject–verb combinations, and write down the question or questions that the expanded verb answers. We've done the first one for you.

a. (Leaves) fall. (Leaves) fall in the autumn. (when?)

   (Leaves) fall if there is not enough rain. (why?)

b. Fires warm. _____ (   )

c. Shoes pinch. _____ (   )

d. Toothaches hurt. _____ (   )

e. Anger festers. _____ (   )

f. Bankers invest. _____ (   )

g. Locker rooms smell. _____ (   )

h. Dieters eat. _____ (   )

i. Grooms march. _____ (   )

j. People travel. _____ (   )

k. Spices enhance. _____ (   )

2. The following short, choppy sentences form a story that doesn't give you much information. We've started to expand the verb of the first sentence so as to make it more interesting. You do the rest. Use carets to indicate where you are inserting your expansions.

who lives in Los Angeles

   a. Kathy ^ calls *her mother long distance every Tuesday.* ^

   b. Her mother scolds _____

   c. Kathy explains _____

   d. Her mother cries _____

   e. Kathy hangs up _____

3. The story below is written in very short sentences. Read it twice. First, read it to understand the content. Second, combine the sentences indicated by expanding the verb of one of the sentences. Write out the new story. We've combined the first set for you.

Combine	
2, 3, 4	[1]Pigeon Cove, Massachusetts, is a town on the north coast of Cape Ann. [2]The winters are long. [3]They are bleak. [4]They are dull. [5]In the winter of 1922, Mr. Ellis Stenman began preparing
5, 6	newspapers. [6]He was going to build a house entirely of newspapers. [7]He made two layers of papers. [8]He pasted them. [9]He folded
7, 8, 9	
10, 11	them. [10]When finished, the walls consisted of 215 thicknesses of newspapers. [11]The walls were made entirely of Boston newspa-
12, 13, 14, 15, 16	pers.
	[12]The walls finished, Stenman and his family worked on the interiors. [13]This consisted of chairs, [14]It contained lamps.
17, 18, 19, 20, 21	[15]It contained a settee. [16]These all were constructed in an octagonal design. [17]Stenman made a desk out of the *Christian Science Monitor*. [18]He made a bookshelf out of foreign papers. [19]He made
22, 23, 24	a grandfather's clock out of newspapers from the capital cities of the United States. [20](There were then only forty-eight.) [21]He
27, 28	made a fireplace mantle from the Sunday supplements of the *Boston Herald* and the *New York Herald Tribune*. [22]Some pieces of furniture are devoted to special events in history. [23]There is a cot made from newspaper articles on World War I. [24]There is a writing desk of Lindbergh's flight across the Atlantic.
	[25]Stenman said he began his work to see what he could do with newspapers without destroying the print. [26]The work took twenty years. [27]Some say that the Paper House is a testament

to Cape Ann winters. [28]The Paper House is now a local tourist attraction.

Pigeon Cove, Massachusetts, is a small town on the north coast of Cape Ann. The winters are long, bleak, and dull.

Practice Expanding Subjects and Verbs

1. Below are ten, two-word subject–verb combinations. Circle the subject and enclose the verb in a box. Then expand the subject and the verb to create a more interesting sentence. Circle the expanded subject and enclose the expanded verb in a box. We've done the first one for you.

   a. (Sheriffs) [arrest.]

   (Sheriffs on duty) [arrest people who commit crimes.]

   b. Hoboes sleep. _____

   c. Fortune-tellers predict. _____

   d. Furnaces heat. _____

   e. Escalators ascend. _____

   f. Plants die. _____

   g. Homeowners worry. _____

   h. Lovers quarrel. _____

   i. Bells startle. _____

   j. Parents scold. _____

2. Reread the sentences you created. Then expand the subject or the verb—or both—in a different way to create a new sentence.

   a. Sheriff s arrest. Sometimes drunken sheriffs arrest the wrong people.

   b. _____

   c. _____

   d. _____

   e. _____

   f. _____

g. _____

h. _____

i. _____

j. _____

3. Write a ten-sentence paragraph about something you saw happen on the street. When you've finished, circle the subject of each sentence and enclose the verb in a box. Expand the subject or the verb or both in at least four sentences.

_____

_____

_____

_____

_____

_____

_____

_____

_____

_____

_____

_____

4. The story below is written in very short sentences. Read it twice. The first time, read it to understand the content. The second time, combine the sentences indicated by expanding the subject or the verb of one of the sentences. Write out the new story. We've combined the first set for you.

Combine	
	[1]The restaurant was noisy. [2]The restaurant was crowded.
1, 2, 3	[3]The restaurant was smoky. [4]My sister Eleanor sat alone at a
4, 5	table. [5]She was waiting for her husband, Paul. [6]Paul arrived late.
6, 7, 8	[7]He was cold. [8]He was tired. [9]"Why did you ask me to meet
	you? he asked. [10]"I thought we should talk about last night's
11, 12	argument," she replied. [11]The people around them were eating
13, 14	their lunch. [12]The people were hungry. [13]Eleanor ordered her
15, 16, 17	lunch. [14]Paul ordered his lunch. [15]The food arrived late. [16]The
18, 19	food was cold. [17]The food was not eaten. [18]Eleanor and Paul
20, 21, 22	just sat at the table. [19]They did not talk. [20]Eleanor sat at the
	table. [21]She was playing with her fingernails. [22]She was looking
23, 24	in the mirror. [23]Paul smoked a cigar. [24]He was anxious to get
	back to work. [25]They did not resolve their argument.

The restaurant was noisy, crowded, and smoky.

_____

_____

_____

_____

_____

_____

_____

_____

_____

FRAGMENTS

A well-formed sentence consists of a subject–verb combination. It can be as short as two words or as long as fifty—or even longer. Begin your sentence with a capital letter, and end it with an end-of-sentence punctuation mark (period, exclamation point, question mark).

No matter how much a sentence is expanded, the basic structure should still be a subject–verb combination, represented by a circle for the subject and a box for the verb.

(Notice the period that comes at the end of the combination.)
Looking at a sentence in this way helps show what a fragment is.

A *fragment* is a piece of something. In writing, it is a piece of a sentence. Fragments often result from not using the basic subject–verb structure to form sentences. Omitting one part or splitting one of the parts can lead to a fragment.

Fragment Type 1: The first type of fragment results from a missing subject or verb, for example,

What Is a Fragment?

What Are the Different Types of Fragments?

a. ⬯　　　　　　　　　　a subject with no verb

b. ▭　　　　　　　　　　a verb with no subject

Most often, this type of fragment is missing the subject:

(John)　got up late.　　Rushed out of the house.

165

Rushed out of the house is an expanded verb with no subject. This kind of fragment has an implied subject; the writer assumes that the reader knows who performed the action. And here it is easy to figure out that *John* rushed out of the house. Nonetheless, a well-formed sentence must have both a *subject* and a *verb*. To repair this fragment, you must supply the missing element—the subject.

(John) | got up late. | | Rushed out of the house. |

Fragment Type 2: The second type of fragment results from splitting the expanded verb, for example,

(John) | got up late. | ⅔ ⅔ | And rushed out of the house. |

You can fix this fragment by removing the punctuation mark and capital letter and joining the two parts of the expanded verb.

(John) | got up late and rushed out of the house. |

You may retain the punctuation by adding a subject, as in Fragment Type 1:

(John) | got up late. | And (he) | rushed out of the house. |

Many people write this kind of fragment because they want to make their sentences short and manageable. For example,

(The fullback on the snow-covered field) | fumbled the ball | ⅔ ⅔ | as he crossed the goal line. |

This fragment also results from splitting the expanded verb *fumbled the ball as he crossed the goal line*. To repair this fragment, reconnect the two parts of the expanded verb.

(The fullback on the snow-covered field) | fumbled the ball as he crossed the goal line. |

Practice Finding Fragments

1. Proofread each set of "sentences." Circle the subject, enclose the verb in a box, and cross out the letter beside each fragment. We've done the first one for you.

   a. Tables and chairs next to each other.

   b. Government spending has been reduced.

   c. Lots of people.

   d. Mother, a kind but steely-eyed woman.

e. The long and exciting story.

f. Juvenile delinquents, once called hooligans, prey on old people.

g. The world full of people of all races, religions, and nationalities waiting for peace on earth and goodwill toward people.

h. Fortunately, the people escaped injury when the train crashed.

i. Schools with happy children doing their work are a pleasure to see.

j. Old battered men, drunk and diseased, on the street corners of the major cities of the country.

2. Read this story twice. The first time, read it to understand the content. The second time, proofread it, and circle the number of each fragment. We've done the first one for you.

> [1]Nora was very lazy when she was younger. [2]She loved school. [3]Hated homework. [4]Her nice and hardworking teachers wrote letters to her parents at least once a week. [5]Her mother and father loved her very much. [6]And wanted the best for her. [7]Never knew what to do with her. [8]At first they talked nicely to Nora at night when they came home from work. [9]They tried to reason with Nora. [10]About her schoolwork. [11]Reasoning didn't help. [12]The teachers wrote. [13]More letters to Nora's parents. [14]Then her father decided what to do. [15]He sat down with Nora every evening and did the homework with her. [16]Made a game out of each assignment. [17]Nora loved. [18]The extra time with her father. [19]And loved talking about the schoolwork. [20]From then on Nora completed her homework. [21]Every day. [22]Now Nora is the best student in the class.

Practice Fixing Fragments

1. Proofread these pairs of "sentences." Circle the subject and enclose the verb in a box. If you find a fragment, fix it. We've done the first one for you.

a. (Marc and Rachel) | strolled along the beach | ∅ | *h*and in hand.

(*Hand in hand* is a fragment. We fixed it by connecting it to the other part of the expanded verb, *strolled along the beach.*)

b. Broken bones must be set so that they will heal properly. Doctors generally put a cast on the affected area to keep it still.

c. Columbus discovered America in 1492. Trying to get to India.

d. The car hit the wall with a tremendous impact. Bounced off and landed on its side.

e. I want a fur coat. With a hood and elegant lining.

f. The elderly are often victims of violent crime. Teenagers prey on them because old people are helpless.

g. I trained to become a nurse. Instead I became a doctor.

h. A long time ago, my mother, sisters, brothers, and I traveled to Brazil. We toured there for three weeks and relaxed for another.

i. The young, frightened immigrants rose. To pledge their loyalty to their new country.

j. The pope apologized to the people of Africa. For any part Christians had played in slavery.

2. After you have read this story once, proofread it and fix any fragments you find.

When Claude was six, he learned that change was not always bad. Claude and his family moved to a new house when Claude was six. Everyone was excited about the move. Except Claude. He didn't want to leave his old house. With his own room and his toys. Claude didn't want to move to a new neighborhood where he didn't know any of the children.

His parents watched the movers take the last boxes to the truck. They were almost out the door when they realized Claude was still inside. Clinging to the bannister. Crying hysterically. "I won't go!" he screamed. "You can't make me!" Claude ran. From room to room. Touching all the walls. His mother and father, very gentle and kind people. Didn't know what to do. "Darling," Claude's mother said, hugging him. "Don't you remember the big yard the new house has and the beautiful school just down the street?" Claude thought about not having to ride on the school

bus for forty minutes and having his own place to play. He stood up.

"Let's go," he announced.

3. Write a ten-sentence paragraph about a job you once held or a task you had to do.

_____

_____

_____

_____

_____

_____

_____

_____

_____

_____

When you're finished writing, number your sentences. Circle each subject and enclose each verb in a box. Fix any fragments you find.

SPELLING

More Homonyns

The following are eight more words that sound alike:

1. altar: center of religious worship. The priest said mass at the *altar.*
   alter: to make different without The dressmaker can *alter* a garment
       changing into something else. when a person loses weight.

*When the deacons met to discuss the renovation of the church, they decided to **alter** the design of the **altar**.*

Write a sentence that uses both words. You try it:

_____

2. berth: **a.** enough distance to maneuver.

The ferry needed a wide *berth* to dock.

     b. a place to sit or sleep in a vehicle.

I always wanted to sleep in the upper *berth* of the sleeping car.

  birth: emergence of a new person in the world.

The child's *birth* was recorded on film.

*The woman prayed she would not give **birth** in the **berth** on the train.*

You try it: _____

3. karat   (or carat): unit of weight for precious stones or metals.

The woman wore a three-*karat* diamond ring.

  caret: a mark ($\wedge$) made in printed matter to indicate where something is to be inserted.

The editor used a *caret* in the manuscript and added information to the text.

  carrot: orange-colored, edible root vegetable.

A *carrot* is a nutritious food.

*The writer used a **caret** to indicate where he inserted the number of **karats** in describing the ring, and he wished he had given his fiance **carrots** instead.*

You try it: _____

4. council: assembly or meeting for advice.

The city *council* met to consider changing the laws.

  counsel: **a.** advice given as a result of a consultation.

Father gave us his *counsel* when we needed it.

     b. a lawyer participating in a trial.

The attorney worked as *counsel* to the Senate committee.

*The **council** met to seek the **counsel** of its advisers.*

You try it: _____

5. naval: relating to the navy.　　　A *naval* ship sat in the harbor.
　　navel: location in abdomen for at-　A baby's *navel* must be kept clean.
　　　tachment of umbilical cord.

*The ensign contemplated his **navel** on the deck of the **naval** destroyer.*

　　You try it: _____

6. pedal:　**a.** a lever activated by the　The piano *pedal* helps control
　　　　　foot.　　　　　　　　　sound.
　　　　　b. to use or work a pedal.　I *pedal* to school on my bicycle.
　　peddle: to sell or offer for sale from　Nowadays many people *peddle* to
　　　　　place to place.　　　　make extra money.

*He **peddles** bike **pedals** for a living.*

　　You try it: _____

7. peer: someone of equal standing.　It is important to get along with one's
　　　　　　　　　　　　　　　peers.
　　pier:　a structure extending into the　We walked out on the *pier* and
　　　　water for use as a landing　watched the sunset over the water.
　　　　place for ships or a walkway.

*I am the **peer** of the woman who dove off the **pier** into the harbor.*

　　You try it: _____

8. waist: narrow part of the body be-　Body builders are concerned about
　　　　tween the hips and chest.　the size of their *waists.*
　　waste:　**a.** sparsely settled region.　The desert is a vast *waste*land.
　　　　　b. rejected material; refuse.　Factory *waste* spilled into the river.
　　　　　c. to cause to shrink.　　Anorexics *waste* away from malnutri-
　　　　　　　　　　　　　　　tion.
　　　　　d. to spend money extrava-　The officials *waste* the taxpayers'
　　　　　　gantly.　　　　　　money

*The dieters swore they would **waste** away to nothing, but few had even lost an
inch on their **waists.***

　　You try it: _____

Practice with Homonyms

1. Write the correct homonym in the blank.

I had planned to arrive at the church in a limousine, but when I saw

the flat tire, I knew we would have to _____ our plans. My family huddled
                                         altar/alter

in a hurried _____, and my father said, "We'll all just have to rent
                council/counsel

bikes and _____ to the church, or the groom will be left alone at the
               pedal/peddle

_____."
altar/alter

"If that's your _____," I told him, "I guess we will have to do
                  council/counsel

it." I touched the one-_____ diamond on my finger and looked
                          karat/caret/carrot

nervously at my wedding gown. I inhaled deeply and adjusted the dress

over my _____. I smoothed it over my _____. I laughed to myself
          naval/navel   waist/waste

as I thought, "When I'm pregnant and ready to give _____, I won't look
                                                        berth/birth

like this." Then I thought of the look that would be on my fiancé's face as

my family arrived at the church on bicycles. He was very proper. He had

spent most of his adult life on a British _____ ship. In fact, his ship
                                             navel/navel

was now at the _____ in our city. I hoped that all these wedding preparations
                 peer/pier

would not be a _____ of time.
                 waist/waste

2. Read this paragraph twice. The first time, read it to understand the content.
The second time, proofread and, if necessary, change the spelling of the
homonyms you've studied in this section. We've made the first change
for you.

alter
Knowing how to revise or ~~altar~~ a piece of writing is an important

skill to learn in school. Many writers believe that a first draft has been

etched in stone. The advice of their piers and the council of their teachers mean nothing. They consider it a waist of time to change one word. But these students are wrong. Knowing where to put a karat and where to add information is crucial. For instance, if you are describing a navel vessel, it may be important to include what war the vessel served in, even if you did not think of it when you wrote your first draft. If is also important to know where and what to delete from, or leave out of, the final draft. Everyone knows, for instance, that a bicycle has two peddles. You probably do not need to include that information. Writing courses in school can be extremely helpful in teaching you these skills.

THE FINAL DRAFT

Now you are ready to proofread the second draft of the essay you began earlier in this chapter. Read your essay again slowly, aloud. Remember what you learned about word order and sense in Chapter 1 and about the conventions of writing in Chapter 2. You may need to look back to these chapters.
    Make sure you can answer yes to these questions as you proofread:

1. Do all your sentences contain both a subject and a verb?
2. Do all your sentences begin with a capital letter and end with the proper punctuation (period, question mark, exclamation point)?
3. Have you eliminated any fragments?

Also check the spelling of any homonyms you may have used. Change anything you think needs changing. Write a clean copy if you make more than one or two changes.

ADDITIONAL WRITING ASSIGNMENTS

Your writer's journal may have some ideas for you to develop into essays. Focus on events that had meaning in your life or others' lives. You may not have known the meaning at the time, but in retrospect you realized the significance of it.
    Other students have found the topics below to be stimulating. Remember to follow the writing process we are developing: Do your focused writing first. Then read it over. You may want to review the Writing and Rewriting

section of each chapter before you start a second draft. Write a main-point statement (or thesis statement) that tells your audience what you want them to know about this incident when they are finished reading, what happened and what significance the event had. When you finish your second draft, proofread it, and write a clean copy.

Topic Suggestions

One of these topics may make a good subject for a story:

1. An accident that turned out all right.
2. An instance of prejudice.
3. An example of sibling rivalry.
4. An incident that proved that "truth is stranger than fiction."
5. A time when you learned that you (or someone else) were different from what you had previously thought.
6. A time when you learned a valuable lesson.
7. A show of concern for someone less fortunate.

You may also want to try writing a story about the time you became aware of yourself as a member of a specific ethnic, religious, racial, social, national, or gender group.

Describing a Place: Showing Versus Telling

Photo by
Arley Bondarin

1. List at least ten things in the room you are sitting in, for example,
   a. a chair.
   b. a table.
2. Expand each item on your list into a descriptive phrase:

   a. battered, yellow ___ with an arm-desk attached
      a ^ chair ^

3. In a group, play "pass the chalk." Pass a piece of chalk from one person to another. Each person must write something different about the chalk.
4. Think of a room in your house. Describe the room in a piece of focused writing. Then draw the room and everything in it to scale as well as you can. When you have finished your drawing, reread your description. Does the drawing remind you of items you left out? If so, put them in your description.

READING

PREVIEW QUESTIONS

As you read "A Mexican House" by Ernesto Galarza and "A Kitchen" by James Baldwin, look for information that helps answer these questions:

"A Mexican House":

1. How many rooms did the house have?
2. What was the purpose of the roof?
3. Does Galarza's use of figurative language help you picture the house?
4. How does Galarza's use of foreign words affect your reading of the description and your feelings about what you read?
5. Does Galarza describe the house in some kind of order? What does he describe first, second, third? Does the order help you picture the house?

"A Kitchen":

1. How dirty was the room?
2. What happened to the mother's face when the boy looked at her?
3. What feelings do you have as you read this selection?
4. Does Baldwin's order and detail influence your feelings?
5. Does Baldwin's use of figurative language help you picture this room?

176

A Mexican House

Ernesto Galarza

Ernesto Galarza was born in Mexico in 1905 and moved to California when he was a small child. He has worked for the Foreign Policy Association and in labor relations, specializing in projects relating to the exploitation of Mexican workers. This essay is taken from his autobiography, Barrio Boy, *published in 1971.*

(1) Our adobe cottage was on the side of the street away from the *arroyo*. It was the last house if you were going to Miramar. About fifty yards behind the corral, the forest closed in.

(2) It was like every other house in Jalco, probably larger. The adobe walls were thick, a foot or more, with patches of whitewash where the thatched overhang protected the adobe from the rain. There were no windows. The entrance doorway was at one end of the front wall, and directly opposite the door that led to the corral. The doors were made of planks axed smooth from tree trunks and joined with two cross pieces and a diagonal brace between them hammered together with large nails bent into the wood on the inside. Next to each door and always handy for instant use, there was the cross bar, the *tranca*. On both sides of the door frame there was a notched stub, mortared into the adobe bricks and about six inches long. The door was secured from the inside by dropping the *tranca* into the two notches.

(3) All the living space for the family was in the one large room, about twelve feet wide and three times as long. Against the wall between the two doorways was the *pretil*, a bank of adobe bricks three feet high, three across, and two feet deep. In the center of the *pretil* was the main fire pit. Two smaller hollows, one on either side of the large one, made it a three-burner stove. On a row of pegs above the *pretil* hung the clay pans and other cooking utensils, bottom side out, the soot baked into the red clay. A low bench next to the *pretil*, also made of adobe, served as a table and shelf for the cups, pots, and plates.

(4) The rest of the ground floor was divided by a curtain hung from one of the hand-hewn log beams, making two bedrooms. Above them, secured to the beams, was the *tapanco*, a platform the size of a double bed made of thin saplings tied together with pieces of rawhide. The top of a notched pole, braced against the foot of the back wall of the cottage, rested against the side of the *tapanco*, serving as a ladder. Along the wall opposite the *pretil*, in the darkest and coolest part of the house, were the big *cantaros*, the red clay jars; the *canastos*, tall baskets made of woven reeds; the rolled straw *petates* to cover the dirt floor where people walked or sat; and the hoes and other work tools.

(5) There was no ceiling other than the underside of the thatch, which was tied to the pole rafters. On top of these, several layers of thatch were

laid, making a waterproof cover thicker than the span of a man's hand. The rafters were notched and tied to the ridgepole and mortared on the lower end to the top of the walls. Between the top of the walls and the overhang there was an open space a few inches wide. Through this strip the smoke from the *pretil* went out and the fresh air came in.

(6) It was the roof that gave space and lift to the single room that served as kitchen, bedroom, parlor, pantry, closet, storeroom, and tool shed. The slender rafters pointed upward in sharp triangles tied at the peak with bows of dark brown rawhide that had dried as tight as steel straps. Strings of thatch hung from the ceiling like the fringe of a buggy top, making it appear that the heavy matting of grass did not rest on the rafters but tiptoed on hundreds of threads. It was always half dark up there. My cousins, Jesus and Catarino, and I slept in the *tapanco*. More than a bedroom, to us it was a half-lighted hideaway out of sight of parents, uncles, aunts, and other meddlesome people.

QUESTIONS OF CONTENT

Circle the letter of the best answer to each question.

1. The living space for the family was in

    a. one room.   **c.** three rooms.

    b. two rooms.   **d.** four rooms.

2. The bedrooms on the ground floor were formed by a wall of

    a. wooden planks.   **c.** adobe bricks.

    b. curtains.   **d.** plaster board.

3. How large was the room?

    a. twelve feet by twelve feet.   **c.** twelve feet by three feet.

    b. twelve feet by thirty-six feet. **d.** twelve feet by ten feet.

4. What did the family use to cover the dirt floor?

    a. wooden planks.   **c.** straw *petates*.

    b. rugs.   **d.** nothing.

5. How many people slept in the *tapanco?*

    a. one.   **c.** three.

    b. two.   **d.** four.

Answer these questions in full sentences:

1. How was the door secured? _____

_____

2. Where and in what was the food cooked? _____

_____

3. What different purposes did the one room serve? _____

_____

QUESTIONS OF INFERENCE ━━━━━━━━━━━━━━━━━

Look back at the text to answer these questions. Answer in full sentences.

1. Why was the *tranca* "always handy for instant use"? _____

_____

2. How many people lived in or spent time in this house? _____

_____

3. Where was the bathroom? _____

_____

4. Where did the family members wash themselves? _____

_____

5. What was the financial status of this family? _____

_____

6. How do you think the narrator feels about his financial status and his house? How does he indicate his feelings? _____

_____

_____

Answer these questions in a short paragraph. You may want to use your own paper.

1. What problems might a large family have living in one room? _____

_____

_____

2. On the other hand, what might be some of the advantages for a family

living in one room? _____

_____

_____

3. What questions would you want to ask the children who live in this house?

(Think of at least three.) _____

_____

_____

4. Do you think Galarza wrote this description for people who are familiar

with this kind of living arrangement? Why or why not? _____

_____

_____

5. Do you think Galarza might have written his description differently if he

had intended it for a different audience? _____

_____

6. Why do you think Galarza wrote this piece? _____

_____

_____

7. If you were to describe where you live, what characteristics would you

emphasize? Why? _____

_____

A Kitchen
James Baldwin

James Baldwin is a novelist, playwright, and essayist who was born in Harlem, New York City, in 1925. This excerpt is from his first novel, Go Tell It on the Mountain, *published in 1953.*

Their mother, her head tied up in an old rag, sipped black coffee and watched Roy. The pale end-of-winter sunlight filled the room and yellowed all their faces; and John, drugged and morbid and wondering how it was that he had slept again and had been allowed to sleep so long, saw them for a moment like figures on a screen, an effect that the yellow light intensified. The room was narrow and dirty; nothing could alter its dimensions, no labor could ever make it clean. Dirt was in the walls and the floorboards, and triumphed beneath the sink where roaches spawned; was in the fine ridges of the pots and pans, scoured daily, burnt black on the bottom, hanging above the stove; was in the wall against which they hung, and revealed itself where the paint had cracked and leaned outward in stiff squares and fragments, the paper-thin underside webbed with black. Dirt was in every corner, angle, crevice of the monstrous stove, and lived behind it in delirious communion with the corrupted wall. Dirt was in the baseboard that John scrubbed every Saturday, and roughened the cupboard shelves that held the cracked and gleaming dishes. Under this dark weight the walls leaned, under it the ceiling, with a great crack like lightning in its center, sagged. The windows gleamed like beaten gold or silver, but now John saw, in the yellow light, how fine dust veiled their doubtful glory. Dirt crawled in the gray mop hung out of the windows to dry. John thought with shame and horror, yet in angry hardness of heart: *He who is filthy, let him be filthy still.* Then he looked at his mother, seeing, as though she were someone else, the dark, hard lines running downward from her eyes, and the deep, perpetual scowl in her forehead, and the downturned, tightened mouth, and the strong, thin, brown, and bony hands; and the phrase turned against him like a two-edged sword, for was it not he, in his false pride and his evil imagination, who was filthy? Through a storm of tears that did not reach his eyes, he stared at the yellow room; and the room shifted, the light of the sun darkened, and his mother's face changed. Her face become the face that he gave her in his dreams, the face that had been hers in a photograph he had seen once, long ago, a photograph taken before he was born. This face was young and proud, uplifted, with a smile that made the wide mouth beautiful and glowed in the enormous eyes. It was the face of a girl who knew that no evil could undo her, and who could laugh, surely, as his mother did not laugh now. Between the two faces there stretched a darkness and a mystery that John feared, and that sometimes caused him to hate her.

QUESTIONS OF CONTENT

Circle the letter of the best answer to each question.

1. Above the stove were

    a. the cupboard shelves.   **c.** pots and pans.
    b. windows.

2. The walls leaned under the weight of

    a. the cupboard.   **c.** the dirt.
    b. the ceiling.   **d.** the cracked paint.

3. How often were the pots and pans cleaned?

    a. every day.   **c.** every Saturday.
    b. once a month.

4. Which of these had cracks?

    a. the pots and pans.   **e.** the dishes.
    b. the paint on the walls.   **f.** the windows.
    c. the stove.   **g.** the ceiling.
    d. the cupboard.

5. What did John notice about his mother?

    a. dark lines on her face.   **d.** weak eyes.
    b. a tightened mouth.   **e.** short, curly hair.
    c. bony hands.   **f.** a perpetual scowl.

Answer these questions in full sentences:

1. What was done to make the room appear clean? _____

_____

2. How many people were in the room? _____

_____

3. What was John's mother like before he was born? _____

_____

182

4. What was his mother like now? _____

_____

Match the statements from the selection (first column) with a similar statement written in a different voice (second column).

1. The pale, end-of-winter sunlight filled the room and yellowed all their faces; and John . . . saw them for a moment like figures on a screen, an effect that the yellow light intensified.

2. The room was narrow and dirty; nothing could alter its dimensions, no labor could ever make it clean.

3. The windows gleamed like beaten gold or silver, but now John saw, in the yellow light, how fine dust veiled their doubtful glory.

4. Then he looked at his mother, seeing, as though she were someone else . . . and the phrase turned against him like a two-edged sword, for was it not he, in his false pride and evil imagination, who was filthy?

a. The windows looked clean, but as you looked closer, there was dust even there.

b. Because the afternoon light in the winter made everything look a hazy yellow, it seemed as if the people in the room were not real, but characters in a movie.

c. He looked at his mother and regarded her as a stranger, and then he realized that the shame he felt because of the dirt was not her fault.

d. The dirt in the room was as permanent as the size of the room.

QUESTIONS OF INFERENCE

Look back at the text to answer these questions. Answer in full sentences.

1. Why could no amount of effort make the kitchen clean? _____

_____

2. What was the financial status of this family? How do you know? _____

_____

3. Whom did John blame for the condition of the room? Why? _____

_____

4. Why did John have such vivid memories of the old photo of his mother?

_____

_____

Answer these questions in a short paragraph. You may want to use your own paper.

1. Why do you think John suddenly had two images of his mother? _____

_____

_____

2. What responsibility, if any, do you think John felt for the change in his

mother's appearance? _____

_____

_____

3. Do you think most children feel somewhat guilty if their parents have a

difficult life? Why or why not? _____

_____

_____

4. Why did John sometimes hate his mother?_____

_____

5. Do you think that it is sometimes all right for children to feel that they

hate their parents? Why or why not? _____

_____

_____

6. In what ways can the size and condition of a kitchen affect a family? ____

_____

_____

7. What questions would you like to ask either John or his mother? (Think

of at least three.) _____

_____

_____

8. How does Baldwin's description make you feel about this kitchen? Would

you want to live there? Explain. _____

_____

_____

_____

VOCABULARY

These words from Galarza's "A Mexican House" and Baldwin's "A Kitchen" may be unfamiliar to you. The exercises will help you learn the meaning of these words and how they function in sentences.

FROM *"A Mexican House"*

adobe	(1)
whitewash	(2)
thatched	(2)
notched	(2)
mortared	(2)
hollows	(3)
hewn	(4)
secured	(4)
saplings	(4)
rawhide	(4)
rafters	(5)
ridgepole	(5)
meddlesome	(6)

FROM *"A Kitchen"*

morbid
intensified
spawned
delirious
communion
corrupted
perpetual
scowl
undo

Word Meanings

Look up the words below in the dictionary. Many of them have more than one meaning, and some are more than one part of speech. Read the entire entry for each word. Choose the meaning closest to the way in which the word is used in the essay. If you're in doubt, write down all the meanings you think are possible, separating them by semicolons. Make sure to include the part of speech next to your definition.

communion _____

corrupted _____

hollows _____

perpetual _____

sapling _____

secured _____

spawned _____

Word Clues

Try to see the words below as the sum of their parts. Consult the list of prefixes and suffixes on pages 10–13, and write a working definition for each word. Check the dictionary entry for each word to see how close your working definition is to it.

meddlesome _____

rawhide _____

ridgepole _____

undo _____

whitewash _____

Seeing Words in Context

The following words appear in either "A Mexican House" or "A Kitchen." You can find clues to the meanings of each word from its context. As you reread the two stories, circle the words or phrases that form the context for each word. Then write (1) your working definition, (2) the dictionary definition that's right for the context, and (3) an original sentence using the word. If you have difficulty figuring out the meaning of the word from the context of "A Mexican House" or "A Kitchen," you may find it helpful to read the following story, in which the words appear in italics:

1. word: *morbid*

   a. working definition _____

   b. dictionary definition _____

   c. your sentence _____

2. word: *delirious*

   a. working definition _____

   b. dictionary definition _____

   c. your sentence _____

3. word: *intensified*

   a. working definition _____

   b. dictionary definition _____

   c. your sentence _____

4. word: *scowl*

   a. working definition _____

   b. dictionary definition _____

   c. your sentence _____

5. word: *rafters*

   a. working definition _____

   b. dictionary definition _____

   c. your sentence _____

6. word: *adobe*

   a. working definition _____

b. dictionary definition _____

c. your sentence _____

7. word: *hewn*

    a. working definition _____

    b. dictionary definition _____

    c. your sentence _____

8. word: *mortared*

    a. working definition _____

    b. dictionary definition _____

    c. your sentence _____

9. word: *thatched*

    a. working definition _____

    b. dictionary definition _____

    c. your sentence _____

10. word: *notched*

    a. working definition _____

    b. dictionary definition _____

    c. your sentence _____

THE ASYLUM

    I had grown up afraid of the asylum that stood in the valley just outside our town. For as long as I could remember, parents threatened to send their children to the asylum if they misbehaved, which often caused me to have unhealthy, *morbid* dreams and to wake in the night crying. When I was sick, fever would make my mind wander, and when I was *delirious* and my fears *intensified,* these thoughts got worse. In my dreams I would see an ugly matron, her face twisted in a *scowl,* walking toward me with ropes. My father told me she used those ropes to hang inmates from the wooden *rafters* in the ceiling.

Of course, I no longer believe these stories, and the asylum has been abandoned for many years. But as I stood on the hill overlooking the group of small buildings, the sight of them still sent shivers down my spine. The reddish *adobe* bricks of the walls were probably shaped by local workmen, not *hewn* by inmates, as we were told. The roofs were made of pieces of slate, which had probably been plastered or *mortared* together to form the ridges that looked like terraced, *thatched* straw. And the bars that secured the doors on the outside rested in the two v-shaped grooves or *notches.* But they did not lock people in. These buildings now penned up horses, not inmates. My adult mind knew this, but the child's heart that still beat within me quaked a bit in fear.

HINT: PERSONIFICATION

Personification is another kind of figurative language. You can see the word *person* in *personification.* Indeed, one of the meanings of the word *personification* is "the act of representing an object or idea as if it were human." We use *personification* to help create pictures with words so that readers will "see" more clearly what we are describing.

In "A Kitchen," James Baldwin wants us to see the dirt in the kitchen. The dirt he is describing is not ordinary; it cannot be easily dusted or vacuumed away. This kitchen is coated with the kind of dirt that nothing will wash away. Baldwin describes the dirt as a person instead of a thing:

> *dirt . . . triumphed*
> *dirt . . . revealed itself*
> *dirt . . . lived behind*
> *dirt . . . crawled*

The verbs on the right side of the ellipsis points (which indicate that words have been left out) are usually used to describe what people do. For example, we would not find it odd to say

> *The runner* **triumphed** *in the race.*
> *The murderer stepped from behind the curtain and* **revealed** *himself.*
> *The people* **lived** *in the house.*
> *The infant* **crawled** *into the corner.*

(These words can also be used with animals and insects, but the extent to which they name human actions permits us to refer to their use as *personification.*) Furthermore, the dirt becomes more overpowering when we see it as possessing the qualities and actions of human beings.

What other nonliving things or ideas could be personified with these words? Write your answers in the blanks:

_____ triumphed
_____ revealed itself
_____ lived   behind
_____ crawled

Column A lists nouns and subjects, things and ideas. Column B lists verbs usually associated with people. Match the words from each list to create some interesting word-pictures. If you don't find any combinations you like, create some of your own, using other words.

A	B
cold	conquers
love	buys
justice	bites
headache	follows
racism	flies
time	tortures

Using Words in Context

One way to make new words part of your vocabulary is to use them in your own writing. Write a paragraph about either a time you were ill or a place in some rural area you once visited. Use at least five of the words in the Vocabulary section in your paragraph, and underline them as you proofread.

_____

_____

_____

_____

_____

_____

_____

_____

_____

_____

WRITING AND REWRITING

The world is full of things to describe: places you have visited, scenes or events you have witnessed, people you have observed. Carry your writer's journal around for a week to write "thumbnail" (brief) descriptions of what you observe traveling to and from school or work.

There are two ways to describe: You can *tell* your audience only the essential facts, as you would if you were filling out an accident report for the police. Or you can *show* your audience the place, scene, or event in such a way that they will feel as if they are sharing the experience with you. You can transport them to a place they have never seen or introduce them to a person they have never met. Or you can give them fresh insight into a place or person they may already know.

What Kinds of Descriptions Will You Have to Write?

What Are the Two Ways to Write a Description?

WRITING: A FIRST DRAFT

Think about a place you know well or that has so impressed you that you remember exactly what it looks like.

1. In the center of the *idea wheel,* write down the name of the place you are thinking about. Then fill in the circles at the tips of the spokes with details about the place: what it looks like, what goes on there, and more. Draw an idea wheel on your own paper, adding more spokes if you need them.

2. Do focused writing about the place. Write the date at the top of a piece of paper. Relax for a moment. Close your eyes. Breathe deeply. As the room starts to quiet, think about this place. See it in your mind's eye. What part of town is it in? What kind of neighborhood forms its immediate setting? What does it look like? What are people doing there? Now open

your eyes. At the signal, start writing and do not stop for ten minutes. Do not stop to think about where to put information. Just let the ideas flow. DO NOT pause if you are unsure about spelling, punctuation, or grammar. DO NOT stop to look up words in the dictionary. If you get stuck momentarily with nothing in your mind, write the word *stuck* until your next idea comes. Okay, begin. After ten minutes, stop. Read what you have written. If you want to add anything, do it now. Consider your focused writing the first draft of an essay. Put it aside for now. We'll come back to it later in the chapter.

WHAT MAKES WRITING GOOD? DETAILS, ORDER, AND FIGURATIVE LANGUAGE

Details

What Is the Most Important Element of Description?

Details are the most important element of description. You must give your audience enough information to enable them to *see* the scene. There are several ways to use detail to enrich description.

1. Write precisely what you see, leaving very little to the reader's imagination, for example,

> Our adobe cottage was on the side of the street. It was like every other house. All the living space for the family was in one large room. The rest of the ground floor was divided by a curtain. There was no ceiling other than the underside of the thatch. It was the roof that gave space and lift to the single room.

Does this description sound familiar? Look again at Ernesto Galarza's "A Mexican House," and underline these sentences in the original passage.

a. Where are these sentences in the original? _____

_____

b. In the original, what kind of information follows each of these sentences? _____

_____

c. Which description do you like better, the abbreviated one or the original? Why? _____

_____

2. Use detail to expand your description. Let's create a fictional place, Dracula's Disco. It's your basic disco: flashing strobe lights, a dance floor, a bar. We'll create more of it as we go on. For the moment, let's suppose Dracula's Disco contains a dining area with red carpeting and furniture upholstered in red and black. You could say,

> Dracula's Disco has red carpeting and red and black upholstered furniture.

Or you could say,

> Dracula's Disco is carpeted in a deep, almost purple, red. All the high-backed chairs are covered in a soft, red velvet, and the low, boxlike benches in a black material.

Why Are Details Important to a Description?

Both sentences describe the same things, but the second is more vivid because of its details. These expansions of the original help the audience see the scene. Underline the words or phrases in the second sentence that help you see Dracula's Disco.

What Are Enhancing Words?

1. Words that tell the size, shape, and color of things enhance description. The following are a few *enhancing* words:

size	shape	color
huge	curved	bright
tiny	rectangular	flaming
extensive	square	somber
cozy	round	neutral
nine by twelve (or any dimension)	oval	yellow
massive	pear-shaped	(any color)

2. What are other *enhancing* words?

_____	_____	_____
_____	_____	_____
_____	_____	_____
_____	_____	_____
_____	_____	_____

Another reminder about details: Your audience is interested in what a place looks like but, even more, in what goes on there. If they have never been to this place, telling them what goes on there will give them a sense of whether or not they might want to go. And if they have been there, they may want to know how your experience compares with theirs.

What Is an Anecdote?

In Chapters 3 and 4 you gained some skill telling stories about your experiences. You can apply that skill here. When you tell a story within a description, you generally have to shorten it; it becomes what we call an *anecdote*. Anecdotes can be very effective in description because they help create an impression of the place as well as provide a reason for your feelings. Remember to include in your anecdote snippets of conversation that you overheard or took part in.

Order

What Is Different About Order in a Story and Order in a Description?

Order in description is different from order in stories. In a story, we retell what happened as it occurred; that is, the order is usually chronological. But in a description, when we see, hear, or react to a place or person, we do it all at once, and it is sometimes difficult to sort out afterwards the order in which these impressions came to us. Actually, it may not be necessary for us to make sense of the experience for ourselves. But when we want to share it, we must give it some order.

For instance, as you enter Dracula's Disco, you are aware simultaneously of the flashing lights, the decor, the crowd of people, and the music. Later, you may see a person you know standing near the bar. But in that first moment, you experience the place as a teeming, pulsing, vivid whole. The day may come when you will be able to simply transfer your thought waves to another person. But until then, you must find a more conventional way to help someone else see and feel Dracula's Disco in the way that you have. You have several options:

What Are Some of the Ways You Can Give Order to a Description?

1. You can begin at a particular spot in the room and "walk" your audience around with you. For instance, start at the door ("As you enter Dracula's Disco, you see . . . "), and describe things as if you were walking around the room. (If you choose this type of order, you may find it helpful to draw a floor plan of the place you are describing.) This is what you did in the preliminary exercises.

2. You can set the scene and write about the most prominent elements first to give the audience a general impression of the place and then develop each element later. For instance, if Dracula's Disco occupies three floors in a large building, you can start with a description of the neighborhood and the outside of the building. Then take your audience inside, briefly outline the main function of each floor (dancing, drinking, dining), and then describe each floor in detail. Look back at "A Mexican House" and note how Galarza uses this approach to set the scene and then shifts to the first method to "walk" the reader through the house.

3. The place you are describing may have one outstanding feature that immediately captures the attention of anyone who enters. If so, you may describe this first. Baldwin does this in "A Kitchen." He first describes the dirt and then relates every detail of the kitchen in some

way to it. In Dracula's Disco, the dance floor is oval with pointed edges, and a huge, revolving strobe light hangs above it. The dance floor so dominates the place that you may want to mention this first and then describe everything else in relation to this one feature.

Whatever pattern you choose should include certain *locating* words to help your audience situate themselves. The following are some *locating* words and phrases:

What Are
Locating Words?

to the left, right (of)   opposite
to the north, south, east, west (of)   near, far away (from)
left, right   inside, outside
above, on top of   vertically, horizontally
next to, beside   diagonally (across from)
below, beneath, under   across
up, down

Add more words you think help establish location:

_____   _____

_____   _____

_____   _____

_____   _____

_____   _____

Figurative Language

The appropriate use of *figurative language* will strengthen your description. Figurative language is the special use of words that compares something the audience may not know with something they do know, thereby giving them a clearer picture of what you are describing. The most familiar types of figurative language (or figures of speech) are *metaphor* (see Chapter 4), *simile* (see Chapter 6), and *personification* (see this chapter).

What Is
Figurative
Language?

Galarza uses two figures of speech in "A Mexican House" to help us see the house more clearly: "Strings of thatch hung from the ceiling *like the fringe of a buggy top.*" (simile) and the matting "did not rest on the rafters but *tiptoed on hundreds of threads.*" (personification). James Baldwin uses figures of speech to bring into clearer focus the dirt in the kitchen: In contrast with the dirt, the freshly cleaned windows "gleamed like beaten gold or silver" (simile); the dirt was a "dark weight" (metaphor); and the dirt "triumphed" (personification).

What Are Some
Types of
Figurative
Language?

We can also use figures of speech to describe Dracula's Disco:

The warm glow of the red velvet chairs offered the patrons a restful haven from the frenzy of the dance floor.

195

A metaphor gives to one thing a quality of another. Chairs don't glow; fires glow, lights glow. However, by giving the chairs the quality of light, the audience gets a new impression of the chairs.

The dance floor looked like a giant checkerboard.

A simile is a metaphor that makes a direct comparison by using the words *like* or *as.*

The pulsating music invited you to join the other dancers.

How Can You Make Your Figurative Language More Effective? Personification is giving something a human quality. Music cannot "invite," people invite.
    Remember:
    1. The comparisons you draw should make sense to the audience, so choose familiar items. For instance, if you want to expand your description of the shape of the dance floor, you might write:

The dance floor was shaped like an egg with its top and bottom pinched in.

(Most readers know what eggs look like.)

But this might bewilder most of your audience:

The dance floor looked like the marquise diamond in the window of Cartier's.

(Unfortunately, all too few of us have experience with diamonds or Cartier's.)

    2. Avoid clichés. Clichés are expressions so overused that they have lost their ability to create fresh images. They no longer help people see. For instance,

The bartender at Dracula's Disco was as busy as a bee.

How many times have you heard someone described this way? Too many! You could create a similar but more effective image by saying,

The bartender at Dracula's Disco was as busy as a store clerk on Christmas Eve.

The audience would know how busy the place is without being bored by the image.

Do These Exercises Before You Revise Your First Draft.

Practice with Details

1. Rewrite each of the sentences below so that it gives a more exact picture. (You may want to underline the words that seem vague so that you will know what to go back to.) You may find that you need more than one sentence to do the job. We've done the first one for you.

a. The *store* was *crowded*. *Macy's was holding its annual sale. The main floor was crowded with anxious shoppers pushing one another to reach the merchandise piled on the tables*

b. The room was big and comfortable. _____

_____

c. The lake was beautiful. _____

_____

d. It was a busy office. _____

_____

e. I live on a quiet street. _____

_____

f. The Christmas decorations in the store window were lovely. _____

_____

g. The kitchen has a lot of furniture in it. _____

_____

h. My old high school is big. _____

_____

i. It was miserable outside. _____

_____

j. The house looked as if the people who lived there were rich. _____

_____

k. The house looked as if the people who lived there were poor. _____

_____

l. The beach was the place to be. _____

_____

m. The train was crowded at that time of day. _____

_____

2. Use enhancing words in each sentence to add detail, for example,

The chair stood in the room.

straight-backed   awkwardly in the middle
The∧chair stood∧   of the room.

a. The children played in the yard. _____

_____

b. People walked toward the trains. _____

_____

c. Flowers grew in the garden. _____

_____

d. Boats passed by. _____

_____

e. The girl fought off her attacker. _____

_____

f. Graffiti covered the walls. _____

_____

g. The garbage spilled onto the street. _____

_____

h. The baby slept in his crib. _____

_____

i. The couple strolled down the boardwalk. _____

_____

j. The cars collided at the intersection. _____

_____

k. *The Scarlet Letter* is the title of a book. _____

_____

l. Accounting is a hard subject. _____

_____

Look back at Chapter 4, More Subjects and Verbs. You may find many similarities to what you have done here.

3. Put yourself in the "pictures" below. For each place listed, jot down details about the place and one word that captures your feeling about it.

	details	*feeling*
bus station	*big, noisy, dirty, crowded, dark*	*scary*
airport	_____	_____
your house or apartment	_____	_____
local movie theater	_____	_____
public park	_____	_____
library	_____	_____
beauty parlor or barber shop	_____	_____
block you live on	_____	_____
high school	_____	_____
college campus	_____	_____
grocery	_____	_____
restaurant, bar, or nightclub	_____	_____

4. Choose one place from this list. Write an anecdote about an experience you had there and how that experience affected your feeling about the place. Use any dialogue, or conversation, you think might help your picture.

_____

_____

_____

_____

_____

_____

_____

_____

_____

_____

Practice with Order

Each of the paragraphs below is a scrambled description. Read each one twice. The first time, read for content. The second time, rearrange the sentences in an order that an audience can follow. Write the numbers of the newly ordered sentences in the spaces following. Remember that there's no absolutely correct way to order these sentences, and so be prepared to explain or defend you decisions. We've done the first one for you.

THE CLOSET

[1]The light cord is attached to a fixture above the door frame. [2]Coats on hangers are crammed on a pole that extends across the length of the closet. [3]A metal cabinet full of old clothes is on the right side. [4]Shelves start above the pole and go up to the ceiling. [5]A trunk packed with more old clothes sits on the floor. [6]Shelves stand along the right side. [7]Towels and boxes are stored on the shelves above the pole. [8]The shelves on the side hold more towels that are not stacked too neatly. [9]As you open the door, a light cord dangles in front of your nose. [10]Sometimes the door of the storage cabinet opens and hits you in the face. [11]As you reach for one towel, several others may fall down. [12]It's a big, full closet.

Reordered sentences:

1.	12	**7.**	6
2.	9	**8.**	8
3.	1	**9.**	11
4.	2	**10.**	3
5.	4	**11.**	10
6.	7	**12.**	5

Explanation: A floor plan for this might help. I started with a main-point statement about the whole closet. Then I described what was right in front of me as I opened the door, then the side, and the floor.

THE PLAYGROUND

[1]The surface is concrete, as in most city playgrounds. [2]The sandbox is also on the left side. [3]Near the kiddie swings are two seesaws and benches for the adults to sit on. [4]The rest of the space is for running and ball playing. [5]There's a large slide in the far right corner of the playground. [6]The kiddie swings are on the left side as you enter. [7]Kids love this playground because there is so much to do here. [8]They are enclosed by a short fence that has a gate with a sign that says, "Please keep this door closed. Children's swings." [9]The playground covers a square block. [10]The swings for older kids are near the slide. [11]You can step down into a circle of sand that has a dome-shaped climbing toy in the center. [12]However, the Parks Department has put down thick rubber mats under some of the play equipment, the things children might fall off. [13]The sandbox is always filled with glass and other debris, which is dangerous because most kids like to play in it with bare feet.

1. _____	**6.** _____	**10.** _____
2. _____	**7.** _____	**11.** _____
3. _____	**8.** _____	**12.** _____
4. _____	**9.** _____	**13.** _____
5. _____		

THE HOUSE

[1]The house is large and comfortable. [2]The dining room is on the left. [3]As you walk in the front door, you see a long hallway and a staircase to the second floor. [4]Behind the dining room is the kitchen. [5]At the end of the hall on the right are two bedrooms. [6]On the left is a guest bath. [7]The living room is on the right with a large picture window overlooking the street. [8]Down the hall is a door leading into the kitchen. [9]The larger bedroom has its own bath. [10]On the second floor are two rooms, a bedroom in the back and a sitting room in front. [11]The last room is a study with a door opening into the back yard. [12]There is also a bathroom upstairs and a great many storage closets.

THE SUPERMARKET

[1]Shopping in my local food market is always an unpleasant experience. [2]The aisles are long and narrow. [3]The fresh vegetables are arrayed on the right side of the store. [4]The freezer compartment is at the rear. [5]The vegetables all are packaged so that you cannot touch them. [6]The dairy case is on the right wall near the back. [7]If a clerk catches you trying to open one of the vegetable packages, he or she will yell in a loud voice meant to embarrass you. [8]The frozen juice is never quite solid, and so you must use it up quickly. [9]Boxes of cookies and crackers are piled too high on the shelves, and so they fall when you reach for one. [10]People bump into one another with their shopping carts. [11]Music blares from loudspeakers. [12]The cash registers are in front. [13]Sometimes the music is interrupted for an unintelligible announcement of a sale. [14]There is no place near the checkout counters to put the unloaded shopping carts, and you can hardly get past them to a line. [15]Then all of a sudden people start pushing carts to where the sale is taking place. [16]It's a madhouse. [17]The checkers are surly and impolite.

1. ⎯⎯   7. ⎯⎯   13. ⎯⎯
2. ⎯⎯   8. ⎯⎯   14. ⎯⎯
3. ⎯⎯   9. ⎯⎯   15. ⎯⎯
4. ⎯⎯   10. ⎯⎯   16. ⎯⎯
5. ⎯⎯   11. ⎯⎯   17. ⎯⎯
6. ⎯⎯   12. ⎯⎯

Practice with Figurative Language

1. Read these paired paragraphs twice, first to understand the content and second to look for figures of speech. Put a check mark next to the paragraph in each pair that contains figures of speech. Put a star next to the one you prefer. Remember that your preference is neither "right" nor "wrong," but be prepared to discuss or defend your choice. For example,

   1a. Smoke came out of the chimney of the factory. Soot fell on all the nearby houses.
   1b. Smoke belched from the chimney of the factory. Soot settled like an unwanted snowfall over the nearby houses.
   Explanation: The second one makes me feel the smoke more and makes me feel like coughing. I also like the image of the snowfall. The other one is okay, though.

2a. The March wind roared like an angry beast. People buttoned up their coats to protect themselves from its wrath. Leaves fled across the ground.

2b. The March wind was strong. People buttoned their coats to protect themselves from the cold. Leaves fell from the trees to the ground.

3a. The children feared the teacher. When she yelled, they started to cry. They wished they were somewhere else, anywhere else, when she punished them for minor misbehaviors.

3b. The children feared the teacher as they would fear a mad dog. Her barking brought them to tears. They wished they were pups protected in a kennel when she nearly bit them for misbehaving.

4a. The house had been the scene of many happy moments. The family had grown up there and left the house. Now that the old people were dead, the house would be torn down.

4b. Laughter once stretched the seams of the house. The family cloaked itself in its warmth but then had outgrown it and left. Now that the old people were dead, it was a frayed, useless garment that would be ripped and discarded.

5a. Inflation was hitting the whole population. People felt like punching bags in a gymnasium. They wondered if they would eventually have to carry suitcases full of money to the grocery store and trunk loads to the car dealerships.

5b. Inflation was affecting the whole population. People wondered if they would have enough money for necessities, let alone luxuries.

2. Underline the figures of speech in the preceding paragraphs. In the margin, label each one M for metaphor, S for simile, and P for personification. Then reread "A Mexican House" and "A Kitchen," and underline the figures of speech and label them.

3. Try creating some images. By yourself or in a group, picture the people or things listed. What do they remind you of? Jot down a few images from the animal world, inanimate objects, or anything you can think of. For example,

1. neighbors   hens in a barnyard/ducks in a pond/
                        hyenas/mismatched bookends

2. parents fighting _____

3. teachers   _____

4. computer dating   _____

5. hot, humid weather _____

6. adolescence   _____

7. amusement park   _____

8. factory   _____

Now circle the images you like best for each item. Write a sentence using that image as a simile. For example,

neighbors   (hens in a barnyard)/ducks in a pond/hyenas/

mismatched bookends

My neighbors sound like hens in a barnyard when they talk at the back fence.

1. _____

2. _____

3. _____

4. _____

5. _____

6. _____

7. _____

8. _____

──────────────────────────── **REWRITING: A SECOND DRAFT**

Now you are ready to turn your focused writing into a second draft. Read it carefully, aloud, and, if you can, to a friend or classmate. Try to get a new vision of your subject. As you rewrite, consider whether or not you want or need a main-point statement that tells your audience the most important thing you want them to know when they are finished reading. Consider whether or not your voice is conveying what you want it to. You should also do the following:

    1. *Revise for detail.* Write precisely what you see; do not leave too much to the audience's imagination. You may find room to put yourself in the picture with an anecdote about what goes on there, if you have

not already. Include dialogue you may have overheard or even used yourself. Use enhancing words to make your picture more vivid.

2. *Revise for order.* Choose one of the options on page 194 to impose order on your subject. Choose the one that seems most suitable to the place you are describing and to your audience, and rearrange your material according to that pattern. (You may find as you are rearranging that you want to add or delete information. You may also find you need to rethink some more.) Make sure that your draft contains locating words that help the audience orient themselves.

3. *Revise for figurative language.* Highlight all uses of figurative language. Then look for other places where figures of speech would make your description livelier. Two or three colorful "pictures" in a piece of writing can be very effective.

Also decide whether you like or dislike the place you are describing, and rewrite your description from that point of view. That is, show how your feeling about the place affects everything in it. You may even want to begin with the main-point statement. "__(the place)__ is the __(most or ——iest)__ place I know."

Then pretend you are an animal, insect, or small child somewhere in this place, and describe the place as you see it from that perspective.

You are beginning to have so much to think about as you rewrite that you may want to write more than one draft. This is a good place to start to think of your "second draft" as one of several "middle drafts"—as many as it takes before you get a version with which you are satisfied.

When you finish a satisfactory middle draft, make a clean copy. Go on to the next section where you'll get some help on the proofreading stage of your writing.

PROOFREADING

COMBINING IDEAS

Sometimes you will want to combine into one sentence two or more ideas you have expressed in separate sentences, for example, the following sentences we've adapted from "A Kitchen":

1. The pale end-of-winter sunlight filled the room.
2. It yellowed all their faces.

The ideas are closely related and can be connected easily. You have two choices: either join the two sentences into one sentence with a conjunction, or link them with a semicolon.

What Are Two Ways to Join Sentences?

Joining

To join two sentences, you must use a joining word, also called a *conjunction*. The most common conjunctions are *and, but, or,* and *nor.* Sometimes *for, yet,* and *so* are also used as conjunctions.

HINT

Although conjunctions are used mainly to join two sentences, you may see them at the beginning of a sentence. Poets and other experienced writers sometimes begin a sentence with a conjunction for special emphasis. For example, Langston Hughes does this in paragraphs 2, 3, and 4 of "Salvation." (Chapter 3)

Use a joining word at the beginning of a sentence sparingly. Like the exclamation point for punctuation, if it is used too much, your audience will not know what you really want to emphasize. Also, inexperienced writers are apt to make mistakes when they try to use a conjunction at the beginning of a sentence. Although it is correct to write

We loved the movie. And we adored the acting.

It is all too easy to leave out the subject of the second sentence ("we") and create a fragment ("And adored the acting.")

Each conjunction has a distinct meaning:

and	= plus, in addition to
but, yet	= opposition
or	= choice of one
for	= reason for something
so	= result
nor	= not one or the other

Use the word that expresses the relationship you intend between the ideas in the sentences you want to join. For example, in the following sentence *and* makes sense, as it indicates that one idea is an addition to the other.

The pale end-of-winter sunlight filled the room, and it yellowed all their faces.

However, you would join the following pairs of sentences with different conjunctions:

1. The pale end-of-winter sunlight filled the room.

but   **2.** It didn't yellow all their faces.

	1. The pale end-of-winter sunlight filled the room.
so, yet	**2.** It yellowed all their faces.
	1. The pale end-of-winter sunlight didn't fill the room.
nor, and	**2.** It didn't yellow all their faces.

HINT

When you use *nor* to combine two sentences, you must change the wording of the second sentence:

The pale end-of-winter sunlight didn't fill the room.
It didn't yellow their faces.
The pale end-of-winter sunlight didn't fill the room, **nor did it** *yellow all their faces.*

Standard English grammar does not allow two negatives in the same clause to express a negative idea (*not didn't* yellow), although many nonstandard dialects do. In standard English, two negatives cancel each other out; for example, "He is *not un*kind" really means that he is not cruel. But it does not necessarily mean he is kind. See Appendix 3 for a discussion of double negatives.

The following narrative is made up of pairs of related sentences. Use a conjunction to join each.

> It started to rain.
> We went home instead of to the park.

> We were tired.
> We were thirsty.

and	We wanted something to drink.
but	There wasn't anything good in the house.
so	
nor	There wasn't any milk.
	There wasn't any juice.
or	
yet	We were thirsty.
for	We were too tired to go to the store.

> We finally dashed out in the rain.
> We wanted a drink badly.

Punctuating Joined Sentences

The simplest way to connect two sentences is to follow these steps:

1. Replace the period at the end of the first sentence with a comma.
2. Insert the joining word (or conjunction).
3. Change the capital letter at the beginning of the second sentence to a lower-case letter.

For example,

> In the 1940s and 1950s, actors often changed their names.
> Then they became movie stars.
>
> In the 1940s and 1950s, actors often changed their names, and then they became stars.

You may decide that you do not want to retain all of the words in the original second sentence. For instance, if you have these two sentences:

> Bernie Schwartz became Tony Curtis.
> He became a star.

You may want to join them in one of these ways:

> Bernie Schwartz became Tony Curtis, and *he became a star.*
> Bernie Schwartz became Tony Curtis and *became a star.*
> Bernie Schwartz became Tony Curtis and *a star.*

When Do You Use a Comma to Join Sentences?

The only time you use a comma with a conjunction is when you join two complete sentences and leave nothing out. *When you delete the subject (and possibly other words) from the second sentence, you do not use a comma.* Many students see the word *and* and use a comma regardless of what follows it. *Use a comma only when you join—and leave intact—two complete sentences.*

Practice Joining Sentences

1. Read these paragraphs twice. The first time, read for content; the second time, join the pairs of sentences indicated, using the words provided. Then write a new version. When you're finished, proofread for punctuation and capitalization. We've done the first one for you.

Join	
2, 3 with *and*	[1]Cold Spring Prison was a low, rectangular building with no windows. [2]Prisoners saw the outside only through
4, 5 with *but*	small slits in the walls. [3]We, the inhabitants of Cold Spring,
6, 7 with *for*	could not see inside at all. [4]We walked by it every day
9, 10 with *yet*	going to and from school. [5]We never glimpsed the inside
11, 12 with *nor*	of the prison. [6]We seldom saw the prisoners. [7]They were

14, 15 with *or*
17, 18 with *so*

rarely allowed to congregate in the large prison yard between the building and the high, barbed-wire fence. [8]It was eery. [9]There were ample grounds. [10]No one used them. [11]The prisoners did not get much fresh air. [12]They didn't get much exercise. [13]When they were in the yard, they acted like zombies. [14]They walked slowly in pairs, not talking. [15]They stood at the fence and stared in the direction of the town. [16]They seemed drugged or crazed or both, more like prisoners in a concentration camp than in a prison. [17]Rumor had it they were a collection of hardened criminals from all over the country. [18]No other prison would have them.

Cold Spring Prison was a low rectangular building with no windows. Prisoners saw outside only through small slits in the walls, and we, the inhabitants of Cold Spring, could not see inside at all.

Join
1, 2
3, 4
5, 6
7, 8
10, 11
12, 13
With
and
but
yet
or
for
so
nor

[1]Queens is a borough of New York City. [2]It is so unlike Manhattan that in some places you sometimes feel as if you are not in the city at all. [3]Queens is in the city. [4]It is not of the city. [5]Queens is mostly a residential borough. [6]You are not surrounded by the tall buildings for which Manhattan is famous. [7]Most homes in Queens are built for one family. [8]They are built for two families. [9]In the outer reaches of the borough, the houses are built on big plots of land. [10]The air is clear far away from the manufacturing areas. [11]You can enjoy sitting in your yard and soaking up the sun. [12]Queens has relatively little noise. [13]It does not have as much crime as Manhattan. [14]It is a quiet and relatively safe place to live.

Queens is a borough of New York City, but it is so unlike Manhattan that in some places you feel as if you are not in the city.

2. Read this paragraph twice. The first time, read it for content, and the second time, proofread it for commas. Correct any problems you find. Insert commas before conjunctions where you think they are necessary.

> Kevin Sullivan really wanted to write the letter but he was almost paralyzed with fear. He had never before answered an ad from the personals column of *True West Magazine.* He had always met women at school, or at work. Lately he had not met many women nor did he find the ones he did meet attractive. He wanted a woman who was good-looking, but not snobbish. He sought intelligence and he valued independence. He had started to read the ads as a joke. He never expected to answer one, yet he was strangely drawn to the column each week. Finally he knew why. The ad read: "Pretty, down-to-earth woman, B. A., own business, desires male counterpart, Box 152TW" He just knew this was it, and that the woman of his dreams was on the other side of that ad. He sat down at his word processor to compose his letter.

3. Write your own ten- to twelve-sentence paragraph describing a place you used to visit as a child but do not go to anymore. Make sure that at least five of your sentences contain joining words to connect two or more related ideas that could have been expressed in separate sentences. (You may want to write the paragraph in short sentences first and then join them in the second draft.) When you have finished, proofread it for capitalization and punctuation. Use your own paper.

Linking Sentences with Semicolons

What Are Two Ways to Link Sentences with a Semicolon?

You can link two sentences with a semicolon—either by itself or with a *linking word* (also called an *adverbial conjunction*). For example,

1. The word *generation* means thirty years.
2. In the microcomputer industry it can mean six months.

Because the ideas are related, these two sentences can be linked:

3. The word *generation* means thirty years; in the microcomputer industry it can mean six months.
4. The word *generation* means thirty years; however, in the microcomputer industry it can mean six months.

When Should You Use a Semicolon?

Sentence 3 links the two sentences with only a semicolon. Sentence 4 uses a linking word that establishes the exact relationship between the two ideas. Remember to link two sentences with a semicolon only when the ideas in them are *very* closely related.

Several familiar words and phrases can be used to link ideas:

211

however	= notwithstanding, in any case
moreover	= besides, in addition
nevertheless	= in spite of, however
therefore	= because of that, as a result
consequently	= as a result
yet	= in spite of, however
still	= even though, in spite of
furthermore	= in addition

These words are useful for linking ideas in sentences and as transitions between paragraphs (see Chapter 7). As with other conjunctions, you must be sure to use the one that signals the relationship you want to establish between the ideas. For example, you could say

> The word *generation* means thirty years;
>
> however,
> still,
> nevertheless,
> yet,
>
> in the microcomputer industry it means six months.

But you could not use the words *furthermore, moreover,* or *therefore.*

The following story is made up of pairs of related sentences. Choose one of the linking words (adverbial conjunctions) to link each pair.

however
moreover
nevertheless
still
yet
furthermore
consequently

1. *Their Eyes Are Watching God* by Zora Neale Hurston is a fascinating book. 2. It is somewhat difficult to read.

3. It is written almost entirely in a dialect. 4. The storyline is sometimes hard to follow.

5. One must read slowly to grasp the meaning. 6. The experience is well worth it.

7. Janie Crawford, the main character, is a proud, beautiful southern woman. 8. She makes decisions that keep her at odds with society.

9. Other characters fear her independence and determination. 10. They constantly try to remold her in their image.

She battles with her fate.
12. Somehow she emerges
triumphant.

Punctuating Linked Sentences

When you link two sentences with a semicolon, you should also replace the capital letter of the second sentence with a lower-case letter. But when you use a linking word, you should place a comma after it:

How Do You Link Sentences with a Semicolon?

> Money can't buy everything.
>
> It does buy many things that make people happy.
>
> Money can't buy everything; it does buy many things that make people happy.
>
> Money can't buy everything; however, it does buy many things that make people happy.

HINT

Linking words (adverbial conjunctions) are somewhat movable. Usually they come just after the semicolon, but they can also appear toward the middle of the second clause:

> *Money can't buy everything; it does, however, buy many things that make people happy.*

Notice that when you put the linking word in the middle of the sentence, you must use two commas to set off the linking word from the rest of the sentence.

Practice Joining and Linking Sentences

1. Read this paragraph twice. The first time, read for content. The second time, join or link the numbered sentences indicated using any of the words listed. Then write the new version below. When you are finished, proofread for punctuation and capitalization. Be prepared to discuss your choice of words. We've done the first one for you.

Join

1, 2
3, 4
6, 7
8, 9
11, 12
13, 14

[1]The Pleasant Street Inn is perfect for a summer vacation with the children. [2]It is an informal, comfortable place with enough room for everyone in the family. [3]The main house is an old, Victorian building. [4]The owners keep it in good condition. [5]The main floor has a huge foyer with a dining room on one side and a living room on the other.

213

15, 16
17, 18
19, 20
22, 23

With
and, but
so, nor
for, or
yet
however
therefore
moreover
nevertheless
still
furthermore
consequently

[6]Neither is very large. [7]They are not particularly charming. [8]The furniture is antique. [9]It is extremely attractive and comfortable. [10]The most prominent feature of the main floor is the bay window in the living room. [11]It is a very large window facing the ocean. [12]You can sip your coffee and watch the gorgeous sunsets over the water. [13]The bedrooms upstairs are very small. [14]They are comfortable. [15]There is enough room to put in a cot or two for the children. [16]You can rent an adjoining room for them. [17]The rooms are not too expensive. [18]Renting two is not impossible. [19]There are also little cottages that have two bedrooms and a kitchen. [20]They have the virtue of more privacy than the main building.

[21]Not too far away are wooded areas for picnics and hiking, a sand beach, and a playground. [22]The inn owns bicycles. [23]You can rent them and ride around the area and to the nearby town. [24]All in all, it is a lovely place.

The Pleasant Street Inn is perfect for a summer vacation with the children, for it is an informal, comfortable place with enough room for everyone in the family.

_____

_____

_____

_____

_____

_____

_____

_____

2. Read this paragraph twice. The first time, read for content. The second, join any sentences you think are closely related. Use any of the joining and linking words listed. Write your new version on your own paper. Then when you are finished, proofread for punctuation and capitalization. Be prepared to discuss your choice of words.

and	[1]Hostess Twinkies taste like cardboard with goo on it. [2]They are harmful to your teeth. [3]Ever since childhood, I have loved Twinkies. [4]I can still imagine their taste, even though I have not eaten a Twinky in fifteen years. [5]Twinkies are little yellow cakes. [6]They have vanilla cream inside. [7]They are sold two to a package. [8]You really get your fill for your money. [9]They are wrapped in cellophane. [10]They stay fresh for a long time. [11]You can eat both at one sitting if you are really hungry. [12]You can rewrap the other one in the cellophane. [13]You can save it for later. [14]Twinkies are full of sugar. [15]They are also full of preservatives and chemicals. [16]Twinkies are not good for your teeth or the rest of your system. [17]They are not good for your waistline. [18]They taste terrible. [19]Worse yet, they have no taste at all. [20]I am still loyal to them. [21]Not to love Twinkies is to forget your childhood.
but	
so	
nor	
for	
or	
yet	
however	
moreover	
nevertheless	
therefore	
still	
consequently	
furthermore	

3. Read "Umbrellas" twice. The first time read for content. The second time proofread it for commas that relate to joining and linking. Make any necessary changes.

UMBRELLAS

No one gives umbrellas a second thought because of their simple design and widespread availability. They are so handy that you don't

215

have to think twice about using them. All you have to do is hear rain forecast on the radio and you reach for your trusty umbrella. You see a drop of rain, and grab your umbrella from the rack.

Umbrellas are lightweight, yet they are sturdy. They are sturdy so you don't often have to replace one; therefore, they are not thought about often. How many of you really care about the umbrella, and appreciate its beauty and design? There are big umbrellas, and there are small umbrellas. There are light umbrellas and heavy ones. Umbrellas can be opened automatically by pressing a button or they can be opened easily with a little push.

Umbrellas are a man's—and woman's—best friend but who extols their virtues? No one writes poems about the umbrella. Poets write about rain; they write about snow but no one sings the praises of the umbrella which protects you from both. It is not exotic enough nor is it expensive enough to trouble about. It is everywhere; therefore it is nowhere.

The lot of the umbrella is unfortunate. Someday you will get caught in the rain, or snow without your umbrella. It will happen; you will, nevertheless not learn to appreciate the umbrella. You will curse it when it does not open easily or when its ribs break. Yes, you will curse it but you will still need it. However, you will not ever love it.

COMMA SPLICES AND RUN-ONS

**What Is a
Comma Splice?**
A *comma splice* is two or more sentences tied together only by a comma, and a *run-on* is two or more sentences strung together with no punctuation between them. Sometimes you will find these problems when you are joining or linking sentences. For example,

The pale end-of-winter sunlight filled the room, it yellowed all their faces.

Look at this comma splice graphically:

If there is no joining word, you *must* have a period between the two sentences, like this:

Sometimes students think a linking word will correct the problem, as in

The pale end-of-winter sunlight filled the room, however it did not yellow all their faces.

This is still a comma splice, because linking words require semicolons when they are followed by complete sentences.

Sometimes students don't use anything to join two sentences, and the result is a run-on sentence:

What Is a Run-on Sentence?

The pale end-of-winter sunlight filled the room it yellowed all their faces.

Look at it graphically:

You can avoid a run-on sentence by using one of the techniques for joining or linking sentences we discussed in this section. (If you are having trouble with run-ons because you don't know where the sentence is supposed to end, review Chapters 3 and 4.)

Practice Finding and Fixing Comma Splices and Run-ons

1. For each numbered "sentence," circle the subject or expanded subject, and enclose the expanded verb in a box. Above the number, identify each "sentence" as S (sentence), CS (comma splice), or ROS (run-on sentence).

   ¹Rachel loved violins. ²She loved the wonderful sound of the instrument when played by a virtuoso violinist, she also loved its shape. ³Every day she walked to school and looked at the violins hanging in the window of the local music shop they were beautiful. ⁴They looked almost like people; they had long necks above sloping shoulders, slightly pinched waists, and rounded hips. ⁵She really loved the look of the violins she wanted to own one very badly. ⁶She saw the price tag hanging from her favorite one it said $150. ⁷She was sure she could earn enough money by mid-May; she baby-sat, walked dogs, and watered plants for the neighbors every day after school. ⁸Of course, she did not play the violin, she would have to take lessons, and that meant even more money. ⁹She thought, however, she might find a violin teacher who needed a child cared for, garden watered, or a dog walked. ¹⁰They could exchange their services.

2. Fix all the comma splices and run-on sentences you found. Change the numbering to reflect your corrections.

3. "Wishing Wells" is written without the help of punctuation and capitalization. As a result, the first time it may be difficult to read. The second time you read it, insert commas, periods, semicolons, and capital letters wherever necessary. Then when you are finished, proofread it.

WISHING WELLS

wishing wells in public places lure thousands of people each year into contributing money to improve the city no one can resist a wishing well for wishing wells are usually attractive moreover they are well marked a person walking past one can hardly miss the sign that says "wishing well" in large letters people want good luck therefore people stop they look at the well they think to themselves that the whole idea is silly but they think again perhaps the wishing well will bring them what they want and no one dares miss a chance at it so they take a coin and drop it in young girls wish for the boys of their dreams boys wish for the girls of their dreams older people wish for health and long life for themselves and their children most people want to wish for money and power however they know they should wish for something else.

4. Write a short paragraph describing a park or playground near your home. When you are finished, proofread the paragraph for comma splices, run-ons, and the appropriate use of commas and semicolons. Use your own paper.

SPELLING

Near-homonyms

What Are Near-homonyms?

In Chapters 2, 3, and 4 we worked on homonyms, words that sound alike but are not spelled alike. In this chapter and in Chapter 6, we shall study *near-homonyms*, words whose spelling is so similar that they sound very much alike and, therefore, often are confusing.

1. accept: **a.** to receive or take.   I *accept* the gifts offered to me.
   b. to agree with.   It's hard to *accept* the mayor's plan.
   c. to understand.   I *accept* the situation as it is.
   except: but, besides   Everyone went *except* Bill.

Most waiters will **accept** *all the tips they are offered* **except** *those left in pennies.*

You try it: _____

2. advice: (n.) opinion, judgment.   The lawyer gave his *advice* about the will.

   advise: (v.) to give advice, recom-   A lawyer's job is to *advise* his clients.
   mend.

The doctor wanted to **advise** *her patient to stop smoking, but the* **advice** *was meaningless because the doctor was a smoker herself.*

You try it: _____

3. affect: **a.** (v.) to assume airs.   When I want to look rich, I *affect* the accent of the rich.
   b. to act or produce an ef-   The disease can *affect* the way the fect or have an influ-   bones grow. ence.
   effect: (n.) the result or outcome   The *effect* of the medicine was to bring of change by an agent;   the fever down. The child's behavior influence.   had a direct *effect* on his mother's nerves.
   (v.) to cause to come into   The therapist wanted to *effect* a being.   change in her patient.

The marchers wanted to **affect** *the onlookers, but the* **effect** *of their protest was limited.*

You try it: _____

4. an: indefinite article before   I sat by *an* oak tree and watched *an* words with a vowel sound,   elf pick up *an* acorn. signaling "one."
   and: conjunction expressing a re-   My sister *and* I went to the movies lation between two items.   *and* then returned home.

We walked along **an** *old pier* **and** *gazed into the inky water.*

You try it: _____

5. desert: worthiness of reward or punishment.[1]   He will get his just *desert.*

Uncultivated, unoccupied land.   The Sahara is the world's largest *desert.*

dessert: a course of fruit, pastry, or ice cream at the end of a meal.   I ate something sweet for *dessert* after dinner.

*The explorer knew it was his just **desert** to end his life far from home in the **desert**, and he fantasized about eating a **dessert** of peaches and cream at his club in London.*

You try it: _____

6. formally: in a formal manner; ceremoniously.   The graduation ceremony proceeded *formally,* according to ancient rituals.

formerly: in times past; once.   She was *formerly* known as Smith, but when she married, she adopted the name Hossenphfeiffer.

*Students like to dress **formally** in the 1980s, whereas **formerly** they would wear only jeans.*

You try it: _____

7. personal: about one person; done in person, private.   Valents tend to one's *personal* comfort.

He made a *personal* call from the office.

personnel: (n.) body of employed persons.   Civil service *personnel* do much of the clerical work at universities.

(adj.) of, about, or having charge of the people who work for a company.   The *personnel* office is responsible for advising employees about their benefits.

*It was my **personal** responsibility to see that my job application was filled out correctly, but the people in the **personnel** department were responsible for answering any questions I had about the application.*

You try it: _____

8. than: comparing one thing with another.   The quarterback was taller *than* the running back.

---

[1] In this meaning, *desert* is a homonym of *dessert.*

then: at that time, following, next.   *Then* we all will be together.
First do this; *then* do that.

*When the children were young, the boy was fatter **than** the girl, but **then** they grew up, and she was bigger **than** he.*

You try it: _____

9. thorough: carried to completion.   He did a *thorough* paint job.
    though: a contraction of   I drank, *though* I wasn't thirsty.
                although.
    through: see page 121.

***Though** the printers were tired, they had to be **thorough** because the customer wanted the brochures early in the morning.*

You try it: _____

10. were: past tense of *are.*   We *were* ready to leave at seven.
     where: at or in what location.   The infants played *where* their mothers put them.

*The books **were** in the library **where** we had left them.*

You try it: _____

Practice with Near-homonyms

1. Write the correct near-homonym in the blank.

It has always been a problem for me to _____ criticism or
                                  accept/except

_____. When I was a teenager, my mother would attempt
advice/advise

to _____ me about the _____ that certain friends of mine
   advice/advise   affect/effect

_____ having on my behavior. I would never listen to her,
were/where

_____ I would continue to make my own _____
an/and   personal/personnel

judgments. I would rather have been wrong _____ _____ what
                                   than/then accept/except

she had to say. Many times, I reaped my just _____ from listening
                                      desert/dessert

only to myself. Most often, my mother, who had been particularly

_____ in her analysis of these people, was right, and I wished
thorough/through

I were in the Mojave _____ rather than face her. For days after, I
desert/dessert

would _____ normal behavior, but actually I was acting very stiffly
affect/effect

and _____. _____ I would ask her to _____ me about
formally/formerly Than/Then advice/advise

the future.

Now that I am an adult, I am _____ old hand at judging people. I
an/and

work in the _____ department of a large company. I am glad I
personal/personnel

learned how to make my own judgments about other people, even

_____ I went _____ some hard times learning
though/thorough though/thorough/through

to make good judgments. I still consult my mother about the _____
affect/effect

certain people will have on others within the company.

2. Read this paragraph twice. The first time, read to understand the content. The second time, proofread this commentary on "Money is the root of all evil" and make any necessary changes in the spelling of the near-homonyms that we have studied in this section.

Many people say that money is the root of all evil; however, the

lack of money seems to have a more evil ~~affect~~ *effect* on people. People cannot

except living with very little money. Formerly, people where able to live a

comfortable life with little cash, but now getting thorough life without

much money is almost impossible. Most of us make a personal decision

about how much money we need to live, and than some people, lacking

what they want, may turn to crime to get what they think they need.

Once people accept a life of crime, no amount of advice will steer

them back to a law-abiding life because the criminals never believe they will get their just desserts. No one accepts the idea of getting caught.

Surely being rich is better than being poor, but being in jail is not better then being free. Insufficient money has a terrible affect on the individual, but crime has a worse effect on the society, and since few criminals are through enough in planning to avoid the law forever, they suffer the affect of their own crimes.

THE FINAL DRAFT

Now you are ready to proofread the second draft of the essay you began earlier in this chapter. Read your essay again slowly, aloud. Remember what you learned about word order and sense in Chapter 1 and about the conventions of writing in Chapter 2. Make sure you can answer yes to these questions as you proofread:

1. Do all your sentences contain both a subject and a verb?
2. Do all your sentences begin with a capital letter and end with the proper punctuation (period, question mark, exclamation point)?
3. If you joined two sentences, did you use the word that signals the relationship you intended between the ideas?
4. Did you use a comma before the conjunction that joins two full sentences?
5. Did you use a semicolon (or a semicolon and a linking word) between linked sentences?
6. Did you eliminate any fragments, comma splices, or run-on sentences?

Also check the spelling of any homonyms you may have used. Change anything you think needs changing. Write a clean copy if you make more than one or two changes.

ADDITIONAL WRITING ASSIGNMENTS

Your writer's journal may have some ideas for you to develop into essays. Focus on places you have been to and things you have seen that had some meaning for you. Think of places that frightened you, brought you happiness or peace; places you visit every day and never gave a second thought to until now, new places you've been to recently.

Other students have found the topics below to be stimulating. Remember to follow the writing process we are developing: Do focused writing first. Then look it over. You may want to review the Writing and Rewriting section of each chapter before you start a second draft. Write a main-point statement that tells your audience what you want them to know about this incident when they are finished reading. When you finish your middle drafts, proofread them and write out a clean copy.

Topic Suggestions

One of the following places may make a good topic for description:

1. a restaurant.
2. a place of worship.
3. a library.
4. a movie theater.
5. a local grocery store.
6. a beauty salon or barber shop.
7. a nightclub or bar.
8. a local tourist attraction.
9. a neighborhood (a place where people congregate).

You may also want to think of a place you know well—for example, your neighborhood, street, the school you attended as a child—that has changed markedly in the last few years. Describe the place as it used to be, and then discuss how and why it has changed.

Describing a Person: Making a Point

6

Photo by
Barbara Smith

1. Write a short paragraph about someone in your class. Do not mention the person's name, but describe him or her so that other members of the class can guess who it is.
2. Think of someone you work with. What is your opinion of this person? State it in one sentence. Then write a brief account of something that happened between you and that person that would explain your opinion.
3. Bring a picture of a famous person to class. It should be someone with whom everyone in the class is familiar. Let each person in the class contribute one line to a description of that person.

READING

PREVIEW QUESTIONS

As you read "Alte Bobbe" by Charles Angoff, look for information that will help answer these questions:

1. Why didn't Alte Bobbe have an English name?
2. What kind of advice and services did she give her family?
3. What was Alte Bobbe's view of love and marriage?
4. What did Alte Bobbe look like, and where in the selection do you find the description of her appearance?
5. Do you think Alte Bobbe's appearance is important to understanding her personality? Are other things more important? What?
6. How does the first sentence of each paragraph help guide you through the selection?

Notes

Czar Alexander II. Ruler of Russia, 1855–1881.
Yom Kippur. Holy day on which Jews ask to be forgiven for their sins.
Rosh Hashanah. Jewish new year.
orthodox. Branch of Judaism that teaches strict interpretation and observance of laws in the Bible.

Alte Bobbe
Charles Angoff

Charles Angoff was born in Russia in 1908 and moved to Boston when he was six. He worked as a newspaper reporter and editor, and he pub-

lished more than thirty books. This selection is condensed from a section in When I Was a Boy in Boston.

(1) How old she was when she died in 1915 I don't know, and neither does anybody else. Whenever one of her thirteen children, ten grandchildren, and about twenty great-grandchildren asked her for the date of her birth, she would smile and say, "Who knows such things? Only in America they remember birthdays. I was born when the good Czar Alexander II was a little boy, God have mercy on his soul. Don't ask me any more foolish questions."

(2) In Yiddish her name was Yente, or Alte Bobbe Yente, Great-Grandmother Yente. Her family called her that in Russia and in Boston, until the census man came around in 1910. He asked one of her grandchildren what Yente's name was in English.

(3) She knew hardly any English, but this question she did understand. It made her laugh. "Tell him I'm too old to have an English name," she said.

(4) The census man persisted. He claimed he couldn't put it down just Yente Schneider. Finally an idea struck him. "Why not call her Jeanette?" he asked.

(5) "Jeannette," my great-grandmother repeated and laughed. The census man also laughed because in those days, at least in Boston, Jeannette was a name assumed by girls who thought they were better than they were. For a while, the mention of Jeannette would cause guffaws of laughter in the house. Then, for some strange reason, the name lost its potency as a laugh inciter, and great-grandmother became Yente again to her friends, and Alte Bobbe to all her offspring, near and far. It sounded more respectful, yet more familiar. Anyway, I, her oldest and favorite grandchild, always called her Alte Bobbe. The name Jeannette never appealed to me. It was at best a joke for grownups, while it lasted, not for us younger fry.

(6) She was short, about five feet two, and she had remarkable bearing to the very end. She weighed only about 100 pounds, walked erect, never wore glasses, and her face was round and kindly and had fewer lines than many women half her age. In accordance with orthodox Jewish rite, her hair was closely shorn and she wore a kerchief instead of a hat. She used a wide variety of kerchiefs, some of them quite colorful, though on Saturdays, Yom Kippur, Rosh Hashanah, and other holidays, she always wore a pure white woolen kerchief. It gave her a truly angelic appearance. She was meticulously tidy, manicuring her fingernails every Friday afternoon in order to greet the Eve of the Sabbath in a worthy manner.

(7) She lived with her oldest daughter, my grandmother, but she really managed the house as if it were her own. She was not dictatorial, but she took an interest in everything that went on, helping out with the housework wherever possible. As long as she lived, her house was the center of the whole family, including all the relatives. Every one of her children and grandchildren visited her at least once a week, and she visited them at least three times a year: on Rosh Hashanah, Passover, and Hanukkah, three important Jewish holidays and feast days.

227

(8) Of course, she would visit a family more often if there was need for her services or advice. She settled domestic difficulties, made sure that the children got proper religious training, and occasionally administered to the physical ailments of young and old. As far as I know, she was never ill herself. She was a great believer in sleep as a healer, and after that she put most stress on chicken soup, boiled beef, black bread, and tea. The only three vegetables that made sense to her were potatoes, carrots, and horse-radish. I often heard her say, "If chicken soup and sleep can't cure you, nothing will. They are God's gift to the poor man." She had little respect for doctors, and there was a slight touch of superstition in her. She cured mild colds and toothaches with a knife and magic words. She would make three circles with a knife around the neck or throat if the patient suffered with a cold, and around the jaw if the patient had a toothache, touching the skin in each case lightly, and whispering holy Hebrew words as she did so. However, she never relied completely on this magic. She insisted on chicken soup and sleep in addition, saying that the incantation wouldn't work otherwise.

(9) While she made sure that all the children got religious training, she didn't push her piety upon the oldsters. She would never light a match on Saturday or even carry a dish across the street. Both were work, which was forbidden on the Sabbath. But she didn't object to her children and grandchildren going to their jobs on the Sabbath. "God does not want the poor to starve," she would say. "He understands and will forgive." The children and grandchildren returned this consideration by not smoking cigarettes or sewing or doing any other forbidden things on Saturday in front of her. This pleased her so much that she at times violated her own convictions. Some of her sons and grandsons, she knew, were heavy smokers, and she was sorry that on Friday night they had to abstain on account of her. So around nine o'clock she would say, "Harry, Fishel, don't you want to take a little walk?" They always did. They knew it meant that if they went into the street and had a cigarette or two, it would be all right with her.

(10) Her advice in the realm of marriage and love helped to smooth out many difficulties. She herself was married at fifteen, and while she thought that was perhaps too early an age, she believed that every girl should have a husband by the time she was eighteen. "A woman must have a man to make up her mind for her," she used to say, "and to give her children." She looked upon childless marriages as a curse. Any family with less than six or seven children was not a real family. She said that in all her life she never knew a woman who was really happy without a flock of her own children.

(11) She had clear and definite ideas about the relationship between husband and wife. I once heard her say to an aunt of mine who complained about her husband, "I don't care what he did or what he said. If there is a quarrel between a wife and her husband, it's always the wife's fault. Look into your heart and change your ways."

(12) While she lived in this country only six years and knew only a few words of English, she loved America almost from the day she arrived. "A

country that has sidewalks," she said, "is God's country. I'm sure there are sidewalks in Heaven," she would add with a smile. The village she came from had no sidewalks. The roads were muddy nearly all year round.

(13) A year or two before she died, she began to weaken perceptibly. I used to walk with her almost every Saturday morning to the synagogue—a journey that meant going down a steep hill and crossing a congested streetcar junction—and I began to notice that she held onto my arm more firmly than before. In the synagogue she used to sit in the balcony, where all women sit in an orthodox synagogue, and I noted that she would doze off occasionally, a thing she had not done previously, to the best of my knowledge. When she returned from the synagogue, she took longer rests before dinner. In the evening she would amble over to the hot-water boiler by the coal stove in the kitchen, lean against it for hours, and apparently go to sleep, though she maintained that she heard everything that was said.

(14) Her children pleaded with her to permit Dr. Golden, the family physician, to examine her thoroughly. She would say, "I'll see him. He's a fine man, but I won't let him examine me. There's nothing wrong with me. I'm only a little tired. When my time comes, he won't be able to help. And besides, I've lived long enough. All my children are married happily, and that's all a woman really wants in life. So don't disturb Dr. Golden."

(15) The inevitable last day came. She was unable to get up from her bed to wash and go to the front room, where she used to pray by herself before breakfast. She asked her oldest daughter to give her a little tea. She finished the tea and then said, "Call all the children. This is the end. I'm not afraid. Don't you be afraid. It's God's will. I thank God I am dying in my own house, with all my children around, and in a good country, where Jews are treated like human beings. I'm sorry I'm not leaving anything of value. I make only two requests: remember me every year by burning a lamp on this my last day, and put a picture of the whole family in my coffin." The entire family had had a group picture taken two years before, at her suggestion.

(16) Her eldest daughter protested such talk.

(17) Alte Bobbe said, "Do as I tell you."

(18) We all came over as soon as possible, some thirty of us, young and old. Dr. Golden was also called. He examined her. She did not object. After the examination he walked out of Alte Bobbe's bedroom, his eyes red. Three or four hours later Alte Bobbe died, fully conscious to the end and as peacefully as anybody could have wished. Her two oldest sons picked her up from the bed and put her down on the floor, in accordance with orthodox Jewish custom, and placed two candles at her head. All of us then walked by her and asked her to plead for us in the other world. My turn came, and I said the Hebrew words my mother told me. I wasn't afraid. Alte Bobbe looked the same as I had always known her, calm, kindly, and as beautiful as snow on a hill not far away. I saw the family picture by her feet. I was inexpressibly glad I was in it, and I always will be.

QUESTIONS OF CONTENT

Circle the letter of the best answer to each question.

1. Where was Alte Bobbe Yente born?

    a. Boston.   **c.** Russia.
    b. New York.   **d.** Israel.

2. Who gave Alte Bobbe Yente the name Jeannette?

    a. her parents.   **c.** the family.
    b. the census man.   **d.** her grandchildren.

3. Why did the name Jeannette incite laughter in the house?

    a. because everyone liked Alte Bobbe.
    b. because Jeannette was a name used by girls who thought they were better than others.
    c. because Jeannette was an American name.
    d. because Jeannette was a funny name.

4. Which is a Jewish rite that Alte Bobbe practiced?

    a. wearing glasses.   **c.** wearing a kerchief.
    b. cooking chicken soup. **d.** manicuring her nails.

5. Which services did Alte Bobbe provide for the family?

    a. settling domestic difficulties.   **c.** mending the children's clothing.
    b. making sure the children received religious training.   **d.** taking care of the physical ailments of young and old.

6. What activities were forbidden on the Sabbath?

    a. carrying dishes across the street.   **d.** smoking cigarettes.
    b. lighting a match.   **e.** reading newspapers.
    c. going to work.   **f.** eating.

Answer these questions in full sentences.

1. What showed that Alte Bobbe was becoming weak? _____

_____

2. When did Alte Bobbe always wear a pure white woolen kerchief? Why?

_____

3. Where did Alte Bobbe sit in the synagogue? _____

_____

4. Why did she believe that a woman should get married by the time she

was eighteen? _____

_____

5. Who was her favorite grandchild? _____

_____

6. In the concluding paragraph, Angoff calls Alte Bobbe "kindly." Summarize
the behavior and mannerisms that led him to this description.

_____

_____

_____

_____

QUESTIONS OF INFERENCE

Look back at the essay to answer these questions. Answer in full sentences.

1. Why was Alte Bobbe unable to remember her birthday? _____

_____

2. Why did the census man say he couldn't put Alte Bobbe's name down

as Yente? _____

_____

3. Why did Alte Bobbe have little respect for doctors? _____

_____

4. Why did she believe that a woman could be happy only when she was

married and had several children? _____

_____

5. Why did she believe that it was the wife's fault if there was a domestic

argument? _____

_____

6. Why was Angoff glad that he was in the picture placed in Alte Bobbe's

coffin? _____

_____

QUESTIONS OF CRITICAL THINKING

Answer each question in a short paragraph. You may want to use your own paper.

1. Alte Bobbe thought a woman needed a man to make up her mind for her. Do you think that once was true or still is true? What could you tell Alte Bobbe about the relationships between men and women today?

_____

_____

_____

2. Alte Bobbe's name was changed. Has anyone in your family changed his or her name? Why did he or she do it? What motivates people to change their names? Is "sounding more American" a good reason?

_____

_____

_____

3. Alte Bobbe's family respected and admired her. Should all elderly people

be treated in a special way? Why or why not? _____

_____

_____

4. Alte Bobbe lived according to orthodox Jewish law and custom, which shaped her daily activity. In what ways do your beliefs shape your life?

_____

_____

_____

5. What questions would you like to ask Alte Bobbe about life in her youth?

_____

_____

_____

6. Why do you think Angoff wrote this description of his great-grandmother?

_____

_____

_____

7. What types of people would be most interested in reading "Alte Bobbe"?

What newspapers or magazines might want to print it? Why? _____

_____

_____

_____

VOCABULARY

These words from "Alte Bobbe" may be unfamiliar to you. The exercises will help you learn the meanings of these words and how they function in sentences.

persisted	(4)	bearing	(6)	incantation	(8)
guffaws	(4)	rite	(6)	piety	(9)
potency	(5)	shorn	(6)	violated	(9)
inciter	(5)	meticulously	(6)	convictions	(9)
fry	(5)	dictatorial	(7)	realm	(10)

| flock | (10) | junction | (13) | inexpressibly | (18) |
| perceptibly | (10) | amble | (13) | | |

Word Meanings

Look up the following words in the dictionary. Many of them have more than one meaning, and some are listed as more than one part of speech. Read through the entire entry for each word and for each part of speech listed. Choose the meaning closest to the way in which the word is used in the selection. If you're in doubt, write down all the meanings you think are possible, separating them by semicolons. Make sure to include the part of speech next to your definition.

violate(d) _____

flock _____

conviction(s) _____

junction _____

potency _____

fry _____

bearing _____

Word Clues

Try to see the words below as the sum of their parts. Consult the list of prefixes and suffixes on pages 10–13, and write a working definition for each word. Check the dictionary entry for each word to see how close your working definition is to it.

inexpressibly _____

perceptibly _____

dictatorial _____

Seeing Words in Context

The following words appear in "Alte Bobbe." You may find clues to the meanings of each word in its context. As you reread the essay, circle the words or phrases that form the context for each word. Then write (1) your working definition, (2) the dictionary definition that's right for the context, and (3) an original sentence using the word. If you have difficulty figuring out the meaning of the word from the context of "Alte Bobbe," you may find it helpful to read the following story, in which the words appear in italics:

1. word: *persist(ed)*

    a. working definition _____

    b. dictionary definition _____

    c. your sentence _____

2. word: *amble(d)*

    a. working definition _____

    b. dictionary definition _____

    c. your sentence _____

3. word: *incite(r)*

    a. working definition _____

    b. dictionary definition _____

    c. your sentence _____

4. word: *realm*

    a. working definition _____

    b. dictionary definition _____

    c. your sentence _____

5. word: *shorn*

    a. working definition _____

    b. dictionary definition _____

    c. your sentence _____

6. word: *flock*

    a. working definition _____

    b. dictionary definition _____

    c. your sentence _____

7. word: *guffaw(s)*

    a. working definition _____

    b. dictionary definition _____

    c. your sentence _____

8. word: *piety*

    a. working definition _____

    b. dictionary definition _____

    c. your sentence _____

9. word: *meticulous(ly)*

    a. working definition _____

    b. dictionary definition _____

    c. your sentence _____

10. word: *rite*

    a. working definition _____

    b. dictionary definition _____

    c. your sentence _____

11. word: *incantation*

    a. working definition _____

    b. dictionary definition _____

    c. your sentence _____

THE FORTUNE-TELLER

    The fortune-teller had *persisted* in working in the tiny storefront for many years, despite rising rents. Everyday as I *ambled* home from work, walking casually, I was tempted by the sign "Fortunes Told. Cards Read." It aroused my curiosity and was the *inciter* of wild fantasies. Finally, one afternoon I walked through the door and entered a *realm* different from any world I had ever experienced.

The room was small and dimly lit by a simple floor lamp. The street windows and doorway were covered by heavy curtains, and the stuffy air made the room smell like a tomb. It was *shorn* of the furnishings most rooms have, as if every nonessential item had been stripped away. What remained were a shabby couch by the wall on the left and in the center a folding table and two straight-backed chairs. Toward the back the room was divided by dark, beaded curtains hung from the ceiling. From behind them I could hear what sounded like a *flock* of children, more than I could count, talking in a foreign language. The woman said something that sent the children into *guffaws* of laughter that did not cease.

I was about to change my mind and leave when a short, plump woman slid through the curtain. She had an air of *piety* that one usually sees only on deeply religious people. "For you, cards are best," she said and gestured for me to sit at the table.

She laid out the cards *meticulously* in neat rows on the table. Clearly, the arrangement of the cards was part of the *rite*. She began to speak in a singsong voice that was more a prayerful *incantation* than an explanation.

HINT: SIMILE

Simile is the easiest figure of speech to identify and write because it most directly compares two things:

> The newly divorced man flitted from one woman to another **like** a bee flying from flower to flower.
> His smile was **as** phony as counterfeit money.

Similes always use the words *like* or *as*.

Similes add detail to description. For instance, Angoff writes that in death Alte Bobbe looked "as beautiful as snow on a hill not far away." He could have simply said that she looked beautiful. But beautiful is a vague word; what is beautiful to one person may not be beautiful to another. (Angoff is describing a corpse!) But by comparing his great-grandmother's beauty to snow on a hillside, he creates a vivid image of her beauty: Fresh, unmarked snow is a very peaceful sight, and in death Alte Bobbe looked serene and tranquil.

Complete these similes to create vivid images. Remember that there are no "right" images, only ones that satisfy your imagination and convey a picture to your audience.

1. The bride stood still like _____

2. Discussing religion or politics on a date is as risky as _____

3. My horoscope says I am as lucky as _____

4. Being able to use the martial arts is like _____

5. After the rain, the streets were as quiet as _____

Watch out for clichés when you write similes. Too often, we are tempted to use the easiest comparison that comes to mind:

*My brother is as strong **as a lion.***

You can be more creative:

My brother is as strong as _____.

(If you don't have a brother, this is really a test of creativity!)
    Watch out for images that are too personal or idiosyncratic:

*Cicely Tyson is as beautiful **as the flowers in my backyard.***

Probably no one reading your essay would be familiar with the flowers in your yard. You can be more creative:

Cicely Tyson is as beautiful as _____.

Using Words in Context

One way to make new words part of your vocabulary is to use them in your own writing. Write a paragraph about either an incident with an older person or an incident involving a minister. Use at least five of the words from the Vocabulary section in your paragraph. Underline the words you use.

_____

_____

_____

_____

_____

_____

_____

_____

WRITING AND REWRITING

Description can make the strange familiar and the familiar special. When we begin reading "Alte Bobbe," Yente Schneider is a stranger. She is a foreign woman who follows customs that many of us do not share or understand and who lived many years ago. But when we finish reading, she has become more like our own grandmothers, and perhaps she has become as special to us as they are. Anyone can be a good subject for description. Each person has some unique quality that is worth writing about.

WRITING: A FIRST DRAFT

Close your eyes and imagine the faces of people you know, as if they were the cast of characters in a movie. Scan your "film" and choose one person to describe. It may be someone you know well and have strong feelings about, or it may be someone you know only casually. For this assignment, it is helpful to choose someone you are likely to see again in the next few days. However, if you are overwhelmed by an image of someone you will probably never see again, you may try to work with that.

Look over the Describe-a-Person Worksheet. Fill in each section with specific characteristics of the person you are describing. Then set the worksheet aside. After you see the person again, add any information you think is important.

DESCRIBE-A-PERSON WORKSHEET

1. WHO is this person? (name, age, relationship to you, and so on)?

2. WHAT does this person look like (facial features, size, physique)?

3. WHAT special mannerisms or traits does the person have (a lisp, a limp, kindness to animals)?

4. WHEN do you see this person (time of day, place, reason)?

5. WHERE does this person fit into your life (how you know the person, how you feel about the person, how you feel about something that happened between the two of you)?

6. HOW does this person dress (flashily, sloppily)?

7. HOW does this person talk (fast, slow, high, low, with any particular expressions)?

When your worksheet is finished, do focused writing about your subject. Write today's date at the top of a piece of paper. Write the title, which can be the subject's name, in the center of the first line. Relax for a moment. Close your eyes. Breathe deeply. As the room starts to become quiet, think about the person. Visualize him or her in your mind's eye. Remember the time or times you have been near the person. How did the person act? What did he or she say or do? Now open your eyes. At the signal, start writing and do not stop for ten minutes. Do not stop to think about where to put information. Just let the ideas flow. DO NOT pause if you are unsure of spelling, punctuation, or grammar. DO NOT stop to look up words in the dictionary. If you get stuck momentarily with nothing in your mind, write the word *stuck* until your next idea comes. Okay, begin. After ten minutes, stop. Read what you have written. If you want to add anything, do it now. Consider your focused writing the first draft of an essay. Put it aside for now. We will come back to it later in the chapter.

WHAT MAKES WRITING GOOD? PURPOSE, DETAILS AND ORDER, UNIFIED PARAGRAPHS, AND VIVID VERBS

Purpose

The purpose of your description should be clear. Why are you writing this description? (Yes, it's a class assignment, but you must have another reason or you won't write a very effective description.) Purposes can be as varied as subjects. Someone's appearance may be so attractive, ugly, or unusual that you want to write about it. You may love or dislike the person. Or you may want to tell your audience about some extraordinary characteristic of your subject.

Think about your subject. What is the most important thing—to you—about this person? Complete these sentences:

_____ is my favorite _____.

_____ is the most _____ person I know.

Sometimes _____ is _____,

but mostly he or she is _____ .

_____ makes me _____ , so I _____

him or her.

These sentences are examples of a *statement of purpose*, one of which could be the first sentence of your paper, like a main-point statement. Descriptive essays do not have to have statements of purpose, but they are extremely helpful in focusing your thinking about the detail and order of your writing.

How Does a Statement of Purpose Help Your Description?

Details and Order

Details and order reflect your purpose. You want your audience to come away from your description with a vivid image of your subject so they will share your feelings about your subject.

Most of your details will relate to your purpose. For example, Angoff devotes most of "Alte Bobbe" to a description of his great-grandmother in action: moving, managing, and tending to her family, which formed the center of her life. Only one paragraph is spent on her physical appearance, because that seems to be relatively unimportant to Angoff's purpose.

How Should You Decide Which Details to Use?

In this kind of descriptive essay, some of your details should be personal. Because the audience knows the subject through you, knowing what's happened between you and your subject will help the readers gain insight into the person's character. Angoff's portrait of "Alte Bobbe" is very personal; through his experiences we see Alte Bobbe, and we may be able to relate them to our experiences with our own grandmothers.

In what order do you share your details? The most important information to share is that related to your purpose, and then everything else will fall into place. Unlike narratives and descriptions of places, you have neither time nor space as a guide to order (although you may include anecdotes that are narratives or a physical description that moves from head to toe).

Unified Paragraphs

What Are Unified Paragraphs? A good way to guide the audience is by means of *unified paragraphs.* Unified means combined or consolidated. In relation to paragraphs, it means linking closely related pieces of information together in one or two paragraphs. For example, all of the information about Alte Bobbe's appearance is in one paragraph, and the details about her folk remedies are also together, as is all the information about her attitudes toward women, love, and marriage. Reread these paragraphs from "Alte Bobbe." Each begins with a *lead* (or *topic*) *sentence* that helps guide the audience toward the information in that paragraph. Look back to Ernesto Galarza's use of lead sentences in "A Mexican House" (pages 177–78).

HINT: PARAGRAPHS

What is a paragraph, and when do we indent to start a new one?

We know we need paragraphs in our writing, but we don't always know why or how many. Experienced writers form paragraphs almost without thinking. Beginning writers are often too uncertain to make them at all and wish the whole topic would disappear. Take heart! The more you read and write, the more easily you will be able to decide where to start a paragraph.

You will want to start a new paragraph when you shift ideas in an essay. Paragraphs are signposts to guide your audience. When you indent to form a new paragraph, you give the audience a visual clue that you are about to shift to something new.

"Ah," you say, hopefully, "my essay is about only one thing, and so I won't need more than one paragraph." That may be so, but probably not. Although most essays are indeed about one main topic, they cover different aspects of the topic. For example, in the description you are working on in this chapter, you may write about someone's appearance, behavior, and speech, and you

---

may tell a story about something that happened between you and that person. Every time you shift to a different aspect of your subject, you can indent to form a new paragraph. You may even want more than one paragraph on one of the aspects if you cover a lot of territory or give many examples.

Paragraphs can be as short as one sentence, although we do not recommend you write such short paragraphs in formal essays. They can also be very long, but we do not recommend that either. A middle range is between five and ten sentences per paragraph.

Learning exactly when to start a new paragraph is a process that takes a long time. At some point, when you've had a lot of practice writing and when you've read a lot of essays and articles that use paragraphs, you will begin to develop a sense of when to signal a new paragraph. But while you are struggling with this process, here are some guidelines:

1. A typewritten page generally contains three to four paragraphs.
2. Only start a new paragraph when you shift from one aspect of an idea to another, and then indent to signal this.
3. Do not separate two closely related thoughts. If you can use a semicolon to link two sentences, you will not want to start a new paragraph with the second sentence.
4. Paragraphing is a somewhat elusive process. Two people revising the same material may indent for new paragraphs in different places. Be prepared to explain your paragraph structure.

If you look back at the narratives and descriptions you wrote in earlier chapters, you may see that you shifted your thoughts more than once in the essay and could now form new paragraphs that you did not see before. You do not have to rewrite an essay just to indent for a paragraph. Simply place this symbol ¶ to the left of the word you want to be the first word of the new paragraph. (If you want to delete a paragraph indentation, write no ¶.)

Vivid Verbs

Vivid verbs increase the precision of your picture. Angoff uses vivid verbs to describe Alte Bobbe:

Vivid Verbs		*Weak Verbs*
She *managed* her house.	rather than	She *ran* her house.
She *administered* to physical ailments.		She *took care of* physical ailments.
She *insisted* on chicken soup.		She *wanted* chicken soup.

Verbs like these can sharpen the image of the subject. Not all verbs in a description should be vivid, but a few can be very effective. (If you are having trouble finding the verb in your sentences, look back at pages 113–14.) Vivid verbs tell us not only *that* something happened but also *how* it happened.

HINT: SYNONYMS

A *synonym* is a word that has the same meaning as another word. Theoretically, one should be able to replace any word with its synonym. But this is only rarely true because words convey feelings and images as well as meanings (that is, connotations as well as denotations). Some dictionaries help the writer who is searching for synonyms, for example, the entry for *rob* in the *Random House College Dictionary*.

rob (rob), *v.*, **robbed, rob·bing.** —*v.t.* **1.** to take something from (someone) by unlawful force or threat of violence; steal from. **2.** to deprive (someone) of some right or something legally due: *They robbed the family of the inheritance.* **3.** to plunder or rifle (a house, shop, etc.). **4.** to deprive of something unjustly or injuriously: *The umpire called the home run a foul ball and we lost the game—we were robbed!* —*v.i.* **5.** to commit or practice robbery. [ME *robb*(en) < OF *robb*(er) < Gmc; c. OHG *roubōn*. See REAVE] —**Syn. 1.** ROB, RIFLE, SACK refer to seizing possessions that belong to others. ROB is the general word for taking possessions by unlawful force: *to rob a bank, a house.* A term with a more restricted meaning is RIFLE, to make a thorough search for what is valuable or worthwhile, usually within a small space: *to rifle a safe.* SACK is a term for robbery on a huge scale during war; it suggests destruction accompanying pillage and the massacre of civilians: *to sack a town.*

Fill in the appropriate synonym for *rob* in these sentences:

The soldiers were ordered to _____ the captured city.

An unoccupied apartment is the easiest to _____.

Travelers in ancient times knew that pirates were likely to _____ their vessels.

We look for the feelings that words convey when we choose strong verbs that tell us *how* something was done as much as *that* it was done. Add to the following list of synonyms for the word *walked:*

strutted	_____	_____	_____
dashed	_____	_____	_____
limped	_____	_____	_____
slithered	_____	_____	_____
skipped	_____	_____	_____

Nouns also convey feelings and images.

The man walked down the street.

Replace the noun *man* with any of the following: boy, jock, dude, geezer, priest. Add more synonyms for *man:*

_____	_____	_____	_____
_____	_____	_____	_____
_____	_____	_____	_____
_____	_____	_____	_____

Sometimes the feeling that a word conveys depends on other words in a sentence. For example, there is nothing remarkable about

The boy skipped.
The geezer limped.

However, if these verbs are linked with different nouns, they can create unusual, sometimes startling, pictures:

The priest skipped.
The jock limped.

A boy can skip, but when a priest skips, we somehow get an image of extraordinary joy. A geezer limping is a common sight, but when a jock limps, we picture some game-losing injury.

Do These Exercises Before You Revise Your First Draft.

Practice Establishing Purpose and Selecting Details

1. The items below are usually found on a desk. Choose one and think about it. Then write a sentence that states a purpose for writing about this item. We've done the first one for you.

Item	Sentence
pencil	*A pencil is a simple writing tool, but when you have to write a first draft, it can be the heaviest object on the desk.*

calendar	_____
telephone	_____
stapler	_____
paper clips	_____
scotch tape	_____
dispenser	_____
dictionary	_____
ruler	_____
typing or writing paper	_____

2. List the details you would put into an essay about the item you chose in Exercise 1. Remember that these details should support your statement of purpose. For example,

> pencil is light, made of wood and lead
> been in use a long time
> can hardly lift it up when you have an assignment
> feels like it weighs a ton
> doesn't cost much

_____

_____

_____

_____

.3. Choose a person from the following list of people associated with a basketball team. Write a sentence that establishes your purpose, the impression you want to give the audience about this person. (If you don't like basketball, choose another sport.) For example:

> person: guard
> sentence: Earl Monroe, former starting guard for the New York Knicks, had the most creative moves to get to the basket.

Person	Sentence
general manager	_____
coach	_____
center	_____
power forward	_____
point guard	_____
"sixth man"	_____
trainer	_____
assistant coach	_____
shooting guard	_____

List details to support your impression:

_____

_____

_____

_____

Practice Personalizing Descriptive Detail

1. Jot down some feelings you have about the people listed here or about the unique traits these people possess:

Ronald Reagan	_____
a grade school teacher	_____
Michael Jackson	_____
an elderly neighbor	_____
a grandparent	_____

a brother or sister   _____

Jesse Jackson   _____

a police officer   _____

Geraldine Ferraro   _____

a clergyman   _____

a close friend   _____

Martin Luther King, Jr. _____

2. Pick someone on the list you know personally, and write an anecdote establishing your connection with that person.

3. Pick someone on the list you do not know personally, and write an anecdote either establishing some connection with that person or justifying your feelings about him or her. Use your own paper.

Practice Using Lead Sentences to Control Paragraphs

1. Read each of the paragraphs below, which could be middle paragraphs in descriptions of famous people. Circle the best lead (or topic) sentence. Draw an arrow from that sentence to the caret (∧) to indicate that in a revision it will be the first sentence in the paragraph. We've done the first one for you.

    a. ∧ He takes one step left and then moves right. He pins away from the basket but goes toward it. He glances behind him. Then he moves the other way. Finally, he fakes left and dribbles down the middle.

    Monroe likes to run up the court.
    Monroe moves toward the basket deceptively.
    Monroe fools around during the game.

    b. ∧ To buy groceries in town in the summer, she wears white-duck jeans and a work shirt and does her hair up in a simple pony tail. To stroll on the beach in the winter, she dons a heavy wool sweater with a sleeveless down vest over it. Patched and faded jeans with work boots complete the outfit. She usually goes hatless, but she's also been seen in a fisherman's knit cap or a heavy wool scarf.

    On vacation in the Hamptons, model Cheryl Tiegs dresses casually.
    Cheryl Tiegs really is not a snappy dresser.
    Model Cheryl Tiegs looked pretty weird on Fifth Avenue.

c. ∧ She was frequently cast as a beautiful society woman. In *Dial M for Murder*, she played the gorgeous wife whom Ray Milland was trying to have murdered for her money. In *Rear Window*, *To Catch a Thief*, and *High Society*, she was the wealthy object of the affections of James Stewart, Cary Grant, and Bing Crosby. She was nominated for Best Supporting Actress for her portrayal of the adultress in *Mogambo* and received an Oscar and the New York Film Critics' Award for her role as the bitter wife in *The Country Girl*.

Grace Kelly made only eleven movies between 1951 and 1956, at which time she married Prince Rainer of Monaco, but her popularity was as strong in 1982 when she died as it was when she was a working actress. Grace Kelly was a magnificent blonde who played rich women full of aloofness and reserve, opposite some of the greatest actors of our time. Because Grace Kelly was often typecast as a beautiful woman, it is easy to forget that she was also an accomplished actress.

2. Read the following paragraphs, which could be parts of descriptions of people you might see on the street. Fill in the information below the paragraph, and then write a lead sentence for each. We've done the first one for you.

a. ∧ *The toddler moved awkwardly.*

His diapers forced his legs wide apart, and so he lurched along, one leg thudding heavily against the pavement while the other leg was in the air. He couldn't bend his knees, which made him look like a miniature robot lumbering down the street.

topic: *a toddler*

purpose: *to show how awkward little kids can be*

lead sentence: *The toddler moved awkwardly.*

b. ∧ _____

Thick eyebrows had been penciled over the real ones. Heavy lines, in a matching color, formed an obscene triangle on her top and lower eyelids, meeting at the outside corner of each eye. Black lashes stood like spiral staircases above and below the vacant eyes. Rough patches of red flared out from her cheeks, and a red heart was painted where her mouth should have been.

topic: _____

purpose: _____

lead sentence: _____

c. ∧ _____

"Me. Me. Me. Me," the man mumbled. He stood on the corner near the bus stop with his rumpled hat in his hand, held out to the passersby with the hope that they would drop some money into it. "Do, re, me. Look at me. I am the one. I am the two. Me and you. Tea for two. Me too. Boo hoo."

topic: _____

purpose: _____

lead sentence: _____

d. ∧ _____

He wore a tan trench coat, buckled at the waist. A plaid wool scarf was tucked inside the collar. Gray flannel trousers with carefully tailored cuffs met carefully crafted cordovan shoes. Despite the wind and cold, he was hatless. An attaché case rested in the slot made by his right hand resting inside his coat pocket. He glanced around. Then his left hand darted to his face, and he quickly inserted his index finger into his left nostril. Then it crept back into his pocket.

topic: _____

purpose: _____

lead sentence: _____

Practice with Unified Paragraphs

Read each of these paragraphs. Underline what you think should be the lead sentence. Then number the rest of the sentences in the order in which you think they belong. Delete any sentences that weaken the unified nature of the paragraph. Be prepared to explain your choices. We've done the first one for you.

    a. ³He is trim and muscular. ⁵His hair is still dark. ¹President Reagan doesn't look his age. ²He holds his six-foot frame erect, and he moves with speed and grace. ⁶His face has few lines. He eats healthy food ⁴Obviously he takes good care of himself and exercises regularly. Nancy Reagan worries about him and sees that he gets a lot of rest. ⁷His teeth look like they all are his own.

    b. It is said that Einstein did not know how to tie his shoe laces until he was six or seven years old. He had a bushy white mustache that always needed trimming. His white hair was rather long and fell carelessly around his head and face. Albert Einstein, one of the greatest scientific minds of the twentieth century, looked in his old age like the typical absentminded professor. His glasses always slid down the bridge of his nose. He was stooped in his later years and walked with a slight shuffle. His suits were baggy and fit him like they had been bought for a larger man. They were slightly rumpled, and they looked like a good pressing wouldn't hurt.

c. In anger, Nastase has thrown and broken tennis rackets. He is a handsome man. He also stalks around the court. Off the court, he is known to be bad tempered but kind and generous to younger tennis players. Sometimes Nastase's curses become quite audible and are directed toward the audience, his opponents, and the tennis officials. Elie Nastase has earned the nickname "Nasty" because of his behavior on the tennis court. He often tries to upset his opponents by delaying play. He has been fined for his behavior many times. When he doesn't like a call, he glares at the linesman and yells at the umpire.

d. She stops, looks around, and says, "Where am I?" She always stays and talks to the students after class. I like Professor Blank. Although her lectures are well organized, she frequently loses her train of thought in an explanation. I think she has three children. Always three or four minutes late for class, she rushes in as if the classroom were the finish line of a hundred-meter dash. Professor Blank, my philosophy professor, has a distracted air about her. She's a tough marker but a fair one. She is trying to quit smoking. Then she sits down, lights a cigarette, and opens her notebook.

Practice Forming New Paragraphs

All the paragraph indentations have been removed from this student essay, "The Neighborhood Old-Timer." Read it carefully and decide where you think shifts in focus should be signaled by a new paragraph. Put the symbol for a new paragraph (¶) in front of the first word of the new paragraph. Remember that your opinion may differ from those of your classmates, and so be prepared to explain yours.

THE NEIGHBORHOOD OLD-TIMER

The human race is a funny race. No matter where you go in the world people will tell you all kinds of stories, especially the old people. I for one always hear stories about the South because my family's roots are from there. I'm constantly being told about all the advantages of today and the disadvantages of fifty years ago, which I know nothing about. One of the stories I hear from my mother is "I had to walk two miles to school when I was a child." Sometimes parents make it sound like it's your fault they didn't have transportation to and from school. Old-timers tend to tell the same or similar stories. This brings me to the neighborhood old-timer. The neighborhood old-timer is a person who's been in or around your neighborhood since the rebuilding of Rome. He is a person who could tell you what was standing, no matter where you stand in your neighborhood, before you moved there; a person who, if your family has been in the neighborhood for quite a lot of years, will say things like, "I remember when your family moved here, you weren't even born yet." and at the present time you are forty years old. "You were one of those kids I used to give nickels and dimes to. Can I have them back now?" I'm quite sure a few of you have come across these types. In my neighborhood there's a man named Mr. Moore, nicknamed Pincus. I believe he has lived in the neighborhood for a thousand years. He's about seventy-six years old and is very friendly. He stands about five-feet-eight with a light complexion. His skin is not as wrinkled as you would expect most seventy-six-year-old men's to be. He has only a few wrinkles around his eyes and under his neck. He looks like he's taken very good care of himself. Pincus is also very active for his age. He rides bikes, tells jokes, and gets along with almost everyone. I've even seen him play basketball and football. He can do most anything you or I can do. You can find Pincus between Sixty-fourth and Sixty-third Street and Amsterdam Avenue. He will be in the company of friends whose ages range from twenty to seventy. He's one of those rare old men who refuses to get old and sit back and say to himself, "I've had my day." The only way it dawns on you how old he is, is because he loves to tell stories about when he came to New York. Then he'll tell you about how the neighborhood has changed and what it was like before the project and the playground, where most of these stories are told. I hope I reach his age and grow old telling people how my neighborhood has changed. If you're ever in my neighborhood—Sixty-third between West End and Amsterdam—look up Pincus and say hello. You can find him any warm day, sitting in the park. He'll be talking and telling jokes about the old days. You'll know him; he'll be the oldest young man there.

Practice with Vivid Verbs

1. Read this paragraph about the day John F. Kennedy was killed. Circle the word in parentheses that best replaces the underlined word. You may insert a word of your own if none of the alternatives pleases you.

FRIDAY, NOVEMBER 22, 1963

Children <u>were</u> in school. Adults <u>were</u> at their offices or homes. At 1:15
    (sat/studied/played)   (worked/lounged/labored)

P.M. (EST), newscasters <u>said</u> that President John F. Kennedy had been shot
             (reported/announced/repeated)

in Dallas. At first, no one <u>thought</u> he was seriously injured. But by 1:45,
                (believed/felt/noticed)

the radio and television newscasters <u>said</u> that Kennedy was dead. The
             (announced/reported/confirmed)

news <u>went</u> fast. In large cities, suddenly hundreds of people <u>came</u> into the
(traveled/spread/moved)   (milled/crowded/arrived)

streets. "Tell me it isn't true!" their tear-choked voices <u>asked</u> one another.
                (inquiredof/begged/entreated)

Strangers <u>held</u> one another for support. Only cries and church
(embraced/clutched/related to)

bells <u>disturbed</u> the quiet that descended on the streets. President
(pierced/punctuated/broke)

John F. Kennedy had <u>died</u> and with him the dreams of millions of Americans.
(been murdered/been assassinated/been gunned down)

2. Change the underlined verbs to more vivid ones. (You may find that you must change a word or two in the sentence so that it will sound right to you.)

    Sister Mary Elizabeth is unique. She <u>has</u> the power of a fullback plunging over the goal line and the agility and speed of a gymnast going for an Olympic gold medal.

    Sister Mary <u>is</u> on the graveyard shift at Sacred Heart Hospital. When most of the city <u>is</u> on its way to bed, Sister Mary <u>gets</u> out of bed to start her night's work. Most nurses <u>get</u> to work ten minutes before their shift begins. Sister Mary <u>is</u> there half an hour early to check on all "her" patients. She <u>has</u> all the charts memorized, and so she <u>is</u> instantly aware of any changes in a patient.

    All night long, she <u>goes</u> from room to room <u>fixing</u> intravenous drips or <u>fixing</u> a pillow, <u>talking</u> with people who are lonely or frightened, <u>relating</u> to people who are sick and in pain. She almost never <u>sits</u> at the nurses' station, and she doesn't even <u>have</u> a coffee break. "Breaks my concentration," she <u>says</u>. She just <u>moves</u> around the floor, <u>looking</u> into rooms to see if anyone <u>wants</u> her.

    One night my father, who was a patient on Sister Mary's floor, <u>fell</u> out of bed. Sister Mary <u>was</u> at his side almost before he <u>made it</u> to the floor. She <u>got</u> him under the armpits and <u>put</u> him back into bed before the other nurses could even <u>come</u> down the hall.

REWRITING: A SECOND DRAFT

Now you are ready to turn your focused writing into a second draft. Read it carefully, aloud, and, if you can, to a friend or classmate. Try to get a new vision of your subject. As you rewrite, consider whether or not you want or need a main-point statement and whether or not your voice is conveying what you want it to. You should also

1. *Revise for purpose.* Choose the most important thing you want your audience to know about your subject. Write a statement that you can use to guide your own thinking (whether or not it becomes the first sentence or main-point statement of your paper).

2. *Revise for detail and order.* Make your details serve your purpose by including any details that support or describe your main point. Place the information related to your purpose close to the beginning of your paper, and order the rest of your information accordingly.

3. *Revise for unified paragraphs.* Keep information about one aspect of the person in one paragraph and shift paragraphs when you shift to a different aspect of the person. You may want to use the Describe-a-Person Worksheet categories as the subjects of paragraphs.

4. *Revise for vivid verbs.* Reread your draft and highlight your verbs. Are they the strongest verbs you can use in this context? Change any you think can be stronger, so as to add more precision to your description. When you finish a satisfactory middle draft, make a clean copy. Go on to the next section, where you'll get some help on the proofreading stage of your writing.

PROOFREADING

SUBORDINATION

What Is Subordination?

Subordination is another way to join sentences. You "subordinate" one of the sentences to make it dependent on the other. For instance, you can join the sentences

Harry went to the candy store.

He bought a lottery ticket.

by subordinating the first sentence to the second.

When Harry went to the candy store, he bought a lottery ticket.

You subordinate the first sentence by adding a special word. *When* is only one of the words and phrases that can establish relationships between ideas in sentences. For example,

He didn't buy a lottery ticket last week.

He didn't have money to spare.

can be combined into

*He didn't buy a lottery ticket last week **because** he didn't have money to spare.*

Because establishes a "cause and effect" relationship between the two ideas. *Cause:* no spare money; *effect:* cannot buy a lottery ticket. Other words form other kinds of logical relationships between ideas. The following are some of these words and phrases, called *subordinating conjunctions:*

Time	*Contrast*	*Condition*
after	although	as long as
as	even though	as though
as soon as	though	if
once	whereas	in case
since	whether	in order that
until	whether or not	in that
when	while	
whenever		
while		

Cause and Effect	*Place*
as	where
because	wherever
since	
so	
so that	
whereby	

You must be sure to use the appropriate word or phrase to establish the relationship you intend between the two ideas. Connect each pair of sentences with the word that signals the most appropriate relationship between each sentence.

Why Must You Be Sure to Choose the Appropriate Word?

because   He didn't buy a lottery ticket last week.
          He didn't have money to spare.

after   He gets paid Tuesday.
      He will have money.

although   He has many other expenses.
         He will buy a lottery ticket next week.

The following pairs of sentences are a paragraph about "The Rocking-Horse Winner," a short story by D. H. Lawrence. Choose the appropriate word or words at the right to join each pair.

although	I had never thought about the unique and possibly dangerous relationship between mothers and their children.
until	I read "The Rocking-Horse Winners."
since	I read it.
because	I've been frightened by the power that mothers exert, unwit-
so	tingly, over their children.
	The mother in the story did not love her children.
because	She believed they'd been "thrust upon her."
so that	She was obsessed by the need for money.
whereas	The family was moderately well-off.
as	Her son developed a mystical ability to predict the winners of horse races.
	He would get her the money she craved.
	He died trying to please her.

Independent and Dependent Clauses

What Do Subordinating Conjunctions Do?

Subordinating conjunctions make one part of a sentence dependent on the other. As a result, the part with the subordinating conjunction can no longer stand by itself as a sentence. In Chapter 4, we defined a sentence as a group of words that contains a subject (noun) and a predicate (verb) and that can stand alone. We can also call a sentence an independent clause.

A *clause* is a group of words containing a subject (noun) and a predicate (verb). If the clause can stand alone, it is independent.

Harry went to the candy store.

He bought a lottery ticket.

What Is a Dependent Clause?

If a clause cannot stand alone, it is a *dependent clause.* In the following sentence, the dependent clause "When Harry went to the candy store" is connected to the independent clause "he bought a lottery ticket" because it cannot stand alone.

When Harry went to the candy store, he bought a lottery ticket.

Punctuating Dependent Clauses

If the dependent clause comes *before* the independent clause in a sentence, you should place a comma at the end of the dependent clause to separate it from the independent clause:

Because he didn't have the money to spare, he didn't buy a lottery ticket.

Dependent clauses can also be the second part of the sentence. When the independent clause comes before the dependent clause in a sentence, a comma is not necessary to separate the two clauses.

He didn't buy a lottery ticket because he didn't have any money to spare.

Practice Joining Sentences with Subordinate Conjunctions

1. Read this paragraph twice. The first time, read it for content; the second time, join the pairs of sentences indicated, using the words provided. Write the new version below. When you are finished, proofread it for correct punctuation and capitalization.

Join

3, 4 since

6, 7, since

9, 10 when

11, 12 as

13, 14 as

16, 17 because

[1] Xanthippe (Zan-tip'-ee) is a small Burmese cat who lives in my apartment building. [2] Her brown short-haired coat is silky, and her eyes are an emerald green. [3] She actually belongs to no one. [4] She belongs to everyone in the building. [5] No one knows where she came from, but everyone has adopted her. [6] She arrived. [7] People have become friendlier. [8] Everyone asks where and how Xanthippe is. [9] Everyone is at work. [10] She prowls the hallways. [11] The evening mealtime nears. [12] She waits on the main floor for someone to board the elevator. [13] The door opens. [14] She dashes in and looks up pleadingly. [15] Some one always takes her home to feed her. [16] It seems as if she runs this game on several people at night. [17] Xanthippe is getting to be a pretty fat cat.

_____

_____

_____

_____

_____

_____

_____

_____

_____

_____

_____

_____

_____

2. Read this paragraph twice. The first time, read it for content; the second time, join the numbered sentences using any one of the conjunctions on the list. Write the new version below. When you are finished, proofread it for correct punctuation and capitalization.

Join
1, 2
3, 4
5, 6
7, 8
10, 11
12, 13
14, 15
With
because
since
as
after
before
as soon as
while
until
unless
once
where
if
although

[1]Brigham Young (1801–1877) was the primary developer of the Church of the Latter-Day Saints (Mormons). [2]He had a greater influence on the church than even its founder, Joseph Smith. [3]He was a house painter in New York State. [4]He heard the call of the new religion. [5]He was baptized in 1832. [6]He became one of the Council of Twelve (Apostles) in 1835. [7]He was a missionary to England. [8]He converted large numbers of people to Mormonism and brought them to the United States. [9]Later, he became director of the Mormon state in Utah. [10]Trouble started between the Mormons and the United States government over the practice of polygamy. [11]Young defied the government's orders and continued to practice what he called his religious freedom. [12]He was married to twenty-seven women. [13]He was not married to all of them at the same time. [14]The government could never prove its case against him. [15]He was once arrested for murder. [16]He was, however, involved in a massacre at Mountain Meadow. [17]Young's influence on the church increased rather than decreased because of his trouble with the government.

_____

_____

_____

_____

_____

_____

_____

_____

_____

_____

_____

_____

_____

_____

_____

3. Proofread this description for appropriate use of commas. Put in any commas that are necessary, and delete those that are not.

Ashley Motorman was voted "smartest," and "most annoying" in our graduating class. While we all agreed that she was the brightest student among the seniors we truly detested the way she flaunted her intellect and demanded attention from the teachers.

Ashley's intellect was awesome. Whether she was in astronomy or zoology class, she knew all the answers. Teachers had to work extra hard in order not to bore her in class. Unless they did their homework Ashley would ask questions that even they could not answer! When new information was presented in lectures, Ashley was always the first to "get" it. If another student didn't get it quickly Ashley was called upon to explain.

We all respected Ashley although we did not like her. She knew how smart she was, since her grades were the highest in the school, and she made our lives miserable. She sat in each class with her hand permanently raised so that we would know she could answer any question. She snickered after someone else answered a question incorrectly.

As long as we were in class with Ashley we were her inferiors. But we tortured her in the cafeteria. We started to ignore her as soon as she entered. No one even looked at her unless she spoke to someone directly. When she complained about our treatment we told her that "turnabout is fair play." We agreed to include her in our social life provided she did not embarrass us in class.

4. Write your own ten- to twelve-sentence paragraph describing a relative or friend who tries to do the right thing but always manages to offend. Make sure that at least five of your sentences contain subordinate conjunctions. When you finish writing, proofread your paragraph for the appropriate use of commas and capitalization. Use your own paper.

Relative Clauses

Another way to join sentences through subordination is with the words *who, whose, that,* and *which* (called *relative pronouns* and, in the case of *whose,* a *relative possessive pronoun*).

1. Mrs. Haggerty is my neighbor.
2. She lives next door.

3. Mrs. Haggerty, *who lives next door,* is my neighbor.

1. Mrs. Haggerty is very lonely.
2. Her husband died last spring.

3. Mrs. Haggerty, *whose husband died last spring,* is very lonely.

1. We chat daily at the fence.
2. The fence separates our back yards.

3. We chat daily at the fence *that separates our back yards.*

1. We must be careful not to trample our flowers.
2. The flowers grow beside the fence.

3. We must be careful not to trample our flowers, *which grow beside the fence.*

What Is a Relative Clause?

In each pair, sentence 2 explains or describes some aspect of sentence 1. The relative pronouns *who, whose, that,* and *which* replace the subject-noun in sentence 2, thus making it a dependent clause no longer able to stand by itself. In this case we can call it a *relative clause.* A relative pronoun begins the dependent clause; in fact, the pronoun is often the subject of the dependent clause. Sentence 3 is the combination of the independent and dependent clauses.

Does It Matter Where You Put a Relative Clause

It's important to put the relative clause next to or near the word or phrase it describes:

1. The police officer, who carried a club, startled the burglar.
2. The police office startled the burglar, who carried a club.

The placement of the relative clause obviously can make a difference in the intended meanings of your sentence. Sentence 1 was derived from

The police officer startled the burglar.
The police officer carried a club.

What two sentences form the basis for sentence 2?

_____

_____

HINT: *WHO, THAT,* AND *WHICH* REFER TO AND REPLACE WORDS FOR DIFFERENT THINGS.

1. *Who* refers to one or more persons.
2. *That* may refer to one or more persons or things.
3. *Which* refers to one or more things.[1]

That and *which* both may refer to things. Later we shall explain how to decide which to use.

When a sentence with a relative clause springs to mind, we do not think about the two sentences from which it might have been formed. But we should be aware of which information is in the independent clause and which is in the dependent (relative) clause and how to divide the one sentence into two.

Each sentence on the left about the courtship of Prince Charles and Lady Diana can be divided into two sentences. Circle the subject-noun of each clause and enclose the predicate-verb in a box. Then replace the relative pronoun with the appropriate noun, and write your two sentences. Remember to check your punctuation and capitalization. We've done the first one for you.

1. 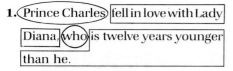 Prince Charles fell in love with Lady Diana, who is twelve years younger than he.

2. Prince Charles fell in love with Lady Diana.
3. She is twelve years younger than he.

---

[1] *Which* is an extremely troublesome word. See Appendix 4 for more information.

261

1. He courted her at Balmoral Castle,
which is his mother's private estate.

2. _____
_____
3. _____
_____

1. He tried to win the affection of the
woman whom he wanted to marry.

2. _____
_____
3. _____
_____

HINT: *WHO* AND *WHOM*

Whom is a form of *who* used when we are talking about the object rather than the subject of a verb. For example, in

Prince Charles fell in love with Lady Diana, who is young and beautiful.

The word *who* is the subject of the clause "who is young and beautiful." To make the clause into a separate sentence, *who* should be replaced by *Lady Diana* (or *she*):

Prince Charles fell in love with Lady Diana.

She is young and beautiful.

However, in the sentence

Prince Charles courted Diana, whom he wanted to marry.

whom is the object of the verb in the dependent clause. The clause can be made into the following sentence:

He wanted to marry her (or Diana).

You will probably use *who* much more often than *whom*.

Why Should We Create Sentences that Contain Relative Clauses?

We can create effective sentences by editing sentences that contain relative clauses.

1. On "General Hospital," Laura schemed to run away from the island, which was her only hope.
2. On "General Hospital," Laura schemed to run away from the island, her only hope.

In sentence 2, the relative pronoun and the verb have been deleted from the relative (dependent) clause. The sentence is shorter and reads more crisply. You won't always want to do this, nor will you be able to. But when you can, the result is often quite elegant.

Look back at the sentences about Mrs. Haggerty at the beginning of this section. If you can change any of them, write down the new version here:

_____

_____

Punctuating Relative Clauses

Some relative clauses are set off by commas:

1. Itzhak Perlman, *who is a famous violinist,* frequently appears on "Sesame Street."
2. He was disabled as a child by polio, *which proves that a physical handicap need not be a barrier to achievement.*

(*Note:* When the relative clause is in the middle of the sentence, you may need two commas.)

Not all relative clauses are set off by commas:

3. People *listening to his music* forget about the crutches *that lie next to his chair.*
4. The person *who focuses on the disability* is rare indeed.

How Do We Decide How to Punctuate a Sentence Containing a Relative Clause?

To punctuate the relative clause correctly, you must decide whether or not the information in the relative clause could be removed without essentially changing what the clause describes. If you decide that removing the information *will* change the meaning of the sentence, then begin the clause with *that* and do not use commas. For example.

An office has fourteen typewriters.
One of them is not working properly.

Thus,

*The typewriter **that needed repair** was stored in the closet.*

This sentence also tells you the location of the one broken typewriter. The information in the relative clause is essential because without it we do not know which of the fourteen typewriters was stored in the closet.

If removing the information in the relative clause will *not* essentially change the meaning of the sentence, you can use *which* and commas to set the clause off from the rest of the sentence. For example:

All police officers in New York City carry .38 revolvers.

Thus,

*New York City Police officers carry guns, **which are .38 revolvers,** in order to enforce the law.*

The relative clause gives interesting, but not essential, information. That is, the meaning of the sentence would be the same if the relative clause were omitted:

New York City police officers carry guns to enforce the law. (The relative clause which are .38 revolvers does not help us distinguish one police officer's gun from another because all of them carry. 38 revolvers.)

When a relative clause begins with *who,* you must decide whether or not the information is essential and use commas accordingly. For example:

There are many ex-convicts on parole. Some should be returned to prison.

Thus,

*Ex-convicts **who break their parole** should be returned to prison.*

We do not want to return all ex-convicts to jail, only those who break parole. Thus the information in the relative clause is essential or necessary to distinguish one ex-convict from another, and so we do not use commas to set off the relative clause.

But study the following example:

All the panel members were honored at a banquet.

All of them were dressed in formal attire.

Thus,

*The members of the panel, **who were wearing formal attire,** were honored at the banquet.*

The relative clause contains interesting information about how the panel members were dressed, but the information is not essential because it does not distinguish one panel member from another. Therefore, we use commas to offset the information in the relative clause.

Look back at the four sentences about Itzhak Perlman. Which ones contain

essential information in the relative clauses? _____

How do you know? _____

Which sentences contain nonessential information in the relative clauses?

_____

How do you know? _____

Practice Using Relative Clauses

1. Read this paragraph twice. The first time, read it for content; the second time, combine the pairs of sentences indicated, using the relative pronouns provided. Remember to put the relative clause close to the word it describes. Write the new version below. When you are finished, proofread it for correct punctuation and capitalization. We've combined the first two sentences for you.

Join
1, 2 with *which*
3, 4 with *whose*
5, 6 with *that*
7, 8 with *which*
9, 10 with *who*
11, 12 with *who*
13, 14 with *that*
15, 16 with *which*
17, 18 with *who*

YOU CAN ALWAYS TELL AN ARIES . . .

[1]Aries is also called the Ram. [2]It is considered the first sign of the zodiac. [3]An Aries has a typical appearance. [4]His or her birthday falls between March 21 and April 20. [5]Both the men and women have sharp facial features. [6]They are very prominent. [7]Their eyebrows knit together at the bridge of the nose. [8]It can be hawklike. [9]An Aries person is generally broad shouldered. [10]He or she has delicate but strong bone structure. [11]You can recognize an Aries by bandages on the head and face. [12]He or she is very prone to injury. ([13]Some Aries are also susceptible to skin rashes, sore knees, and stomach ailments. [14]They are born in late March and early April.) [15]But the real symbol of the Aries personality is the eyes. [16]They look straight at you. [17]An Aries focuses right on you and sends off signals of power and energy. [18]He or she never just glances about.

Remember that if a relative clause with nonessential information falls in the middle of a sentences, the clause should be set off with two commas.

Aries, which is considered the first sign of the zodiac, is also called the Ram.

_____

_____

_____

_____

_____

_____

_____

_____

_____

_____

2. Read this passage twice. The first time, read it for content; the second time, combine those sentences you think should be combined, using the relative pronouns *who, which, that,* or *whose.* Write the new version below. When you are finished, proofread it for correct punctuation and capitalization. We've done the first one for you.

. . . BUT YOU CAN'T TELL HIM (OR HER) MUCH!

[1]Aries's energy is partly based on conceit. [2]It is legendary. [3]The Aries wants what he or she wants. [4]It means someone who will pursue a challenge and master it but also someone who may trample over others in his or her way. [5]The Aries does not mean to offend or hurt. [6]He or she is not malicious, merely heedless.

[7]But the Aries is also charming and romantic. [8]The Aries can dominate a party with fascinating conversation. [9]It has his or her audience enraptured. [10]The Aries man will dazzle his current love with romance, but he will leave her if he gets bored or if he suspects infidelity. [11]The Aries woman can sustain great passion. [12]She is an independent woman. [13]She wants a man she can admire, and once she finds him, she's a tigress. [14]She'll defend her lover against any insult. [15]His reputation is sacred to her.

Aries's energy, which is legendary, is partly based on conceit.

_____

_____

_____

266

_____

_____

_____

_____

_____

_____

_____

_____

_____

_____

_____

3. Read this passage twice. The first time, read it for content; the second time, proofread it for commas. Delete or insert commas where you think they are necessary.

Roland Gladstone was bald. Bald as a ball, he was, which is pretty bald. Hardly a hair grew on his neck or scalp. The few that did he had taken to shaving off. He oiled his scalp daily which doctors told him would keep his scalp healthy. Thus a naked and gleaming head topped his six-foot frame.

Roland whose friends were all quite used to his baldness, never remembered to inform his blind dates of his condition.

Women are either repelled or fascinated by a man's baldness. Women, who want to play Delilah to someone's Samson were disappointed in their evenings with Roland. They hated to be seen with him, which was upsetting to them and to him, and they spent most of the evening looking at everyone except him which was embarrassing for everyone. However, women, who liked the bizarre appearance of this tall, hairless man, delighted in being seen with him in public. Roland, who was a bit of a showman, enjoyed preening for his date and for the crowd.

4. Reread the paragraphs you wrote in Exercises 1 and 2, and change any relative clauses you think sound better in shortened form. Put brackets around the words you intend to delete. Make sure not to change the meaning of the sentence. For example:

(1) Aries, [which is considered] the first sign of the zodiac, is also called the Ram.

_____

_____

_____

_____

Fragments

In Chapter 4 we discussed fragments that result from omitting one of the principal parts of the sentence—namely, the subject-noun or the predicate-verb. Another kind of fragment is caused by treating a dependent clause as if it were an independent clause, as if it could stand alone as a sentence:

> In the autumn the leaves turn brown. <u>Which is always a beautiful sight.</u>
> Maxine decided to check the directions one more time. <u>Even though she was fairly certain how to get to the school.</u>
> The hidden microphone didn't record their voices. <u>Because it had been disconnected by the mobsters.</u>

Can a Dependent Clause Be a Complete Sentence?

The dependent clauses that are underlined are fragments because they cannot stand alone. They begin with a capital letter and end with a period and therefore look like sentences, but they are not. We can correct this kind of fragment by connecting it to an independent clause so as to make one complete sentence:

> In the autumn the leaves turn brown, which is always a beautiful sight.
> Maxine decided to check the directions one more time, even though she was fairly certain how to get to the school.
> The hidden microphone didn't record their voices because it had been disconnected by the mobsters.

Correcting Comma Splices and Run-on Sentences

In Chapter 5 we discussed several ways to correct comma splices and run-on sentences. There is still another way to handle these problems: subordination. For example, we can eliminate the comma splice in this sentence:

How Do We Use Subordination to Fix Run-ons and Comma Splices?

Sharon ate her breakfast, then she went to work.

by making one of the sentences a dependent clause. For example, we can do this in two ways, (1) by adding the word *after*.

After Sharon ate her breakfast, *she went to work.*

or (2) by adding the word *before*.

Sharon ate her breakfast **before she went to work.**

Practice Finding and Fixing Fragments

1. Circle the number of each fragment.

BEWARE THE GOAT

[1]If a person born under the sign of Capricorn the Goat stood next to one born under Aries the Ram, no one would notice the Capricorn. [2]Capricorns are by nature gloomy, self-effacing types. [3]Who melt into their surroundings. [4]They are the quiet ones, the watchers. [5]That triumph at the finish. [6]Because they possess the determination of the goat rather than the aggressiveness of the ram.

[7]Capricorns come in all sizes and shapes. [8]Although they each have different builds. [9]Most of them are dark haired and dark eyed. [10]Capricorns, who are known for being well disciplined. [11]Frequently look serious or sad. [12]Even when they are happy. [13]Although they feel the same emotions as people born under other signs. [14]They have more trouble showing them.

[15]Capricorns generally have small noses and good teeth, unless they are the unlucky ones. [16]Who are constantly plagued by tooth decay. [17]As

are all people who worry a lot, Capricorns are distinguished by nervous allergies and rashes. [18]You will frequently see them bent because of stomach ailments. [19]Unless it is depression that is laying them low.

[20]Capricorns mellow with age. [21]Provided they can endure a gloomy childhood. [22]Those that do. [23]Find love and success more enjoyable in their maturity.

2. Look back at Exercise 1. Fix any fragments you found. Make sure to renumber the sentences.
3. Proofread this passage for comma splices and run-on sentences. Correct them by using the appropriate subordinate conjunctions. Refer to the list in the Subordination section on page 255.

Count Dracula, the most famous vampire in literature, film, and theater, was based on the Rumanian Prince Vlad, the Impaler, who lived in Transylvania in the fifteenth century. According to the author of the original novel, Bram Stoker, Dracula appeared only between sundown and sunup, during the day he slept in a coffin. Dracula did not eat he nourished himself by drinking blood from the necks of his neighbors. They thought he was a harmless eccentric. They did find it a bit odd that he had no reflection in the mirror.

Dracula has been the subject of at least ten plays and movies, beginning in 1897 and continuing into the 1980s, his looks have been quite consistent. The count is a tall, dapper gentleman in his thirties or forties. A mustache is optional, it depends on the fashion of the era. Some may find him handsome, he is thin lipped and cruel looking. Sharp little white teeth protrude over ruby lips he obviously got the red lips from sucking blood. Somewhat pointed ears stick out from under his elegantly styled hair. But it is the hands that truly betray him. Dracula's hands are too coarse for a titled gentleman. Look closely, you will see tiny hairs growing out of his palms. He has manicured his fingernails to dangerous, fine points. The hands are cold as ice, as cold as death. Touch him you will think you are touching a corpse.

The actors Bela Lugosi, John Carradine, Christopher Lee, and Frank Langella all matched Stoker's descriptions of Prince Vlad in appearance, their appearance could be altered where they differed slightly.

4. All of the punctuation and capitalization have been removed from this passage about the Scorpio personality. Read it until you are certain you know what it means. Then insert commas, periods, and capital letters where necessary.

scorpio the birth sign that extends from october 24 through november 22 is one of the most deceptive of the signs of the zodiac although scorpios can be the deadly scorpion they can also be the lowly lizard or the proud eagle because they can take on so many guises they are hard to distinguish that's the way scorpios want it they enjoy the mystery so long as they are not the ones who are in the dark

but certain characteristics point you to scorpios who are generally powerful physical specimens their features are well defined and sharp their noses are prominent and their eyes are piercing while their eyebrows tend to meet over their noses male scorpios are known for the hair on their arms and legs which has a reddish tint to it.

scorpios cultivate a blank expression on their faces they want to appear uninterested and nonchalant which is how they find out all that they know people just tend to ignore them because they look so bland but beware the scorpion may strike or the lizard may sneak up on you although scorpios are capable of ruthless behavior they are also capable of the soaring generosity and greatness of the eagle they know no fear unless it is the fear that their greatness will be discovered for they prefer to be anonymous and stay behind the scenes they will rise above any adversity and meet any challenge

5. Write your own description of someone whose astrological sign fits him or her. Begin with the sentence:

   (name of person)   is the perfect   (name of sign .

If you are not interested in astrology, write about someone you consider a "perfect __(name a quality)__ ." You might begin with

__Jeffrey Jerome__ is a perfect __idiot__ .

After you have finished writing, proofread your paragraph for fragments, run-on sentences, and comma splices, and eliminate them by using subordination. Make sure your use of commas with subordination is appropriate. Use your own paper.

More Near-homonyms

The following are ten more sets of words that sound enough alike to cause trouble. Supply your own hints where you can.

1. allusion: indirect mention or casual reference.

illusion: false idea or opinion; deceptive appearance.

This salesman made an *allusion* to his customer's weight.

It was an *illusion* to think the world was flat.

*The drama critic made an **allusion** to the fact that several cast members in* Oh Calcutta! *appeared nude, but he assumed it was merely an optical **illusion.***

You try it: _____

2. been: past participle of be (used with *have* or *had*).

being: **a.** present participle of *be* (used with *am, is, are, was, were*).

b. one who exists.

The drunk had *been* in the bar for two hours.

The children were *being* obnoxious, and so their mothers ignored them.

Every human *being* is entitled to freedom.

*A person who has **been** or is **being** confined in jail should still be considered a human **being.***

You try it: _____

3. decent: proper and fitting; conforming to approved social standards.

descent: **a.** coming down.

b. lineage, ancestry.

Even unidentified corpses are given a *decent* burial by the state.

The jalopy's *descent* of the hill was slow and noisy.

Princess Grace was not of royal *descent*.

dissent: (v.i.) to differ in. When I feel I must, I *dissent* from what my friends are doing.

(n.) an act of differing; rendering a minority opinion. Justice Thurgood Marshall issued his *dissent* in the case.

*Many people believe that those of royal **descent** set standards of **decent** behavior for everyone, but others **dissent**, believing that royalty is not a proper model of behavior.*

You try it: _____

4. know: to have certain information. Teenagers think they *know* everything.

now: **a.** at the present moment or a time close to the present. The performance begins *now* and ends at 6 P.M.

b. (no definite meaning, used for emphasis.) *Now* listen my children, and you shall hear.

***Now** is the time for all gymnasts to demonstrate what they **know** about the parallel bars.*

You try it: _____

5. loose: free; not confined or restrained. The horse ran *loose* in the fields.

lose: (v.t.) to become unable to find, to get rid of. I *lose* an umbrella whenever I use one.

(v.i.) to undergo or suffer a loss, to be defeated in a contest, to go astray. It hurts to run an entire marathon in first place and then *lose* in the last quarter-mile.

*The girl wore her hair **loose** because she was afraid she would **lose** the barrette she needed to hold a ponytail.*

You try it: _____

6. quiet: (adj.) still, calm, motionless. Before a tornado, the air is strangely *quiet.*

(v.t.) to calm or pacify, to allay fear. The sitter tried to *quiet* the crying baby.

quite: completely or entirely. The food was *quite* burned by the time I reached the stove.

to a considerable degree. I was *quite* angry with myself.

*The **quiet** water of the ocean made it **quite** impossible to surf.*

You try it: _____

7. statue: the form of a person or animal carved in stone or other material.

A *statue* of Atlas holding the world stands in Rockefeller Center.

stature: height of a person or object; development or growth or level of achievement.

Harry Truman gained *stature* after he became president.

statute: a rule or law.

The *statute* prohibits parking in a "red zone."

*By **statute,** any person over seven feet in **stature** should not have a **statue** erected in his or her memory at public expense.*

You try it: _____

8. trail: (v.i.) to move along behind.

Because I dawdle, I always *trail* the other hikers.

(n.) a mark, footprint, scent left by a thing that has passed.

The skunk left a distinct *trail* for us to follow.

trial: a trying, testing, putting to the proof; examination of facts.

The race was a *trial* to see which runners would qualify.

Lizzie Borden stood *trial* for the murder of her parents.

*The prosecutor at the **trial** pointed out that the murderer had set out to **trail** the victim to his own apartment.*

You try it: _____

9. went: past tense of *go.*

My mother *went* to live in Florida because of its mild climate.

when: at whatever time.

When you make a decision, you must stick to it.

***When** Egyptian President Anwar Sadat **went** to Jerusalem, he took a great step toward peace in the Middle East.*

You try it: _____

10. woman: one female human being.

A *woman's* place is in the house—and the Senate.

women: more than one female. The men as well as the *women* in this country have been affected by the feminist movement.

*One **woman** with a tractor can do the work of ten **women** with shovels.*

You try it: _____

Practice with Near-homonyms

1. Write the correct near-homonym in the blank.

_____ short is a terrible burden thrust upon a person by two
Been/Being

_____ but unknowing parents. They, too, are short, and proba-
decent/descent/dissent

bly they hate it, but they _____ themselves in love and have the
loose/lose

_____ that they cannot be _____ certain that they will create
allusion/illusion   quiet/quite

a new person doomed to be small of _____. But heredity tri-
statue/stature/statute

umphs _____ short parents have short children.
went/when

And it is the way of human _____ that _____ is
beens/beings   statue/stature/statute

all. Life for a short person is a continual _____. I _____ from my own
trail/trial   know/now

experience. Do you _____ that because they are hassled so much in
know/now

public, short people must constantly decide if they really need to leave their

houses? People on street corners make bad jokes that begin: "_____
Know/Now

this short person wanted to cross the street. . . ." They do it to make short

people self-conscious.

Life is worse for short men. Maybe short _____ do not care
woman/women

as much as men. People do not look twice at a short _____ with a
woman/women

tall man. But woe to the short man seen with a tall _____. Social
woman/women

life for a short man is very difficult, even though people often make an

_____ to the idea that short men are attentive suitors. Who would
allusion/illusion

ever _____? No _____ of _____
        know/now   woman/women   decent/descent/dissent

_____ will accept a date with a short man. It's as if there is
statue/stature/statute

a _____ against it. A _____ only wants a man with
   statue/stature/statute   woman/women

the body of a _____, and not a miniature _____ either!
          statue/stature/statute   been/being

This kind of _____ prejudice is enough to drive a short
             quiet/quite

man _____ mad.
   quiet/quite

2. Proofread this essay and make any changes necessary in the spelling of the near-homonyms we have studied in this section.

Once again, the use of the death penalty is been debated. Most

states voided their death penalty statues in the 1970s, although juries

could still impose a death penalty at the conclusion of a trail. Know some

states have begun to use their death penalty statutes again.

Proponents of the death penalty see it as quiet an effective deterrent

to crime. They point to countries like Saudi Arabia with severe penalties

and quite low crime rates. It is true that in that country, people are safe

when they are at home, and went they walk in the streets they are not

afraid of being mugged. However, those who oppose the death penalty

see the comparison of the two countries as an illusion. Saudi Arabia, they

say, is a tightly knit, homogeneous society, whereas American society is

a lose, heterogeneous one. What will work in one culture may not work

quiet so well in another. Moreover, they point out, went people commit

murder, they frequently do not plan it in advance, or they do not believe they will get caught, or they see themselves as being above the law. Thus, the death penalty does not deter them.

People who favor the death penalty point out that we all are equal before the law. They believe that society deserves retribution for the crime committed. Those who descent see the death penalty as been inherently prejudicial. More men than woman are now on death row. A woman seems to inspire a jury to be lenient in a way a man does not. Also, went members of minority groups commit crimes, they frequently cannot afford expensive defenses, and they, too, are disproportionately represented on death row.

THE FINAL DRAFT

Now you are ready to proofread the second draft of the essay you began earlier in this chapter. Read your essay again slowly, and aloud. Remember what you learned about word order and sense in Chapter 1 and about the conventions of writing in Chapter 2. You may need to look back at these chapters. Check to see that each sentence you've written contains a subject and a verb.

Make sure you can answer yes to these questions as you proofread:

1. If you have joined two sentences, have you used either a conjunction or a subordinating conjunction that signals the relationship you intended between the ideas?
2. Is your punctuation and capitalization of your joined sentences correct?
3. Did you use *who*, *whose*, *that*, and *which* appropriately, and did you correctly punctuate the sentences that use these words?
4. Have you used subordination to eliminate any fragments, run-on sentences, and comma splices?

Read also for the correct spelling of any of the homonyms you may have used. Change anything you think needs changing. Write a clean copy if you make more than one or two changes.

ADDITIONAL WRITING ASSIGNMENTS

Your writer's journal may have some ideas for you to develop into essays. Focus on people you know. They may be people you know well, with whom you have developed relationships over a long period of time. They may be people you saw in a crowd, on a bus, or in a train, who interested you. Carry your writer's journal around with you for a few days and see who you see.

The following are topics that students have found stimulating. Remember to follow the writing process we are developing: Do focused writing first. Then look it over. You may want to review the Writing and Rewriting section of each chapter before you start a second draft. Write a main-point statement that tells your audience what you want them to know about this person when you are finished reading. When you finish your middle drafts, proofread them and write a clean copy.

Topic Suggestions

One of these people may make a good subject for description:

1. your sister or brother.
2. a grandparent.
3. close friend (but not a boy friend or girl friend).
4. a teacher.
5. a boss or supervisor.
6. a neighborhood "character."
7. your "hero."
8. a relative (other than a parent[2]).
9. the most popular or unpopular person in your class.
10. a coworker or teammate.

Also, on your travels to or from school or work, observe someone traveling with you. Talk to the person if you can. Because you do not know him or her, you will have to infer, or even invent, certain details from what you can observe. Write a description of this person based on your observations and inventions.

---

[2] You may be surprised to be advised *not* to write about your parents or your boy friend or girl friend. You should write about people who are important to you, but you do need some objectivity about your subject as well. It is very hard to be objective about parents or people with whom you are romantically involved.

Giving Directions

7

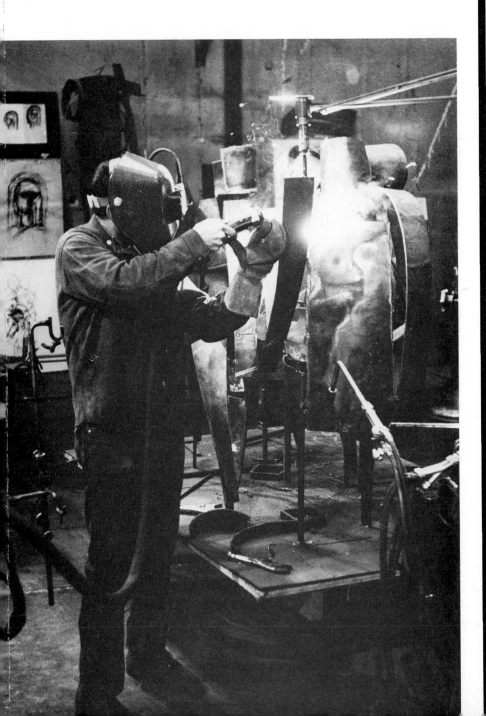

Photo by
Arley Bondarin

1. Write a set of directions to guide someone from your classroom to where you live.
2. Choose a popular card or board game, and write a set of directions explaining how to play the game.
3. Write directions that would help teach a child how to cross the street safely.
4. Write the recipe for your favorite dish.

READING

PREVIEW QUESTIONS

As you read "Fried Chicken" by Jim Villas, look for information that will help answer these questions:

1. Look at the title of the article and the subheadings. On the basis of these, write two questions you would expect the article to answer:

   _____

   _____

2. How seriously does the author take fried chicken?
3. Does Villas explain the process of making fried chicken in a way that you can follow?
4. Do the subdivisions help you understand the process?
5. For what audience is Villas writing? What words or phrases give you this information?
6. Can you read and enjoy this selection if you are not southern?
7. How does Villas's use of abbreviations and numbers differ from what you learned in Chapter 2?
8. How and where does Villas's punctuation differ from the punctuation rules you have learned?

Notes

Julia Child. The "French Chef" on public television.
James Beard. The writer of several famous cookbooks.
Craig Claiborne. The food editor of the *New York Times.*

Fried Chicken

Jim Villas

Jim Villas is from North Carolina. He taught comparative literature and languages before becoming the food and wine editor for Town and Country *magazine. He also contributes to many other popular magazines. This selection is an excerpt from the book* Mom, the Flag, and Apple Pie, *compiled by the editors of* Esquire.

(1) When it comes to fried chicken, let's not beat around the bush for one second. To know about fried chicken you have to have been weaned and reared on it in the South. Period. The French know absolutely nothing about it, and Julia Child and James Beard very little. Craig Claiborne knows plenty. He's from Mississippi. And to set the record straight before bringing on regional and possible national holocaust over the correct preparation of this classic dish, let me emphasize and reemphasize the fact that I'm a Southerner, born, bred, and chicken-fried for all times. Now, I don't exactly know why we Southerners love and eat at least ten times more fried chicken than anyone else, but we do and always have and always will. Maybe we have a hidden craw in our throats or oversize pulley bones or . . . Oh, I don't know what we have, and it doesn't matter. What does matter is that we take our fried chicken very seriously, having singled it out years ago as not only the most important staple worthy of heated and complex debate but also as the dish that non-Southerners have really never had any knack for. Others just plain down don't *understand* fried chicken, and, to tell the truth, there're lots of Southerners who don't know as much as they think they know. Naturally everybody everywhere in the country is convinced he or she can cook or identify great fried chicken as well as any ornery reb (including all the fancy cookbook writers), but the truth remains that once you've eaten real chicken fried by an expert chicken fryer in the South there are simply no grounds for contest.

(2) As far as I'm concerned, all debate over how to prepare fried chicken has ended forever, for recently I fried up exactly twenty-one and a half chickens (or 215 pieces) using every imaginable technique, piece of equipment, and type of oil for the sole purpose of establishing once and for all the right way to fix great fried chicken. In a minute I'll tell you what's wrong with most of the Kentucky-fried, Maryland-fried, oven-fried, deep-fried, creole-fried, and all those other classified varieties of Southern-fried chicken people like to go on about. But first *my* chicken, which I call simply Fried Chicken and which I guarantee will start you lapping:

(3) *Equipment* (no substitutes)
A sharp chef's or butcher's knife 12 to 13 in. long
A large wooden cutting board
A small stockpot half filled with water (for chicken soup)

A large glass salad bowl
A heavy 12-in. cast-iron skillet with lid
Long-handled tweezer tongs
1 roll paper towels
2 brown paper bags
1 empty coffee can
A serving platter
A wire whisk
A home fire extinguisher

(4) *Ingredients* (to serve 4)
3 cups whole milk
½ fresh lemon
1½ lbs. (3 cups) top-quality shortening
4 tbsp. rendered bacon grease
1 whole freshly killed 3½- to 4-lb. chicken
1½ cups plus 2 tbsp. flour
3 tsp. salt
Freshly ground black pepper

(5) *To Prepare Chicken for Frying.* Remove giblets and drop in stockpot with neck. (This is for a good chicken soup to be eaten at another time.) Cut off and pull out any undesirable fat at neck and tail. Placing whole chicken in center of cutting board (breast-side up, neck toward you, grab leg on left firmly, pull outward and down toward board, and begin slashing down through skin toward thigh joint, keeping knife close to thigh. Crack back thigh joint as far as possible, find joint with fingers, then cut straight through to remove (taking care not to pull skin from breast). Turn bird around and repeat procedure on other thigh. To separate thigh from leg, grasp one end in each hand, pull against tension of joint, find joint, and sever. Follow same procedure to remove wings. Cut off wing tips and add to stockpot.

(6) To remove pulley bone (or wishbone to non-Southerners), find protruding knob toward neck end of breast, trace with fingers to locate small indentation just forward of knob, slash horizontally downward across indentation, then begin cutting carefully away from indentation and downward toward neck till forked pulley-bone piece is fully severed. Turn chicken backside up, locate two hidden small pinbones on either side below neck toward middle of back, and cut through skin to expose ends of bones. Put two fingers of each hand into neck cavity and separate breast from back by pulling forcefully till the two pry apart. (If necessary, sever stubborn tendons and skin with knife.) Cut back in half, reserving lower portion (tail end) for frying, and tossing upper portion (rib cage) into stockpot. Place breast skin-side down, ram tip of knife down through center cartilage, and cut breast in half.

(7) (Hint: Level cutting edge of knife along cartilage, then slam blade through with heel of hand.)

(8) Rinse the ten pieces of chicken thoroughly under cold running water,

dry with paper towels, and salt and pepper lightly. Pour milk into bowl, squeeze lemon into milk, add chicken to soak, cover, and refrigerate at least two hours and preferably overnight.

(9) *To Fry Chicken.* Remove chicken from refrigerator and allow to return to room temperature (about 70°). While melting the pound and a half of shortening over high heat to measure ½ inch in skillet, pour flour, remaining salt and pepper to taste into paper bag. Remove dark pieces of chicken from milk, drain each momentarily over bowl, drop in paper bag, shake vigorously to coat, and add bacon grease to skillet. When small bubbles appear on surface, reduce heat slightly. Remove dark pieces of chicken from bag one by one, shake off excess flour, and, using tongs, lower gently into fat, skin-side down. Quickly repeat all procedures with white pieces; reserve milk, arrange chicken in skillet so it cooks evenly, reduce heat to medium, and cover. Fry exactly 17 minutes. Lower heat, turn pieces with tongs and fry 17 minutes longer uncovered. With paper towels wipe grease continuously from exposed surfaces as it spatters. Chicken should be almost mahogany brown.

(10) Drain thoroughly on second brown paper bag, transfer to serving platter *without* reheating in oven, and serve hot or at room temperature with any of the following items: mashed potatoes and cream gravy, potato salad, green beans, turnip greens, sliced homegrown tomatoes, stewed okra, fresh corn bread, iced tea, beer, homemade peach ice cream, or watermelon.

(11) Now, that's the right way, the only way to deal with fried chicken. Crisp, juicy on the inside, full of flavor, not greasy and sloppy, fabulous. Of course one reason my recipe works so well is it's full of important subtleties that are rarely indicated in cookbooks but that help to make the difference between impeccable fried chicken and all the junk served up everywhere today. And just to illustrate this point, I cite a recipe for "Perfect Fried Chicken" that recently appeared in *Ladies' Home Journal.*

1. Rinse cut-up 2½- to 3-lb. broiler-fryer and pat dry.

2. Pour 1 in. vegetable oil in skillet, heat to 375. Combine ½ cup flour, 2 tsp. salt, dash of pepper in bag. Coat a few pieces at a time.

3. Preheat oven to 250°. Place paper towels in shallow baking pan.

4. Fry thighs and drumsticks, turning occasionally, for 12 minutes until golden. Pierce with fork to see if juices run clear. Remove to baking pan and place in heated oven. Fry remaining pieces for 7 to 8 minutes. Serves four.

(12) Snap! That's it. A real quicky. Fast fried chicken that promises to be perfect. Bull! It tastes like hell, and if you don't believe me, try it yourself. The pitfalls of the recipe are staggering but typical. First of all, nobody in his right mind fries a skinny two-and-a-half-pound chicken for four people, not unless everyone's on some absurd diet or enjoys sucking bones. Second, the recipe takes for granted you're going to buy a plastic-wrapped chicken that's been so hacked and splintered by a meat cleaver that blood from the bones saturates the package. What help is offered if the chicken you happen to have on hand is whole or only partially cut up? Third, what type of skillet, and what size, for heaven's sake? If the pan's too light the chicken will burn on the bottom, and if you pour one full inch of oil in an eight-inch skillet,

you'll end up with deep-fried chicken. And as for sticking forks in seared chicken to release those delicious juices, or putting fried chicken in the oven to get it disgustingly soggy, or serving a half-raw thick breast that's cooked only seven or eight minutes—well, I refuse to get overheated.

(13) Without question the most important secret to any great fried chicken is the quality of the chicken itself, and without question most of the three billion pullets marketed annually in the U.S. have about as much flavor as tennis balls. But, after all, what can you expect of battery birds whose feet never touch the dirty filthy earth, whose diet includes weight-building fats, fish flours, and factory-fresh chemicals, and whose life expectancy is a pitiful seven weeks? Tastelessness, that's what, the same disgraceful tastelessness that characterize the eggs we're forced to consume. How many people in this country remember the rich flavor of good old barnyard chicken, a nearly extinct species that pecked around the yard for a good fifteen weeks, digested plenty of barley-and-milk mash, bran, grain, and beer, got big and fat, and never sent one solitary soul to the hospital with contamination? I remember, believe you me, and how. I pity the millions who, blissfully unconscious of what they missed and sadly addicted to the chicken passed out by Colonel Sanders, will never taste a truly luscious piece of fried chicken unless they're first shown how to get their hands on a real chicken. Of course, what you see in supermarkets are technically real chickens fit for consumption, but anyone who's sunk teeth into a gorgeous, plump barnyard variety . . . would agree that to compare the scrawny, bland bird with the one God intended us to eat is something more than ludicrous.

(14) I originally intended to tell you how to raise, kill, draw, and prepare your own chickens. Then I came to my senses and faced the reality that unless you were brought up wringing chickens' necks, bleeding them, searching for the craws where food is stored, and pulling out their innards with your hands—well, it can be a pretty nauseating mess that makes you gag if you're not used to it. Besides there's really no need to slaughter your own chicken, not, that is, if you're willing to take time and make the effort to locate either a good chicken raiser who feeds and exercises his chickens properly (on terra firma) or a reliable merchant who gets his chickens fresh from the farm. They do exist, still, be their number ever so dwindling. If you live in a rural area, simply get to know a farmer who raises chickens, start buying eggs from him and tell him you'll pay him any amount to kill and prepare for you a nice 3½- to 4-pound pullet. He will, and probably with pride. If you're in a large city, the fastest method is to study the Yellow Pages of the phone book, search under "Poultry—Retail" for the words "Fresh poultry and eggs" or "Custom poultry" or "strictly kosher poultry," and proceed from there.

(15) Now, if you think I take my fried chicken a little too seriously, you haven't seen anything till you attend the National Chicken Cooking Contest held annually in early summer at different locations throughout the country. Created in 1949, the festival has a Poultry Princess; vintage motorcar displays; a flea market; a ten-feet-by-eight-inch skillet that fries up seven and a half tons of chicken; ten thousand chicken-loving contestants cooking for cash

prizes amounting to over $25,000; and big-name judges who are chosen from among the nation's top newspaper, magazine, and television food editors. It's a big to-do. Of course, I personally have no intention whatsoever of ever entering any chicken contest that's not made up exclusively of Southerners, and of course you understand my principle. This, however, should not necessarily affect your going to the National and showing the multitudes what real fried chicken is all about. A few years back, a young lady irreverently dipped some chicken in oil flavored with soy sauce, rolled it in crushed chow mein noodles, fried it up, and walked away with top honors and a few grand for her Cock-a-Noodle-Do. Without doubt she was a sweetheart of a gal, but you know, the people who judged that fried chicken really need help.

QUESTIONS OF CONTENT

Circle the letter of the best answer to each question.

1. According to Villas, to know fried chicken you must have been born and raised in
   a. the North.
   b. France.
   c. the South.
   d. your home.

2. Villas refers to his chicken as
   a. Kentucky-fried.
   b. fried.
   c. oven-fried.
   d. deep-fried.

3. Which piece of equipment is *not* needed to prepare Villas's fried chicken?
   a. a large wooden cutting board.
   b. a home fire extinguisher.
   c. a wire whisk.
   d. a roll of aluminum foil.

4. Which ingredients are not the same as those in Villas's list?
   a. one whole, freshly killed, 3½- to 4-lb. chicken.
   b. three teaspoons of salt.
   c. one fresh lemon.
   d. three cups of skimmed milk.

5. To finish separating the thigh from the leg, you must
   a. pull against tension of joint.
   b. grasp one end in each hand.
   c. find joint and sever.
   d. drop thigh into hot fat.

6. Non-Southerners call a pulley bone a
   a. thigh joint.
   b. leg bone.
   c. neck bone.
   d. wishbone.

7. Chicken cooked correctly should be
   a. light brown.
   b. crispy brown.
   c. mahogany brown.
   d. golden brown.

8. The most important secret to a great fried chicken is
   a. the subtleties of the recipe.   **c.** the utensils.
   b. the size of the skillet.   **d.** the quality of the chicken.

Answer these questions in full sentences:

1. Why does Villas think Craig Claiborne "knows plenty" about fried chicken?

_____

2. How did Villas prove his recipe was the best? _____

_____

3. What happens to fried chicken that is put in the oven to warm? _____

_____

4. Summarize Villas's attitude toward how chickens are raised in the United

States and his advice on how to find and buy the best chicken. _____

_____

_____

_____

_____

QUESTIONS OF INFERENCE

Look back at the essay to answer these questions. Answer in full sentences.

1. Why are some chickens more likely than others to send a person to the

hospital? _____

_____

2. Why does Villas single out the French (as opposed to any other nationality)
when he discusses those who know nothing about fried chicken?

_____

3. Can a non-Southerner ever learn to make good fried chicken? _____

_____

4. Why does Villas provide the "hint" in paragraph 7? _____

_____

5. Why does Villas say "no substitutes" in his lists of equipment and ingredi-

ents? _____

_____

6. What suggestions does Villas give about how to write a set of directions?

_____

_____

QUESTIONS OF CRITICAL THINKING

Answer each of these questions in a short paragraph. You may want to use your own paper.

1. Villas says that mass-produced chicken like Kentucky Fried Chicken "never

tastes truly luscious." Do you agree or disagree, and why? _____

_____

_____

_____

2. Villas pities the millions of people who are "blissfully unconscious" of the good food they are missing. If people are happily unaware of something—chicken or anything else—should they be pitied? Give examples.

_____

_____

_____

3. Villas is angered by the presence of chemicals and contaminants in chicken. Do you share his feelings about additives in the food you eat? How do your feelings affect your food-buying and -eating habits? _____

_____

_____

_____

_____

4. Why do you think Villas wrote this article? And for whom? _____

_____

_____

_____

5. Do you think Villas's "tone" (or voice) is appropriate to get his message across? What effect do his attitude and word choice have on you?

_____

_____

_____

6. What questions would you like to ask Villas about this article? _____

_____

_____

_____

VOCABULARY

These words from "Fried Chicken" may be unfamiliar to you. The exercises will help you learn the meaning of these words and how they function in sentences.

weaned	(1)	tendons	(6)	extinct	(13)
reared	(1)	cartilage	(6)	species	(13)
holocaust	(1)	reserve	(9)	contamination	(13)
classic	(1)	subtleties	(11)	blissfully	(13)
craw	(1)	impeccable	(11)	ludicrous	(13)
ornery	(1)	cite	(11)	innards	(14)
staple	(1)	staggering	(12)	terra firma	(14)
reb	(1)	absurd	(12)	dwindling	(14)
classified	(2)	saturates	(12)	vintage	(15)
protruding	(6)	seared	(12)	irreverently	(15)
indentation	(6)	battery	(13)	multitudes	(15)
severed	(6)	consume	(13)		

Word Meanings

1. Look up the words below in the dictionary, and write down their meanings:

holocaust _____

reb _____

terra firma _____

2. Look up these words in the dictionary. Each has more than one meaning, and some are listed as more than one part of speech. Read the entire entry for each word, including that for each part of speech listed. Choose the meaning closest to the way in which the word is used in the selection. If you're in doubt, write down all the meanings you think could be the right one, separating the meanings by semicolons. Make sure to include the part of speech next to your definition.

rear[ed] _____

indentation _____

battery _____

consume _____

extinct _____

species _____

staple _____

subtlety [subtleties] _____

cite[1] _____

sear[ed] _____

Word Clues

1. Try to see the following words as the sum of their parts, and then write
a working definition for each. (The list of prefixes and suffixes on pages
10–13 will help you with some of the words.) Check the dictionary entry
for each word to see how close your working definition is to it.

irreverent[ly] _____

contamination _____

blissful[ly] _____

reserve _____

impeccable _____

absurd _____

Star the words whose prefixes and suffixes *did not* help you define them.

  Prefixes and suffixes are not very helpful for some words because the
root of the word does not mean anything when it stands alone—for instance,
absurd. The list of prefixes and suffixes informs us that *ab* means "away
from." Thus you have "away from *surd*." But what is *surd?* It is a Latin word
meaning *deaf* or *insensible*. Consult the dictionary for words like this.

2. "Fried Chicken" contains two words that have the same root: *classic* and
classified. Look up both words in the dictionary. What is the root? What

does it mean? _____

Seeing Words in Context

These words appear in "Fried Chicken." You may find clues to the meaning
of each in its context. As you reread the essay, circle the words or phrases

[1] This word is often confused with its two homonyms *site* and *sight*. If you are unsure of
their meanings, check them now.

that form the context for each word. Then write (1) your working definition, (2) the dictionary definition that is right for the context, and (3) an original sentence using the word. If you have difficulty figuring out the meaning of the word from the context of "Fried Chicken," you may find it helpful to read the following story, in which the words appear in italics:

1. word: *protruding*

    a. working definition _____

    b. dictionary definition _____

    c. your sentence _____

2. word: *dwindling*

    a. working definition _____

    b. dictionary definition _____

    c. your sentence _____

3. word: *weaned*

    a. working definition _____

    b. dictionary definition _____

    c. your sentence _____

4. word: *innards*

    a. working definition _____

    b. dictionary definition _____

    c. your sentence _____

5. word: *craw*

    a. working definition _____

    b. dictionary definition _____

    c. your sentence _____

6. word: *ornery*

   a. working definition _____

   b. dictionary definition _____

   c. your sentence _____

7. word: *staggering*

   a. working definition _____

   b. dictionary definition _____

   c. your sentence _____

8. word: *severed*

   a. working definition _____

   b. dictionary definition _____

   c. your sentence _____

9. word: *tendons*

   a. working definition _____

   b. dictionary definition _____

   c. your sentence _____

10. word: *saturates*

   a. working definition _____

   b. dictionary definition _____

   c. your sentence _____

11. word: *vintage*

   a. working definition _____

   b. dictionary definition _____

   c. your sentence _____

12. word: *ludicrous*

    a. working definition _____

    b. dictionary definition _____

    c. your sentence _____

FRANKLIN INVESTIGATES

It was an ordinary night in the Eighty-ninth Precinct when Detective Oliver Franklin caught the squeal: a body *protruding* from an alley between West and Main streets, its head sticking out into the filthy street and its feet hidden in the darkness of the alley.

What was it doing there, Franklin thought as he edged his car into Main Street. No one wanted to be in that part of town at night—if he had a choice. The winos and addicts who sprawled on the sidewalks or slept in the nearby flop houses didn't have a choice. Franklin watched the "right side of the tracks" grow smaller in his rearview mirror, *dwindling* into the distance.

The body was no wino. Franklin saw that even before he stepped out of the car. Long blond hair covered her face, but Franklin knew immediately that she was young. She'd been *weaned* from her mother's milk for fewer than the sixteen years he'd been on the force. He could feel his stomach tighten. His *innards* still churned against useless death. It stuck in his *craw* like a fish bone he couldn't swallow. He was an *ornery* cuss, stubborn in tracking a killer. And even though he was aware of the *staggering* number of murders each year, too many to be counted except by computer, he never stopped being overwhelmed by the thought of the victim, a body *severed*, abruptly cut off, from its soul.

The medical examiner was talkative: "Rough one, this. Guy must have been real angry. Real angry. Broke the bones in her legs. Cut clear through the *tendons.* Took the muscles right off 'em. Ripped the *cartilage* out of the knees. Wonder why he went for the fleshy parts?" Franklin wished the M.E. would stop. "That's not how she bought it, though," the M.E. continued. "All that blood soaking her clothes. *Saturates*, it does. That's what killed her. This guy was real angry."

Franklin was no longer listening. Something caught his eye. For the second time, a *vintage* Maserati, a classic car, one of the best ever made, circled the block. A car like that in a neighborhood like this was so laughable as to be *ludicrous.* Franklin had something to go on.

Using Words in Context

One way to make new words a part of your vocabulary is to use them in your own writing. Write a paragraph about an accident you once had or witnessed. Use at least five of the words in the Vocabulary section in your paragraph. Underline them when you proofread.

_____

_____

_____

_____

_____

_____

_____

_____

_____

_____

HINT: HYPERBOLE

Hyperbole (pronounced hy-per'-bo-lee) is the use of exaggeration for effect. We use it all the time:

Q: Are you hungry?   A: I'm starved!
Q: Did you like the movie?   A: I died laughing!

The answers to both questions are *hyperbolic,* that is, obvious exaggerations to emphasize a point.

Villas loads his first paragraph with hyperbole to prod his audience into attention: "To know fried chicken you have to have been weaned and reared on it in the South." We could take Villas literally until he tells us why Southerners know fried chicken so well: "Maybe we have a hidden craw in our throats or oversized pulley bones. . . ." And "any ornery reb has better taste buds for fried chicken than anyone else in the world." Villas's statements are too much to be believed, which probably means they are not meant to be believed. Rather, Villas uses hyperbole to get the audience to pay attention to the directions he is going to give.

Look through "Fried Chicken" and jot down any other words or phrases you think are examples of hyperbole:

_____

_____

_____

Write any hyperbolic expressions you often use:

_____

_____

_____

One of the words Villas uses hyperbolically is *holocaust.* You have already found its two meanings, and your dictionary may also have listed another meaning. In World War II, the Nazis slaughtered more than ten million civilians (among whom were six million Jews, three million gypsies, and one million Catholics), many in specially built gas chambers. This is known as the Holocaust, and the word has come to be associated almost entirely with this event.

Do you think Villas wanted his audience to make this association? _____
Why or why not? _____

Do you agree with Villas's word choice, given this special meaning of the word?
_____ _____

Villas also invokes God and a special context of religious vocabulary in a hyperbolic way. In paragraph 13, he complains about the chickens sold in supermarkets and how different they are from the fowl "God intended us to eat." Does Villas believe that God takes a special interest in the chicken we eat? Then in paragraph 15, he invites the audience to "show the multitudes" the glories of his recipe.

Do you agree with Villas's choice of context? _____

Why or why not? _____

WRITING AND REWRITING

A young woman stops you on the street and asks how to get to the Rialto Theater, or a young man corners you in the laundromat and begs to know how to get his whites whiter and his colors brighter. Clear directions may

Why Are Clear Directions Important?

not seem important when you are the "giver" in a casual encounter, but they may be crucial to the "receiver." For example, the woman may be on her way to audition for her first acting job, and the man may be expecting his parents to visit his new apartment.

Sometimes, however, you may be passionately involved with something, in the way that Jim Villas is with fried chicken. Whether it is decorating cakes, playing baseball, or programming a computer, you will want people to share your passion and do this task correctly.

WRITING: A FIRST DRAFT

Everyone has something that he or she does well. Perhaps it is something world changing like knowing how to splice genes or how to build a nuclear weapon, but it may be a more modest accomplishment like how to get the kitchen floor sparkling clean or how to service a car.

Think of something you do well that you can teach to someone else.

1. Do focused writing teaching someone to do the task you have chosen. Write today's date at the top of a piece of paper. Relax for a moment. Close your eyes. Breathe deeply. As the room starts to get quiet, think about the task or skill you have chosen. See yourself going through the process. Now open your eyes. At the signal, start writing and do not stop for ten minutes. Do not stop to think about where to put information. Just let the ideas flow. DO NOT pause if you are unsure about spelling, punctuation, or grammar. DO NOT stop to look up words in the dictionary. If you get stuck momentarily with nothing in your head, write the word *stuck* until your next idea comes. Okay, begin. After ten minutes, stop. Read what you have written. If you want to add anything, do it now.
2. List all the equipment or ingredients you will need to complete your task.
3. List all the steps in the task.
4. To test the clarity of your directions, give them to someone to read. Ask that person to "walk through" the task.
   a. Can the person follow the procedure accurately?
   b. If not, where does he or she get lost?
5. Revise your draft based on this feedback.

Consider this the first draft of an essay. Put it aside for now. We'll return to it later in the chapter.

WHAT MAKES WRITING GOOD? TOPIC, PURPOSE, AND AUDIENCE; DETAILS; ORDER; AND TONE

Topic, Purpose, and Audience

An effective essay is a combination of an interesting topic and purpose aimed at the appropriate audience. The writer must be interested in the topic. Otherwise why write about it? If you look back to "The Transaction" by William Zinsser in Chapter 1, you will find him saying that writers communicate their enthusiasm about a topic to their audience. And as noted in Chapter 6, you must be clear about your purpose: What do you want to convey about the subject? For instance, suppose you want to write directions for "How to Get the Most Out of Your Exer-Cycle." Are you most interested in emphasizing its weight-reducing capabilities, or do you want to stress its ability to strengthen muscles?

Should Writers Be Interested in the Topics They Write About?

Being clear about your purpose depends heavily on understanding your audience. For whom are you writing? Is your "How to Stop Smoking" geared to the National Cancer Society or the American Tobacco Growers Association? You will need to approach each group differently, taking into consideration what each knows about the topic and is prepared to accept. You may have to modify your purpose to satisfy your audience. Topic, purpose, and audience will therefore influence the order, details, and tone of your paper.

Does the Audience Influence the Purpose?

Details

The amount and variety of details will depend on your topic, purpose, and audience. For example, the directions for "How to Diet Successfully" would differ depending on whether you were writing for an audience of fat people you wish to encourage to try one last diet or for an audience of Weight Watchers graduates you want to encourage to maintain their newfound slimness. You need enough details and of the right kind to enable your audience to follow your directions.

What Do Details Depend on?

You may use personal anecdotes in directions. Your own experience can highlight certain steps in the process your are describing and—like Jim Villas in "Fried Chicken"—can tell your audience your attitude toward your topic.

Order

Consider two kinds of order: the order of the steps in the process and the order of your explanation of the process.

What Are Two Kinds of Order?

What is the proper order for the steps in a task? Some tasks are clearly sequential: one step follows another. For instance, if you are making an omelet, you must break the eggs before you beat them. In other tasks the order of the steps may be optional. Some photographers, for example, (those who still use nonautomatic cameras) set their lens opening first and then the shutter speed. Others reverse the order. When you have a choice, you impose an order the audience should follow.

There's more to your essay than just the steps in the task. You may include extra details, a way to interest the audience, and a list of everything necessary to carry out the directions. (For example, you can't teach "How to Make an Omelet" without eggs!) You will probably establish separate paragraphs, each focused on one kind of information.

What Are Transitions?

Often you will want to use *transitions* to link two ideas in the process or two paragraphs in the paper. Transitions are word or sentence bridges that help the audience move from one idea to another. For example:

To Relate Ideas that Follow in Time	To Relate Ideas that Result from Others	To Summarize Ideas
first (second, third, last, and so on)	and so	all in all
then	because of this	in summary
in addition	as a consequence	in conclusion
furthermore	as a result	on the whole
moreover	consequently	
also	so	
as well	therefore	
besides	thus	
next		
finally		
lastly		

Tone

What Is Tone?

Tone refers to your choice of words that conveys your feelings about your topic. Words show your enthusiasm as well as your distaste. Jim Villas makes his feelings very clear about who can and cannot cook and understand fried chicken. Each writer decides how much and what kind of feelings to show through his or her choice of words. Again, the relationship among the topic, purpose, and audience helps you set the tone.

Do These Exercises Before You Revise Your First Draft.

Practice Choosing Topic, Purpose, and Audience

1. List ten tasks you could describe. They may range, for example, from "How to Make a Persistent Suitor Give Up and Go Away" to "How to Operate an IBM Personal Computer." Indicate your feeling about each topic.

Topic	Interesting	Dull	Undecided
_____			
_____			
_____			
_____			
_____			
_____			
_____			
_____			
_____			

2. Write a short statement of purpose for each "interesting" topic, declaring what you want to convey about each.

Topic	Purpose
_____	_____
	_____
_____	_____
	_____
_____	_____
	_____
_____	_____
	_____

3. Below is a list of potential audiences for your directions. Specify where necessary, and add others. Make sure that any audiences you add differ in some significant way from those already listed (for example, at least ten years of age, degree of intimacy with you, job they hold).

a. classmates _____

b. family members (specify) _____

c. mayor or other public figure (specify) _____

d. newspaper or magazine (specify) _____

e. close friend (specify) _____

f. teacher (specify level of school, subject) _____

g. other _____

Now experiment with some combinations of topic, purpose, and audience. Use the "interesting" topics you devised. Add the purpose and audience. We've given you one as a sample. (Remember that sometimes it is enough of a purpose to want to share your knowledge and enjoyment of something with another person.)

Topic	*Audience*	*Purpose*
how to do laundry	people who live alone	to simplify a common chore
_____	_____	_____
_____	_____	_____
_____	_____	_____
_____	_____	_____
_____	_____	_____
_____	_____	_____
_____	_____	_____

Practice with Details

The following are abridged versions of the lists of equipment and ingredients from "Fried Chicken."

Equipment	*Ingredients*
knife	milk
cutting board	lemon
pot	shortening
bowl	grease
skillet	chicken
tongs	flour
paper towels	salt
bags	pepper
can	
platter	
whisk	
fire extinguisher	

Were you able to follow Villas's instructions with these lists? Why or why not? _____

_____

Star the items that need more detail to be useful.
Now compare these lists with Villas's originals. What general kinds of information are missing from the abridged lists?

_____   _____

_____   _____

_____   _____

Practice Adding Details According to Topic, Purpose, and Audience

Indicate the audience you want to address. Then check the appropriate answer in the yes/no/maybe column, and explain your reasoning. Be prepared to defend your choices.

In a Set of Directions for	Should You Include	For what Audience	Yes/No/ Maybe	Why
climbing a mountain	description of the beauties of the countryside; how you got started mountain climbing.			
riding a bike	anecdote on how you broke your leg while learning to ride; statement that you were once afraid to ride but overcame your fear.			
organizing an antinuke rally	story of Gandhi; description of a nuclear reactor; anecdote about your previous participation in similar rallies.			
producing a play	your dreams of being a producer; description of "backstage."			

Practice Ordering the Steps of a Task

Below are scrambled versions of two tasks. Put the steps in order. Be prepared to defend your choices.

HOW TO DIAPER A BABY

Correct Order

_____ **1.** Place clean diaper under baby.

_____ **2.** Place baby on any flat surface, such as a bed, the floor, or a changing table.

_____ **3.** Place fresh diaper, washcloth (or paper "wet wipes"), and baby powder within easy reach.

_____ **4.** Clean baby.

_____ **5.** Put waterproof sheet under baby.

_____ **6.** Remove old diaper.

_____ **7.** Strap baby down or hold with free hand.

_____ **8.** Secure diaper (pins with cloth; tabs with disposable).

HOW TO PLAY RUMMY

_____ **1.** Turn over top card and place next to pack.

_____ **2.** Remove jokers.

_____ **3.** Player to dealer's left may take overturned card or pick from deck and keep or discard this or any other card from his or her hand.

_____ **4.** Start with deck of fifty-two playing cards.

_____ **5.** Stack remaining cards face down on table.

_____ **6.** Next player may pick up last discarded card or pick from deck and so forth until someone reaches the object of the game.

_____ **7.** Deal one card at a time, face down, to each player, beginning with player on dealer's left. Repeat until each player has seven cards.

_____ **8.** Shuffle deck.

_____ **9.** Object of game: To obtain a combination of a "run" of three or more cards of the same suit (like the four, five, six, and seven of diamonds) and three or four of a kind (three fours, fives, or whatever).

Practice Ordering a Process Paper

1. The numbers below correspond to the paragraph numbers in Villas's "Fried Chicken." Reread the selection, and next to each number, jot down the purpose of the paragraph.

(1) *introductory: get audience attention* _____ (9) _____

(2) _____ (10) _____

(3) _____ (11) _____

(4) _____ (12) _____

(5) _____ (13) _____

(6) _____ (14) _____

(7) _____ (15) _____

(8) _____

Do you think Villas's order makes sense? _____ yes; _____ no. Do you think any of the paragraphs could have been left out? _____ yes; _____ no. Star the numbers of the paragraphs you think could have been omitted.

2. Column A lists the information often found in the paragraphs of a set of directions. Column B shows the "empty" paragraphs necessary to a set of directions; column C shows "empty" paragraphs considered optional. Write the appropriate letter for each kind of information (from column A) into the boxes in columns B and C. Then draw arrows to show where into column B the paragraphs from column C would fit.

A-*Information*   B-*Necessary*   C-*Optional*

a. equipment
b. steps in process
c. get audience atten-
   tion
d. anecdote
e. results of process
f. miscellaneous infor-
   mation
g. background or his-
   tory of process
h. alternative process

Practice Using Transitions

Write the appropriate transitions in the blanks in this process paper. Consult the list of transitions in the Order Section.

HOW TO SET A TABLE

Setting an attractive table may seem to you like a skill needed only by bored housewives, but it is really a task work doing to make one's guests feel welcome. Whoever they are—friends, roommates, family members—they will enjoy their meal more and appreciate your thoughtfulness.

You need only the standard equipment: knives, forks, spoons, plates, napkins, and glasses or cups. The number of each item will, obviously, depend on how many people you intend to serve. For the most simple meals, one utensil of each kind per person will do. If you are serving soup, you will want to add a large spoon per person; for a first course or dessert, add either a fork or spoon each, or both, depending on what you serve. *Hint:* If your silverware is in limited supply, be prepared to sneak into the kitchen and wash utensils between courses. Don't worry! It's done even in the best of families.

To set your table, _____ lay out your plates in the places on the table where each person will sit. _____, position the forks to the left of the plate and the knives and spoons to the right—the knife next to the plate and the spoon next to the knife. The bottom edge of each utensil should _____ be even with the bottom edge of the plate. _____ the bottom of each place setting will be a straight line. _____, arrange your napkins in your favorite style. The simplest method is to fold each one in half and place it, lengthwise, to the left of or on top of the forks. Some people like to fold napkins into flower shapes and put them on the dinner plate. _____, place your cups or glasses above your plates—wine glasses above the knife, water and juice glasses above the fork. Coffee cups may be placed directly above the plate, in the middle of the setting.

_____, you may want to add some decorative touches. Candles are an attractive addition to any table, even if they are simple utility candles melted into a small, flat plate. One or two flowers, even in a juice glass, look romantic _____. _____, none of this is too difficult, and it is a nice way to welcome friends and family to your table.

Practice with Tone

Each of the paragraphs below could be the opening paragraph of a process paper, the paragraph that grabs the audience's attention and sets the tone for the essay. As you read each one, decide whether or not the tone is appropriate to the topic, purpose, and audience. If not, rewrite the paragraph. (You may also want to suggest an alternative audience to which this tone would be more appropriate.) In the space provided, explain your reasons for your decision.

1. Topic: How to choose a nursing home
Purpose: Provide information about alternatives
Audience: Children of aging parents

> Most nursing homes are the pits. They're filthy, vermin infested, and the inmates—clients, they're called—are not in much better shape. They walk around in dirty clothes, eyes vacant. They linger in hallways waiting for nonexistent relatives to visit them or flop in the dayroom, staring at the blank TV. Surly attendants toss rotten food at them, and half the time there's no one available to help an old person to the bathroom. You know what happens then. If you want better than this, you've got to invest a lot of time and money to find a decent place.

Appropriate: _____ yes _____ no

Analysis/Explanation: _____

_____

_____

_____

Rewrite: _____

_____

_____

_____

_____

2. Topic: How to recharge a car battery
Purpose: Informational
Audience: People who drive cars

You think it can never happen to you, but you suddenly find yourself kicking the you-know-what out of yourself and your car. You left your lights on overnight, and when you get to the car in the morning, the battery is dead. It's raining. The AAA says it can't send a truck for an hour, and you have to get to work. Not to worry. If you are properly prepared and not too chicken to flag down a passing car, you can recharge your own battery.

Appropriate: _____ yes _____ no

Analysis/Explanation: _____

_____

_____

_____

Rewrite: _____

_____

_____

_____

_____

_____

3. Topic: How to sell real estate
Purpose: To encourage young people to enter the field
Audience: College students at a campus career conference

Don't waste your time finishing school. Smarts are what count, not the degree. You can start right now. This is the way to go. I used to be a teacher, and I earned $20,000. Now I sell houses to teachers, and I earn more than double that. So get with it. Start selling real estate today.

Appropriate: _____ yes _____ no

Analysis/Explanation: _____

_____

_____

_____

Rewrite: _____

_____

_____

_____

_____

_____

REWRITING: THE SECOND DRAFT

Now you are ready to turn your focused writing into a second draft. Read it carefully, aloud, and, if you can, to a friend or classmate. Try to get a new vision of your subject. As you rewrite, consider whether or not you want or need a main-point statement, whether or not your voice is conveying what you want it to. You should also

1. *Revise for topic, purpose, and audience.* Make sure you have a topic that interests you. Decide what you want your audience to know, and gear your presentation to that particular person or set of people.

2. *Revise for order.* Put the steps in your task in an order your audience can follow. Structure the paragraphs of the entire presentation so that they interest the reader and make sense.
3. *Revise for transitions.* Where needed, use transitional words or phrases to move the audience from one idea to another.
4. *Revise for detail.* Use enough steps in your directions to satisfy your audience. Include anecdotes and descriptions where you think they will help stimulate the audience's interest and understanding.
5. *Revise for tone.* Choose words that reflect your feelings and that are appropriate to your topic, purpose, and audience.

When you finish a satisfactory middle draft, make a clean copy. Go on to the next section, where you'll get help on the proofreading stages of your writing.

PROOFREADING

NOUNS AND THEIR PLURALS

In Chapter 3 we defined a noun as

a word that identifies a person, place, thing, or idea.

What Is a Noun?

Words like *man, lamp, computer,* and *sanity* are *common nouns.* They answer the questions *who* or *what.* (If the answers to these questions are *proper nouns,* names like John and Atari, you capitalize them.)
A noun can function as the subject of a sentence. In the sentence

My aunt fixes fried chicken every Saturday.

How Do Nouns Function in a Sentence?

the word *aunt* is a noun that identifies a person. It answers the question *who* (Who fixes fried chicken? My aunt.) It also functions as the subject of this sentence.

Nouns can have other functions in sentences. They can be the objects of verbs or prepositions. In the example sentence, the word *chicken* is a noun that identifies a thing. It answers the question *what,* and it functions as the object of the verb *fixes.*

There are several ways to identify nouns:

How Can We Identify Nouns?

1. Most nouns change their spelling to form the plural:

singular	*plural*
hat	hats
party	par*ties*
fresh*man*	fresh*men*

309

2. Most nouns change their spelling to show possession:

Sam	Sam's
baby	baby's
car	car's

3. The words *a, an,* or *the* can often introduce a singular noun:

love	a love (or the love)
building	a building (or the building)
umbrella	an umbrella (or the umbrella)

4. The words *this, that, these,* and *those* can often introduce a noun:

people	these people (or those people)
desk	this desk (or that desk)

You may become confused by a word you recognize as a noun that can also function as another part of speech. For example, the word *store* is a noun when it identifies a place where merchandise is sold, but it also can function as a verb when it means to gather and put something away for future use. In the sentence below, *store* is used as a noun and a verb. Circle the noun and underline the verb:

The clerk was told to store the unsold Christmas ornaments in the back room of the store.

HINT: NOUNS AS ADJECTIVES

If you were asked what kinds of words *brick, glass,* and *computer* are, you would probably say that they were nouns because they identify things, for example,

*Many people live in houses made of **brick** and **glass**.*
*My neighbor bought a new keyboard for his **computer**.*

However, knowing what part of speech a word is does not always tell you how the word functions in a sentence. Sometimes nouns can function as adjectives. That is, nouns can be used to describe other nouns, just as adjectives do. It is easy to be confused by words we recognize as nouns that seem to be

---

functioning as adjectives. Notice how *brick*, *glass*, and *computer* function as adjectives:[2]

> People who live in **glass** houses shouldn't throw stones at **brick** houses.
> My neighbor's **computer** keyboard had to be repaired.

Making Nouns Plural

What Is the Most Common Way of Making a Noun Plural?

The most common way to make a noun plural is to add an *s* or *es* ending to the noun. For example:

The crowd overflowed the theater for the Michael Jackson concert.
*The crowd**s** overflowed the theater**s** for the Michael Jackson concert**s**.*

Had my wish been granted, I'd have gone to the beach.
*Had my wish**es** been granted, I'd have gone to all the beach**es** on the island.*

You probably know these standard English plural forms but do not always use them. You may proofread your essays without noticing that you have not added a plural ending to a word that calls for it. Proofreading more carefully—preferably aloud—helps solve this problem.

You may have difficulty using standard English plural forms because you use different forms in your conversational speech or dialect. See Appendix 5 for a discussion of dialect usage.

Practice with Nouns and Their Plurals

1. Underline all the nouns. (For additional practice, circle the subject of each sentence.) We've done the first one for you.

College freshmen experience many differences between high school and college. At first, many students find it difficult to adjust to college.

The atmosphere of a college campus, be it on a rolling hill in West Virginia or in an office building in downtown Chicago, is much freer than high school. Men and women gather in lounges, cafeterias, hallways, and quadrangles. Their behavior is not restricted, except for rules of common

---

[2] When a noun is used as an adjective, it is called an *attributive noun*. That is, like an adjective, the noun is used to identify a characteristic or an attribute of another noun.

decency and personal safety. In high school, there is usually no place for students to relax together, and their behavior is controlled much more.

No one tells college students when or if they should attend class. There are no monitors or deans patrolling the hallways with report slips. Moreover, many college professors do not even take attendance in their classes. This, again, is a big change from high school, where hallways are patrolled and attendance is taken scrupulously.

Further, college instructors expect students to budget their time appropriately and be prepared for exams. Teachers seldom remind students of assignments or tests once a syllabus has been distributed. This sheet is the students' only guide to when their work is due. Students coming straight from high school are used to teachers who hound them for assignments and guide them in every detail.

Many young people who move directly from a high school to a college find this freedom too much to handle. They are used to being told not to smoke and not to cut classes, and they rely on teachers to tell them to be prompt and to study. Without these guidelines, freshmen get confused and depressed. The lucky ones find their way into a counselor's office or capture the attention of a sympathetic professor. The unlucky ones are likely to drop out.

2. Below is a description of the "plain people" of Pennsylvania. After the first paragraph, most of the nouns are written in their singular form. Read the passage carefully. Change the singular nouns to their plural forms wherever it makes sense to do so. Changes in some other words will also be necessary.

Lancaster, Pennsylvania, is the center of "Pennsylvania Dutch" country, an area populated by groups of German (*Dutch* was a mispronunciation of the word *Deutsch*, which means "German.") Protestants. Among the "plain people" are Mennonites, Brethren, and the Amish.

The plain person prefers a simple way of life that preserves his tradition. Thus, a plain person uses no electricity in his home. A home is lit by candlelight. Each article of furniture is handcrafted. A chair is most often a high-backed, wooden chair with a rush seat. A plain person does not watch a television or listen to a radio. His contact with the outside world is limited. A plain person works his farm with a horse-drawn tractor and drives a horse-drawn buggy. Driving through Bird-in-Hand or Intercourse, the tourist often finds herself behind the gray, boxlike buggy with an orange, metallic triangle indicating "slow traffic." Only recently has the plain person agreed to use this symbol, and now only for the public good. The symbol was originally thought to imply more contact with the world than the plain person wanted. The plain person is, however, polite to a more modern driver. He will move his buggy to the right of the road when traffic permits to allow a more modern conveyance to pass.

A plain person dresses in plain garb that satisfies his desire for simplicity and modesty. A male wears a hat, a cloth one for a man and a straw one for a boy, a black cloth jacket and trousers, and a white shirt. An adult man wears a beard because of a biblical injunction against shaving the hair on his face. A female wears a gray or black long dress with a white collar and cuff. The head covering varies from sect to sect, but each girl and woman keeps her head covered. An Amish woman wears a dark bonnet that shades her face and ties under her chin.

3. Look up these singular nouns in the dictionary, and write down their plural forms.

alumnus	_____	appendix	_____	basis	_____
bus	_____	criterion	_____	datum	_____
dwarf	_____	edifice	_____	fish	_____
foot	_____	incubus	_____	ibex	_____
larva	_____	louse	_____	medium	_____
mouse	_____	ox	_____	parenthesis	_____
phenomenon	_____	quiz	_____	sheep	_____
scarf	_____	tooth	_____	truth	_____
Vietnamese	_____	wharf	_____		

4. Read this process paper twice. The second time, proofread it, and change any inappropriate noun forms.

HOW TO FIGURE OUT YOUR HOROSCOPE

Everybody has a horoscope signs, although only some people care about them. Those who do regulate their life around them; the others ignore them. Your horoscope is the position of the planets and stars, in relation to one another, at the moments of your birth. According to astrologers, this configurations can influence many important aspect of your life.

To figure out your horoscope, you must know the exact dates of your birth and the times of your birth. (It is also important to know where you were born because of the time changes across the United States and the world. Suppose you were born in Omaha, Nebraska, at 6 P.M. on July 11. That is in the central time zone and would be daylight savings time because it is summer. These factors make a difference to your sign.)

Armed with this knowledge, you can consult any astrological charts to find out your "sun sign," which is based on your date of birth. What you will find are twelve sign, which run roughly from the twenty-first day of one month to the twenty-first day of the next month, for instance, June 21 to July 21, inclusive. If you were born on the first or the last day of the months, you need to know the exact longitudes and latitude of your birthplace to determine whether or not the sun had already moved into the next signs. Otherwise, you might spend your entire life thinking you were a Libra if you were born on October 23, when in fact, you are a Scorpio. Some difference!

Once you have established exactly what your sign is, you must start to gather information about that sign and apply its general principles to yourself. Remember that horoscope sign are very general. They are based only on the position of the sun, which is very general, and not on the position of the moon and the other planets. Therefore, the informations you gather about yourself from your sun sign can be applied only in general terms. Your horoscope may say that all Leo men are egotistical, and you are too self-effacing for words; your horoscope may say that all Aquarian womens are realistic, and you always have your head in a cloud. These discrepancy do not invalidate all the information about your sign. You may find many similarity between what you know about yourself and element of looks, personalities, and behaviors you find in your horoscope.

You may never become a person who makes dates only on "good days" or cancels a business meeting because it is a "wary day." However, could you resist buying a lottery ticket on the day your horoscope reads, "Today is the day for fame and fortune"?

PRONOUNS AND THEIR ANTECEDENTS

**What Is a
Pronoun?**

In Chapter 3 we defined a pronoun as

a word that stands for or replaces a noun.

It, he, they, and *who* are pronouns. Each can replace a noun. For example, the pronoun *it* can replace the noun *book:*

*The girl brought the **book** to class and gave **it** to the teacher.*

**What Is an
Antecedent?**

The noun that the pronoun refers to is its *antecedent.*[3] In the preceding example, *book* is the antecedent of *it.* The antecedent usually comes before but can also be somewhere near the pronoun it stands for. The antecedent can be in the same sentence:

***Mary** worried because **she** didn't know if **she** could pass the test.*

Or it can be in a previous sentence:

***People** should not cross the street without first looking in both directions. **They** risk their lives when **they** don't observe approaching cars.*

Pronoun Agreement

**In What Ways
Must a Pronoun
Agree with Its
Antecedent?**

A pronoun must agree with its antecedent in number, gender, and person. *Number* means that the pronoun is either singular or plural. For example, *she* can refer to a singular noun like *Mary,* and *they* can refer to a plural noun like *students.*

Singular	Plural
he (his, him) *she* (her, hers)	*they* (their, theirs, them)
it (its)	
I (my, me, mine)	*we* (our, ours, us)
you (your, yours)	*you* (your, yours)

Notice that the pronoun *you* can be both singular and plural:

***Students,** I want all of **you** to read The Catcher in the Rye by J. D. Salinger.*

*It is a book any **student** will enjoy, and each of **you** is just the right age to identify with the main character.*

The following are some examples of singular and plural pronouns and their antecedents:

---

[3] Remember that the prefix *ante* means "before."

*In the book, **Holden Caulfield** loves **his** sister **Phoebe** because **she** is "real."*

*He dislikes most other **people** because **they** are "phony."*

*And he detests his **school** most of all because of **its** phoniness. **Holden and Phoebe** manage merely to tolerate **their** parents and most other adults.*

*Holden longs to be a "catcher in the rye" and save **children** from **their** miserable fate in the adult world.*

Gender means that pronouns can be masculine, feminine, or neuter. Neuter refers to words that cannot be classed as masculine or feminine, such as *chair, table, bottles, desks, happiness,* or *misery.*

What Is Gender?

Masculine	*Feminine*	*Neuter*
he (his, him) *you* (your, yours), *they* (their, theirs, them)	*she* (her, hers), *you* (your, yours) *they* (their, theirs, them)	*it* (its), *they* (their, theirs, them)

Notice that the pronoun *you* can refer to both males and females and that *they* can refer to both people and things. Here are some examples of pronouns that match their antecedents in gender:

    Masculine: *Jack* wanted *his* shoes shined.
                   Hank, do *you* know the answer to this question?
                   Some of the *men* lied to *their* wives.
     Feminine: *Maxine* sews most of *her* dresses.
                   Kim, do *you* have to see *your* doctor again next week?
                   All of the *women* wanted *their* leadership abilities recognized.
       Neuter: He didn't want to buy the *car* because *it* had too many
                   dents in *its* fenders.
                   Both of the *tables* were returned to the store because *they*
                   were damaged during shipment.

Another type of agreement between a pronoun and its antecedent is *person.* In this sense, the word *person* is a grammatical term used to indicate the following:

1. *First person* indicates the person or persons speaking (I, we). For example: *I* am a student. *We* are high school graduates.
2. *Second person* indicates the person or persons spoken to (you). For example: *You* are my best friend. *You* all are in this together.
3. *Third person* indicates the person (or persons) or thing (or things) spoken about (he, she, it, they). For example: *He* is the captain of

the debating team. *She* is a straight-A student. *They* make a good couple.

First Person	*Second Person*	*Third Person*
I (my, me)	*you* (your)	*he* (his, him)
we (our, us)		*she* (her)
		it (its)
		they (their, them)

When you need to check your pronoun–antecedent agreement, follow these steps:

1. Find the antecedent. (Make sure you have one.)
2. Determine the antecedent's number—singular or plural.
3. Determine the antecedent's gender—masculine, feminine, or neuter.
4. Determine the antecedent's person—first, second, or third.
5. Select a pronoun that agrees with the results of steps 2, 3, and 4.

HINT

Sometimes two or more singular nouns are joined by *and;* they are then considered plural and require a plural pronoun. For example:

> **Susan and Harvey** said **they** needed more time to study for the test.

Some Pronoun Agreement Problems

How Can We Avoid Vague and Ambiguous Pronouns?

Lack of agreement between pronouns and their antecedents can confuse the reader because it's hard to tell what the writer is talking about.

1. Vague Pronouns

A pronoun is vague when it has no direct antecedent:

*In my high school **they** do not allow the students to be late more than five times.*

Who are *they?* This question need not arise if the vague pronoun is replaced by a specific noun:

In my high school the teachers do not allow the students to be late more than five times.

Make changes in the following excerpt from a student paper to clarify the vague pronouns:

Another reason that I don't like hamburgers is that I cannot bear to think of the cows they kill to get the meat to make the hamburgers. I was not so much against hamburgers until the summer of 1982 when I got a job in a fast-food restaurant and saw for myself how they prepare the food. I got sick to my stomach and quit a few weeks after. Since then the hamburger joints have never made a dime from me again.

2. Ambiguous Antecedents

What Is an Ambiguous Antecedent?

Each pronoun should have an obvious antecedent. Sometimes the antecedent is present but ambiguous:

*John told Harry that **he** needed a haircut.*

Who needs a haircut, Harry or John? It is not clear, as the pronoun *he* can refer to either John or Harry. The revised version is clear:

John told Harry that Harry needed a haircut.

There is also a confusing pronoun in this sentence:

*Gerard sat beside Eric and fixed **his** tie.*

Whose tie did Gerard fix, Eric's or his own? Revise this sentence to eliminate the problem of ambiguous antecedents:

_____

3. Shifting Pronouns

What Is Wrong With Shifting Pronouns?

Abruptly shifting pronouns changes the focus of the writing. In the passage below, the writer shifts the focus from himself (my, I), to the audience (you), and then back to himself (me).

> *My* reading is not too good. *I* like to read only mystery stories. Textbooks bore *me.* As soon as *you* start reading one of them, *you* get tired and sleepy. Reading makes *me* fall asleep right away.

It's best to stick to one focus:

> *My* reading is not too good. *I* like to read only mystery stories. Textbooks bore *me.* As soon as *I* start reading one of them, *I* get tired and sleepy. It makes *me* fall asleep right away.

You should avoid shifting pronouns when you want to make a general statement about someone or something. Notice the use of *their* and *you* in these sentences:

*If a person reads many books, **their** reading will improve.*
*Once a person learns how to ride a bicycle, **you** never forget.*

Although the general statements are true (most of us improve our reading as we read more; most of us never forget how to ride a bike), you must be careful that the pronouns and antecedents agree in number, gender, and person. Rewrite these statements as

*If a **person** reads many books, **his** or **her** reading will improve.*[4] OR
*If **people** read many books, **their** reading will improve.*

*Once a **person** learns how to ride a bicycle, **he** or **she** never forgets. OR*
*Once **people** learn how to ride a bicycle, **they** never forget. OR*
*Once **you** learn how to ride a bicycle, **you** never forget.*

4. Unnecessary Pronouns

Sometimes pronouns are used unnecessarily. One example is a "double subject":

*My **Mother, she** always helps me with my problems.*

Only one subject—the noun—is needed; the pronoun should be omitted:

*My **mother** always helps me with my problems.*

The inclusion of a pronoun with a noun as antecedent is also unnecessary in these sentences:

*I strongly believe that America, **it** is ready for a new president.*

*By her doing volunteer work **it** made her a better person.*

These sentences should be rewritten as

I strongly believe that America is ready for a new president.

Doing volunteer work made her a better person.

---

[4] For years writers used the pronoun *he* when the gender of the antecedent was not specified. The feminist movement has changed that! Now writers use *he or she* or *he/she*. To avoid this sometimes-clumsy construction, you can simply make your antecedent noun plural and use the pronoun *they*, which can refer to either males or females.

Indefinite Pronouns

Indefinite pronouns are those that do not refer to a specific person or thing. Below is a list of some of them. Can you think of others?

What Are Indefinite Pronouns?

anyone	everybody	nothing
anything	everyone	one
anybody	everything	some
another	none	something
somebody	someone	

_____	_____	_____
_____	_____	_____

In this excerpt from a journal, a student plays with indefinite pronouns:

> I heard a very interesting story today about four people: Everybody, Somebody, Anybody, and Nobody. Here's how the story goes. There was an important job to be done, and Everybody was asked to do it. Everybody was sure that Somebody would do it. Anybody could have done it, but Nobody did it. Somebody got angry about that because it was Everybody's job. Everbody thought Anybody could do it, but Nobody realized that Everybody wouldn't do it. It ended up that Everybody blamed Somebody when actually Nobody asked Anybody.
>
> When I heard this, it was so funny, but when I thought about it, it is really a fact that people stuck stuck stuck this free writing is too, but then again I could never forget a story like this.

Pronouns can be antecedents for other pronouns. Indefinite pronouns are often antecedents for personal pronouns. Most indefinite pronouns are singular; the clue is that most of them end in *body* or *one*. However, you must always be aware of the intent of indefinite pronouns in a sentence. That is, you should use a singular pronoun to refer to an indefinite pronoun whose intent is singular:

Write	*Instead of*
Somebody left *his* or *her* books on the desk.	*Somebody* left *their* books on the desk.
Everybody wanted *his* or *her* picture taken.	*Everybody* wanted *their* picture taken.
No *one* should yell out *his* or *her* answers.	No *one* should yell out *their* answers.
Everyone fixed *his* or *her* own lunch for the picnic.	*Everyone* fixed *their* own lunch for the picnic.

"Dummy" Pronouns

Pronouns do not always have antecedents:

It is a sunny day.
It is going to rain.

In these sentences the pronoun *it* is a "dummy filler" that functions as the subject of the verb. *It* does not have an antecedent. Another word that sometimes functions in this way is *there:*

There is nothing on the table.

Practice with Pronouns and Their Antecedents

1. Read this passage. Circle the personal pronouns, and draw an arrow from the pronoun to its antecedent.

On *its* "Swap the Old Lady for a New Woman" page, the magazine

New Woman defines the term *old lady* as an attitude that women have

toward themselves in relation to their men. In the April 1984 issue, three

actresses expressed their feelings:

Zsa Zsa Gabor said that for her, "To a smart girl, men are no problem;

they're the answer."

Mitzi Gaynor advised a woman that to get along with her man, she

has to play his game. "If he likes watching sports, start off the game by

sitting on his lap. If he likes to eat, learn to be a good cook."

And Raquel Welch contributed, "A smart wife is one who knows

her body is a temple, and she'd better take care of it or her husband will

worship somewhere else."

On that same page, *New Woman* gives a "Thump on the Head

to . . ." the novelist Taylor Caldwell, who has stated her opinion on women

as follows: "I don't like women, I never did. . . . Women are the inferior

sex in every way. . . . With all the opportunity in the world—all the leisure—

all the shelter—if women had any genius, it would've come out. It never did."

These attitudes differ from those that *New Woman*'s editors listed in the "Sounds Like a New Woman" column, represented here by the writer Meridel Le Sueur, who said at the age of eighty-four, "I don't admit age. I call it ripening. Like all of nature, we are transformed into future seed. Ripening has distinct advantages for women—they have a chance to regain their full identity as a person."

2. Write the appropriate pronoun in the blanks. We've done the first one for you. Remember that pronouns must agree with their antecedents in number, gender, and person. When you think that using a pronoun might be too vague or ambiguous, use a noun.

    Personal pronouns: I (my, me, mine); you (your, yours); he (his, him); she (her, hers); it (its); we (our, ours, us); they (their, theirs)

    Indefinite pronouns: another, anyone, anything, anybody, another, everybody, everyone, everything, one, none, nothing, one, some, somebody, someone

HOW TO MAKE ICE CUBES

This is an old recipe that ___*my*___ family has used for generations. Perhaps _____ is also an old _____ in _____. Although not a complicated recipe, _____ requires patience, if not skill. _____ in _____ family has learned _____ over the years. Children, at about the time of _____ fifth birthday are initiated into the rite by _____ in the family who is older than _____ are, although not necessarily wiser. Almost _____ can learn the process, but to do _____ correctly, _____ must have certain equipment and follow certain steps.

First, _____ need to have drinkable water. (What's the point of making ice out of water that will give you dysentery?) _____ also need a freezer or a refrigerator with a freezer. _____ is preferable to have trays in which to form the ice, although _____ can be made in any metal or plastic container. *Hint:* Do not use glass containers to make ice. _____ have a tendency to expand and crack, thus making _____ and the ice unusable.

_____ are ready to begin. Fill _____ container with water to about one-quarter inch from the top. Open the freezer door. (Sometimes this operation requires only one hand, but _____ sometimes needs two; _____ must be prepared for both eventualities, or have _____ else nearby to assist.) The next step is crucial: Carefully raise the ice tray and place _____ in the freezer, so that the _____ bottom is level, being careful not to tip _____ so that water spills over _____ hand or into the freezer. When _____ say crucial, _____ mean it! How many times _____ remember hearing _____ mother singing as _____ worked in _____ the kitchen. Then _____ would hear a scream. When _____ came running to see what had happened, _____ was standing at the refrig-erator, _____ hand in the freezer, staring at a puddle on the floor _____ had created by tipping the ice tray. "_____ can learn," _____ would say, shaking her head, "but _____ must continue to be careful each time."

Assuming _____ have reached this point, _____ are ready to finish the process. Close the freezer door tightly and let the water stand for at least two hours. After an hour _____ may check the progress of the ice by putting _____ finger gently into _____. If _____ breaks through _____ and gets freezing and soaking wet, _____ are not finished.

3. Change all the nouns to their plural forms and make all the necessary changes in pronoun forms, verb endings, and any other words. Remember to delete any unnecessary words.

A joke is a great social icebreaker at a dance. It allows the teller a ritual opening line for conversation ("Did you ever hear the one about . . . ?"), and at the same time it enables the listener to enter the conversation with an easy reply ("No."). This simple mechanism, the joke, also provides a total stranger with insight into his companion. For instance, from the teller's point of view, he knows as soon as he has finished the joke whether or not the person he is talking to has a sense of humor and whether it matches his own. The listener finds out not only about the other person's humor but also about his character. The person who tells a joke to a stranger must be pretty secure about his own personality and his ability to tell a joke; otherwise, he is a fool. Either characteristic quickly becomes apparent. At the end of the joke, assuming that the listener has stayed around that long, each person in the conversation can decide what he wants to do. A joke helps establish a sound basis for continuing a conversation or a reason for ending one.

4. Find the vague pronouns in this student paper. Change each to make clear what it refers to.

The transit system is inefficient. Half of the time the trains are never on time. The platforms and cars are always dirty. The prices for tokens are too doggone high for the service you get and the protection is lousy.

Anytime I take the transit system there always seems to be a mechanical problem. There's either a train ahead of us or it has to go out of service because of mechanical difficulties. This gets me very angry. First of all they need to have more modern trains and take out these old trains which are of no use.

If I pay ninety cents for a token,[5] the least they can offer me is that the trains come on time and not to have me wait for the train for a half hour. I leave my job at eleven o'clock at night, but the train seems to slow down in the late hours. Why do they do this? I will never know. I feel that if they're going to decrease the service in the night, then they can decrease the token fare at night also.

The platforms are so dirty, and the train floors are so messy with garbage. They need to hire more people to clean up the subway platforms and the train floors. Also they need to clean up the subway tracks so this way they will have fewer subway fires on the track.

When I take the train to come to school in the morning, there is an abundance of cops on the trains and on the platform. When I leave work to come home it seems like they're all off duty. The nighttime is the worst time to take the train home because that's when something most likely will happen to you. I remember one night I was coming home

[5] In New York City, transit riders must purchase tokens to gain entrance to the trains.

from work. I was by myself getting ready to get on the train. These two big burly guys were getting off. One of them took my hat off my head and threw it onto the train tracks. I got so scared I said to myself, "Where are the cops when you need them?"

Each night when I leave work to come home. I pray that I will reach home safely. Luckily, nothing drastic has ever happened to me. I hope it will always remain this way until the transit system becomes safer.

5. Write in the appropriate pronouns in these examples of folk wisdom.

    a. If you give a dance, _____ have to pay the band.

    b. Anyone can get what _____ wants, if _____ tries.

    c. Once a person learns how to swim, _____ never forgets.

    d. Am I _____ brother's keeper?

    e. Someone who sticks _____ nose into other people's business is apt to get a sore nose.

    f. A fool and _____ money are soon parted.

    g. Everyone has a right to _____ own opinion.

    h. Some people cannot keep _____ mouths shut.

    i. None of us is perfect, but _____ of us aren't so bad either.

    j. Everyone should mind _____ own business.

    k. A man's best friend is _____ dog.

    l. When opportunity knocks on a person's door, _____ should not hesitate to open _____.

    m. God bless the child that's got _____ own.

    n. Don't count your chickens before _____ are hatched.

o. The person who pays the piper is the _____ who calls the tune.

p. A man's home is _____ castle.

6. Proofread this discussion of mental health and self-image. Make sure that all pronouns agree with their antecedents in number, gender, and person. Change any vague or ambiguous pronouns, and delete any overused pronouns. Make sure the focus of the pronouns remains consistent.

MENTAL HEALTH AND SELF-IMAGE

Mental health professionals believe that positive self-concept is the key to mental health in this ever-changing society we inhabit. Everything else around the individual is moving too fast for you to use as an anchor for mental health. Jobs, which people used to hold for a lifetime, are too fluid for one to attach any permanent significance to. Even housing is now too mobile to serve a person as a symbol of its security. Thus, the only stability one can find is within himself.

Self-image, then, it is the only thing a person can hold on to because it is the only thing that cannot be taken away. It may change in time, as an individual matures, but they cannot take it away from you because it is within the individual.

Thus, it is important that a person safeguards their feelings of self-worth. People need that core of good feelings about themselves to go out and confront the many changes and adversities we all are faced with each day. People should maximize their potential for acting independently and forcefully. This may mean *not* pushing ahead in the supermarket line, even though everyone else is pushing their cart, simply because the individual knows it is wrong. Or it may be standing firm on a jury for acquittal when eleven other jurors vote for conviction. These are the situations that maximize an individual's feelings of self-worth and make it possi-

ble for them to withstand continued onslaughts to their mental health.

SPELLING ━━━━━━━━━━━━━━━━━━━━━━━━━━━━

Some Rules

Most of the following rules relate to spelling changes that occur when you make a noun plural. Three general spelling rules appear at the end of this section.

> ### HINT
>
> The English alphabet is divided into vowels and consonants. The vowels are *a, e, i, o, u* (and sometimes *y*). These are the letters that change their sound, alone or in combination with other vowels, according to their position in a word. All the other letters of the alphabet are consonants: *b, c, d, f, g, h, j, k, l, m, n, p, q, r, s, t, v, w, x, y,* and *z*.

Pluralization Rules

1. We form the plurals of many nouns by adding the letter *s* to the end of the word.[6]

capitalist	capitalists
bureaucrat	bureaucrats
school	schools
writer	writers
desk	desks
location	locations
headache	headaches

2. Nouns that end with *s, z, x, ch,* or *sh* add the letters *es*.

fox	foxes
brush	brushes
kiss	kisses
watch	watches
witness	witnesses

---

[6] This *s* is different from the *s* that is added to third-person (or *s*-ending) verbs.

3. Most proper nouns add the letter *s*.

Reagan	Reagans
Ford	Fords
Lincoln	Lincolns
Kennedy	Kennedys
Jackson	Jacksons
Ferraro	Ferraros

4. Proper nouns that end in *s, z, x, ch,* and *sh* add the letters *es.*[7]

James	Jameses
Williams	Williamses
Fitz	Fitzes
Reich	Reiches

5. Nouns ending in *y* and immediately preceded by a consonant change *y* to *i* and adding *es.*

baby	babies
army	armies
sky	skies
fly	flies
ally	allies

6. Nouns that end in *y* and are preceded by a vowel add the letter *s*.

monkey	monkeys
day	days
boy	boys
joy	joys
alley	alleys

7. Most nouns that end in *o* add the letter *s*.

piano	pianos
memo	memos
radio	radios

However, there are certain exceptions to rule 7. These nouns add *es* as an ending:

echo	echoes
potato	potatoes
tomato	tomatoes
veto	vetoes
hero	heroes

---

[7] Do not confuse these plural forms with possessive forms that require an apostrophe. For example:

The *Jameses* came to our house for dinner. (plural)
Then all of us went to the *Williams's* for a party. (possessive)

Further, some nouns that end in *o* may add either *s* or *es*.

buffalo	buffalos/buffaloes
motto	mottos/mottoes
zero	zeros/zeroes

8. Certain nouns that are holdovers from Old English form their plurals irregularly.

man	men
freshman	freshmen
woman	women
goose	geese
foot	feet

9. Some nouns have the same form for the singular and the plural and so do not add any letters to form the plurals.

deer	deer
moose	moose
sheep	sheep
fish	fish[8]
Chinese	Chinese
Guyanese	Guyanese
Vietnamese	Vietnamese
series	series
species	species

10. Some nouns ending in a single *f* change the *f* to *v* and add *es*.

wolf	wolves
knife	knives
life	lives
self	selves

11. Nouns ending in *sis* (from Greek) form their plural as *ses*.

basis	bases
parenthesis	parentheses
analysis	analyses
crisis	crises

12. Some nouns ending in *us* (from Latin) change the *us* to *i*.

alumnus	alumni
radius	radii
fungus	fungi

---

[8] *Fish* can be pluralized when it refers to multiple species, as in: Among the fishes of the world are sharks, flukes, and bass.

13. Some nouns ending in *um* (also from Latin) change the *um* to *a*.

addendum	addenda
datum	data
medium	media

14. Some nouns ending in *on* (another Greek ending) change the *on* to *a*.

phenomenon	phenomena
criterion	criteria

Three General Spelling Rules

1. In English, the letter *q* is always followed by the letter *u*.

quack	quarter
quart	quadrangle
equal	equitable
quit	quote
query	

2. Remember, *i* before *e*   except after *c*   and when sounded like *a*, as in neighbor and weigh.

believe	ceiling
friend	conceive
mischief	receive
niece	receipt
review	
yield	

However,

cod*ei*ne	sc*ie*nce	n*ei*ther	w*ei*rd
caff*ei*ne	suffic*ie*nt	forf*ei*t	h*ei*ght
l*ei*sure	consc*ie*nce	s*ei*ze	g*ei*ger

3. One word in English ends in *sede:* supersede.
   Three end in *ceed:* exceed, proceed, and succeed.
   All others end in *cede:* precede, recede.

Practice with Spelling Rules

1. Change the underlined nouns to their plural forms. As you do this, you will find that other words need to be changed or deleted. Make all the necessary changes.

What a curious phenomenon it is that an American doctor knows so little about nutrition. A Chinese doctor works almost entirely with diet and herbs, whereas the American counterpart relies almost totally on a chemical compound. The basis of Western medicine seems to be the alleviation of a symptom in a crisis, whereas the major criterion of Asian medicine is the prevention of illness.

The American physician must become the ally of nature, for the benefit of the life of every American baby, woman, and man. Every freshman in medical school should be required to study the importance of food to human growth and health; he or she should examine the datum on the role of a dish of fish, meat, a dairy product, and vegetable like the potato and a fruit like the tomato in the daily life of a member of the species. Even the importance of an edible fungus should be the subject of analysis. (Much experimentation is needed; if a human subject is not appropriate, a monkey can be substituted.) Further, every medical school alumnus should receive a monthly memo with the latest nutritional information. A severe penalty should be imposed on a physician who treats only illness and does not first try to prevent it.

The medical consumer must also become aware of the importance of nutrition in human life. The radio should broadcast the "Nutritional Slogan of the Day." A child should learn that "One apple a day keeps the antibiotic away." The person who learns good nutritional habits as a youth will probably live to a longer and healthier old age.

2. Supply the missing letters in the following words. Use General Rules 2 and 3 as guides.

From the moment a woman conc__ves a child, she forf__ts the right to abuse her body with poor eating habits. Doctors now bel__ve that prenatal growth and development are determined by maternal nutrition. Thus, pregnant women must follow the advice of sc__ntists; they must rec__ve adequate amounts of prot__n and complex carbohydrates but must not y__ld to the temptations of fr__nds who tell them to "eat for two." A doctor's advice super____s that of n__ghbors.

Most doctors tell women that a w__ght gain of between thirty to forty pounds is suffic__nt, but that women should not exc__d that c__ling. Women who are s__zed by cravings for ice cream and cake should listen to th__r consc__nces, not their stomachs.

Doctors also advise women to indulge in n__ther coffee nor drugs during pregnancy. Many women feel tired during the early months of pregnancy, and they resort to coffee to stay awake. But caff__ne reduces the w__ght of the fetus. Moreover, as soon as the hormone women secrete in early pregnancy rec____s, their feeling of tiredness will disappear. Drugs such as cod__ne and marijuana have been implicated in miscarriage, birth defects, and infant respiratory ailments. Women who want their pregnancies to succ__d are warned away from drug use.

3. Proofread this essay for spelling errors:

The recent phenomenas of micro and macro audio equipment makes allys as well as enemys of the older and young generations. Youths and middle-aged people alike love the microes in the form of Sony Walkman and other radios made by both the Japaneses and Americans. These devices allow their owners to amble the streetes plugged into their favorite station, oblivious to the sounds around them. It is common to see childrens on buses tapping out their favorite rhythms while their older nieghbors tap their feets to a different sound. Most people love this new electronic medium, but there are those who oppose it. They say Walkmans are turning us into a nation of sheeps who follow electronic gods. They also point out a health hazard. People plugged into Walkmen may not be sufficeintly aware of what goes on around them to yeild for oncoming traffic at an intersection. But those who love them, young and old, will not forfeit their right to use them.

On the other hand, the young and the old part company on the macro equipment. From the vacant lots of the urban ghettos to the public squares of small towns, youthes hang out with enormous radioes. Their sound levels excede noise-pollution standards. The young seem to love them. The old are driven mad by them. Youngsters say that the radios are harmless; their owners are not getting into mischeif, nor are they assaulting people with knives. These kids see themselfs as unfairly portrayed as delinquents in the news medias. Older people see the macro radios as ugly funguses. They look for the psychological basises of the need to carry and listen to what they call "noise boxes." Older people see these youthes as having no social conscience at best, and at worst as having dangerous antisocial tendencys.

Now you are ready to proofread the middle draft of the essay you began earlier in this chapter. Read your essay again slowly, and aloud. Remember what you learned about word order and sense in Chapter 1 and about the conventions of writing in Chapter 2. You may need to look back at these chapters. Check to see that each sentence you've written contains a subject and a verb.

Make sure you can answer yes to these questions as you proofread:

1. Have you used plural forms where they are required?
2. Have you used the appropriate endings on the plural forms?
3. If you have used any personal pronouns, does each one have an obvious antecedent?
4. Does each personal pronoun agree in number, gender, and person with its antecedent?
5. If you have used any homonyms, near-homonyms, or words covered by any of the spelling rules we have studied, have you spelled them correctly?

ADDITIONAL WRITING ASSIGNMENTS

Your writer's journal may have some ideas for you to develop into essays. Focus on things you know how to do. It may be something you do every day and take for granted, like doing the laundry. Or it may be some special skill you have for which you are known, like playing basketball, writing computer programs, or decorating cakes.

Other students have enjoyed giving directions for the tasks below. Remember to follow the writing process we are developing: Do focused writing first. Then look it over. You may want to review the Writing and Rewriting section of each chapter before you start your middle drafts. When you finish them, proofread them, and write a clean copy.

Topic Suggestions

1. how to wash a car.
2. how to do the laundry.
3. how to study for a final exam.
4. how to live alone and enjoy it.
5. how to decorate a cake.
6. how to be aggressive without being pushy.
7. how to play poker (whist, canasta, bridge, crazy eights).
8. how to shop for groceries efficiently.
9. how to get your life back in order after the breakup of a relationship.
10. how to get the kids to bed.

You may want to describe another task with which you are familiar. Instead of teaching someone how to do it, describe in detail how it works. For instance, if you know something about automobiles, you might want to write a paper on "How a Car Engine Works" (rather than "How to Tune an Engine"). The emphasis in this paper should be on the function itself.

Defining

8

Photo by
Kathy Sloane

Choose one of these sentence openings. Finish the sentence, and then write a short paragraph to explain your meaning:

1. A good teacher is someone who _____

2. A good friend is _____

3. Love means _____

4. Racism is _____

5. Poverty means _____

6. An educated person is someone who _____

7. Success means _____

8. A slave is someone who _____

9. If you are an addict, you _____

10. Peace means _____

READING

PREVIEW QUESTIONS

As you read "Why I Want a Wife" by Judy Syfers, look for information that will help answer these questions:

1. Is Syfers married?
2. Each paragraph of "Why I Want a Wife" is devoted to one set of a wife's responsibilities. How would you label each?
3. As you read this article, does it make you think about yourself or someone in your family? If so, who? Why? How does this article make you feel?
4. How often does Syfers repeat the phrase "I want a wife"? What effect does the repetition have on you as you read?
5. Circle all the uses of the words *I, me, my,* and *mine.* These are forms of the pronoun *I.* Why does Syfers use all these different forms?

6. Change the phrase "I Want a Wife" into the question "Why does she want a wife?" Does Syfers answer the question?
7. Why would anyone want a wife? List three reasons. How do your reasons compare with those Syfers gives?
8. What is the role of narration, or storytelling, in this essay? Why does Syfers tell little stories, or anecdotes? How would the essay be different if she did not use them?

Why I Want a Wife
Judy Syfers

Judy Syfers is a free-lance writer who lives in San Francisco. This selection first appeared in Ms. *magazine in December 1971.*

(1) I belong to that classification of people known as wives. I am A Wife. And, not altogether incidentally, I am a mother.

(2) Not too long ago a male friend of mine appeared on the scene fresh from a recent divorce. He has one child, who is, of course, with his ex-wife. He is obviously looking for another wife. As I thought about him while I was ironing one evening, it suddenly occurred to me that I, too, would like to have a wife. Why do I want a wife?

(3) I would like to go back to school so that I can become economically independent, support myself, and, if need be, support those dependent upon me. I want a wife who will work and send me to school. And while I am going to school I want a wife to take care of my children. I want a wife to keep track of the children's doctor and dentist appointments. And to keep track of mine, too. I want a wife to make sure my children eat properly and are kept clean. I want a wife who will wash the children's clothes and keep them mended. I want a wife who is a good nurturant attendant to my children, who arranges for their schooling, makes sure that they have an adequate social life with their peers, takes them to the park, the zoo, etc. I want a wife who takes care of the children when they are sick, a wife who arranges to be around when the children need special care, because, of course, I cannot miss classes at school. My wife must arrange to lose time at work and not lose the job. It may mean a small cut in my wife's income from time to time, but I guess I can tolerate that. Needless to say, my wife will arrange and pay for the care of the children while my wife is working.

(4) I want a wife who will take care of *my* physical needs. I want a wife

who will keep my house clean. A wife who will pick up after me. I want a wife who will keep my clothes clean, ironed, mended, replaced when need be, and who will see to it that my personal things are kept in their proper place so that I can find what I need the minute I need it. I want a wife who cooks the meals, a wife who is a *good* cook. I want a wife who will plan the menus, do the necessary grocery shopping, prepare the meals, serve them pleasantly, and then do the cleaning up while I do my studying. I want a wife who will care for me when I am sick and sympathize with my pain and loss of time from school. I want a wife to go along when our family takes a vacation so that someone can continue to care for me and my children when I need a rest and change of scene.

(5) I want a wife who will not bother me with rambling complaints about a wife's duties. But I want a wife who will listen to me when I feel the need to explain a rather difficult point I have come across in my course of studies. And I want a wife who will type my papers for me when I have written them.

(6) I want a wife who will take care of the details of my social life. When my wife and I are invited out by friends, I want a wife who will take care of the babysitting arrangements. When I meet people at school that I like and want to entertain, I want a wife who will have the house clean, will prepare a special meal, serve it to me and my friends, and not interrupt when I talk about the things that interest me and my friends. I want a wife who will have arranged that the children are fed and ready for bed before my guests arrive so that the children do not bother us. I want a wife who takes care of the needs of my guests so that they feel comfortable, who makes sure that they have an ashtray, that they are passed the *hors d'oeuvres*, that they are offered a second helping of the food, that their wine glasses are replenished when necessary, that their coffee is served to them as they like it. And I want a wife who knows that sometimes I need a night out by myself.

(7) I want a wife who is sensitive to my sexual needs, a wife who makes love passionately and eagerly when I feel like it, a wife who makes sure that I am satisfied. And, of course, I want a wife who will not demand sexual attention when I am not in the mood for it. I want a wife who assumes the complete responsibility for birth control, because I do not want more children. I want a wife who will remain sexually faithful to me so that I do not have to clutter up my intellectual life with jealousies. And I want a wife who under-stands that *my* sexual needs may entail more than strict adherence to monog-amy. I must, after all, be able to relate to people as fully as possible.

(8) If, by chance, I find another person more suitable as a wife than the wife I already have, I want the liberty to replace my present wife with another one. Naturally, I expect a fresh, new life; my wife will take the children and be solely responsible for them so that I am left free.

(9) When I am through with school and have a job, I want my wife to quit working and remain at home so that my wife can more fully and completely take care of a wife's duties.

(10) My God, who *wouldn't* want a wife?

QUESTIONS OF CONTENT ████████████████████

Circle the letter of the best answer to each question.

1. Which reasons does Syfers give for wanting a wife?
   a. Syfers wants to return to school.
   b. She wants a good sexual partner.
   c. She needs someone to take care of her social life.
   d. She needs someone to manage her office affairs.
2. Why does Syfers want to return to school?
   a. She wants to become a successful lawyer.
   b. She wants to get a job in a big corporation.
   c. She'd like to become economically independent.
   d. She needs to make important social contacts.
3. When Syfers finishes school and gets a job, why would her wife have to quit working?
   a. to enable the wife to go to school.
   b. to have more time to take care of her duties.
   c. to be able to take part in important community affairs.
   d. to take care of the children.
4. If there were a divorce, what would happen to the children?
   a. They would be sent to their grandparents.
   b. Syfers would take complete responsibility for them.
   c. The wife would have sole responsibility for them.
   d. Syfers and the wife would have joint custody.

Answer these questions in full sentences:

1. What things could a wife do to enable Syfers to return to school? _____

_____

2. What are some of the physical needs a wife is supposed to take care of?

_____

_____

3. What should a wife do for dinner guests? _____

_____

4. List five reasons Syfers wants a wife. _____

_____

_____

343

Look back at the essay to answer these questions. Answer in full sentences.

1. How might Syfers know that her male friend is "obviously looking for another wife"? _____

_____

_____

2. Why does Syfers say that "of course" her friend's children were with his ex-wife? _____

_____

3. Why does Syfers tell us she was ironing as she thought about her friend?

_____

_____

4. Why does Syfers say that "not altogether incidentally, I am a mother"?

_____

_____

_____

5. What does the remark "My God, who *wouldn't* want a wife?" suggest about the value of a wife? _____

_____

_____

6. What is the main point of this story?

_____

344

Answer each question in a short paragraph. You may want to use your own paper.

1. What kind of a wife—and mother—do you think Syfers is? _____

_____

_____

_____

2. This article was first published in *Ms.* magazine. Who was the intended

audience? How do you think this audience responded to the article? _____

_____

_____

_____

_____

3. What does Syfers suggest about the role of men in this society? Do you

think she is unfair to men? Why or why not? _____

_____

_____

_____

_____

4. What is the tone of the article (for example, serious, humorous, sad)? Do
you think the tone is appropriate to the subject matter? Why or why not?

_____

_____

_____

_____

5. Imagine that you are writing an article about the relationship between men and women. Who would be your intended audience? What tone would you adopt? What impact do you think your article would have on the

audience? _____

_____

_____

_____

_____

QUESTIONS OF CRITICAL THINKING

1. Does Syfers give accurate explanations of a wife's duties? What are the

essential qualities of a good wife? _____

_____

_____

_____

_____

2. What is "women's work"? Why do you think only women can or should

perform this work? _____

_____

_____

_____

_____

3. List a wife's duties, according to Syfers. Next to each item, estimate the amount of time it takes to perform the task. Next to that, guess the cost of hiring someone to perform this task. Add up your figures. How many hours a week does a wife work? What is this labor worth? Use your own paper.

4. What kind of spouse do you want to be? What are the duties you will perform? Which of those do you think you would like, and which would

you dislike? _____

_____

_____

_____

_____

5. How do you feel about "house husbands," men who stay home and care for the house and the children while the wife works? Would you feel comfortable having or being a "house husband"? Why or why not?

_____

_____

_____

6. Using the help wanted section of your local newspaper as a guide, write an advertisement for a person to perform all the duties you listed in question 3. What job titles do you find in the want ads that seem to cover these duties? Use your own paper.

7. Write a paragraph entitled, "Why I Want a Husband." Use your own paper.

VOCABULARY ■■■■■■■■■■■■■■■■■■■■■■■■■■■■■■■

These words from "Why I Want a Wife" may be unfamiliar to you. The exercises will help you learn the meaning of these words and how they function in sentences.

classification	(1)	rambling	(5)	entail	(7)
incidentally	(1)	hors d'oeuvres	(6)	adherence	(7)
nurturant	(3)	replenished	(6)	monogamy	(7)
peers	(3)	clutter	(7)	solely	(8)
tolerate	(3)	intellectual	(7)		

Word Meanings

Look up the words below in the dictionary. Each has more than one meaning, and it may be listed as more than one part of speech. Read the entire entry for each word, including that for each part of speech listed. Choose the meaning closest to the way in which the word is used in the selection. If you're in doubt, write down all the meanings you think are possible, separating them by semicolons. Make sure to include the part of speech next to your definition.

hors d'oeuvres _____

intellectual _____

entail _____

peer[s] _____

Word Clues

Try to see the words below as the sum of their parts, and then write a working definition for each word. The list of prefixes and suffixes on pages 10–13 will help you with some of them. Check the dictionary entry for each word to see how close your working definition is to it.

incidentally _____

nurturant _____

adherence _____

solely _____

Seeing Words in Context

The words below appear in "Why I Want a Wife." You may find clues to the meaning of each word in its context. As you reread, circle the words or phrases that form the context for each word. Then write (1) your working definition, (2) the dictionary definition that's right for the context, and (3) an original sentence using the word. If you have difficulty figuring out the meaning of the word from the context of "Why I Want a Wife," you may find it helpful to read the following story, in which the words appear in italics:

1. word: *replenish*

    a. working definition _____

    b. dictionary definition _____

    c. your sentence _____

2. word: *rambling*

    a. working definition _____

    b. dictionary definition _____

    c. your sentence _____

3. word: *tolerate*

    a. working definition _____

    b. dictionary definition _____

    c. your sentence _____

4. word: *monogamy*

    a. working definition _____

    b. dictionary definition _____

    c. your sentence _____

5. word: *clutter*

    a. working definition _____

    b. dictionary definition _____

    c. your sentence _____

A TOAST

"Ah, Jeeves," Chester Q. Wiltshire III summoned his butler. *"Replenish* our glasses. Fill them up again. Master Henry has brought news that we have cause to celebrate. My son and only heir has come to announce his engagement to Willfreda U. Allingham."

Lord Wiltshire continued his *rambling* speech long after Jeeves had left the room. He had no particular point; he simply bubbled with delight that his bachelor son, whose eye for the ladies the village had had to *tolerate*, was going to settle down. The village would no longer have to put up with his behavior.

"Ah, Henry, my boy, my boy," he now addressed his son. *"Monogamy* is a challenge. Staying married to the same woman all your life, just being married to one woman at a time, heh, heh—I'm sure you know what I mean—is difficult. Women do tend to *clutter* up one's life. Take up a lot of room and make a mess, they do. But it is expected of the future Lord Wiltshire."

Master Henry, at age fifty-two, looked unimpressed.

HINT: IRONY

Irony is the use of words to express the direct opposite of the literal meaning of the words used. Judy Syfers entitled her article "Why I Want a Wife." Does Syfers really want a wife, or does she want to

1. expose the real roles that women play in a marriage.
2. heighten people's awareness of how wives are taken for granted.
3. change what she believes are unfair differences in the responsibilities of men and women.
4. all of the above.

If Syfer's purpose was one of these, then it was the opposite of what she stated in "Why I Want a Wife," and her use of these words was ironic, or an example of irony.

Irony is a useful technique in writing because it is an indirect way of conveying a message to an audience. Sometimes an audience will respond better to an indirect message. Why do you think Syfers chose to use irony?

Irony is sometimes a variation of *satire* and *sarcasm*. Look up these words in the dictionary, and write definitions of each:

_____

_____

_____

Using Words in Context

One way to make new words a part of your vocabulary is to use them in your writing. Write a paragraph about a couple you know. Describe how the man acts, the role he plays in the relationship. Then describe how the woman acts, the role she plays in the relationship. Use at least five of the words in the Vocabulary section in your paragraph. Underline them when you proofread your paragraph.

_____

_____

_____

_____

_____

_____

_____

_____

_____

WRITING AND REWRITING

Much of what we say and write is an attempt to explain something to somebody. Sometimes facts help. For example, a child may ask, "What is rain?" If we know the facts, we may explain that rain is "water falling to earth in drops that have been condensed from the moisture of the atmosphere." Sometimes more important than the facts, however, are the understanding of a topic that we gain from experiences and the point of view we develop based on what we have observed, read, or heard about. For instance, someone asks, "What is a good marriage?" We are not authorities on marriage. However, we have probably thought about marriage, know people who are married, and have read books and seen movies in which people marry and divorce. And we've seen the effect that their parents' marriages have had on our friends.

How Do Facts Help Us Explain Things?

Based on these kinds of information, we may be able to define a good marriage and its characteristics. Your definition of marriage may not be scientific, but your examples may be so thought provoking that your audience will be influenced by your explanation when they consider the topic for themselves.

What Other Kinds of Information Can We Use to Help Us Explain Things?

**Why Are
Students
Worried that
They Can't Write
About Certain
Topics?**

Students often worry that they cannot write about a topic because they "don't know enough." Some types of explanation require specific, technical knowledge, but others require only your own definition and examples.

WRITING: A FIRST DRAFT

Many things in this world need explaining. No matter how many times certain topics appear as the subjects of newspaper and magazine editorials, no matter how many student essays explore them, new points of view add to our understanding of the issue. Look at this list of topics:

addiction	success
censorship	divorce
prejudice	education
nutrition or diet	fitness
careers	

1. Choose an issue that interests you. Write the word on the top line of a page, and *brainstorm*. That is, write down all the words and ideas that come into your mind based on your original word. Write single words, phrases, or whole sentences. Fill up your page with ideas. For instance:

    ISSUE: A FRIEND

    Difference between friends and acquaintances.
    Friends are there when you need them.
    Trust with confidences—tell secrets.
    Best friends: Judith, Susan.
    Very different from one another; very different from me—love them both very much.
    Call up with problems—give advice.
    Knows when I need her.
    Willing to do anything for me—and me for her—very important.
    Wouldn't want to live without friends. I didn't have a lot of friends when I was a child, and I missed that.

2. Do focused writing. Write today's date on the top of a sheet of paper. Write the topic in the middle of the first line. Relax for a moment. Close your eyes. Breathe deeply. As the room starts to quiet, think about your topic. What does the term really mean? What do you know about it? How have you or people you know or read about experienced it? Try to think of at least three situations or examples that fit your definition. Now open your eyes. At the signal, begin to write and do not stop for ten minutes. Do not stop to think about where to put information. Just let the ideas flow. DO NOT pause if you are unsure about spelling, punctuation, or grammar. DO NOT stop to look up words in the dictionary. If you get stuck momentarily with nothing in your mind, write the word *stuck* until

your next idea comes. Okay, begin. After ten minutes, stop. Read what you have written. If you want to add anything, do it now.

3. Compare your brainstorming with your focused writing. Put a check next to any ideas in the brainstorming that also appear in the focused writing. Look over the unchecked items. If you wish to include any of them in your focused writing, or if they make you think of something you did not put in, revise your focused writing.

4. Look up in the dictionary the word you chose, and write its meanings.

_____   _____

            _____

            _____

            _____

5. Now reread your own definition of the issue. What does the dictionary's definition contain that yours does not? What does your definition contain

that the dictionary's does not? _____

_____

_____

_____

       Consider your focused writing as the first draft of an essay. Put it aside for now. We'll come back to it later in the chapter.

WHAT MAKES WRITING GOOD? PURPOSE, AUDIENCE, TOPIC; EXAMPLES, DETAILS, ORDER

Purpose, Audience, and Topic

Your purpose is to inform your audience about certain facts or help them gain some understanding of an issue. For instance, you are explaining the phenomenon of homelessness in the 1980s. Perhaps you should tell your audience what percentage of the American population is homeless. You should certainly create a picture of homelessness that the audience will not soon forget. This might include an example of a family you know who lost their home and who now live in their car.

What Is the Purpose of Explanation?

What Can Your Audience Learn from Your Explanation?

Some knowledge of your audience helps. Who are they? How much do they know? How much do they need to know? What kind of examples will appeal to them? For instance, you are explaining "the VCR craze." Are your audience television watchers and moviegoers? If so, you need only mention the availability of certain films. However, if your audience are not television watchers or moviegoers, you will need to write something about the content of the films so that the appeal of owning them will become obvious.

What Should You Know about Your Audience?

Finally, you will want to define the topic you are explaining. Use one of three kinds of definition:

Why Should You Define Your Topic?

1. The most common way to define a word is to use a synonym, a word or phrase very close in meaning to the word you are defining. For instance:

What Is a Synonym Definition?

   A **carnivore** is a **meat-eating animal.**
   An **aardvark** is similar to an **anteater.**
   Inane means **silly.**

   You can find synonyms in the dictionary.

What Is a Group Definition?

2. Another way to define a word or phrase is to place it in a general context, that is, to identify the group to which it belongs and then to specify its place within that group. For instance:

   A **crossword puzzle** is a **word game** (group, like Scrabble or Boggle) **in which synonyms are given for words that are written in numbered squares either down or across** (specific, different from other word games).
   A **pain** is a **reaction by the senses** (group, like hearing, seeing) **caused by injury, or disease transmitted through the central nervous system** (specific, different from other reactions by the senses).

   Group and specific definitions can also be found in the dictionary.

What Is an Extended Definition?

3. Still another way to define is to use an extended definition, which goes beyond the dictionary to give the audience a "picture" of a word, phrase, or concept. For instance, in the dictionary,

   friendship is the **act of being a friend,** and
   a **friend** is a **person** (group) **whom one knows well and is fond of** (specific).

We know that friendship is really

   . . . that state of grace of being connected to the world through people unrelated to you by blood who nonetheless help you maintain your sanity, the quality of your life, and sometimes your very existence. Friends know secrets they do not betray; they feel your pain and need and manage—sometimes at great personal cost—to ease the pain and fill the need.

354

The preceding definition not only explains friendship but also gives a picture of what friends do. However, it is a unique definition. Not everyone would define friendship in the same way. This definition gives the writer's own perspective, based on her experience, and it indicates what aspects of friendship she might develop if she wrote an essay on friendship.

Examples

After you write an extended definition of your word, you can find examples from your personal experiences; books, newpapers, or magazines; television or movies; or incidents you've heard about from friends, relatives, and acquaintances. Your examples must be relevant to the definition. For instance, in the essay "What Is a Friend?" the ideas that good friends dress well, don't smoke, or get along with your parents may be irrelevant.

Let's continue to build an essay on friendship. Most of us have friends with whom we have shared experiences. An extended definition and two examples follow. Only one of them is focused on the definition and, therefore, is relevant to the essay:

> Friendship is that state of grace of being connected to the world through people unrelated to you by blood who nonetheless help you maintain your sanity, the quality of your life, and sometimes your very existence. Friends know secrets they do not betray; they feel your pain and need and manage—sometimes at great personal cost—to ease the pain and fill the need.

> 1. Judith knows more about me than anyone else, sometimes more than I know myself. She sees the "whole" me, not just the parts that other friends and even family see because they look through lenses of their own needs. Judith's vision is unadulterated by ego. Thus, I can confess my weaknesses, gloat over my successes, and confide my fears. She listens, she laughs, she prods, and she advises. "You knew what he was like when you married him," she says. "You know he can't make plans in advance. Buy the tickets yourself or be content not to go to the theater." Sometimes I'd like to kill her, but I know she's right, and she's saved my marriage at least five times.

> 2. My friend Zoe is not the same. Her needs always come first. We went through college together and have maintained our friendship, but it gets more and more strained as our lives change. Zoe married before I did, and for a whole year she could not talk on the phone because "Harry didn't like it." We spoke less and less. I lasted longer than Harry, and since the divorce, we speak more often. But now I have a child and Zoe can't understand that after work I'd rather go home and see my daughter than meet for a drink. The conflicts of working mothers don't mean much to her.

Paragraph 2 may be interesting, but it is not an example of friendship as we have defined it.

Details

How Do We Develop Our Examples?

Each example you use to develop your extended definition requires details. Your paragraph may begin with a general statement, a *topic sentence*, that applies to more than one person or thing. It then should be followed by more specific statements that clarify and explain the topic sentence and relate to someone or something specific. It is possible, however, to write your paragraph in reverse beginning with the details and ending with the topic sentence.

The following paragraph could be included in an essay about friendship:

> Sometimes easing my pain is painful for my friends. Susan is terrified of illness. She's a nurse—of course—who thinks she or her daughter has every disease she treats in the hospital or reads about in a medical textbook. If there's a flu in Hong Kong, she's certain she will be the first American victim. Naturally, my husband's heart attack scared her to death. She complained of chest pains all the time he was in the hospital. But still she called every night, listened to me cry, and explained his condition to me as well as she could.

Why Is the Topic Sentence the Most General?

The topic sentence ("Sometimes easing my pain is painful for my friends") is the most general statement of the paragraph. It is not about a particular friend but about friends in general. The next sentence starts, more specifically, to discuss one friend, and the rest of the paragraph provides more specific details about how that friend behaves.

Syfers also moves from a general statement to specific details in each of her paragraphs. The topic sentence in paragraph 4 reads: "I want a wife who will take care of my physical needs."

What specific needs does Syfers say must be met? _____

_____

Order

Your group/specific and extended definitions, supported by relevant examples, make up your essay. These definitions may form the introductory paragraph, with or without additional information. The order of the examples is optional.

In What Order Should You Put Your Examples?

If one order doesn't "flow" for you, you may want to look at your definition and cite examples in the same order that you mentioned them in the extended definition. For instance, in the essay on friendship, you could cite examples of (1) how friends help you maintain your sanity and life, (2) how they keep secrets, and (3) ease your pain. The last paragraph should contain some restatement of the definition and of the information in the body of the essay.

What Is a Topic Sentence?

The parts of an essay won't fit together well without topic sentences and appropriate transitions. A topic sentence often does double duty by informing the audience what the writer will be showing and linking the ideas in the paragraph with those in other parts of the essay. For instance, the introduction (group and extended definition) and an example of friendship are as follows:

> Friendship is that state of grace of being connected to the world through people unrelated to you by blood who nonetheless help you maintain your sanity, the quality of your life, and sometimes your very existence. Friends know secrets they do not betray; they feel your pain and need and manage—sometimes at great personal cost—to ease the pain and fill the need.
>
> 1. Judith knows more about me than anyone else, sometimes more than I know myself. She sees the "whole" me, not just the parts that other friends and even family see because they look through lenses of their own needs. Judith's vision is unadulterated by ego. Thus, I can confess my weaknesses, gloat over my successes, and confide my fears. She listens, she laughs, she prods, and she advises. "You knew what he was like when you married him," she says. "You know he can't make plans in advance. Buy the tickets yourself or be content not to go to the theater." Sometimes I'd like to kill her, but I know she's right, and she's saved my marriage at least five times.

In this draft, the two paragraphs seem a bit unconnected. Adding the topic sentence "Judith is a friend like that." ties the two together. The sentence tells the audience that they will be reading an example of friendship. The word *that* serves as a transition between this paragraph and the introduction.

Judy Syfers effectively uses topic sentences in "Why I Want a Wife." Starting with paragraph 3, her topic sentences tell the audience which aspects of being a wife she will focus on. Review "Why I Want a Wife" and underline the topic sentences in each paragraph. Then examine the complete essay "Friendship":

roduction: /specific itions

> Friendship is that state of grace of being connected to the world through people unrelated to you by blood who nonetheless help you maintain your sanity, the quality of your life, and sometimes your very existence. Friends know secrets they do not betray; they feel your pain and need and manage—sometimes at great personal cost—to ease the pain and fill the need.

c → ence · *il/ nple*

> Judith is a friend like that. Judith knows more about me than anyone else, sometimes more than I know myself. She sees the "whole" me, not just the parts that other friends and even family see because they look through lenses of their own needs. Judith's vision is unadulterated by ego. Thus, I can confess my weaknesses, gloat over my successes, and confide my fears, She listens, she laughs, she prods, and she advises. "You knew what he was like when you married him," she says. "You know he can't make plans in advance. Buy the tickets yourself or be content not to go to the theater." Sometimes I'd like to kill her, but I know she's right, and she's saved my marriage at least five times.

c → tence

> Sometimes easing my pain is painful for my friends. Susan is terrified of illness. She's a nurse—of course—who thinks she or her daughter has every disease she treats in the hospital or reads about in a medical textbook. If there's a flu in Hong Kong, she's certain she will be the first American

*detail /
example*

victim. Naturally, my husband's heart attack scared her to death. She complained of chest pains all the time he was in the hospital. But still she called every night, and listened to me cry, and explained his condition to me as well as she could.

*conclusion:
restate main-
point and
topic sentences*

Friendship is very special. A friend knows you as you really are, with all your warts and faults, but still listens. And, even when it's difficult, a friend helps you when you need help.

Do These Exercises Before You Revise Your First Draft.

Practice with Topic, Purpose, and Audience

1. Write "synonym" definitions for these terms. Use the dictionary if you need it.

A *scalpel* is ⎯⎯⎯⎯⎯⎯⎯⎯⎯⎯⎯⎯⎯⎯⎯⎯⎯⎯⎯⎯⎯⎯⎯⎯⎯.

A *qualm* is ⎯⎯⎯⎯⎯⎯⎯⎯⎯⎯⎯⎯⎯⎯⎯⎯⎯⎯⎯⎯⎯⎯⎯⎯⎯.

A *curmudgeon* is ⎯⎯⎯⎯⎯⎯⎯⎯⎯⎯⎯⎯⎯⎯⎯⎯⎯⎯⎯⎯⎯⎯.

Lasers are ⎯⎯⎯⎯⎯⎯⎯⎯⎯⎯⎯⎯⎯⎯⎯⎯⎯⎯⎯⎯⎯⎯⎯⎯⎯.

2. Write group/specific definitions for these terms:

Sanity is ⎯⎯⎯⎯⎯⎯⎯⎯⎯⎯⎯⎯⎯⎯⎯⎯⎯⎯⎯⎯ (group)

⎯⎯⎯⎯⎯⎯⎯⎯⎯⎯⎯⎯⎯⎯⎯⎯⎯⎯⎯⎯ (specific)

Poverty is ⎯⎯⎯⎯⎯⎯⎯⎯⎯⎯⎯⎯⎯⎯⎯⎯⎯⎯⎯ (group)

⎯⎯⎯⎯⎯⎯⎯⎯⎯⎯⎯⎯⎯⎯⎯⎯⎯⎯⎯⎯ (specific)

Love is ⎯⎯⎯⎯⎯⎯⎯⎯⎯⎯⎯⎯⎯⎯⎯⎯⎯⎯⎯⎯ (group)

⎯⎯⎯⎯⎯⎯⎯⎯⎯⎯⎯⎯⎯⎯⎯⎯⎯⎯⎯⎯ (specific)

Fascism is ⎯⎯⎯⎯⎯⎯⎯⎯⎯⎯⎯⎯⎯⎯⎯⎯⎯⎯⎯ (group)

⎯⎯⎯⎯⎯⎯⎯⎯⎯⎯⎯⎯⎯⎯⎯⎯⎯⎯⎯⎯ (specific)

Happiness is ⎯⎯⎯⎯⎯⎯⎯⎯⎯⎯⎯⎯⎯⎯⎯⎯⎯ (group)

⎯⎯⎯⎯⎯⎯⎯⎯⎯⎯⎯⎯⎯⎯⎯⎯⎯⎯⎯⎯ (specific)

3. Jot down a list of topics or ideas that need to be well defined before you can work with them. Rate them according to your interest in writing about them.

Topic   *Interesting*   *Dull*   *Undecided*

_____

_____

_____

_____

_____

_____

4. Write a group/specific definition for each topic you rated as "interesting."

Topic   *General Definition*

_____   _____

                                         _____

_____   _____

                                         _____

_____   _____

                                         _____

5. Write an extended definition for two of the "interesting" topics you selected.

Topic: _____

Definition: _____

_____

_____

_____

Topic: _____

Definition: _____

_____

_____

_____

Practice with Examples

Put a check next to the examples that are relevant to the definition and an X next to those that aren't.

COLLECTIVES

1. Group/specific definitions: *Collectives* are groups of people acting together as a group under a system of joint ownership.
2. Extended definition: When you live or work in a collective, you do everything with the other members of the group. All decisions are made by agreement, and all money is shared.

Example 1: Last year the student government of Acorn College rebelled against the high prices charged by the company that ran the student cafeteria. Students organized picket lines, protest rallies, and a letter-writing campaign. The college administrators were forced to close the cafeteria and appoint a committee to negotiate a new price structure with the vendor. Had the students not acted together, they would not have been so effective.

Example 2: In rural Vermont and New Hampshire, local women have traditionally knitted through the long winters and sold the finished products to designers. Recently the women organized their own "cottage industry." They pool their money to buy yarn, and one member of the group markets their products to retailers.

GUILT

1. Group/specific definition: *Guilt* is a feeling of having done something wrong or immoral for which one should atone.
2. Extended definition: People who feel guilty force themselves to do things that they would ordinarily not do to "right" whatever wrong they feel they have committed. Often they do nearly impossible things, but they are rarely satisfied.

Example 1: My cousin Linda was always sure she had killed her mother because my aunt died when she gave birth to Linda. Linda was wrong, of course, but there was no way to convince her. All during her adolescence, she would come home after school, clean the house, and cook elaborate meals for her father. She did not "hang out" with the kids or date because she felt it took too much time away from her household duties. She never married so that she could tend to her father in his old age. These are the things she thought her mother would have done.

Example 2: My mother used to let us run her ragged when she got home from work. She figured we'd been all day without a mother to talk to and to do things with. So if one of us asked for an apple, she'd run and get it, and if someone else asked for milk, she'd get that too. She became our slave as soon as she walked through the door.

GENTRIFICATION

1. Group/specific definition: *Gentrification* is a process of urban renewal in which old housing occupied by poor people is remodeled and converted into high-income–producing property for the middle class.
2. Extended definition: By gentrification, I mean the poor getting pushed out of their houses because the yuppies, with their hanging plants and hammocks, move into the neighborhood, buying the property to fix up and live in. All of a sudden, what was a low-income neighborhood has fancy wooden doors with door knockers, and the poorer people move who knows where.

Example 1: West Main Street was always on the wrong side of the tracks. If you could live anywhere else, you did. The two-story frame houses had peeling paint and ripped screens. But to the poor people who rented these houses, the neighborhood was home. Then the Joneses were evicted. No one knew why, and two days later a big moving truck drove up and workmen started to unpack oak furniture and brass lamps. The house had been bought by a young dentist who wanted a "good property."

Example 2: The house I lived in as a child was torn down to make room for an interstate highway. I remember when my parents got the notice from the city that we had to move and that we'd be compensated. However, nothing satisfied my mother, who was also born in that house.

NARCISSISM

1. Group/specific definition: *Narcissism* is a personality trait characterized by self-love or excessive interest in one's own appearance, importance, abilities, or anything else connected with oneself.
2. Extended definition: When people are narcissistic, they think only of themselves and what will bring them pleasure. They believe they are the most beautiful, the most talented, and the smartest.

Example 1: My roommate can stand in front of a mirror for an hour putting on her makeup and smiling at herself. When she's finally finished, she emerges from the bathroom and says, "Don't I look wonderful." She complains that no one she dates is as smart as she, nor as interesting or witty. What she's really saying is that no one is a carbon copy of her, which is what she's looking for.

Example 2: My friend Fritz thinks only of himself. When he calls on the phone, he prattles on and on about what he's doing, how he's feeling, what's new in his life. He doesn't even bother to ask how I am. I am not sure why he calls, except to hear himself recount his latest adventure. You'd think he'd make some attempt to listen to someone else, but he doesn't. He's really interested only in himself and in having someone listen to him.

Practice with Detail

1. Circle the number of each "general" statement in the following groups of sentences:
   a. (1) On "Knot's Landing," "Falcon Crest," and "Dynasty," most of the characters are rolling in money and are not above murder to reach their goals.
      (2) "Miami Vice" devotes most of its footage to slow-motion carnage.
      (3) TV programs promote the image of Americans as rich, violent, and nasty.
      (4) In "Dallas," Larry Hagman as J. R. Ewing has raised viciousness to a high art.
   b. (1) Health and fitness clubs charge enormous fees but have waiting lists of people wanting to join.
      (2) Joggers will not stop even in a sudden rainstorm but will continue on, slipping and sliding in the mud.
      (3) Just to lose ten pounds, some people will eat only grapefruit for weeks at a time.
      (4) People will do anything for the "perfect body."
   c. (1) My uncle Mario thought he would find gold in the streets, but the only money he has "found" he works very hard for.
      (2) Immigrants come to the United States searching for the "American dream," but they often settle for much less than they expected.
      (3) My grandparents came here looking for religious freedom, but they found a lot of discrimination as well.
      (4) My aunts and uncles thought that in America, education made everyone equal, but they realize now that despite equal education, class and race still make people unequal.
   d. (1) Muslims and Christians fight and kill each other in Lebanon.
      (2) In Northern Ireland, Protestants and Catholics have been at war for more than one hundred years.
      (3) Strife between Hindus and Sikhs in India has led to massacres.
      (4) Religious differences between people often cause bloodshed.
   e. (1) Statistics show that there are more suicides among teenagers than in any other age group.
      (2) Many adolescents spend a lot of time feeling stupid or frightened.
      (3) Physical changes and braces on teeth discomfort teenagers.
      (4) Adolescence, far from being a period of joy and freedom, is too often one of stress and unhappiness.

2. For each general statement, write three specific examples that could form a paragraph.

a. Television soap operas portray problems that are true to life.

(1) _____

(2) _____

(3) _____

b. Despite increasing public attention to good health practices, too many Americans continue habits that lead to disease and illness.

(1) _____

(2) _____

(3) _____

c. Now that people are buying their own telephones, they are concerned with style as well as convenience.

(1) _____

(2) _____

(3) _____

d. Cocaine and heroin are escapes from daily problems, but in the long run they cause more problems than they solve.

(1) _____

(2) _____

(3) _____

e. The media promote the desirability of being thin.

(1) _____

(2) _____

(3) _____

Supply a general statement (or topic sentence) that tells the reader what to expect from the examples that follow:

a. _____

   (1) My sister Eileen went to college because she thought it would help her get a better job.
   (2) I am attending college because I can't find a job, and I have nothing else to do with my time.
   (3) One of my friends is going to college because she wants to learn what's in all the books in the library.

b. _____

   (1) Doctors recommend diets low in fats and cholesterol, salt, and sugar to keep arteries from clogging and to keep blood pressure low.
   (2) Thirty minutes a day of aerobic exercise keeps heart action at a healthy level and raises the level of high-density cholesterol, which helps prevent heart attacks.
   (3) People can learn to reduce the amount of stress in their lives and to handle the remaining stress in order to lessen the danger to their hearts.

c. _____

   (1) Many business people bring work home from the office to finish on their home computers, and many do their personal banking and other record keeping on the computer.
   (2) With the hundreds of software programs available for home computers, children can practice lessons learned in school or learn material not covered in the standard school curriculum.
   (3) Adults and children enjoy the many games of skill and strategy marketed for use with personal computers.

d. _____

   (1) Thirty years ago only 3 percent of first-year law students were women, whereas today the proportion is closer to 35 percent.
   (2) Women are getting M.B.A.'s and joining the ranks of big business.
   (3) More women are becoming medical doctors, engineers, and even construction workers.

REWRITING: THE SECOND DRAFT

Now you are ready to turn your focused writing into a second draft. Read it carefully, aloud, and, if you can, to a friend or classmate. Try to get a new vision of your subject. As you rewrite, consider whether or not your voice is conveying what you want it to. You should also

  1. *Revise for topic, purpose, and audience.* Your purpose is to explain something new to your audience. Make sure you know something about your audience and what they need to know. Define your term or issue. Use the dictionary to help you form a group/specific definition, and use your own experience to write an extended definition that shows what the group/specific definition looks like in action.

  2. *Revise for examples.* Choose examples that relate directly to your definition.

  3. *Revise for topic sentences and transitions.* Begin each paragraph with a sentence that will announce what your example is and will tie the example to the definition in the introduction.

  4. *Revise for order.* Use your group and extended definitions as your opening paragraphs. Then decide which of your examples to place first, second, and third. In your last paragraph, restate your definition and summarize each of your examples.

  When you finish a satisfactory middle draft, make a clean copy. Go on to the next section, where you'll get help on the proofreading stages of your writing.

PROOFREADING

POSSESSIVE FORMS OF NOUNS

We can state that someone owns something in several ways:

How Do We Show Possession?

Singular (One boy owns the hat):   Plural (Several babies have diapers):

The hat of the boy   *The diapers of the babies*
The boy owns the hat   *The babies own the diapers*
The hat belongs to the boy   *The diapers belong to the babies*

These ways of indicating possession tend to sound a bit awkward and require more words than necessary to express a relationship. We can express possession much more simply by using the possessive form of the noun; that is, by adding an apostrophe and an *s* to a singular noun or just an apostrophe to a plural noun that ends in *s:*

the boy's hat   *the babies' diapers*

Follow these rules when you use an apostrophe for possession:

What Are the Rules for Using an Apostrophe?

  1. Add an apostrophe and *s* to singular words like *child, mother, computer,* and *idea:*

He tripped over the child's skate that lay in the doorway.
A mother's work is never done.
The computer's fan made too much noise.
The idea's usefulness made it worth considering.
One man's meat is another man's poison.

2. Add only the apostrophe to nouns whose plurals are formed by adding *s* or *es*, like *mothers, glasses, Joneses:*

   The mothers' baby-sitting co-op has disbanded for the summer.
   The wine glasses' stems were very fragile.
   All of the Joneses' cars were parked in the driveway.

3. Add an apostrophe and an *s* to plural nouns that are formed in other ways, like *women* (singular: *woman*), *alumni* (singular: *alumnus*), and *data* (singular: *datum*):

   The women's complaints of sex discrimination made an impact on their employers.
   The alumni's money helped finance the new library.
   The scientists worried about the data's completeness when they submitted their report.

(See Appendix 6 for a discussion of dialect forms of possession. You may also want to review the use of the apostrophe for contraction in Chapter 2.)

Practice with Possessive Forms of Nouns

1. Rewrite this paragraph, changing each underlined phrase to a possessive noun form. We've done the first one for you. Remember that you will need to shift some words in the paragraph as you rewrite.

Shirley Jackson's
"The Lottery" [by Shirley Jackson] is the story of a not-so-typical

New England town. The people of the town gather in the public square

of the town for an annual lottery. Jackson shows the reader the excitement

of the children and the nervousness of the adults. She describes the ritual

of the lottery, which has developed over many years. Then it begins. The

head of each family draws for his family. The anticipation of the crowd

mounts. The Hutchinsons win. Then each member of the family draws.

Tessie Hutchinson wins. What is the prize of Tessie Hutchinson? Read

"The Lottery."

2. Proofread this paragraph. Insert or delete apostrophes where necessary.

Young childrens parent's get more upper respiratory infection's than other adults. It's not hard to understand. Normally adults catch one or two colds a year. Adults' colds may be severe, but do not last long. Adult's ability to fight off viruses is good, and they do not normally catch colds from casual encounters with one another. However, kids have runny noses and coughs all the time. Kids' noses run, and they wipe them with their arm's and go on playing. Kids germs are tossed into the air because kids sneeze and cough without covering their noses and mouth's. They give their colds to all their friends at school, but they are also spreading them to their own parents and the other kids' parents. Parents' ability to withstand germs is no match against the attacks from their own kids, and what the kids' bring home from their friends. These little disease carriers can empty their parents' tissue boxes fifty-two weeks a year.

PRONOUN FORMS

Unlike nouns, pronouns have possessive forms that do not require apostrophes:

*Mary lost **her** book.*
*The dog wagged **its** tail.*
*The letter was **mine.***

As in other uses of pronouns, the use of possessive forms requires agreement between the pronouns and their antecedents in number, gender, and person. In the sample sentence, the pronoun *her* agrees with its antecedent *Mary* because both words are singular, feminine, and in the third person. Knowing the rules of agreement will help you select the appropriate pronoun; however, you also must choose the correct form of the pronoun. For example, *her* has two possessive forms, *her* (which we use as an adjective to describe a following noun):

What Is Pronoun–Antecedent Agreement

*Monica didn't know that it was **her** ticket that was lost.*

and *hers* (which we use when no noun follows):

*Monica didn't know that the lost ticket was **hers.***

Other Forms of Pronouns

The form of the pronoun that you should use depends on its grammatical function, that is, whether the word functions as the subject, the object, or an adjective. For example,

On What Does the Pronoun's Form Depend?

***Me** was uncertain the mechanic would return **I** car to **my** this afternoon.*
***I** was uncertain the mechanic would return **my** car to **me** this afternoon.*

My and *me* are forms of the first-person singular pronoun *I*, but as you can see, the three pronouns are not interchangeable. The first sentence sounds awkward because the pronouns are in the wrong place. The second sentence sounds better because the pronouns are rearranged to fit their function.

PERSONAL PRONOUN FORMS

	Subjective	*Objective*	*Possessive*	*Possessive Adjective*
Singular				
first person	I	me	mine	my
second person	you	you	yours	your
third person	he, she, it	him, her, it	his, hers, its	his, her, its
Plural				
first person	we	us	ours	our
second person	you	you	yours	your
third person	they	them	theirs	their

The pronoun takes a *subjective form* when it functions as the subject of the sentence, that is, the subject of the verb (usually at or near the beginning of the sentence):

*The **disc jockey** played the music.*
***He** played the music.*

The pronoun takes an *objective form* when it functions as the direct object or the indirect object of the verb:

*The disc jockey told **the caller** to hang up. (direct object)*
*The disc jockey told **him** to hang up. (direct object)*
*The caller told **the disc jockey** bad jokes. (indirect object)*
*The caller told **him** bad jokes. (indirect object)*

The pronoun also takes an *objective form* when it functions as the object of a preposition:

*The disc jockey lost his patience and shouted at **the caller** to hang up.*
*The disc jockey lost his patience and shouted at **him** to hang up.*

The pronoun can also have a possessive form:

*The disc jockey shouted "Hang up **your** telephone."*
*The caller shouted back, "No, hang up **yours.**"*

HINT

The pronoun *who* has other forms, *whose* and *whom,* that are related to their function. Use the subjective form, *who,* when the pronoun functions as the subject of the verb (or sentence):

> ***Who*** *spilled the hot chocolate on Mary's dress?*
> *No one knew* ***who*** *spilled it.*

Use the objective form, *whom,* when the pronoun functions as the object of the verb or a preposition:

> ***Whom*** *will Elizabeth Taylor marry next?*
> *With* ***whom*** *are you going to the prom?*

Use the possessive form, *whose,* to indicate a possessive relationship between words:[1]

> ***Whose*** *book is on the desk?*
> *I wondered* ***whose*** *turn it was to pay for dinner.*

Pronoun Problems

Students often have difficulty choosing the appropriate pronoun form when the sentence contains more than one pronoun.

When Do Students Have Problems With Pronouns?

    1. Which sentence in each pair sounds better to you?

    a. *He* and *I* have been buddies for ten years.
    b. *Him* and *me* have been buddies for ten years.
    c. *Gerard and me* are saving our money to buy a home computer.
    d. *Gerard and I* are saving our money to buy a home computer.

In some dialects, sentences b and c sound appropriate, but in standard English, a and d are more appropriate.

    Use the subjective form of both pronouns in the subject position. If you are not sure which is the subjective form, try saying aloud the sentence using only the pronoun that refers to yourself. For example, "I have been a good buddy" sounds more appropriate than does "Me have been a good buddy." Once you have chosen the form of the personal pronoun in the first person, you can choose the other pronoun from the same column in the Personal Pronoun Forms table.

    2. Which sentence in this pair sounds more appropriate?

---

[1] Do not confuse *whose* with *who's* (a contraction of *who is*).

369

a. The argument was between *him* and *me.*
b. The argument was between *he* and *I.*

Standard English uses the objective form of the pronoun directly after a preposition, thus making the first sentence the better choice.

3. Finally, choose the more appropriate sounding sentence from each of the following pairs:

a. Talya did it better than *I.*
b. Talya did it better than *me.*

c. Daniel swims as well as *me.*
d. Daniel swims as well as *I.*

e. Arielle is not quite as tall as *I.*
f. Arielle is not quite as tall as *me.*

In standard English, a, d, and e are preferred. The subjective form is used because the pronoun is the subject of an implied verb, that is, one that is understood but not actually included. One way to decide which form to use is to add a verb after the pronoun at the end of the sentence: Talya did it better than *I did* (rather than Talya did it better than *me did*); Daniel swims as well as *I swim;* and Arielle is not quite as tall as *I am.*

Practice with Pronouns

1. Write the appropriate form of the pronoun in the blank.

My mother and _____ are good friends. _____ maintain cordial relations
           I, me   I, Me

with_____ father, a host of uncles, aunts, cousins, friends, and acquain-
    me, mine, my

tances, but there is no hope for even amicable relations between my sister

and _____.
  I, me

_____ is a relationship of mutual antagonism; _____ simply cannot
Ours, Our   we, us

get along. When the two of _____ were young, there were constant fights
                we, us

between _____. "This is _____!" one of _____ would shout. "No, its not,
    we, us   mine, my   we, us

_____, it's _____ book (or whatever)," the other would yell.
your, yours   mine, my

_____ parents could barely tolerate the noise. _____ patience
Our, Ours   Theirs, Their

370

was often stretched to the limit. _____ wrecked one another's nerves, but
We, Us

we also wrecked _____.
theirs, their

It's not much different now that _____ are grown. The subjects of the
we, us

arguments have changed, but the relationship between _____ is still unhappy.
we, us

2. Proofread this dialogue between two bums for appropriate use of pronouns:

"Just between you and I," the wino whispered, "there's a place over

there for us to sleep." He pointed to an alley between two warehouses.

"Me and you can bed down there for the night."

"You're smaller than me, so you sleep over there."

"I don't want to sleep near him," he said, pointing to a body already

stretched out alongside one building. "Last week there was a fight between

he and I, and I took the worst of it."

"Me and him don't get along either. He stole something of my yester-

day."

"I heard about that. He said it belonged to he."

"It was mine!"

"Okay, don't get huffy. I don't care whose it is. You and me had

better stay friends. We're going to Florida next week, aren't we?"

3. Choose one of these phrases to begin a sentence:

My sister's clothes . . .
The policeman's club . . .
Our neighborhood . . .
Their haughtiness . . .
My personality . . .

Finish the sentence and continue your thoughts in a ten- to twelve-sentence
paragraph. When you are finished writing, proofread it, with special attention to your use of possessive forms of nouns and pronouns. Use your
own paper.

Students worry more about commas than about any other part of their writing. Many students believe that if they learn to put commas in the "right" places, they will solve all the problems in their writing.

Commas are important, although not as important as some people may think. Commas set off words, phrases, and clauses *within* a sentence (unlike a *period,* which separates one sentence from another). Commas help the reader understand how the writer has grouped words together in sentences.

What's a Comma?

However, commas are punctuation marks, and therefore, you need to consider them only when polishing the final draft. You don't have to spend much time thinking about commas in the early stages of the writing process. Even in the final draft, commas should be used sparingly.

There are two common "rules" for the use of the comma; one is helpful, one not:

1. Not helpful: Put a comma where you pause. Actually, the reverse is true. We pause when we read a comma, but we don't write a comma whenever we pause. Pause where you see a comma. As we write, we pause often—to think about what we are writing, to decide if we have left anything out, to think about word choice—but we don't insert a comma each time we pause for these reasons.
2. Helpful: When in doubt, leave it out. Many commas we use are unnecessary.

Where do commas go? We have already discussed commas in coordination (Chapter 5), in subordination (Chapter 6), and with transitions (Chapter 7). Below are some additional rules for using commas, many of which may already be familiar to you. Use a comma or commas

1. In dates to separate the day from the year:

   July 4, 1776

2. In the names of places to distinguish a part from the whole:

   Denver, Colorado
   Plaquemines Parish, New Orleans

3. In names to identify the surname (last name), when it appears first:

   Lincoln, Abraham
   Washington, George

4. In numbers to indicate denominations of one thousand or more:

   1,000
   10,000 (The comma indicates thousands.)
   4,000,000 (The commas indicate millions and thousands.)

5. In a series of three or more words, phrases, or clauses. Commas must be used to separate all the items except the last two in the series. The last two are connected with a conjunction, and the use of the comma is optional (However, if you decide to use that comma, use it consistently throughout):

Words: *The best wedding presents I received were the* toaster, silverware, linens, *and* glasses.

Phrases: *The old hiking trail led us* along a creek, down a mountainside, across an old wooden bridge, *and* through a dense rain forest.

Clauses: *We couldn't reach a decision about the recreation activity for this afternoon because* Gerard wanted to go swimming, Eric wanted to play tennis, *and* Kim wanted to go horseback riding.

6. To set apart any nonessential word or phrase that interrupts the main flow in a sentence:

The astronauts were, to be sure, *ready for all eventualities in space.* (*Note that we used two commas.*)

7. Between two or more adjectives or adverbs that could stand alone but that are used together to describe the word that follows:

We arrived home from the trip very, very tired.
All the ushers at the wedding wore blue, oversized jackets.[2]

8. To set off words or phrases that explain another word or phrase in the sentence:

Two distinguished guests, both university trustees, *spoke at the banquet:* Herbert Cook, *the president of the alumni association, and* Dorothy Bennett, chairperson of the board of directors.

9. For the opening and closing phrases in letters:

Dear Helen, (*Note that we usually use a colon in business letters.*)
Sincerely,

10. After a verb of "saying" that introduces a quotation:

Claudia screamed, "Shut the door!"
The theater usher said, "Form a single line."

---

[2] No commas are used in a series of adjectives whose order is unchangeable.

      Write: I own one blue van.
Rather than: I own a blue, one van.

Practice with Commas

1. Read this letter from a Pilgrim settler to her family in England, and insert commas wherever necessary. If you haven't done so already, review the earlier chapters' discussions of the uses of commas; you need the information now.

Provincetown America

November 1621

Dearest Family in England

    We have just finished a feast of Thanksgiving for all the blessings of our lives in this new wondrous land. With our friends the Indians who are native to this part of the earth who welcomed us and have sustained us since our arrival we broke bread and shared the plenty of the harvest. We have much for which to be thankful.

    First the land is rich and fruitful. We planted and harvested rutabagas turnips potatoes and corn. Every vegetable that we plant thrives; every tree bears fruit. We have blessedly canned apple butter cranberry relish sour tomato chutney and pear sauce for next year enough to see us through 'til another harvest.

    Second and perhaps more important we are grateful for our neighbors the Indians. They are a peaceful people and they are willing to share their knowledge of the terrain with us the newcomers. They understand the changes of the seasons far better than we do since we did not have such cold nor such heat in England and they must know 1000 ways to cook maize which grows in abundance in this terrain. They are of course believers in many gods. However they are very receptive to our teachings about Christianity and we have every hope of converting them to a life of Christ. It will be a good exchange. They will bring up the fullness of the land and we will bring them the fullness of the Lord. Theirs are also unseen gods so when they ask "To whom do you pray?" we do not have trouble explaining ourselves.

    As we prepare ourselves for a long winter of cold and solitude we think of you and of our homeland. We would not indeed return to your lovely shores but we are very very lonely for you our family. We wish you a Christmas of joy and peace a new year of hope and fruitfulness a life of plenty and fellowship. From all of us who have traveled beyond the ocean

With love

Your daughter sister cousin and aunt

Martha Wellington

2. Proofread this more contemporary letter for its use of commas:

540 Atlantic Avenue

Brooklyn New York

May 12 1979

Chrysler Corporation

1500 Front Street

Detroit Michigan

Dear Sirs

Four months ago, I purchased a Plymouth K car, from my local dealer, Chrysler Motors, Incorporated, of Brooklyn, New York. From the minute I drove it out of the dealership, I knew I had purchased, as they say, a lemon. I have had, at least, three kinds of difficulties in the last four months: The heating/air-conditioning system, which is so highly rated in *Consumer Reports*, the carburetor, and a "mystery" odor, that none of your service personnel can solve.

The heating/air-conditioning system has never worked correctly. I bought the car in the winter and should, presumably, have been able to use the heater. However, when I did, I discovered that even on the lowest setting, the blower generated more heat than I could stand. In the summer, I discovered, much to my dismay, that the air-conditioner only, rarely, started when I pushed the buttons. The mechanic in your service department said, "Lady, it's a machine. Machines don't always work, do they?" Strangely, I do not find that answer comforting. I want the air-conditioner to function, when I turn it on.

When the air-conditioner does start in hot weather, which is the only time I plan to use it, the car, immediately, begins to overheat. Even if I turn the air-conditioner off, the car loses power, and I cannot drive. Your mechanics have diagnosed this as carburetor trouble, but they have adjusted the carburetor three times already, and the problem is, as yet, unsolved.

Finally, the car has a mysterious odor. I can smell it from inside the car, and from outside. It is greatest in the back, left-hand seat, and over the left, rear wheel. It is almost always present, but it's worst when I have been driving a long time, and using either the heater or the air-conditioning. Thus far, none of your service people can diagnose it, or get rid of it. They say, "All of these models are like that."

Your customer service literature explains the process by which a consumer may complain about a product. I am beginning this process, with this letter. I shall expect to hear from you, shortly.

Very truly yours,

Mrs. Janice, Malone

Now you are ready to proofread the middle draft of the essay you began earlier in this chapter. Read your essay again slowly, and aloud. Remember what you learned about word order and sense in Chapter 1 and about the conventions of writing in Chapter 2. You may need to look back at these chapters. Check to see that each sentence you've written contains a subject and a verb.

Make sure you can answer yes to these questions as you proofread:

1. Have you used possessive forms where necessary?
2. Have you used apostrophes correctly?
3. If you used pronouns, are their antecedents obvious?
4. Do the pronouns agree with their antecedents in number, gender, and person?
5. Are the forms of the pronouns appropriate for their place in the sentence?
6. Have you checked the commas to make sure that you need them and that they are in the appropriate places?

ADDITIONAL WRITING ASSIGNMENTS

Your writer's journal may have some issues or ideas for you to develop into essays. Focus on ideas you think need to be explained, particularly by means of definition and example. They may be things you do not really understand and want to explain for your own knowledge; or they may be things you understand but think others need to understand better. You may want to imagine you are explaining some aspect of American culture and society to a new immigrant or tourist.

Other students have found these issues need to be explained. Remember to follow the writing process we are developing: Do focused writing first. Then read it over. You may want to review the Writing and Rewriting section of each chapter before you start your middle drafts. When you finish them, proofread them and write out a clean copy.

Topic Suggestions

1. fast foods.
2. art.
3. personal identity.
4. ball playing.
5. vintage cars.
6. education.
7. public assistance.
8. vigilantism.
9. sexuality.
10. martial arts.

You may also want to discuss what you think is the worst social problem in the United States as a whole or in the city or town where you live. Define the problem and give examples of it.

Comparing, Contrasting, and Giving Examples

9

Photo by
Arley Bondarin

1. Go to a local fruit market or supermarket and examine two pieces of fruit or two fresh vegetables. Write the name of each fruit or vegetable at the top of Columns A and B, and write one word in each space:

		A	B
Name of Item			
Categories:	size		
	shape		
	color		
	texture		
	taste		
	price		

Then write a paragraph comparing and contrasting the fruits or vegetables. Below are two graphic ways of organizing information. Choose the one that best organizes your information. Draw it on your own paper and insert the information.

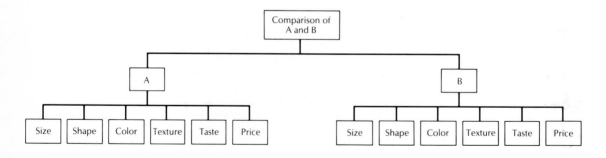

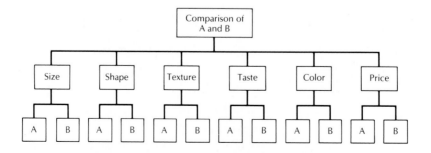

What is the difference in the ways in which the information is presented in the two graphic organizers? Compare the paragraph you wrote with what you wrote in the graphic organizers. Is the information in your paragraph organized in the same way? Did you list all the features of one item and then all the features of the other? Or did you compare and contrast each feature point by point? If you handled the information in another way, draw a graphic organizer that fits the order of your information. Use your own paper.

2. Choose one of the pairs of items from this list:

> high school and college.
> movies and books.
> computers and typewriters.
> hamburgers and hot dogs.
> basketball and baseball.
> cities and towns.
> women and men.

Jot down some of the important differences and similarities between the two items:

Differences   *Similarities*

_____   _____

_____   _____

_____   _____

_____   _____

_____   _____

Write a paragraph comparing the two items:

_____

_____

_____

_____

_____

_____

Draw a graphic organizer to represent how your ideas are organized and presented in your paragraph. Use your own paper.

READING

PREVIEW QUESTIONS

As you read "Blessings of Emptiness" by Elizabeth Hanson, look for information that will help answer these questions:

1. Think about the title. Does it make sense? How can emptiness be a blessing? What in your experience gives meaning to this expression?
2. What aspects of American and Japanese life does Hanson compare?
3. Why does Hanson tell the anecdote about herself and the Hiratas at the beginning of the essay?
4. In paragraph 4, Hanson states, "The effects of this poverty of space are everywhere." Could this be the main-point statement of the essay? Why or why not?
5. What is the purpose of the personal anecdote in paragraphs 5 and 6? How does it relate to the essay's main point?
6. Recall Galarza's and Baldwin's essays in Chapter 5. Both describe spaces. Do you think the inhabitants of these spaces felt a "poverty of space?" Why or why not?
7. Notice Hanson's use of pronouns. To whom does the "we" refer in paragraph 2? What audience is Hanson addressing? To whom does "one" refer in paragraph 10? And to whom does "her" refer in paragraph 13?
8. Notice the use of transitional words and phrases, such as "in Japan," "in America," "yet," and "better than." How do they help the reader?

Notes

samisen: a Japanese musical instrument similar to a banjo but with three strings.
Beatles: a British group (John Lennon, Paul McCartney, George Harrison, and Ringo Starr), very popular in the 1960s and 1970s.

Blessings of Emptiness
Elizabeth Hanson

This essay first appeared in the National Observer *in 1975.*

(1) I returned to the United States for a visit this summer after living for two years in Kyoto, Japan. While I was home I learned a lesson about affluence that might serve Americans as a "survival tactic." On the way back to Kyoto, my husband and I helped an elderly Japanese couple, the Hiratas, find their way through the big, empty Seattle airport. Mrs. Hirata looked around in awe as she went down the escalator. "You can hardly see a human shadow," she said. "My daughter says she likes living in America better than in Japan, and after three months here, maybe I agree."

(2) When we landed at Haneda airport in Tokyo, we were immersed in a baggage-claim area that was packed with people. I understood then that Mrs. Hirata wasn't attracted to American life because we have cars and big television sets and lots of appliances. The Japanese have those things too. She liked the United States because of the emptiness.

(3) I realized after living in Japan that emptiness is a natural resource like oil or topsoil, yet in America we take our large country for granted.

(4) The United States has its share of congested urban areas, and many Americans live close together without the benefit of some private green area. Yet the crowded conditions of some cities in the United States are standard in Japan. The effects of this poverty of space are everywhere. In Japan, a population half the size of the United States' is packed into a land area about the same size as California, and only about 16 percent of that land is habitable. Housing that would be considered middle class in the United States—a pre-fabricated three-bedroom house with a quarter-acre lot, for example—is out of the reach of all but the richest Japanese families.

(5) My husband and I were lucky enough to rent a house in Kyoto with two small rooms upstairs and two downstairs. The kitchen is large enough for only one cook. Our yard is a narrow concrete area in the front and back, with a hardy Japanese maple growing over the wall. There is no central heating, no running hot water, no washing machine. We thought the place would be big enough for the two of us, though. We smugly told ourselves that it would be good experience to live Japanese-style in this "typical" house.

(6) We learned soon after moving in that our house is not typical. It is large. Japanese friends comment on the size the minute they take their shoes off and step into the entry hall. They are amazed at how quiet and private it is, despite the fact that we can hear the rumblings of the streetcar a block away and the unique sound mixture of one neighbor playing a samisen, another practicing classical piano, and a third playing Beatles' records. Japanese friends have asked several times why we don't rent our upstairs room to a student boarder. Surely, they say, the house is lonely with just two people.

(7) A white-collar worker typically lives in a three-room apartment with his wife and two or three children; a recent advertisement in Kyoto listed the cost of such a 760-square-foot condominium apartment at $60,000. The rooms are converted from sleeping to living rooms and back again. There is no place for a private children's room, much less a den. Children play in a communal patch of packed earth between the buildings, in a parking lot, or on the streets.

(8) Because their homes are small, the Japanese don't spend as much time in them as Americans do. Men don't bring colleagues home for dinner because a quiet, leisurely meal is impossible in a tiny apartment shared with active children. Japanese meet close friends at restaurants or bars instead of having parties at home. Coffee shops in nearly every neighborhood serve as substitute living rooms, not just as places to grab a snack.

(9) A poverty of space also affects the way people spend their free time. Because many people have only one day off each week, a Sunday outing to a park, zoo, or beach is a constant struggle against crowds. Trains and buses to recreation areas are packed to rush-hour capacity. Families sit nearly side by side in parks, eating their picnics and politely ignoring the people around them.

(10) One has to reserve a tennis court a month in advance to play on a weekend. Golf courses are luxuries; persons may have to pay fees of $30 to $50 to play 18 holes. Japanese who say they often play golf get on a real course only a few times a year; usually they must be satisfied with practicing on a driving range. Movies are full on weekends and holidays, with people standing in the aisles.

(11) This summer when I visited my home state, Illinois, I was entranced by the rich, flat grain fields. Just outside the center of Japanese cities one can find rice plots wedged between houses and apartment buildings. The Japanese rely desperately on imports of grain and other rice.

(12) Most Japanese are well fed, but families spend 40 to 50 percent of their income on food. A dozen eggs cost $1.25; a quart of milk, 73 cents; ground beef, $3 a pound. It embarrassed me to hear American friends in the United States complain about food prices and having to eat fish, chicken, or hamburger instead of roast or steak. Most Japanese don't consider eating large pieces of meat every day any more than people in Kansas expect to eat freshly caught seafood.

(13) Sometimes the strains of living in such a society are overwhelming. Each year several teenagers commit suicide because of the pressure of studying for entrance examinations to crowded colleges. A few years ago, a man killed his neighbor and her daughter because he could no longer stand to hear their piano playing.

(14) Yet the Japanese seem to appreciate what they have and to accept, more or less, that some things are impossible to obtain. If there is no room around the house for a yard, then a garden enthusiast substitutes a row of carefully tended potted plants.

(15) I realize after living in Japan how precious mere emptiness can be. I didn't know what an advantage it is to live in a big country until I lived in a small one. If we Americans understand what a blessing space is, perhaps we can accept problems of inflation with a sense of balance and perspective.

QUESTIONS OF CONTENT

Circle the letter of the best answer to each question.

1. How long did Hanson live in Japan?

    a. two months.   **c.** two years.
    b. two weeks.   **d.** five years.

2. Mrs. Hirata was attracted to American life because Americans have

    a. cars.   **c.** appliances.
    b. televisions.   **d.** space.
                                  e. all of the above.

3. What proportion of the land in Japan is habitable?

    a. 50 percent.   **c.** 100 percent.
    b. 25 percent.   **d.** 16 percent.

4. Which features does Hanson's house in Japan have?

    a. hot and cold running water.   **c.** two small rooms upstairs.
    b. narrow lawn in front and back.   **d.** a small kitchen.

5. What percent of a Japanese family's income is spent on food?

    a. 10 to 20 percent.   **c.** 30 to 40 percent.
    b. 20 to 30 percent.   **d.** 40 to 50 percent.

Answer these questions in full sentences:

1. In what ways was the house the Hansons rented not typical? _____

_____

2. Why did the Hansons' Japanese friends suggest that they rent a room to

a student boarder? _____

_____

3. Where do Japanese children play?_____

_____

4. Why was Mrs. Hirata in awe when she reached the Seattle airport? _____

_____

5. Where do the Japanese entertain their friends and colleagues? _____

_____

6. Summarize Hanson's descriptions of America and Japan. _____

_____

_____

_____

_____

_____

QUESTIONS OF INFERENCE

Look back at the essay to answer these questions. Answer with full sentences.

1. What places might Hanson have had in mind when she wrote, "The United States has its share of congested urban areas"? _____

_____

2. Why do the Japanese have to import much of their food? _____

_____

3. Why don't the Japanese expect to eat meat every day or the residents of Kansas expect to eat fish? _____

_____

4. Why don't most American teenagers feel the same pressure to get into college that Japanese teenagers feel? _____

_____

5. If the Hansons' Japanese house was not typical, what would you imagine a typical Japanese house to be like? _____

_____

6. Do you think Mrs. Hirata might have had a different reaction if she had landed at Chicago's O'Hare Airport at 6 P.M. on a Friday evening? Why?

_____

QUESTIONS OF CRITICAL THINKING

Answer each of these questions in a short paragraph. You may want to use your own paper.

1. What questions would you like to ask the Hiratas about living conditions in Japan? (Write at least three.) _____

_____

_____

2. List three or four characteristics of the Hanson's Japanese house. How is where you live similar to or different from the Hansons' house in these respects? _____

_____

_____

3. Describe your own house. Do you consider your living arrangements "poverty" or "richness" of space? Why? How do your living arrangements affect your life? _____

_____

4. How do you think people are affected by "richness of space" or "poverty of space"? Give examples of how people can live in either large or small spaces. Explain what happens to them. _____

_____

_____

_____

5. Is Hanson's intended audience people who are familiar with life in Japan, life in the United States, both, or neither? How do you know?

_____

_____

_____

6. Why do you think Hanson wrote this essay? Does the title offer a clue to the purpose of the essay? (Underline her main-point statement in the text.) _____

_____

_____

7. How does the comparison of the two places help you understand the purpose of the essay? _____

_____

_____

8. Hanson lists the price of an apartment and of some food items in Japan in 1975. How do these compare with prices where you live now? What percentage of your income or your family's income is spent on food? What does it cost now to buy a home or rent an apartment?

_____

_____

_____

9. In the library, consult an old newspaper and look up the price of (a) a three-room apartment in your hometown in 1975, (b) a dozen eggs, (c) a quart of milk, and (d) a pound of ground beef. How do these prices compare

with the prices in Kyoto then? _____

_____

_____

_____

_____

10. Do you agree or disagree with Hanson that space is a blessing because it enables one to look at other problems—like inflation—with more "bal-

ance and perspective"? Why? _____

_____

_____

_____

11. Hanson says that lack of space is a major strain in Japanese life. What do you think are some major strains in American life?

_____

_____

_____

_____

12. Hanson gives an example of how the Japanese accept their lack of space and adjust to it. What have you wanted but found impossible to attain?

Give an example of how you have adjusted. _____

_____

_____

_____

These words from "Blessings of Emptiness" may be unfamiliar to you. The exercises will help you learn the meanings of these words and how they function in sentences.

affluence	(1)	habitable	(4)	colleagues	(8)
awe	(1)	prefabricated	(4)	entranced	(11)
immersed	(2)	smugly	(5)	enthusiast	(14)
resource	(3)	unique	(6)	inflation	(15)
topsoil	(3)				

Word Meanings

Look up the following words in the dictionary. Each has more than one meaning and may be listed as more than one part of speech. Read the entire entry for each part of speech listed. Choose the meaning closest to the way in which the word is used in the selection. If you're in doubt, write down all the meanings you think are possible, separating them by semicolons. Make sure to include the part of speech next to your definition.

immerse[d] _____

resource _____

entrance[d] _____

enthusiast _____

inflation _____

Word Clues

Try to see the words below as the sum of their parts, and then write a working definition for each. (The list of prefixes and suffixes on pages 10–13 in Chapter 1 will help you with some of the words.) Check the dictionary entry for each word to see how close your working definition is to it.

topsoil _____

habitable _____

prefabricate[d] _____

Seeing Words in Context

The words below appear in "Blessings of Emptiness." You may find clues to the meaning of each word in its context. As you reread, circle the words or phrases that form the context for each. Then write (1) your working definition, (2) the dictionary definition that's right for the context, and (3) an original sentence using the word. If you have difficulty figuring out the word from the context of "Blessings of Emptiness," you may find it helpful to read the following story, in which the words appear in italics:

1. word: *smug(ly)*

   a. working definition _____

   b. dictionary definition _____

   c. your sentence _____

2. word: *unique*

   a. working definition _____

   b. dictionary definition _____

   c. your sentence _____

3. word: *awe*

   a. working definition _____

   b. dictionary definition _____

   c. your sentence _____

4. word: *colleague(s)*

   a. working definition _____

   b. dictionary definition _____

   c. your sentence _____

5. word: *affluence*

   a. working definition _____

   b. dictionary definition _____

   c. your sentence _____

J. RALPH OF EAST MAIN STREET

J. Ralph Hutchinson sat in the meeting room of the East Main Street Neighborhood Improvement Association. No one knew what "J." stood for, and no one asked. At six-foot-five, with a body like Mr. T., he could smile *smugly*—deeply satisfied with himself—and everyone just nodded when he said, "None of your business." J. Ralph, as he was known in the neighborhood, was *unique*. There was no one like him: part-time hoodlum, longtime troublemaker, self-educated community organizer. Neighborhood residents were in *awe* of him; both afraid and respectful, they treated him like a minor god. And that's why they elected him chairman of the association. If anyone could change their luck, J. Ralph could.

The meeting began. J. Ralph stood up. "My dear *colleagues*, fellow association members," he began. "If we can persuade people to invest their money in new businesses in the neighborhood, we will achieve a new *affluence*. Now who here doesn't want to be rich?" No one raised a hand. "Let's get down to business."

Using Words in Context

One way to make new words a part of your vocabulary is to use them in your own writing. Write a paragraph describing the neighborhood you live in or some area of your town or city. Use at least five of the words in the Vocabulary section in your paragraph, and underline them as you proof-read.

_____

_____

_____

_____

_____

_____

_____

_____

In Chapter 7, we studied certain words—called transitions—that help move the reader from one point to another in an essay and see the relationships between ideas. Elizabeth Hanson uses transitions sparingly but effectively in "Blessings of Emptiness." It is easy to skim over them, not realizing they are there.

In paragraph 2, she writes "I understood *then* that Mrs. Hirata wasn't attracted to American life because we have cars and big television sets and lots of appliances." Hanson's use of the word *then* tells us that she realized this fact about Mrs. Hirata when they reached the crowded baggage area of Haneda Airport.

In paragraph 4, she writes, "*Yet* the crowded conditions of some cities in the United States are standard in Japan." And again in paragraph 14, she uses *yet*. "*Yet* the Japanese seem to appreciate what they have and to accept, more or less, that some things are impossible to obtain." In both paragraphs, *yet* functions as a transition word meaning *nevertheless* or *still*, and in both cases, *yet* establishes a bridge between two contrasting ideas.

In paragraph 9, Hanson writes about how the Japanese respond to lack of space in their homes. What else does a lack of space affect? Hanson then uses the word *also* as a transition: "A poverty of space *also* affects the way people spend their free time." Again, the transition word moves the reader from one idea to another.

WRITING AND REWRITING

What Is an Effective Way of Explaining?

Comparing and contrasting are effective ways to explain something. Often, we gain insight into something when we understand its similarity to or difference from something else. For instance, if you are interested in buying a car, you may need to know how a Toyota is like or unlike a Chrysler. If you are looking for a good diet to lose weight and maintain good health, you may want to compare and contrast the Pritikin and Scarsdale diets. Comparing and contrasting are also good ways to understand something that changes over time. For instance, you could compare your childhood with your current views of your neighborhood, your family, or even yourself.

WRITING: A FIRST DRAFT

Comparing and contrasting may reveal different aspects of ideas that you have already considered. The list below contains areas of comparison for some of the topics developed in Chapter 8:

addiction: cigarettes and cocaine.
censorship: children's TV or adult entertainment.
prejudice: the 1960s versus the 1980s.
diets: safe and dangerous.
careers: private sector or public service.

success: at work and at love.
divorce: friendly or hostile.
education: high school and college.
exercise: jogging and weight lifting.

1. Choose a topic that interests you. You do not have to choose the same topic you worked on in Chapter 8, although you may want to develop it now in a different way. Write the topic and the two items on the top line of a page, and brainstorm. Write down everything you can think about these two things. You may write single words, phrases, or whole sentences. Just fill up your page with ideas. Look at the results of brainstorming for an essay on child abuse.

CHILD ABUSE

disgusting
who would want to hit a kid
young parents
poor parents
broken bones
kids look so forlorn
not just physical abuse—mental as well
parents: short tempered
they're sorry, but the damage is done
some parents are out of money
hit kids out of frustration
parents cry when they see what they've done—but it's too late
kids look all bruised
parents feel powerless, out of control
ugly welts on their bodies

2. Read your brainstorming, and *cluster* the information, that is, put together the ideas that seem to be related to one another. You may simply want to draw arrows from one related idea to another, or you may want to jot down the information in a series of circles:

CHILD ABUSE

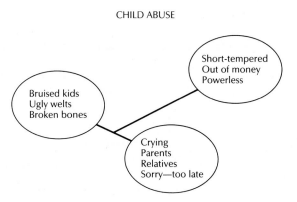

3. Do focused writing. Write today's date at the top of a piece of paper. Write your topic in the middle of the top line. Relax for a moment. Close your eyes. Breathe deeply. As the room gets quiet, think about the items you have chosen. How are they similar? How are they different? Now open your eyes. At the signal, start writing and don't stop for ten minutes. Do not stop to think about where to put information. Just let the ideas flow. DO NOT pause if you are unsure about spelling, punctuation, or grammar. DO NOT stop to look up words in the dictionary. If you get stuck momentarily with nothing in your head, write the word *stuck* until your next idea comes. Okay, begin. After ten minutes, stop. Read what you have written. If you want to add anything, do it now.

4. Based on your brainstorming, your clustering, and your focused writing, use one of these graphic organizers to help you organize your information:

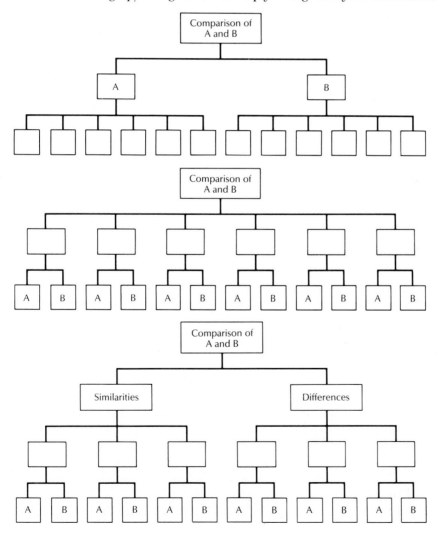

Consider your focused writing as the first draft of an essay. Put it aside for now. We shall come back to it later in the chapter.

WHAT MAKES WRITING GOOD? PURPOSE, AUDIENCE, AND TOPIC; DETAILS; ORDER; AND LANGUAGE

Purpose, Audience, and Topic

What Is Your Purpose for Writing?

Your purpose is to inform. You need not convince your audience that one item is "better" than another; they can decide for themselves when they have all the information. Rather, you should give them detailed information in a straightforward manner.

You must know something about your audience. The audience that wants data comparing Toyotas and Plymouths may not be the same audience that wants to know about Rolls Royces and Mercedes Benzes. What might be some of the differences between the two audiences?

What Should Your Introduction Do?

Of course, you can stimulate the interest of almost any audience with a strong introduction. An introduction should tell the audience what you are writing about (your main idea) and why you are writing about it. William Zinsser says in "The Transaction" (Chapter 1) that readers are attracted to a piece of writing when they can feel the writer's interest and emotion. We develop an interest in and a feeling for something because of our experience with it. So one good way to introduce the topic is telling the audience what you have experienced.

Some topics are based on stronger feelings than others are. A comparison of apartheid in South Africa and racial inequality in the United States is more emotionally charged or "hotter" than is a comparison of daytime and evening TV "soaps." But whether your topic is hot or cold, you still have a reason for writing about it (even if it is a topic you choose from a list).

Let's look at an introduction for an emotionally hot topic. You are writing about child abuse. You have defined the term; now you are comparing physical abuse with mental abuse. You want your audience to understand your main point. Physical and mental abuse are different, but they both harm children.

Why are you writing about this topic? Perhaps you've known or seen an abused child (or at least seen a picture of one), and it affected you deeply. Perhaps you yourself were abused either physically or mentally. "Showing" the audience your experience will give them a picture of your commitment to and concern for the topic. For instance:

> When I worked in the emergency room of Boise General Hospital, I frequently saw children who'd been scalded or beaten or both. I will never forget their bruised and broken bodies, or the screaming parents who regretted what they'd done too late. But I've also seen abused children

who didn't have a mark on them. How is that possible? They were victims of mental abuse, not physical abuse. Physical and mental abuse are different, but they both harm children. Whether children's bodies or minds are hurt, they suffer the consequences.

The writer shares his experience with his audience and establishes his personal connection to the topic. Having explained why the topic is important to him, he also makes it important to the audience. Look back at Hanson's "Blessings of Emptiness," and note how she introduces her topic by telling us about her experience and feelings.

Details

Your details and examples let the audience see the differences and similarities more clearly and make better judgments about the merits or demerits of the items. Your most important task is deciding what your points of comparison and contrast will be. Of course, it's easiest to compare concrete objects. Return to the Preliminary exercises. When you compared the two supermarket items, you saw how they were both alike and different, and so the categories *size*, *shape*, *color*, *taste*, and *price* seemed to be good categories for comparison. What other categories might you add to this list? Why do you think these other categories should be included? If you were going to compare living in a large city and in a small town, what categories would you choose? At least one might be "availability of entertainment." (In large cities, many movies play at the same time; live shows and concerts take place every night. But in a small town, there may be only one or two movie theaters, and shows and concerts may be less frequent.) List your categories for this topic:

What Do Details Do?

_____

_____

_____

_____

_____

The less concrete your topic is, the more difficult it may be to come up with categories. For instance, if you compare rural poverty with urban poverty, categories will be harder to find than if you compare dogs with cats.

Although you may think in advance of some categories for your comparison, you will most often need to brainstorm, cluster, and free-write about your topic before you can decide. Then, when you have some information in hand, the categories will seem more obvious.

Within each category, you usually move from a general statement to specific details. Suppose you compare urban and rural poverty. One of your categories might be "housing." You should begin the paragraph with a *general statement:*

In rural and urban areas, many poor people live in substandard housing, but the buildings look very different.

You then can follow it with *specific statements* that describe the differences among the kinds of substandard housing:

In large cities, tenements in poor neighborhoods are tall, to make the most out of very little urban space. It is not unusual for tenements in New York to have thirty stories. In rural areas, where space is not a problem, public housing is rare. Poor people live in small shacks, surrounded by lots of open space. Their houses, however, often lack hot and cold running water and toilet facilities.

Details should always be relevant to your categories. For example, for an essay comparing two fast-food restaurants, your categories may include the quality of food, atmosphere, and attitude of employees. You may also have some information about one restaurant that doesn't match anything you know about the other: Burger King will make a hamburger "your way," but you don't know McDonald's policy about special orders. What do you do? You could investigate this, get the information about McDonald's, and add the category "handling special orders."

Sometimes writers do not provide details on both sides of some comparisons. Elizabeth Hanson assumes that her audience knows how spacious America is but doesn't know much about Japan. Therefore, she gives us a lot of information about the lack of space in Japan, but she does not always contrast it directly with information about how we use space in America. For instance, in paragraph 9, Hanson describes Sunday outings in Japan, but she does not give an example of a comparable outing in America. We are meant to infer, based on our knowledge of America, that many Americans would use cars to get to parks and beaches, which would not be as crowded as those in Japan. Comparing by inference will, therefore, only be effective if you make the right assumptions about your audience.

Order

What Are Three Ways to Arrange Details in Your Essay? You must be concerned about two kinds of order: the order in which you present your details and the order of the entire essay. You have three ways to handle the information that you want to compare and contrast. You may state your main point and then (1) write thoroughly about one item first and then about the other,

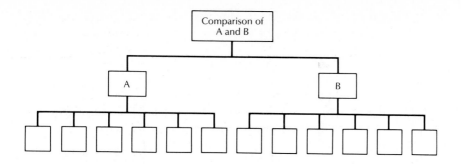

(2) point out the similarities between the two items and then the differences,

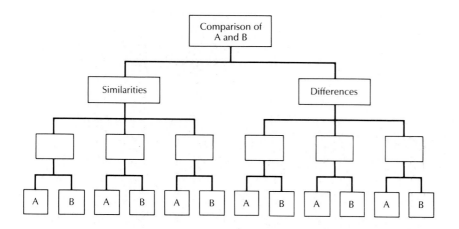

or (3) work through a set of categories, comparing and contrasting the two items with respect to each category:

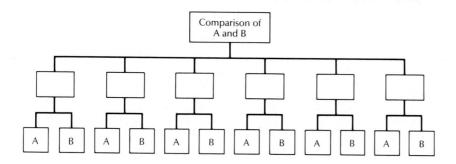

Certain topics lend themselves to particular methods of organization. An essay comparing two types of fruit may be clearer if one piece of fruit is described fully, and then the other. However, an essay that compares two different car models may work better if you develop a set of categories for comparing them. An essay comparing high school and college may work best if all the similarities between the two are discussed and then the differences. Look back at Hanson's "Blessings of Emptiness." According to which method does she organize her essay?

What Are the Three Parts of the Essay? Like other essays that explain, the body of your essay—the part that compares and contrasts—will be preceded by an introduction that states your main point and followed by a conclusion that summarizes the information you have given.

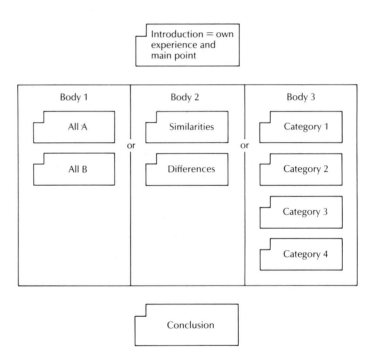

What Are Some Words that Can Help You Compare and Contrast?

Language

Certain words and phrases help you compare and contrast and often also function as transitions between ideas. Look at this list of *comparing and contrasting* words:

Words and Phrases of Comparison	*Words and Phrases of Contrast*
alike	after all
like	but
likewise	different from
the same as	in contrast (with)
similar to	less than
as of	more than
also	notwithstanding
	on the contrary
	on the other hand
	other than
	than
	unlike
	whereas
	while
	yet

HINT

Many people are confused whether to use *different than* or *different from*. Most grammar books encourage using *different from*, as in the expressions:

> *Apples taste **different from** pears.*
> *Although they all are literature, essays are **different from** novels, which are **different from** poems.*

The expression *different than* is often used informally.

We can also compare and contrast with only one word if we use comparative or superlative endings or words. For instance,

Olympic marathon champion Frank Shorter ran fast.

*Bill Rogers ran fast**er**. (comparative form, **er** ending)*

*However, Alberto Salazar ran the fast**est**. (superlative form, **est** ending)*

One- or two-syllable words may use these endings:

*Gas stoves heat food fast. Convection ovens heat food fast**er**. Microwave ovens heat food the fast**est** of all.*

*Pearls are costly. Opals are costl**ier**. Diamonds are the costl**iest**.*

What Are Some of the Word Endings Used to Compare and Contrast?

When Should We Avoid Word Endings for Comparison and Contrast?

What Should We Use Instead?

These endings are not used with polysyllabic words (words of several syllables). Instead, with words of three or more syllables we use *more* or *most* to express comparatives and superlatives. For instance,

*The queen was courteous. She was **more** courteous than the king. But the princess was the **most** courteous person in the royal family.*

*The ending of the story was fantastic. The students each contributed what they thought was a **more** fantastic ending. The teacher gave a prize for the **most** fantastic ending.*

What Forms of *Bad* and *Good* Do You Use for Comparison and Contrast?

Three common words use entirely different forms for their comparatives and superlatives:

*After the game, all the athletes were in **bad** shape. The losers were in **worse** shape than the winners were. But the losing coach was in the **worst** shape of all.*

*Ice cream cones are **good**. Ice cream sodas are **better**. Sundaes are the **best**.*

*Mennonites use **little** modern equipment in their homes. Church Amish use **less**. House Amish use **the least**.*

Some words do not have comparative forms. For instance, if a bottle is *empty*, there is nothing in it. It cannot be "emptier" than something else. Empty is empty. Other words like this are *only* and *unique*.

HINT

A great debate ranges over the appropriate use of the words *less* and *fewer*. English professors and advertising copywriters do not agree! With the exception of people who write ads, most people agree that *fewer* should be used when referring to items that can be counted, which are usually identified by words in their plural form:

> *I have **fewer** doubts about marriage than I did years ago.*
> ***Fewer** and **fewer** plays open on Broadway every season.*
> *Inflation brings **fewer** problems to the middle class than to the working class.*
> ***Fewer** people like Wagner than like Bach.*

We use *less* when referring to amounts that are usually not counted with numbers, usually identified by words that do not form plural endings:

> *Most people have **less** money to use for luxuries than they had last year.*
> *My uncle has **less** hair on his head than he had five years ago.*
> *The gym at my school has **less** equipment than it should.*
> *I wish there were **less** sand to walk through to get to the ocean.*[1]

---

[1] See Chapter 7 for a discussion of the differences between mass nouns and countable nouns.

Comparisons must make sense to your audience. For example, sometimes you may make a comparison in a kind of shorthand:

Going to the beach in the summer is better than winter.

What, exactly, are you comparing? Summer and winter? Going to the beach in one season or another. Most likely, it is the second, but you must make that clear:

*Going to the beach in the summer is better than **going to the beach** in the winter.*

Although most writers strive to be concise, they must be ready to add a few extra words for the sake of clarity.

Do These Exercises Before You Revise Your First Draft.

Practice with Introductions

1. Reread the first four paragraphs of Hanson's "Blessings of Emptiness." Place brackets around what you consider to be the introductory material. Underline what you think is the main-point statement. Put a star next to the part of Hanson's introduction that stimulates you to read on. Compare what you starred with what your classmates selected.
2. Choose three of the following five topics. For each, write a personal experience with or connection to the topic that might make a good introduction for an essay.
   a. topic: kinds of music
      main point: I like disco better than rock. (You may choose two other kinds of music.)

   _____

   _____

   _____

   _____

   _____

   _____

b. topic: teachers

main point: My current English teacher is different from the teacher I had last year. (You may choose a teacher from a different subject.)

_____

_____

_____

_____

_____

_____

c. topic: relating to people with serious illness

main point: Some people are afraid to have anything to do with a seriously ill friend or relative, whereas others are not.

_____

_____

_____

_____

_____

_____

d. topic: pets

main point: Cats are easier pets to take care of than dogs are but are not necessarily more satisfying. (You may choose other animals.)

_____

_____

_____

_____

_____

_____

e. topic: watching sports events

main point: Basketball is more interesting to watch than baseball. (You may choose other sports.)

_____

_____

_____

_____

_____ _____

3. Read the two paragraphs below. Compose a suitable introduction, including a main-point statement.

_____

_____

_____

_____

_____

_____

     Older sisters can do anything, whereas younger sisters just have to sit around and be little. When you're the older sister, you get to wear makeup, see any movie you want, and go out at night. The younger sister constantly is told: "Nail polish is for grownups," "You can't see that movie until you're at least fourteen," and "You have to go to bed now." It's a drag. My older sister wears eyeshadow and rouge, but my mother screams if she sees me touch her lipstick. I was dying to see _Creepshow_, but only my sister was allowed to go. And I remember having to stay home with a baby-sitter while my sister and my parents went to a cousin's club meeting.

     But life's not perfect for older sisters. They fight with their parents and cry all the time, whereas younger sisters don't have too much trouble. The older sister is the trailblazer, fighting for rights that younger sisters take for granted. For instance, my sister once wanted to go to a party with her friends, stay out all night, and have breakfast with her friends in the morning. My parents had never heard of such behavior; "nice girls" didn't do that sort of thing. My sister cried and explained that all her friends were doing it. Finally, my parents gave in, but the arguments lasted for hours. In a few years, I'll want to go to a party like that, and no one will give me any trouble. My sister fought my battle for me in advance.

Practice with Details

1. Reread Hanson's "Blessings of Emptiness." Determine the categories she uses to show the differences between the United States and Japan, and list them in the middle column. We've already listed two. Then put a check in the right or left column (or both) to indicate to which country Hanson is referring for that category.

America		*Japan*
_____	size of houses	_____
_____	crowded conditions	_____
_____	_____	_____
_____	_____	_____
_____	_____	_____
_____	_____	_____
_____	_____	_____
_____	_____	_____

2. Choose any two topics in Exercise 2 in Practice with Introductions. Brainstorm, cluster, and then establish categories for your comparison.

Topic: _____
Brainstorming/clustering

Categories: _____   _____

_____   _____

Topic: _____
Brainstorming/clustering

Categories: _____   _____

_____   _____

3. Choose the most general statement in each group.

   a. Stamp collecting transports you to faraway places.
   b. Rock climbing teaches you about nature.
   c. Building model boats helps you develop coordination in your hands.
   d. Hobbies are educational ways of passing the time.
   e. Growing roses teaches you how to care for living things.

   a. *Hamlet* tells of guilt and the relationship between mothers and sons.
   b. *King Lear* analyzes aging and the relationship between fathers and daughters.
   c. *Macbeth* is about the use and abuse of power.
   d. *A Midsummer Night's Dream* bursts with visions of love and deception.
   e. Shakespeare wrote plays about eternal themes.

   a. You can spend most of the summer outdoors, but in winter you are cooped up inside.
   b. Summer is a more enjoyable season than winter.
   c. In the summer, you can go to free concerts and movies in the park, but in winter, municipalities support almost no free activities.
   d. You can find a place to swim more easily than you can find a place to ski.
   e. In the summer, school's out and you have plenty of time to enjoy yourself, but in winter, you must study and prepare for exams.

   a. Cantaloupe is dense and chewy, whereas watermelon is light and airy.
   b. Watermelon has a thick rind, but cantaloupe has a paper-thin rind.
   c. Watermelons and cantaloupes both are melons, but they are not alike at all.
   d. Cantaloupes have seeds in the middle, but watermelons do not.

4. Write at least three specific statements to explain these general ones:

    a. Telephones always ring at the wrong times.

_____

_____

_____

    b. Being young is better than being old.

_____

_____

_____

    c. Some books make a lasting impression on you.

_____

_____

_____

_____

    d. People with power can be very dangerous.

_____

_____

_____

5. Write general statements to fit these specific ones.

    a. _____
    b. Doctors can often detect kidney failure through the eyes.
    c. Eyes can tell you whether a person is happy or sad.
    d. Eyes can tell you what a person is thinking.

    a. _____
    b. Hot dogs and hamburgers both are meat that tastes best grilled.
    c. Both are eaten on rolls with catsup or mustard.
    d. Children and adults love hamburgers and hot dogs.

a. _____

b. Computers are useful for writing letters and reports.

c. You can play Pac Man and Zork on a computer.

d. Computers can be used for storing recipes, figuring bank balances, and practicing musical scales.

Practice with Order

1. Choose the graphic organizer that best fits the order of Hanson's "Blessings of Emptiness." Draw it on your own paper and fit the information from the essay into the organizer.

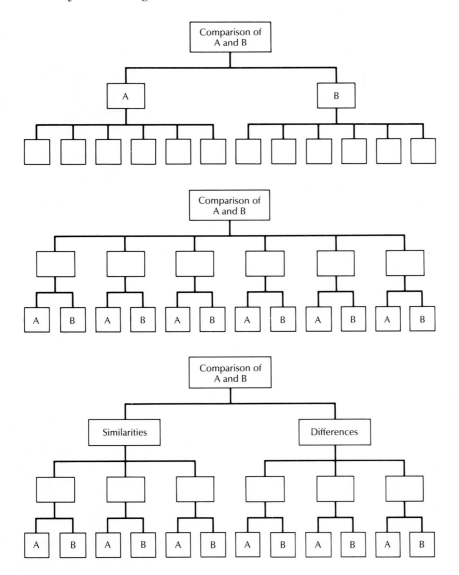

2. In each of these graphic organizers we provide some information and omit some. Add the missing information. You may want to use your own paper.

A.

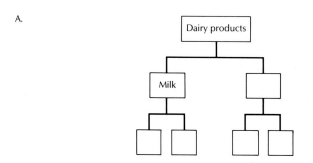

B.

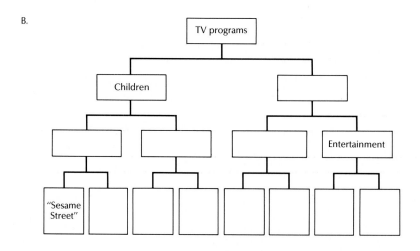

C.

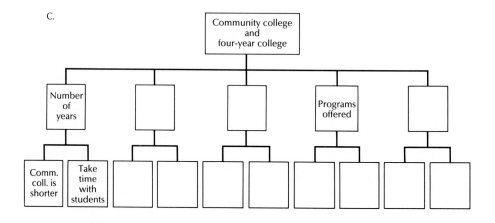

3. Some information about the cities of Boston and Philadelphia follows. Organize it in the pattern of one of the graphic organizers. Use your own paper.

BOSTON

Forty-eight square miles.
Population of 640,000.
Nation's tenth largest city.
Founded in 1630.
Extensive bus and subway system.
Home of the Boston Pops Orchestra and the Boston Symphony.
Children's Museum—"touch me" exhibits for all ages.
Isabella Stewart Gardner Museum—one of the best private collections in the United States.
Museum of Fine Arts—second most comprehensive art collection in the Western Hemisphere.
Museum of the American–China Trade.
Also: Paul Revere's House, Hayden House (stop on the Underground Railroad), Quincy Market, Freedom Trail.
Neighborhoods: North End—Italian; Beacon Hill and Back Bay—fine houses; South End—mixed, many Syrians and Hispanics.
Site of Boston Tea Party, important event leading to the Revolutionary War.

PHILADELPHIA

Founded in 1682.
For a time during the Revolutionary War, the capital of the United States.
130 square miles.
Large subway and bus system.
Site of Independence Hall and the Liberty Bell, Congress Hall, Ben Franklin's grave, Betsy Ross House.
Chinatown and Germantown; also many ethnic neighborhoods: Greek, Italian, Hispanic, Jewish, Asian.
Home of the Philadelphia Orchestra, Philadelphia Folk Festival, Mummers' Parade.
Pennsylvania Academy of Fine Arts—oldest museum and art school in United States.
ILE-IFE Black Humanitarian Center Museum—African and Caribbean artifacts.

Practice with Comparative Language

1. Look through Hanson's "Blessings of Emptiness." Circle the words and phrases of Comparison and Contrast from the lists on page 399.

If Hanson uses any other words that you think fulfill the same function, write them here:

_____ _____ _____

_____ _____ _____

2. Fill in the missing words and phrases listed on page 399:

Cape Cod and Cape Ann both are New England summer resorts, but they are very _____ each other. Cape Cod is a narrow strip of land with the calm bay on one side and a peaceful ocean on the other, _____ Cape Ann is a thick chunk of land jutting into the sea. The waters around Cape Cod tend to be warm in the summer (at least by New England standards), _____ Cape Ann waters are cold and almost unswimmable, even in August. _____, natives of the region do dash in for a dip, at least a quick dip. The beaches are quite different. Cape Cod is known for its sand dunes and great stretches of white sand beaches, _____ Cape Ann has many rocky shores and relatively few expanses of sand. Cape Cod, _____ Cape Ann, has a very small winter population. Most of the winter residents own small stores or work as service personnel, like police officers and fire fighters. _____, Cape Ann's winter community of fishermen and retirees who've migrated from other parts of the state thrives.

3. Write the appropriate comparative or superlative ending or word in the blank.

I like staying home and watching movies on the VCR _____
                                                          good
than going to a theater to see a movie. Home is _____ than
                                                      comfortable
a theater. I can sit in my favorite chair or stretch out on the couch,

which is the _____ position for watching a movie. Refreshments are
                good
_____ and _____ at home. I can put the VCR on "pause"
   convenient   cheap
and go make fresh popcorn, _____ and _____ than I usually get
                               hot   fresh
at the theater, and my popcorn costs much _____ money than
                                               less/fewer
I pay at the movies. But the very _____ thing about staying home is
                                      good
that it is _____ than a movie theater. First, there are _____
              quiet   less/fewer
people. At home, there's just me, but at the movies there are hundreds

of people. Second, it's my _____ luck to always sit in front of the
                              bad
_____ mouth in the place, some pseudointellectual who wants to
  loud
show his date he's the _____ person she ever went out with. Some-
                          smart
times I sit near the _____, _____ and _____ person
                        old   crazy   annoying
in the theater, who mumbles and sings during the movie. Finally, the

_____ part of going to the movies, and the _____ part of stay-
  bad   good
ing home, is the cost. Going out to movie can cost $10, but renting a

movie costs me $1.99.

4. Proofread the passage below for the appropriate use of comparative forms,
inserting or deleting them as needed:

Being male is better than being female. Men have less problems in

employment than women. Men move up the corporate ladder more quickly

than women do, and men usually earn more money than women do for

the same work. Similarly, less people will stand for having a woman boss,

even if the man is the worse tyrant in the place.

Social life is also more easy for a man. For example, a man can order a drink in a bar and no one will bother him, but a woman is a target for being "picked up." A man who dates many women is called "manly," but a woman who sees many men is considered a "tramp."

REWRITING: THE SECOND DRAFT

Now you are ready to turn your focused writing into a second draft. Read it carefully, aloud, and, if you can, to a friend or classmate. Try to get a new vision of your subject. As you rewrite, consider whether or not your voice is conveying what you want it to. You should also

1. *Revise for a strong introduction.* Make your personal connection to the topic clear to your audience, for this is what will engage their attention. Make sure, also, to state your main point, so that the audience will know what they are about to read.

2. *Revise for details.* Decide on several points of comparison based on your material. If you need to, you can brainstorm some new information and cluster it to get some new categories.

3. *Revise for general and specific statements.* Once you have your categories, make sure you include examples or anecdotes that support each category. The more specific your examples are, the better your audience will understand your comparison. Your examples must be relevant to your category and should be contrasted with another example, unless you are sure your audience can infer contrasting information from their own knowledge, background, and experience.

4. *Revise for order.* Choose a suitable order for your presentation. It may help you to use graphic organizers to decide how to present your information. After you have written your information in the body of the paper, you can write your introduction and conclusion.

5. *Revise for comparative language.* Use transitional expressions that are suitable for the comparisons. Use the appropriate comparative forms of words and phrases.

When you finish a satisfactory middle draft, make a clean copy. Go on to the next section, where you'll get help on the proofreading stages of your writing.

PROOFREADING

To understand how verbs work in sentences, you will need many of the sentence-writing skills you've already learned. You already know that each sentence has a subject and a verb and that both the subject and verb can be expanded. You know about nouns (and their plural forms) that are the subjects of sentences and about pronouns that take the place of nouns. These topics are also important to the study of verbs.

Let's review. What's a verb?

A verb is a word that tells the reader what the subject of a sentence is or is doing.

Now for some new information:

*A verb also tells the reader **when** the action, event, or state (the subject) takes place.*

VERBS AND TIME

We divide time into three phases: present, past, and future. For verbs, these phases are called *present tense, past tense*, and *future tense*. Sometimes sentences contain "time words" or "time phrases" that indicate when something happened; for instance, a football game was played *last week* or is to be played *tomorrow* or even *today*. The *time line* below is divided into three periods: past, present, and future. There already are some time words and time phrases in the appropriate columns. Add more words and phrases to each column, in the spaces *above the line with the arrow*.

What Are Tenses?

Past	*Present*	*Future*
yesterday	today	tomorrow
a few days ago	at this time	next week

————————————————————————————————>

413

Time words and phrases tell when something happens, and they are clues to the tenses of the verbs in the sentence. When sentences don't have time words or phrases, the verbs must do all the work of telling the reader when something happened:

*The Jets' quarterback **threw** the ball into the end zone. (past tense)*

*The Jets' quarterback **throws** the ball into the end zone. (present tense)*

*The Jets' quarterback **will throw** the ball into the end zone. (future tense)*

*I **walked** to work every day for sixteen years. (past tense)*

*I **walk** to work every day. (present tense)*

*I **will walk** to work when I get a job. (future tense)*

Why Do Verbs Change Forms?

Place the verbs from these sentences in the appropriate columns of the time line, in the spaces *below the line with the arrow.* Notice that the verb changes its form to indicate different time periods.

Let's turn now to variations of the present, past, and future verb tenses.

Simple Present Tense

What Is the Simple Present Tense?

The simple present tense indicates actions or events that are happening in the present or that happen all the time, repeatedly or habitually. For example, if someone asks you, "Do you go to school?" you may answer, "Yes, I *go* to school everyday." The simple present tense shows that an action takes place all the time, that someone does the same thing repeatedly, or that something is always or generally true:

*Veronica always **leaves** the light on when she goes to sleep.*

*Every night the actors **recreate** their roles.*

*You usually **arrive** at school at 8:00 A.M.*

We use the simple present tense unless we want to indicate that an action or event is happening at the very moment we are talking about it.

Continuous Present Tense

What Is the Continuous Present Tense?

The continuous present tense tells about something that is happening *right now.* For example, if someone asks you, "Are you going to school now?" you might answer, "Yes, I *am leaving* for school now." Other examples of the present continuous tense are

*It **is snowing.***

*The balls **are rolling** off the shelf.*

How Do You Form the Present Continuous Tense?

Form the continuous present tense by using a verb phrase made up of a *helping verb* (sometimes called an *auxiliary verb*) and a *present participle* (*ing* ending). Some of the helping verbs are

am	be	has	can	may
is	been	have	could	might
are		had	shall	must
was			will	ought to
were			would	
			should	

The helping verbs we use with the continuous present tense are *am, is, are, was,* and *were.* See Appendix 7 for a discussion of other helping verbs.

Practice with Present Tenses

1. Choose the simple present or the continuous present tense of each of the verbs in parentheses.

a. Right now, raindrops _____ on my head.
(fall)

b. The rain in Spain always _____ mainly on the plain.
(stay)

c. Mrs. Brown, you _____ a lovely daughter.
(have)

d. Sleigh bells often _____; are you listening?
(ring)

e. In the lane at this moment, snow _____.
(glisten)

f. Right now, I _____ of a white Christmas.
(dream)

2. Choose the best form of the verb:

On weekday mornings the inhabitants of my house _____ like statues
(look)

in a museum; each one ___ about his or her task oblivious to everyone else.
(go)

The alarm _____ at 6:30 A.M. I _____ and _____ my legs over the side of
(ring) (grumble) (drop)

the bed while my husband _____ a few minutes more sleep. While I _____,
(grab) (shower)

he _____ to the kitchen to start breakfast. Frequently, I _____ from the
(dash) (shriek)

bathroom because I am hit by freezing pellets of water, but my husband

_____ me and _____ his work. I ____ out of the shower and, still draped
(ignore) (continue) (run)

in my towel, _____ my daughter. She _____ to dress—with my help—
(wake) (manage)

without opening her eyes. As I gently _____ her off to the kitchen, hairbrush
(push)

in hand, I _____ back to my room. While my husband _____ the child's
(race)   (brush)

hair, ___ her lunch, and _____ her breakfast (and _____ some down himself),
(fix)   (feed)   (gulp)

I _____ and _____ to the bathroom and _____ my makeup. I ___ out of
(dress)   (return)   (apply)   (be)

the bathroom by the time my daughter and husband _____ for their turns.
(come)

We _____ our coats, ___ out the door, and _____ one another at the elevator.
(grab)   (fly)   (kiss)

By contrast, on weekends, we are more like three solitary turtles at the

zoo. For instance, today is Sunday, and as always my daughter ___ up first.
(get)

"It _____," she ____. While we _____, she _____ TV for an hour by herself.
(snow)   (say)   (sleep)   (watch)

By 9 A.M., my husband _____ in the kitchen, and I _____ the newspaper.
(putter)   (read)

No one _____ to any one else. In fact, no one ____ the least attention to
(talk)   (pay)

another person. Right now, I _____ how much I ____ Sundays. I _____ to
(think)   (love)   (listen)

music, my husband _____ in his darkroom, and my daughter _____ at the
(work)   (paint)

kitchen table. No one _____. Sunday ___ our day to rest.
(rush)   (be)

3. Write a paragraph about how you feel about school, beginning with "This
   year, I _____ school very much." When you are finished, put a box around
   the main verb in each sentence, and check to see that it is in the appropriate
   tense.

_____

_____

_____

_____

_____

_____

SUBJECT–VERB AGREEMENT

Subjects and verbs have a special relationship, because one talks about the other. However, the particular kind of relationship that linguists call *agreement* is often difficult to understand. Look at the following table. Under "Subject" are listed personal pronouns, and under "Verb" are the various forms of the verb *know* in the simple present tense:[2]

Subject (pronoun)	Verb (know)
I	know
you (singular)	know
he, she, it	know*s*
we	know
you (plural)	know
they	know

Notice that for almost every subject, the verb has the same form. The only verb with an *s* ending is the one with the subject *he*, *she*, or *it*. If the verb itself is spelled with the final consonants *z*, *s*, *sh*, or *ch*, the ending becomes *es*, as in

*The teacher **quizzes** the students on verbs.*

*The farmer **kisses** the maiden behind the barn.*

*Everyone **wishes** to win the lottery.*

*The shoe **pinches** because it is too small.*

Most speakers of standard English automatically add this *s* ending on the verb but speakers of nonstandard dialects and nonnative speakers of English must proofread carefully for this form (see Appendix 8).

When working on subject–verb agreement, your knowledge of nouns (and their plurals) and pronouns will begin to pay off. For every subject–verb combination, you can do a subject–verb agreement "test":

1. Look to see whether the noun (subject) is singular. (Frequently, a singular subject has no *s* at the end, nor does it have any of the special plural forms.)

When Does the Verb Get the *s* Ending?

When Does the *s* Ending Become es?

How Do You Find Out Whether the Subject Agrees With the Verb?

---

[2] *Know* is the "base" form of the verb. We use the base form in exercises to show what verb we are using. It is used in sentences as well:

She can *go* with you.

The base form is really the "infinitive" form without *to* before it:

She wants *to go* to China.

When a verb has *to* or words like *can* and *should* before it, it *never* has an ending.

2. Substitute the appropriate personal pronoun for the noun (subject).
3. If the noun (subject) is singular and you substituted *he, she,* or *it* for the noun, then the verb should have an *s* or *es* ending.

Noun	Singular/plural		Pronoun substitute	Verb (start)
I	x		I	start
flowers		x	they	start
doctor	x		she	starts
soldier	x		he	starts
typewriter	x		it	starts
illness	x		it	starts
scarves		x	they	start
inflation	x		it	starts

What Are Irregular Verbs?

Some verbs, called *irregular* verbs, change in a different way:

Subject	Verbs		
	(*do*)	(*have*)	(*be*)[3]
I	do	have	am
you (singular)	do	have	are
he, she, it	does	has	is
we	do	have	are
you (plural)	do	have	are
they	do	have	are

HINT

Substituting pronouns for nouns will work only when the subjects form their plurals by adding *s* or *es*. When the subject has an *s*, the verb will not have an *s*, for example,

*The soldier**s** train for the drill.*

But when the subject does not have an *s*, the verb will:

*The soldier train**s** for the drill.*

Of course, the rule doesn't work for nouns that do not form their plurals by adding *s* or *es*. With these plural nouns, the verb will still not end in an *s* or *es*:

*The people **stand** in line for the movies.*
*Children **love** to hear stories read aloud.*

---

[3] *Be* is the base form.

What is particularly difficult about subject–verb agreement is that a singular noun "agrees" with a verb with an *s*. The *s* on the verb is not the plural *s* or the possessive *s*. The same letter ending (or suffix) is used for three different purposes.

We have avoided labeling verbs as singular or plural because we do not think these labels are accurate or helpful. Instead, we have chosen to note the *s* ending added to the verb when the subject is *he*, *she*, or *it* or is a noun that can be replaced by one of these pronouns. This rule can be particularly helpful when dealing with the irregular verbs *do*, *have*, and *be*. Although these verbs do not have an *s* ending, they are spelled with a final *s* (*does*, *has*, and *is*) when the subject is *he*, *she*, or *it*. Focusing on the final *s* in the spelling of these irregular verbs will help you remember the forms used with the subjects *he*, *she*, or *it*.

Practice with Subject–Verb Agreement

1. Write in the "Noun" column the subjects you find in the essay you are writing in this chapter. Then fill in the rest of the table. First, decide whether the subject is singular or plural. Next, substitute the appropriate pronoun for the information you have put in the "Noun" column. Then, put in any verb that comes to mind and makes sense to you.

Noun	Singular/ plural	Pronoun substitute	Verb
_____	_____	_____	_____
_____	_____	_____	_____
_____	_____	_____	_____
_____	_____	_____	_____
_____	_____	_____	_____
_____	_____	_____	_____
_____	_____	_____	_____

2. To help you in subject–verb agreement, replace each noun with the appropriate personal pronoun. Use each of these nouns as the subject of a sentence of your own, using the appropriate form of a verb in the present tense.

419

love   daydreams   war   hormones   dictionary
status   fiction   envelope   computer   Taiwanese

_____

_____

_____

_____

_____

_____

_____

_____

3. Describe yourself in a paragraph beginning with the words "I am _____."
When you are finished, imagine that you are someone else, a good friend
of yours, and that that person is describing you to a third person. Change
the word *I* to *she* (or *he*) throughout the paragraph, and change all the
verbs accordingly.

_____

_____

_____

_____

_____

_____

_____

4. Read this comparison of the Taurus and Sagittarius personalities.[4] Circle all uses of *s* as the final letter of a word. Then, in the appropriate column, list each word you have circled.

Tauruses are born between April 21 and May 21. They are the strong, silent types whom nothing disturbs. They do not budge once their minds are made up. It's a rare Taurus who is anything but patient, calm, and placid. Taurus's temper, however, is characterized by blind fury. A true Taurus leads a quiet life; change upsets him or her, although each bears pressure with grace. The Taurus is solid looking, big shouldered, thick necked. A Taurus likes members of the opposite sex but doesn't go out looking for love. Tauruses prefer a quiet evening at home to a noisy night out.

Sagittarians, on the other hand, are the life of the party. These characters, born six months later, between November 23 and December 21, are very lively. There's nothing silent about a Sagittarian, who is friendly, outgoing, lively, and totally innocent that his or her behavior embarrasses somebody or makes someone else's life uncomfortable. The Sagittarian is blunt and gets away with it because of sparkling eyes and good intentions. Sagittarians share a temper with Tauruses. However, the Taurus must be pushed; the Sagittarian naturally rebels against authority. The Sagittarian tends to be big, athletic, and restless. He or she falls in love quickly but is hard to lead to the altar. Marriage's attractions are not for the person who wants to be the life of the party.

[4] Based on an exercise in Mina Shaughnessy's *Errors and Expectations* (New York: Oxford University Press, 1977), pp. 138–39.

plural s   *subject–verb agreement*   *possessive* s

last letter   *contraction*

Problems with Subject–Verb Agreement

Problems with subject–verb agreement are caused by not being able to find the subject of the sentence or not knowing whether the subject is singular or plural.

Sometimes the subject is separated from the verb. When you expand the subject part of the sentence, you may insert words or phrases between the subject and the verb:

1. The man whistles.
2. The man in the middle of the huddle whistles.
3. The man eating lunch with his friends whistles.

This separation is sometimes confusing because other nouns appear in the sentence, and you may be tempted to choose one of them to agree with the verb. For instance, if you chose *friends*, in sentence 3, you'd get the subject–

verb combination of *friends whistle*. But *friends* is not the subject of this sentence: *man* is. Circle the expanded subjects of the following sentences and enclose the verbs in boxes. Check the subject–verb agreement:

1. *Invisible Man*, by Ralph Ellison, one of the most highly regarded novels ever written in the United States, was published in 1948.
2. The main character of the novel, an unnamed black man who was born and raised in the South and migrates to the North, believes that white people do not really see him because of his blackness.
3. However, other people in the novel, black people as well as white, do not see him either.
4. Most of the characters, because of political attitudes or economic goals, do not understand who the main character really is.
5. Invisibility—the quality of not being noticed by other people—becomes both a prison for and the liberation of the main character.

Sometimes you ignore quantifiers (words that signify number or amount) that tell you whether a subject is singular or plural. Some quantifiers are easy to find:

A ticket is still available for the concert.

Sixty minutes comprise an hour.

Some quantifiers are hard to pick out:

One of the players needs to help the coach empty the lockers.

One is the key word because it is the subject and it is singular, even though it refers to the plural *players.* Underline the key words in these sentences:

1. None of the bags is big enough to contain all my art supplies.
2. Some of the people in the balcony are laughing too loudly.
3. Another one of the cartons has rotten eggs in it.
4. Several of the teachers in my school skip their lunch breaks to help students with problems.

Here is a list of quantifiers to consult:

a	some	several	few
any	none	each	many
all	both	one	much

Sometimes it is difficult to pick out plural subjects:

Shirley and Cathy skip rope well.

The subjects are connected with the joining word *and* to form a plural subject. Thus there is no *s* ending on the verb. The key word here is *and.* Whenever it is used to join two subjects, it will produce a plural subject. But this does not hold for other expressions that appear to combine subjects. Underline the phrases in the sentences below that look as if they join subjects:

1. The pastor, together with his congregation, is leaving for a spring retreat.
2. Susan, in addition to all the other students, needs a doctor's note to explain the prolonged absence from school.

---

[5] The term *mass noun* refers to nouns that can't be counted with numerals. For example, we can count a noun like *hat* (one hat, two hats), but we can't count nouns like *sand, traffic, mud, tar,* and *equipment.* The term also refers to nouns that are abstractions, like *peace, infinity, courage,* and *despair.*

The phrases *together with* and *in addition to* do not function in the same way as does the conjunction *and* to form a plural subject. *Pastor* and *Susan* remain singular noun-subjects.

HINT

There are two important exceptions to remember about joined noun-subjects. One is that the conjunction *and* is used in several expressions that are regarded as single units because the items occur together so often. For instance:

Ham and eggs is a nutritious breakfast.

The verb form *is* is used with *ham and eggs* because the expression is regarded as a single unit.

The other exception occurs when nouns are joined with the expressions "either . . . or" or "neither . . . nor." For example:

Neither the president nor the White House aides favor the new income tax bill.
Either the committee members or the chairperson decides the date for the next meeting.

The verbs in the sentences do not agree with both the nouns joined by these expressions. Rather, each verb agrees with the noun nearest to it. That is, in the first sentence, *favor* agrees with the plural subject *White House aides*, and in the second sentence, *decides* agrees with the subject *chairperson*.

The noun-subject can be a "collective" noun. Some nouns, like *team, class,* and *Congress,* refer to a group of people acting as a single unit. Although these words refer to more than one person, they are treated grammatically as singular nouns because the people they refer to are functioning together as a group:

The orchestra plays in the park on weekends.

The basketball team recruits new players in the spring.

Although *orchestra* and *team* refer to more than one person, the people play or act together, and so the entire group is considered to be one unit. Thus the verbs *plays* and *recruits* have the *s* endings that agree with singular subjects.

When the plural forms of these nouns are used, they function as plural subjects:

The orchestras from several cities play in the park on weekends.

All basketball teams recruit new players in the spring.

The subject can be a verb or verb phrase that functions as a noun. It is sometimes difficult to identify subjects when they are derived from verbs:

1. Watching football on Sundays is my father's favorite pastime.
2. Jogging is one of America's rituals.
3. Shopping for birthday presents always excites me.
4. To forgive is divine.
5. To go out in the rain without an umbrella is foolish.

In these sentences, the verbs are in their *ing* form (present participle)—*watching, jogging,* and *shopping*—or they are in their base form with *to* (infinitive)—*to forgive, to go.* Bracketing the expression and substituting a pronoun make it easier to see that these expressions operate as nouns:

It
[Watching football on Sundays] is my father's favorite pastime.

It
[Jogging] is one of America's rituals.

It
[Shopping for birthday presents] always excites me.

It
[To forgive] is divine.

It
[To go out in the rain without an umbrella] is foolish.

HINT

Sometimes the subject of the verb is difficult to find because it is not one word or even a phrase, but an entire clause:

Whatever Bill Cosby does makes me laugh.

The subject of the sentence is the clause "Whatever Bill Cosby does." Substituting the pronoun-subject *it* for the clause can help identify the subject:

It
[Whatever Bill Cosby does] *makes me laugh.*

Noun-subjects can be indefinite pronouns like *anybody, somebody, everyone,* and *nobody.* All of these pronouns are treated grammatically as singular, even though some of them (like *everybody* and *everyone*) may have a plural meaning:

Everybody needs to learn patience.

Nobody likes to be a loser.

The *s* ending is on both verbs so that they will agree with their singular subjects.

Additional Practice with Subject–Verb Agreement

1. Read the following comparison of two fruits, the kiwi and the apple, and write the appropriate present tense verb form in the blanks.

The kiwi and the apple ___ very different kinds of fruit. The egg-shaped
            (be)

kiwi, imported from New Zealand and until recently considered only a gour-

met food item, _____ fifty-nine to eighty-nine cents each. Eighty-nine cents
        (cost)

___ a lot of money for such a small, ugly fruit. It ___ brown, rough, hairy
(be)   (has)

skin, like the stubble of a day-old growth of beard, which ___ peeled off
                             (be)

before eating the fruit. The inside of the kiwi ___ a gentle green color. When
                   (has)

you slice a kiwi in rounds, you ___ even lighter shades of green coming
                   (see)

from the center of each piece; small black, edible seeds _____ a circle near
                   (form)

the center of each slice. To bite into a kiwi ___ to delight your sense of
               (be)

taste. When ripe but not too mushy, a kiwi _____ juicy and sweet, with just
               (taste)

a hint of tartness.

Although it _____ in many varieties, the domestic apple ___ much
       (come)   (be)

less exotic than the kiwi. Apples _____ in many parts of the United States.
         (grow)

They, of course, ___ less too. In the fall, when apples of all sorts and varieties
      (cost)

___ in season, eighty-nine cents ___ two whole pounds of apples. Apples
(be)   (buy)

___ also less trouble to eat. Their shiny, smooth skins—green or red or yellow—
(be)

_____ crunchy and sweet. The skins also _____ a substance called pectin,
(taste)   (contain)

which _____ blood cholesterol. Many different varieties of apples, from the
    (lower)

familiar MacIntosh and Delicious to the rarer Jonathans and Mutsus, ___
                                     (be)

available in most supermarkets. Almost anyone _____ afford them; everyone
                                                      (can)

_____ them. Each variety of apple _____ different; some apples ___ sweet
(enjoy)   (taste)   (be)

and some ___ tart; some ___ dense and some ___ light.
         (be)   (be)   (be)

2. Proofread the following comparison of pizza and tacos for problems with
subject–verb agreement.

Pizza and tacos are ethnic foods that has always been favorites in
their own communites, but now their popularity extend far beyond their
origins. They is convenience foods; hand-held portions can be eaten while
walking or standing at a counter.

Pizza and tacos contains some of the same ingredients. Each have
some kind of dough, tomatoes, or tomato sauce, cheese, and spices. The
dough, of course, is different. Pizza dough are usually thick and crunchy,
whereas the tortilla used for tacos are thin and crisp. Some of the spices
used in Italian and Mexican cooking is the same: garlic, sweet and hot
peppers, and oregano. However, the tomato sauce used for pizza also
contain bay leaf, parsley, thyme, and onion. The salsa we puts on tacos
contain chilies, cumin, and cilantro. A mild Mozzarella cheese make up
a large part of a pizza, and a mild cheese, like Monterey Jack, just tops a
taco. Some pizzas come with meat, but most tacos does. Sausage can be
ordered on a pizza, whereas tacos contains ground beef.

3. Write a paragraph in which you compare either radio and television or
cars and buses. When you're finished, circle each subject and draw a box
around each verb. Then proofread the paragraph for subject–verb agreement. Use your own paper.

Simple Past Tense

The simple past tense describes an action that was started and completed at a specific time in the past. For example, if someone asked, "Did you go to school yesterday?" you might answer, "Yes, I went to school yesterday." The word *yesterday* tells the specific time, and the verb *went* indicates that your going to school started and ended yesterday.

Circle the words or phrases in the sentences below that indicate the specific time each event or action took place.

*Several entertainers **sang** at the rock concert last night.*

*We **visited** our cousins last week.*

*The airplane **arrived** at the airport at 8:00 A.M.*

You do not have to state the specific time if it is understood that something happened in the past. For example, if you were asked, "Did you go to school yesterday?" you might respond, "Yes, I went to school," or "Yes, I did go to school," or "Yes, I did."

Form the simple past tense by adding *ed* to the base form of the verb. We shall discuss the exceptions to this rule later in this chapter.

HINT

When we use the helping verb *did* to form the simple past tense, as in the sentence "I did go to school," we form a verb phrase with the base form of the main verb *go*. Notice that the past tense is indicated only by the helping verb *did*, not the main verb *go* (that is, not *did went*). The present tense is indicated by the helping verb *does*, the past tense by the helping verb *did*. The main verb does not change when it is combined with the helping verb. See Appendix 7 for a further discussion of *do*.

The tense of verbs affects the meanings of sentences. What differences do you notice in the meanings of these sentences? How do the shifts in verb tenses affect the meanings of the sentences?

1. Vickie likes school very much.
2. Vickie once liked school very much.
3. Josephine is playing the piano.
4. Josephine once played the piano.

Which sentence indicates that Vickie has stopped liking school? ____
Which sentence indicates that Josephine has stopped playing the piano? ____

Which sentence indicates that Vickie still enjoys school? _____

Which sentence indicates that Josephine continues to play the piano? _____

Continuous Past Tense

When Do We Use the Continuous Past Tense?

We use the continuous past tense mainly when we want to indicate that an action or event occurred while something else was happening. For example,

> Samantha was crawling on the floor when she accidentally bumped her nose on a chair.
> Something happened—Samantha bumped her nose on a chair—while another action was occurring—she was crawling.

These sentences also show actions occurring simultaneously:

> The train was leaving the station as I arrived at the platform.
> When the boss entered the office, the receptionist was talking on the telephone.

Forming the Past Tense

How Do We Form the Continuous Past Tense?

To form the continuous past tense, we use the helping verb *was* (or *were*) and the *ing* form of the main verb, for example,

> I was driving.
> We were driving.

The helping verb has two forms that must agree with their subjects:

Subject (*pronoun*)	Verb (*wait*)
I	was waiting
you (singular)	were waiting
he, she, it	was waiting
we	were waiting
you (plural)	were waiting
they	were waiting

Subject–verb agreement is necessary only for forms of the verb *to be* because this verb has two forms in the past tense (*was, were*). All other verbs have one simple past tense form for all subjects.

To form the simple past tense, we add *ed* to the base form of regular verbs. For example,

Present	Past
I *talk* on the telephone.	I *talked* on the telephone.
I *hope* to win the lottery.	I *hoped* to win the lottery.

Examples of this rule are on the following verb chart:

Base form	Present tense	Past tense
(to) look	look/looks	looked
(to) ridicule	ridicule/ridicules	ridiculed
(to) write	write/writes	wrote
(to) bite	bite/bites	bit
(to) spend	spend/spends	spent
(to) lend	lend/lends	lent
(to) set	set/sets	set
(to) bet	bet/bets	bet

This chart also contains examples of the many exceptions to the rule that you add *ed* to form the past tense:

1. Some verbs form the past tense by changing the vowel sound (for instance, *speak* becomes *spoke*). Star two examples of this on the verb chart.
2. Some verbs form the past tense by changing the final letter *d* to *t* (for instance, *bend* becomes *bent*). Put two stars next to examples of this in the verb chart.
3. Some verbs do not change to form the past tense (for instance, hit remains *hit*). Put two checks next to examples of this in the verb chart.

If you think of other exceptions, add them in the blank spaces of the chart.

HINT

A special group of words does not add the present tense *s* or the past tense *ed* endings:

can	shall
could	should
may	will
might	would
must	ought

These are often called *helping verbs* or *auxiliary verbs*. We combine them with *regular* or *main verbs* to form *verb phrases*:

The mechanics **can fix** all kinds of cars.

Can fix is a verb phrase. If we change the subject to *mechanic* or *he* or *she*, the verb phrase will remain the same:

The mechanic **can fix** all kinds of cars.

Helping verbs tell us something about the main verb:

Can expresses capability.

Susan **can jog** four miles a day.

Could is sometimes used as the past tense of *can*.

Susan **could jog** four miles when she was eighteen years old.

May and *might* express doubt.

Felix **may get** an award for his community service.
Wally **might retain** the presidency of the student government.

Must expresses strong obligation or certainty.

> Veronica **must pay** for the tickets by Friday.

Note: Use *had to* for the past tense of *must:* Veronica *had to* pay for the tickets by Friday.

Shall is used in the first person to express future time or strong intention.

> I **shall do** my homework when I finish my dinner.

Should and *ought to* express obligation.

> Cheryl **should share** her clothes with her sister.
> Brenda **ought to marry** Bart.

Will indicates future time.

> She **will wash** the car this weekend.

Would indicates a condition.

> Tracy **would go** roller skating if she were not sick with the flu.

Notice that the main verbs in these verb phrases do not have any *s* or *ed* endings. When main verbs are joined to certain helping or auxiliary verbs, they do not change endings or forms.

Practice with Past Tenses

1. Change all the present tense verb forms in this story of Fleda Starr, private investigator, into the past tense. Add time words if you need them to help express the meaning. (Do not change words inside quotation marks.)

STARR'S FIRST CASE

"I am hungry," Starr says to herself. "I am just going to hop over to Ellen's for the fried clam special." She speaks aloud, but there is no one in the room to hear her. She pushes in the drawer of the battered oak desk, wheels the old swivel chair back along the plank floor, and stands up.

Before she can reach the door, the sight from the window catches her attention. The second floor of a Bearskin Neck house is a perfect place to view the ocean at dusk. The pleasure boats are gliding in through the placid water. Starr sees old *Miss Rockport* stop at Tuna Wharf and her last passengers scurry off. She knows that after leaving the wharf, they write their "I love Rockport" postcards at the Heart Shop, dash for their cars, and head for Route 128 before dark.

Lights begin to sparkle, on shore and off. The lighthouses on Thacher's Island twinkle in the waning light. Starr loves Thacher's Island, the romantic mystery of Rockport.

"This is what keeps me here," she thinks, and sighs. "I can get more work in Boston. Who needs a private investigator on Cape Ann? But where else can I see this view from my window?"

Starr shifts her eyes from the view and starts for the door when she hears footsteps on the stairs. Starr knows it is a woman, from the sound. And the woman is hesitant. She lightly jiggles the door knob before she knocks.

2. Insert the appropriate past tense form of the verb in the passage that follows. In this exercise you may change even those words inside quotation marks.

STARR'S FIRST CASE (CONTINUED)

She ____ not from Rockport or Gloucester. Starr _____ that immediately.
　　　(be)　　　　　　　　　　　　　　　　　　　　(know)

This lady _____ the look of Magnolia, Starr _____: the neatly styled blond
　　　　　(have)　　　　　　　　　　　　　　(think)

hair, the white gloves and small purse, the black and white pumps. She _____
　　　　　　　　　　　　　　　　　　　　　　　　　　　　　　　　　(sleep)

on satin sheets, Starr _____.
　　　　　　　　　　(surmise)

"I _____ you are a private detective," the lady _____. Her hands,
　　(understand)　　　　　　　　　　　　　　　　　(begin)

carefully folded in her lap, ___ shaking. The lights on the Neck _____ through
　　　　　　　　　　　　　　(be)　　　　　　　　　　　　　　(shine)

the window.

Starr _____ silently, waiting for the woman to speak. She _____ for the
　　　(sit)　　　　　　　　　　　　　　　　　　　　　　　　　　(wait)

woman to begin her story.

"My name is Alice Wharton. My son and I _____ a great deal. He _____
　　　　　　　　　　　　　　　　　　　　　(fight)　　　　　　　(lose)

every job he _____ at. And when he ___ not get fired, he _____. Then he
　　　　　　(work)　　　　　　　　　(do)　　　　　　　　(quit)

_____ all day and ___ around the house all night. We _____. Then he _____.
(swim)　　　　　(lay)　　　　　　　　　　　　　　　(fight)　　　　　(leave)

He _____ in a few days, and I _____ him."
　(return)　　　　　　　　　　(forgive)

"How old ___ your son on his last birthday? Starr _____.
　　　　(be)　　　　　　　　　　　　　　　　　　(ask)

"Nineteen."

It _____ like a familiar enough pattern. Starr ___ so.
　(sound)　　　　　　　　　　　　　　　　(say)

"Yes, but the pattern _____." Mrs. Wharton's voice _____ deeper.
　　　　　　　　　　(change)　　　　　　　　　　　　(grow)

"Money ___ missing from the house. I ___ him all he _____, but he ___
　　　(be)　　　　　　　　　　　　(give)　　　　(need)　　　　(tell)

me he _____ more." She _____ in disgust. "He _____ his own mother's money!"
　　(want)　　　　　(sigh)　　　　　　(steal)

she nearly _____. "Then he _____ a lamp to the floor, and he _____ the
　　　　(shriek)　　　　　(throw)　　　　　　　　　　　　　(leave)

room. He ___ on a swim suit, _____ off the rocks and _____ toward Norman's
　　　(put)　　　　　　　(dive)　　　　　　　　(swim)

Woe."

"Do you want me to find him?" Starr _____.
　　　　　　　　　　　　　　　　　(ask)

". . . the best I _____," Mrs. Wharton _____ to herself.
　　　　　　　(can)　　　　　　　　　(murmur)

"Do you want me to find him?" Starr _____.
　　　　　　　　　　　　　　　　　(repeat)

"Yes," the woman _____.
　　　　　　　(whisper)

Starr _____ out the window. The moon _____ and _____ on the ocean;
　(glance)　　　　　　　　　　　　(rose)　　(shine)

the water ___ calm. But trouble _____ in paradise. Maybe Cape Ann ___
　　　(be)　　　　　　　　　　(brew)　　　　　　　　　　　　　(do)

_____ a detective.
(need)

Starr _____ a pad out of her desk drawer. She _____ her first case.
　(take)　　　　　　　　　　　　　　　　　(begin)

3. Read this excerpt from a *New York Times* editorial by William Safire about the Bernhard Goetz case. Goetz shot three teenagers on a New York City subway train after they asked him for money. Draw a box around each verb and verb phrase. Note any words you do not understand.

(1) . . . conservatives hailed the Goetz response as a courageous and long-overdue act of self-defense, symbolic of the need for the potential victim to fight criminal fire with fire, especially when the forces of law in New York City are able to put only one in jail for every 50 crimes reported.

(2) . . . liberals, slow to react for fear of getting mugged on the way to the ramparts, finally found their voices to protest what seemed to them the excessive use of force by a vengeance-bent white against four black youths. The police records of these subway swaggerers will be explained as root-caused by poverty and society's neglect, and the blazing reaction of the gun-toting man they accosted will be held up as the product of the right-wing Reagan fanatics who oppose gun control.

(3) Psychojournalists have had a field day explaining the pent-up outrage of the put-upon citizen. His appetite for the immediate gratification of vigilante justice, we are informed, was whetted in recent years by the actors Charles Bronson and Clint Eastwood.

(4) Sociologists and depth-pollsters will turn out doctoral theses on the six-week turn in public opinion, as the original shy hero turns out to be a publicity-seeker who reportedly pleaded mental ailments to avoid military service, and one of the original threateners, who had been armed with a screwdriver, may be paralyzed for life.

The tenses of the verbs make a difference in the meaning of the sentences.

1. Are conservatives still hailing Goetz?
2. Are liberals already protesting?

3. Have the police records been explained?
4. How would the meaning of paragraph 3 be different if it read "Psycho-journalists *will have* a field day . . ."?
5. When was Goetz's interest in vigilantism formed?
6. Was the "publicity-seeker" in paragraph 4 already called for military service?
7. Are we positive that "one of the original threateners" will remain paralyzed? If we are, what word should we use to express our certainty?

Future Tense

What Is the Future Tense?

The future tense indicates that an action or event will take place in the future:

We will play the baseball game tomorrow at 7:30 P.M.

Veronica will lend you five dollars so you can go with us to the movies.

How Do We Form the Future Tense?

We form the future tense with the helping verb *will* (or *shall*) and the base form of the main verb, as in *will play* (or *shall play*) and *will lend* (or *shall lend*).[6]

Practice with the Future Tense

1. Draw a box around the main verb in each sentence of the passage below. Change each to the future tense. Do not change the verbs inside the quotation marks.

> Learning to drive is a terrifying experience. You sit behind the wheel of the car, and you feel like a two-year-old in front of a computer. The dashboard looks like a maze of dials. Letters and numbers look as though they can jump out at you. The floor is no less intimidating. Pumps and levers wait to be used. Your instructor's voice drones. "You turn the key in the ignition and step on the accelerator."
>
> "Hey, wait a minute," you want to scream. "I am too scared to understand what you are saying."

---

[6] There is another way to express the future, for example,

Ted Kennedy says he *is not going to run* for president in 1988.

437

Finally, the instructor gets you moving. You are in traffic. Cars are

moving all around you. "You need your signal to turn," she says.

"Signal?" you answer. "What's a signal? I can't learn to drive."

2. Write a paragraph about what you hope to achieve in the next five years of your life, beginning with "In the next five years, I hope to _____." When you are finished, check to see that you have used the future tense appropriately. Use your own paper.

SPELLING

Rules for Simple Past Tense Verb Forms and *ing* Forms

Three spelling rules govern the formation of the simple past and *ing* forms.

1. Some verbs double the final consonant when adding *ed* or *ing* (*stop* becomes *stopped* and *stopping*). Two types of verbs do this:

   a. A verb with a one-syllable base form that ends in a single vowel plus a single consonant, for example, *rob, jog.*

   b. A verb with a base form of more than one syllable, whose accent is on the last syllable and which ends in a single vowel and a single consonant, for example, *permit, control.*

2. Some verbs ending in *y* change it to *i* when adding *ed.* (*Study* becomes *studied*).

3. Some verbs ending in *e* drop it when adding *ed* or *ing* (*hope* becomes *hoped* and *hoping*).

HINT

The expression *used to* frequently appears in verb phrases to indicate an action or event that occurred in the past:

> Eric **used to play** cards with us on Saturday nights.
> Maxine **used to be** a member of the Committee on Public Housing.

The sound of the *d* ending is lost because of the word that follows. Students often forget to write it because they do not hear themselves say it. Knowing that a *d* should go "somewhere," some people put if on the main verb: "use to played." Some people put it on both, "used to played." Remember that the *d* ending goes on *use* and that the base form does not take an ending.

438

Practice Spelling Past Tense Verb Forms and *ing* Forms

Proofread this passage for spelling errors. Check the verb chart in Appendix 9:

Because of recent scandals, national attention is focussing on college sports, and some coaches are admiting that they don't teach their athletes that playing the game well and honorring their obligations to their studies are more important than wining the game. Instead, these coaches say they've been forgeting their responsibilities as teachers, and as a result, college athletes are running wild.

On the field, athletes are hurtting fellow players and even sluging it out with opponents, because controling the point spread of games is important to betting on the outcome. In effect, the athletes are selling their integrity to gamblers. Off the field, athletes are swiming in drugs, and one college football player was even found to be robing from fellow students to pay for his habit. No one, the coaches now say, wins in this situation, and it is begining to change. Coaches are running their teams more aggressively. Athletes found to be cuting classes are bared from playing, and those who take drugs are being refered to treatment programs. The athletes are whining about it, but the coaches are also stoping the illegal gambling connections. College sports are entering a cleaner era.

THE FINAL DRAFT

Now you are ready to proofread the middle draft of the essay you began earlier in this chapter. Read your essay again slowly, and aloud. Remember what you learned about word order and sense in Chapter 1 and about the conventions of writing in Chapter 2. You may need to look back at these chapters. Check to see that each sentence you've written contains a subject and a verb.

Make sure you can answer yes to these questions as you proofread:

1. Is the verb of each sentence in a tense that tells you when the event occurred?
2. If you are writing in the present tense, did you use the simple present and the continuous present appropriately?
3. Do your subjects and verbs agree? Do all the verbs that need *s* endings have them?
4. Do you know why you have *s* endings on all the words (verbs and other words) that have them?
5. If you are writing in the past tense, did you use the simple past and the continuous past appropriately?
6. Did you use *d* and *ed* endings, and did you spell the past tense forms correctly?

ADDITIONAL WRITING ASSIGNMENTS

Your writer's journal may have some issues or ideas for you to develop into essays. Focus on ideas you think need to be explained, particularly by comparing and contrasting them with something else. These may be things you do not understand and want to explain to yourself. Or they may be ideas you wish to share with others. You may want to imagine that you are a "time traveler" explaining something to a person who lived in 1822 or who will live in 2135.

Here are some issues that students have found need to be explained by means of comparison and contrast. Remember to follow the writing process we are developing: Do focused writing first. Then look it over. You may want to review the Writing and Rewriting section of each chapter before you start your middle drafts. When you finish, proofread them and write a clean copy.

Topic Suggestions

1. your neighborhood now and when you were young.
2. jazz and rock music.
3. two teachers you remember.
4. the city you live in and one you've visited.
5. "Dallas" and "Dynasty."
6. saints and sinners.
7. two rooms in your house.
8. Wendy's and McDonald's.
9. two friends.
10. writing and talking.

You may also want to think about yourself. What do you look like? Where do you live? What is your life like? What do you believe in? What do you value? Then think of what you will be like in ten years. Compare yourself as you are now with the person you may be in a decade.

Taking a Stand

Photo by
Kathy Sloane

1. Read these statements:

a. Baseball is more exciting than basketball.

b. Women should be drafted into the armed forces.

c. Prayers should be said in public schools.

d. The United States should not have business dealings with South Africa.

e. Law-abiding citizens should arm themselves against muggers, thieves, and rapists.

Check each statement you agree with, copy it in the appropriate space below, and then write down two reasons why you support it.

statement: ＿＿＿＿＿＿＿＿＿   statement: ＿＿＿＿＿＿＿＿＿

＿＿＿＿＿＿＿＿＿＿＿   ＿＿＿＿＿＿＿＿＿＿＿

reason 1: ＿＿＿＿＿＿＿＿   reason 1: ＿＿＿＿＿＿＿＿

＿＿＿＿＿＿＿＿＿＿＿   ＿＿＿＿＿＿＿＿＿＿＿

＿＿＿＿＿＿＿＿＿＿＿   ＿＿＿＿＿＿＿＿＿＿＿

reason 2: ＿＿＿＿＿＿＿＿   reason 2: ＿＿＿＿＿＿＿＿

＿＿＿＿＿＿＿＿＿＿＿   ＿＿＿＿＿＿＿＿＿＿＿

＿＿＿＿＿＿＿＿＿＿＿   ＿＿＿＿＿＿＿＿＿＿＿

Jot down some reasons that people might not agree with each of the statements:

＿＿＿＿＿＿＿＿＿   ＿＿＿＿＿＿＿＿＿

＿＿＿＿＿＿＿＿＿   ＿＿＿＿＿＿＿＿＿

＿＿＿＿＿＿＿＿＿   ＿＿＿＿＿＿＿＿＿

＿＿＿＿＿＿＿＿＿   ＿＿＿＿＿＿＿＿＿

2. From the following list of topics from a class discussion on "what students write about," choose three you might want to write about:

a. mass transit.

b. crime/punishment.

c. money.

d. sex.

e. personal independence.

f. future.

g. marriage/divorce.

h. relationships between parents and children.

i. racism.

j. drugs.

Then for each topic, write one sentence that reflects your feelings about the issue. For example:

> [I believe] drugs can cost you your health and, possibly, your life. [I think] children must respect their parents but parents should also respect their children.

Topic 1: _____

Sentence: [I think] _____

Topic 2: _____

Sentence: [I think] _____

Topic 3: _____

Sentence: [I think] _____

READING

PREVIEW QUESTIONS

As you read "Smokers Have Rights, Too," by Ernest van den Haag, look for information that will help answer these questions:

1. What side does van den Haag take at the beginning of the essay? List the reasons that he takes this side.
2. Read the title and the introductory and closing paragraphs. Can you determine from them the problem that van den Haag is addressing and his solution to it? What do you expect the body of the essay to contain, based on your analysis of these two paragraphs?
3. Notice van den Haag's use of *we* in the first three paragraphs. Do you feel you are one of the persons included in the *we?* Who do you think van den Haag is addressing?
4. Van den Haag directs many questions to his audience. Read carefully the questions in paragraphs 3 and 7. Do they help van den Haag make his points? Does he answer his own questions? Does he want you to answer them? How would you answer the questions in paragraph 3?

5. Van den Haag also uses comparisons to illustrate his points. For example, he says that smoking is a dependence, like reliance on a lover.
He also suggests that smoking is like eating and drinking. How effective
are these comparisons? Do you agree with him?

Notes

Winston Churchill (1874–1965). British statesman, orator, writer, and prime
minister during and again after World War II. Churchill chain-smoked
cigars.

Smokers Have Rights, Too
Ernest van den Haag

*Ernest van den Haag is a professor of law and public policy at the Fordham
University Law School in New York City. This article appeared originally in
the* New York Times *on April 9, 1985.*

(1) Enough is enough, and we have seen enough of the harassment and intimidation of smokers.

(2) True, smoking is bad for the smoker's health, and when he finally
suffers his heart attack, or gets lung cancer, abstinent taxpayers have to pay
for his hospitalization. As a result, many nonsmokers favor laws prohibiting
smoking, at least in public and semipublic places. This may seem logical,
but it puts us, as a society, on a dangerous, slippery slope, raising the prospect
that we will soon be preventing all kinds of other people from doing what
they want because of hazards to their health and our pocketbooks.

(3) After all, taxpayers are also compelled to help pay for the hospitalization of drinkers, obese overeaters and those too lazy to exercise. Should we,
then, have legal regulation of eating, drinking and exercising? How much
liberty—the liberty to enjoy one's own habits and even vices—are we willing
to sacrifice?

(4) People smoke, or drink, or eat the wrong things, despite bad physical
effects, because of the psychological gratification they obtain. In his 60's, Sigmund Freud underwent the first of more than 30 painful operations for oral
cancer. He was told that it was caused by cigar smoking, but he continued
nevertheless. In his 72d year he wrote: "I owe to the cigar a great intensification
of my capacity to work and . . . of my self-control." By then, he had an
artificial jaw and palate. He smoked till he died, in his 80's.

(5) Most nonsmokers simply cannot understand this, and they scornfully
label it "addiction." I prefer to call it a dependence, like reliance on a lover.
Such a reliance may be enjoyable and productive; and it may have bad, even

tragic, effects as well. But even when the bad effects become clear, one may want to continue because of the gratifications: the habit, once formed, is usually hard to shake. If one is deprived of the lover, or of the cigars, one suffers withdrawal symptoms, be they physical or psychological. Love is seldom called an addiction. Why should smoking be?

(6) The nonsmoking taxpayer is right about one thing: he should not have to pay for hospitalizations caused by smoking. Instead, we should impose a Federal tax on tobacco sufficient to pay all the extra costs that smoking causes. Insurance companies, too, might charge higher rates to smokers and drinkers.

(7) But what about the health effects of "passive smoking" and the annoyance that smoking may cause?

(8) Some people are indeed allergic to smoke, and any civilized person will avoid smoking when they are around. Allergic people should, in turn, avoid places and occasions known to be smoky—discotheques, bars or dinners with Winston Churchill. But allergies to smoking have increased amazingly in recent years—a sudden increase that suggests that many of them are hysterical, or faked, to justify the imposition of the nonsmoker's preference on smokers.

(9) In fact, dubious statistics to the contrary and except in instances of rare genuine allergies, smoking does not ordinarily endanger the health of nonsmokers unless they are exposed to smoke for a long time in an unventilated space.

(10) As for annoyance, life is full of annoyances, some hazardous to health, that we must tolerate for the sake of other people, who want, or need, to do what annoys us. We all have to breathe polluted air, even if we never ride in a car or bus, simply because others want to.

(11) Far more people refrain from smoking now than in the past—which is fine. But harassment will not increase their number. Nor will the prohibitions of cigarette advertising. Marijuana does quite well without such promotion. People learn to smoke, or drink, from others, not from advertisements.

(12) Is there nothing to be done? Certainly, wherever possible we should separate nonsmokers from smokers and provide ventilation. We do so now on big airplanes. But in most other places, in offices and restaurants, for instance, smokers and nonsmokers will have to rely on mutual tolerance. Courtesy cannot be replaced by one-sided and unenforceable regulations which, even if temporarily effective, will in the long run simply discredit the law.

QUESTIONS OF CONTENT

Circle the letter of the best answer to each question.

1. Despite the bad physical effects, people continue to eat, drink, and smoke the wrong things because

a. their parents did these things.

b. they obtain psychological gratification from them.

c. they have adequate health insurance.

d. they have a death wish.

2. Instead of an addiction, the author calls smoking a

    a. dependence.   **c.** tragedy.

    b. substitution.   **d.** burden.

3. The recent increase in allergies to smoking suggests that

    a. more people are smoking than ever before.

    b. more nonsmokers are becoming hysterical.

    c. low-tar cigarettes are not effective.

    d. too much pollution is fouling the air.

4. People learn to smoke cigarettes from

    a. reading advertisements.

    b. watching others smoke.

    c. drinking alcohol.

    d. associating with the wrong crowd.

Answer these questions in full sentences:

1. According to the author, under what conditions does smoking endanger the health of nonsmokers? _____

_____

2. Why did Sigmund Freud continue to smoke, even though he developed oral cancer? _____

_____

3. What should people do who are allergic to smoke? _____

_____

4. What ailments are smokers almost certain to suffer from? _____

_____

5. Summarize van den Haag's major arguments for the rights of smokers.

_____

_____

_____

QUESTIONS OF INFERENCE ■■■■■■■■■■■

Look back at the essay to answer these questions. Answer in full sentences.

1. In the opening paragraph, van den Haag states that "we have seen enough of the harassment and intimidation of smokers." What kinds of things is he referring to that might have been done to smokers? _____

   _____

2. How harmful does van den Haag think smoking is? How does comparing it with drinking and eating affect your judgment of it? _____

   _____

3. How do you think van den Haag would feel about gambling, prostitution, and dope? Would he also oppose legislation to combat these vices? Explain.

   _____

   _____

4. In paragraph 8, van den Haag uses the term *civilized person*. What seems to make a person civilized? _____

   _____

5. In paragraph 3, van den Haag asks, "Should we, then, have legal regulation of eating, drinking and exercising?" What answer does he expect us to give? Why? _____

   _____

QUESTIONS OF CRITICAL THINKING ■■■■■■■■■■■

Answer each of these questions in a short paragraph. You may want to use your own paper.

1. Does van den Haag's use of the anecdote about Freud strengthen his

argument? Explain. _____

_____

_____

2. Van den Haag chooses to label smoking as a "dependence," not as an "addiction." Why is this difference important to him? Is it important to

you? Explain. _____

_____

_____

3. List some habits or vices that other people have that annoy you. Would you favor legal restrictions on any of these? Why or why not?

_____

_____

_____

4. In paragraph 3, van den Haag asks, "How much liberty—the liberty to enjoy one's own habits and even vices—are we willing to sacrifice?" How would you answer this question based on your own habits and vices?

_____

_____

_____

5. Van den Haag uses Freud as an example of someone who got great satisfaction from smoking despite its "bad physical effects." Can you think of someone else who has both benefited and suffered from smoking or some

other habit or vice? Explain. _____

_____

_____

_____

6. Van den Haag compares smoking with drinking and eating. In what ways are they similar and in what ways are they different? Do you think it is a fair comparison? Explain. How does the comparison help strengthen

his argument? _____

_____

_____

7. Van den Haag notes that in most public places (offices and restaurants) "smokers and nonsmokers will have to rely on mutual tolerance." What does he have in mind? What kinds of things would they have to do to

accommodate each other? _____

_____

_____

8. Van den Haag argues that people don't learn how to smoke from advertisements. If this is so, what do they learn about smoking from advertisements?

_____

_____

_____

9. In paragraph 10, van den Haag states that life is full of annoyances (for example, air pollution from car emissions) that we must learn to live with. Is this a good argument for smoking? Explain.

_____

_____

_____

10. How does the tone of the article change when van den Haag uses the terms *hysterical* and *faked* to describe the allergic reactions of nonsmokers to smoking? What effects may the author's use of these terms have on

his audience? _____

_____

_____

11. Do you think van den Haag is a smoker or nonsmoker? Is there anything in the article that suggests what he is? Would it make a difference to you if you knew whether or not he smoked? Do you think that a smoker can present better arguments against smoking than a nonsmoker can?

Why or why not? _____

_____

_____

_____

VOCABULARY

These words from "Smokers Have Rights, Too" may be unfamiliar to you. The exercises will help you learn the meanings of these words and how they function in sentences.

harassment	(1)	oral	(4)	dubious	(9)
intimidation	(1)	intensification	(4)	endanger	(9)
abstinent	(2)	palate	(4)	hazardous	(10)
semipublic	(2)	dependence	(5)	refrain	(11)
prospect	(2)	reliance	(5)	ventilation	(12)
compelled	(3)	withdrawal	(5)	tolerance	(12)
obese	(3)	impose	(6)	discredit	(12)
vices	(3)	passive	(7)		
gratification	(4)				

Word Meanings

Look up the words below in the dictionary. Each has more than one meaning and may be listed as more than one part of speech. Read the entire entry for each part of speech listed. Choose the meaning closest to the way in which the word is used in the selection. If you're in doubt, write down all the meanings you think are possible, separating them by semicolons. Be sure to include the part of speech next to your definition.

prospect _____

vice[s] _____

palate _____

oral _____

impose _____

refrain _____

Word Clues

The words below are made of prefixes (or suffixes) added to a root word. If you know the root words and look up the prefix or suffix in the list on pages 10–13, you should be able to figure out the meanings. On the line next to each word, write the separate parts. (You may need to change the spellings somewhat to see a root word in some.) Write a working definition for each word. Check the dictionary entry to see how close your working definition is to it.

semipublic _____

discredit _____

withdrawal _____

hazardous _____

The two words below have similar suffixes: *ence, ance.* What does the suffix

mean? _____. Write the root word and your working definition:

dependence _____

reliance _____

The words below have the same suffix: *tion.* What does it mean? _____.
Write the root word and your working definition:

intimidation _____

ventilation _____

gratification _____

intensification _____

Word Classes

Many words in "Smokers Have Rights, Too" have other forms that you may know:

Verbs	Nouns	Adjectives	Adverbs
annoy	annoyance	annoying	annoyingly
depend	dependence	dependable	dependably
	dependent	dependent	
rely	reliance	reliable	reliably
produce	producer	productive	productively
	production		
	product		
amaze	amazement	amazing	amazingly
impose	imposition	imposing	imposingly
prefer	preference	preferred	preferably
		ordinary	ordinarily
hazard	hazard	hazardous	
prohibit	prohibition	prohibited	
advertise	advertisement	advertising	
	advertising		
promote	promotion	promotable	
tolerate	tolerance	tolerant	
effect	effect	effective	effectively
intimidate	intimidation	intimidated	
harass	harassment	harassed	
gratify	gratification	gratified	

Notice that certain word classes frequently have certain endings. For instance: the suffixes *ance, ence, tion,* and *ment* are noun suffixes; the suffixes *able, ive,* and *ous* are adjective suffixes, and *ly* is an adverb suffix.

What's most important to know is how the word functions in a sentence. Does it name something (noun), tell you what something is or is doing (verb); tell you more about the doing (adverb); or describe the noun (adjective)?

Choose the form of the word in parentheses that fits best in each blank. Add *s* to verb forms where necessary.

1. When the children play, the little girl _____ her brother, but the sound of their screeching is a constant _____ to their grandmother. (annoy)

2. _____ is a form of emotional blackmail; a person who _____ others is an emotional criminal. (intimidate)

3. My _____ for champagne is well known; my friends know I _____ it to any other wine. (prefer)

4. The snow made driving _____, as the blinding white stuff made each

curve a new _____. (hazard)

5. _____ is a major industry in the United States. Retailers _____ to sell

their products, spending large amounts on each new _____ campaign.
(advertise)

6. An _____ day for a Himalayan *sherpa* consists of climbing mountains,

which are _____ covered with ice and snow. (ordinary)

7. I _____ on aspirins to cure a headache, but my _____ on these pills is

tempered by the knowledge that no medication is totally _____. (rely)

8. Each television _____ is the successful completion of the _____ efforts

of a director, actors, and _____. (produce)

Seeing Words in Context

These words appear in "Smokers Have Rights, Too." You may find clues to
the meaning of each word in its context. As you reread, circle the words or
phrases that form the context for each word. Then write (1) your working
definition, (2) the dictionary definition that's right for the context, and (3) an
original sentence using the word. If you have difficulty figuring out the meaning of the word from the context of "Smokers Have Rights, Too," you may
find it helpful to read the following story, in which the words appear in italics:

1. word: *obese*

    a. working definition: _____

    b. dictionary definition: _____

    c. your sentence: _____

2. word: *passive*

    a. working definition: _____

    b. dictionary definition: _____

    c. your sentence: _____

3. word: *dubious*

   a. working definition: _____

   b. dictionary definition: _____

   c. your sentence: _____

4. word: *compel(led)*

   a. working definition: _____

   b. dictionary definition: _____

   c. your sentence: _____

5. word: *endanger*

   a. working definition: _____

   b. dictionary definition: _____

   c. your sentence: _____

6. word: *abstinent*

   a. working definition: _____

   b. dictionary definition: _____

   c. your sentence: _____

7. word: *harass(ment)*

   a. working definition: _____

   b. dictionary definition: _____

   c. your sentence: _____

McDERMOTT VERSUS XEROX

In 1974, Mrs. Catherine McDermott was denied a job with the Xerox Corporation because at five-feet-six and 246 pounds, she was considered *obese*. Mrs. McDermott did not sit back and take it. Instead of being *passive*, she filed suit against Xerox.

Acting as her own lawyer, Mrs. McDermott argued that Xerox's grounds for not hiring her were *dubious*; she doubted that Xerox was concerned for her health more than their own disability-insurance rates.

Xerox should be forced, *compelled,* to hire Mrs. McDermott or their actions might *endanger* everyone's freedom. If Xerox can make a rule about obesity, another company can force *abstinent* eaters—people who don't eat and are underweight—to gain weight. These rules constitute *harassment,* repeated attacks, on civil liberties.

Mrs. McDermott won her case, although she turned down a $100,000 settlement offered by Xerox and then could not take a job with the company because of a back problem. She recovered, however, and went back to Xerox, worked for a few weeks, collected her back pay, and retired.

Using Words in Context

One way to make new words a part of your vocabulary is to use them in your own writing. Write a paragraph about some habit you have that you suspect might make other people uncomfortable. Use at least five words from the Vocabulary section in your paragraph, and underline them when you proofread it.

_____

_____

_____

_____

_____

_____

_____

_____

_____

_____

_____

_____

_____

WRITING AND REWRITING

Why Do We Choose Sides?

Every issue has at least two sides, and we often take one side or the other. What prompts us to take that side? Perhaps it's a "spur of the moment" decision. Your date asks if you want to see a movie, and without even thinking, you say no. You like movies, but at that moment you don't want to go to one. We also choose sides based on our experience and knowledge. As you and a friend are looking for a place to eat, you pass a Burger Town. Your friend suggests that you eat there. You say you'd rather not. You've eaten there before, and the food was terrible.

When you take sides, therefore, you are (1) expressing your preference (like or dislike) for one thing over another:

What Do We Express When We Take Sides?

Walking is more fun than jogging.

or (2) making a judgment about something (deciding on the basis of some evidence that something is better or worse than something else):

Satisfaction on the job is more important than job security.

or (3) expressing an attitude toward how something should or should not be:

Couples should live together before they get married.

What Does Our Main-point Statement Express?

The expression of your preference, judgment, or attitude is your main-point statement, which you must explain by means of your reasons for holding the position you do. Perhaps you do not like Burger Town because (1) all the food tastes the same and (2) there is too much fat, salt, and sugar in the food. Your reasons are general statements that you explain by means of specific details and examples. When you ate at Burger Town you ordered the "Big Town" and your date ordered a "Super Town." They looked alike, and to figure out which was which, you bit into both burgers, only to discover that it was impossible to distinguish between them.

How Do We Explain Our Main-point Statement?

Your goal in an essay that takes sides is thus to explain your preference, judgment, or attitude. You don't necessarily have to convince your audience to accept your point of view.

What Is the Goal of a Good Essay?

WRITING: A FIRST DRAFT

In Chapters 8 and 9 you explained aspects of these topics by defining them or comparing and contrasting them:

addiction.
censorship.
prejudice.
diets.
careers.
success.
divorce.
education.
exercise.

Examine one of these issues in a different way. Are you for or against it? Are some aspects of the issue acceptable to you and others not? How do you feel about it? What makes you feel this way? You don't have to use the same issue you used in Chapter 8 or 9, but you may be interested in pursuing that topic further.

1. If you are ready to express a preference, judgment, or attitude, do it (if not, go to step 2).

   [I believe] _____

2. You may need to brainstorm first. On a piece of your own paper, jot down any ideas, words, or phrases that come to mind about the issue.

3. Cluster the information you brainstormed.

4. If you wrote about this issue previously, look over the drafts of your essays from Chapters 8 and 9. You will very likely find information you can use in your essay.

5. If you have not written a statement of preference, judgment, or attitude yet, write one now. Look at your brainstorming, clustering, and any other information. Decide which way you seem to be leaning on the issue. Then write your statement:

   [I believe] _____

6. Now do focused writing. Write today's date at the top of a piece of paper. Write your judgment (main-point) statement at the top of the page. Relax for a moment. Close your eyes. Breathe deeply. As the room starts to quiet, think about the judgment you've made. Why do you take this side? Now open your eyes. At the signal, start writing and do not stop for ten minutes. Do not stop to think about where to put information. Just let the ideas flow. DO NOT pause if you are unsure about spelling, punctuation, or grammar. DO NOT stop to look up words in the dictionary. If you get stuck momentarily with nothing in your head, write the word *stuck* until your next idea comes. Okay, begin. After ten minutes, stop. Read what you've written. If you want to add anything, do it now.

7. Try to fit your ideas into this graphic organizer:

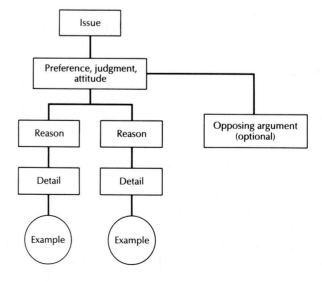

Consider your focused writing to be the first draft of an essay. Put it aside for now. We'll come back to it later in the chapter.

WHAT MAKES WRITING GOOD? TOPIC, AUDIENCE; DETAILS; ORDER; LANGUAGE

Now that you've begun to experiment with essays in which you take a stand on an issue, consider the following elements of an effective essay of this type.

Topic and Audience

Your topic is the side you take on an issue—the preference, judgment, or attitude you express. Although people express their position in many different ways, certain words can make your preference, judgment, or attitude very clear:

Preference	Judgment	Attitude
like, dislike	good/bad	should/should not
appreciate	right/wrong	may, must/may not,
hate, love	worthwhile/useless	
disgust	better/worse	
_____	_____	_____
_____	_____	_____
_____	_____	_____

Add other words you use to express preferences, judgments, and attitudes.

You should state your preference, judgment, or attitude—that is, the side you're on—very clearly. For instance, how do you feel about capital punishment? Are you completely for it, or do you lean, with reservations, to one side or the other? Do you favor it only for hired assassins and those who murder law-enforcement officers, but are you against it for those guilty of treason? When you have decided which side you are on, tell your audience as clearly as possible.

How does your audience feel about the issue? If you cannot be sure, gear your essay to the "average" audience who will have a range of opinions on the issue. Consider the sides different from your own. You may want to incorporate one of these opinions in your essay. Some understanding of your audience will also help you establish the tone of your essay.

Details

Most of your essay is devoted to your reasons for feeling as you do about the issue and to the specific details that show your reasons to be sound. There can be any number of reasons. But each one should be developed with specific details. If you offer only one reason, it will need extensive development because it alone is supporting your position. But if you have three reasons, you can divide the support for your side among them.

Let's suppose your judgment is that capital punishment should be lawful. What are your reasons? Consider these:

1. The only just payment for taking a human life is the life of the murderer.
2. Capital punishment deters crime.
3. It costs the taxpayer less to execute a murderer than to keep him or her in jail.

What specific details support these reasons?

Main-point statement

First reason

Details (examples)

Details (anecdote)

Second reason

Details

Third reason

Details

FIRST DRAFT

[I believe] Capital punishment should be lawful. The only just payment for taking a human life is the life of the murderer. Life is precious to those who live it, their friends, and their families. How can you compensate a child for the loss of a parent, a husband for the loss of a wife, a parent for the loss of a child? No amount of money or time can make up for the loss. The only payment is something equally valuable—another life. The parents of one of the young girls murdered in New Jersey were interviewed on TV last week after the execution of the killer. They said they were satisfied that, at the very least, justice had been done.

Knowing that they may forfeit their own lives, would-be murderers may decide the price is too high and be deterred from committing the crime. In an interview from his death row cell in a Texas prison, John Singleton said that he believed he would not have killed if he had known he would get the electric chair.

Capital punishment is also cheaper than its alternative, life in prison. The law-abiding citizens of my state spend $30,000 a year to keep a murderer alive and well in prison, eating three meals a day, getting exercise, seeing a doctor when necessary, and having books to read and a job to keep him or her busy. Every year my taxes go up because there are more people in jails for me to support. And every year I resent it more. Why do I need to support a person who has destroyed a human life? It would be cheaper, for all of us, to let him or her pay in kind.

Notice that in each paragraph the writer states a reason for believing in capital punishment and then uses details and examples to support each.

Thinking About Opposing Views

You may also want to think and write about the ideas of those people who disagree with your side of the issue. You may be in favor of the death penalty, but equally intelligent people may not. Think about their side. State what they might say, and then use their position to strengthen your own:

Your Side

Knowing that they may forfeit their own lives, potential murderers may decide the price is too high and be deterred from committing the crime. In an interview from his death row cell in a Texas prison, John Singleton said that he believed he would not have killed if he had known he would get the electric chair.

Opposing Side

People may say that they would not commit murder if they knew they'd die for it, but murder is not the act of a reasonable person. At the moment someone murders, emotion rules, not reason. The person is overcome by passion—envy, hatred—whatever; the last thing the murderer is thinking of is what will happen afterward.

How do you handle opposing arguments in your essay? You may mention an opposing point of view (like the preceding one) and then disagree with it: "Yes, I know many murderers are not rational, but those involved in premeditated crimes—burglary with a gun—might choose not to carry a weapon so that they will not be tempted to use it." Or you may just want to keep the opposing arguments in mind as you write.

Often the most convincing details are personal details. If, for instance, you know someone who was murdered or seriously injured by a criminal, you might want to write about your own feelings (or the feelings of the person's family) regarding what should happen to the murderer. If you know someone who's been convicted of murder, you might want to put yourself in that person's position and include that side of the issue.

Order

There are several ways to order information in an essay that takes a side. We provide one that has worked well for basic writers:

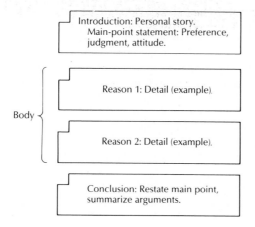

Introduction: Personal story.
Main-point statement: Preference, judgment, attitude.

Body

Reason 1: Detail (example).

Reason 2: Detail (example).

Conclusion: Restate main point, summarize arguments.

How Do You Write Your Introduction?

First, start with an introduction that gets the audience's attention, for example, van den Haag's statement, "Enough is enough." You may want to go right to the point, as van den Haag does, ". . . we have seen enough of the harassment and intimidation of smokers." Or you may want to use a personal story, like the ones you used in the essays you wrote in Chapters 8 and 9. Or you may want to start by anticipating objections, similar to the way that van den Haag does in the second paragraph of his essay when he acknowledges that "smoking is bad for the smoker's health." Somewhere near the beginning of your essay, you should tell the readers what you are arguing for.

What Goes Into the Body of the Essay?

Second, build the body of the essay with reasons for holding your opinion, supported by specific details and examples.

With What Do You Develop Your Reasons?

Last, write a conclusion that restates your main point and summarizes the major arguments, so that you will leave a strong, lasting impression with your audience. You may also want to add some novel solution to the problem, as van den Haag does when he suggests the separation of smokers and non-smokers and mutual courtesy. Your conclusion must be linked to your original argument; it should not introduce a new idea you are not going to expand.

What Goes Into the Conclusion?

At some point between your first and last draft, you should try to fit your ideas into a graphic organizer to see that you have all the pieces you will need for a well-rounded essay.

If we put together all the information we now have for an essay on capital punishment, it might look like this:

MIDDLE DRAFT

main-point statement ← Capital punishment should be lawful. Many people may disagree with me, but most of them have not lived my life. My family owned a small variety store, which my father opened at 7 A.M. and closed at 7:30 P.M. One winter night, two teenagers ran into the store at 7:15 P.M., robbed the cash register, and shot my father. My father died.

Introduction

Personal story to get reader's attention

The police caught them. They were convicted of murder, sentenced to prison, and paroled within five years for "good behavior." Six months later, they robbed and murdered again.

My mother and I and the family of the other victim have to live with our tragedy. I'd like others not to suffer the same fate.

First reason

The only just payment for taking a human life is the life of the murderer. Life is precious to those who live it, their friends, and their families. How can you compensate a child for the loss of a parent, a husband for the loss of a wife, a parent for the loss of a child? No amount of money or time can make up for the loss. The only payment is something equally valuable—another life. The parents of one of the young girls murdered in New Jersey were interviewed on TV last week after the execution of the killer. They said they were satisfied that, at the very least, justice had been done.

Body

Details

Second reason

Knowing that they may forfeit their own lives, would-be murderers may decide the price is too high and be deterred from committing the crime. In an interview from his death row cell in a Texas prison, John

Singleton said that he believed he would not have killed if he had known he would get the electric chair. I know that murderers are not acting rationally when they commit murder, but if there were capital punishment, perhaps people—like the teenagers who shot my father—would think before they took a gun along to commit a crime. Had these boys not had a gun, they couldn't have used it.

Body {

Capital punishment is also cheaper than its alternative, life in prison. The law-abiding citizens of my state spend $30,000 a year to keep a murderer alive and well in prison, eating three meals a day, getting exercise, seeing a doctor when necessary, and having books to read and a job to keep him or her busy. Every year my taxes go up because there are more people in jails for me to support. And every year I resent it more. Why do I need to support a person who has destroyed a human life? It would be cheaper, for all of us, to let him or her pay in kind.

Third reason

Details

Conclu-sion {

I don't like the idea of the state's taking a human life, but those who murder give up their right to life. Capital punishment is payment in kind for what they have done; it may, in fact, cause a would-be murderer to think before acting, and it is the cheapest method of handling those who do commit murder.

Restatement of main point

Summary of three reasons

Language

How Do You Establish the Proper Tone in an Essay?

The language you use in the essay should be evenhanded. You want your audience to know and understand your position. Thus, to establish the proper tone for your audience, you must respect their opinions and ideas. For instance, you would not want to say, "Anyone who doesn't believe in capital punishment either has so much money that he can throw it away on taxes or is so stupid that it doesn't matter." Van den Haag uses an evenhanded tone for most of his essay. However, in paragraph 8 he says that the "sudden" increase in allergies to cigarette smoke are "hysterical" or "faked"; there he risks offending the very people he wants to win over to his side.

Why Do You Need Transitions?

As in any essay that attempts to explain, you need good transition words to keep your audience on the right track. You may also want some special "conclusion" words in your last paragraph:

What Words Help You Conclude Your Essay?

Conclusion Words

therefore	as I have said (shown, stated)	finally
in conclusion	to summarize	consequently
all in all	as a result	thus
in summary	in other words	

If you use any of these conclusion words, make sure you use the one best suited to what you are saying.

Special Dos and Don'ts When You Are Taking Sides

1. *Do* respect your audience. Many people who hold strongly to one side of an issue often simply dismiss opposing arguments as irrelevant. People who believe in capital punishment often scoff at those who say they don't feel that the state has the right to "play God"; in fact, says the procapital punishment side, the murderer has already done so. It's tempting, when you feel strongly about an issue, to "put down" the other side and the people who support it. But you will be more effective if you assume your audience is as intelligent and sensitive as you are.

2. *Do* argue against an idea, not a person. If you believe that capital punishment should be lawful in your state, say so and state your reasons, supported by details. Perhaps someone famous disagrees with you, as does Governor Mario Cuomo of New York. You may want to mention Cuomo and his position, but you should avoid insulting him. Capital punishment is the issue, not Governor Cuomo. For example, it seems reasonable to say, "Unlike the governor, I believe capital punishment should be lawful in New York because it might reduce the huge number of homicides in that state." It takes away from your position to say, "Governor Cuomo is foolish for allowing homicides to continue in New York because there is no death penalty."

3. *Don't* jump to conclusions. Almost any topic worth debating has many reasons to support both sides. Try to include more reasons rather than fewer and to see the issue in all its complexity. Just because the number of violent crimes increased after capital punishment was suspended does not necessarily mean that the lack of capital punishment *caused* the increase in violent crime. The population also rose in those years, as did unemployment.

4. *Don't* oversimplify or engage in "either/or reasoning." Your side is reasonable, but the opposing side also may be reasonable. Although you may believe capital punishment is an important deterrent to crime, you cannot say that murderers will be loose in the streets without capital punishment.

Do These Exercises Before You Revise Your First Draft.

Practice with Topic and Audience

1. Read each set of statements. Circle the letters of the ones that do *not* express a side of an issue. (*Hint:* Look for words that signal preferences, judgments, and attitudes.)

   issue: relationships between men and women.

   a. There are more women than men in the United States.
   b. Men should emulate some of the qualities of women.
   c. Men do not take orders well from women supervisors.

d. Women must become more comfortable with their natural leadership abilities.

issue: college bookstores

a. College bookstores should stock used copies of current texts.
b. It's convenient to shop right on your own campus.
c. The bookstore is a good place to socialize as well as to buy books.
d. Most college bookstores are managed by outside companies.

issue: travel

a. Most Americans never travel beyond the borders of their own country.
b. Americans generally speak only one language.
c. Traveling is educational and fun.
d. People who want to consider themselves educated should experience life in other cultures.

2. The following are some issues on which people take sides. For each one, write a statement that expresses your preference, judgment, or attitude toward some aspect of the issue.

horror movies   Children under age thirteen should
                                 not be allowed to see horror movies.

a. financial aid to college students.
b. TV soap operas.
c. nursing homes.
d. famine relief.
e. choosing a career.
f. school cafeteria food.

a. _____

b. _____

c. _____

d. _____

e. _____

f. _____

3. Look back to van den Haag's "Smokers Have Rights, Too."

State the issue he addresses: _____

What side is he on? _____

Practice with Details

1. Read each set of reasons related to one side of an issue. Cross out the ones that are not relevant to the argument.

issue: space travel

side: The United States should continue to explore space.

reasons: **a.** Many medical discoveries result from space exploration.
             b. The United States wants to beat other countries for ownership of space.
             c. The movie industry makes many space adventures.
             d. The space industry creates many jobs.

issue: toxic wastes

side: Private industry should be free from regulations governing the disposal of its waste products.

reasons: **a.** Any restraint on industry is unconstitutional.
             b. Industry must be free to explore new ways to manufacture its products.
             c. The health and safety of citizens are very important.
             d. Regulations are almost impossible to enforce.

issue: food

side: Much of what is called "health food" is frequently not particularly healthy.

reasons: **a.** Many products sold in health food stores contain fat in excess of recommended proportions.
             b. Health food stores are not always very clean.
             c. Large food manufacturing companies sell their products under special "health food" labels.
             d. What is called health food frequently contains fructose, which is just as bad for the system as processed sugar is.

2. Choose two of the issues you worked on in Exercise 2 on the previous page. For each, write down two reasons for taking the side you do.

issue:

side:

reasons: **a.** _____

             b. _____

issue:

side:

reasons: **a.** _____

            b. _____

3. Draw a line through those details that do not relate directly to the reasons for taking a side.

issue: word processing

side: Word processing takes the drudgery out of writing.
reason: When you use a word processor, you can correct errors without retyping the entire page.
details: Your copy appears on a screen or monitor. The letters are green or amber. You can delete or substitute letters, words, or sentences. You can move whole blocks of type right on the screen. Then you hit the "print" key, and your new copy slides out of the printer. But you'd better remember to "save text" or it all will disappear when you turn off the machine.

issue: credit cards

side: People shouldn't use credit cards.
reason: Credit cards make you spend more than you have.
details: Credit card companies offer card holders high "credit lines" as an available balance. Many people think of it as money they have when it is really only a potential debt. Most people are staggered by the amounts the companies put at their disposal. They are frequently unaware of the 18.5 percent or higher interest charged by most companies. Card holders feel very powerful with that little piece of plastic, and no price seems too much to pay. Most people figure, "Who cares! I have until the end of the month to pay the bill." Then the end of the month comes, and with it credit card bills, and they have no money to pay for that new living room sofa they probably could have lived without.

issue: day care

side: Local governments should impose strict standards for day-care workers.
reason: Without standards, people with records of child abuse and unstable personalities may be employed by day-care centers.
details: Too often, we read in the newspapers about a day-care worker molesting a child in the closet of the day-care center. The parents left the child there to be cared for, not abused, by people the municipality said were trustworthy. But who really checked these

people? How was it decided that they were qualified? Currently local governments have no standards for day-care workers. Hundreds of people apply for these jobs every year. No one is even sure how many. Anyone who "looks okay" may be accepted.

4. We already know the issue in the van den Haag essay and the side he takes. What are his reasons for taking this side? List two. What are the

details he uses to explain his reasons? _____

_____

_____

_____

_____

_____

5. Choose an issue you worked on in Exercise 2. Jot down the issue, your side, and one reason. Then write a paragraph of details to explain that reason.

   issue:

   side:

   reason:

   details: _____

   _____

   _____

   _____

   _____

   _____

6. Copy two preferences, judgments, or attitudes you expressed in Exercise 5. Then jot down some ideas that people on the opposite side of the issues might have.

statement:
opposing ideas: _____

_____

_____

_____

statement:
opposing ideas: _____

_____

_____

_____

Practice with Order

1. Van den Haag states his opinion clearly but doesn't use a personal introduction to capture the audience's attention. Write a paragraph of personal anecdote that could begin "Smokers Have Rights, Too." Make sure the theme of the paragraph is harassment, smoking, or whatever you feel is appropriate. Use your own paper.

2. Fit the information from "Smokers Have Rights, Too" into a graphic organizer. Use your own paper.

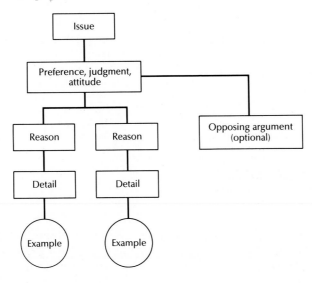

Practice With Language

In paragraphs 8 and 9 of "Smokers Have Rights, Too," van den Haag changes the tone of his essay and uses words that may offend his audience. Look back at these two paragraphs. Underline the words or phrases you think might cause trouble. Revise these paragraphs to make their tone more appropriate. Use your own paper.

REWRITING: THE SECOND DRAFT

Now you are ready to turn your focused writing into a second draft. Read it carefully, aloud, and, if you can, to a friend or classmate. Try to get a new vision of your subject. As you rewrite, consider whether or not your voice is conveying what you want it to. You should also

1. *Revise for topic and audience.* Write a statement that expresses your preference, judgment, or attitude toward the topic. Make the side you are taking on the issue clear to the audience. Think about what your audience might know about the issue and what their opinions about it may be.

2. *Revise for details.* State your reasons for taking the side you do, and develop those reasons by means of details and examples. Consider opposing ideas, and if appropriate, work them into your argument.

3. *Revise for order.* Write an introduction that captures the audience's attention and makes them sensitive to your point of view. A personal anecdote is often very helpful. Make sure that your statement of preference, judgment, or attitude is near the beginning of your essay. Devote a paragraph to each reason and your details and examples. Write a conclusion that restates your side and summarizes your main points. You may find it helpful to draw a graphic organizer and fit your ideas into it.

4. *Revise for language.* Be diplomatic. Demonstrate the reasonableness of your side without offending people who hold a different view. If they are helpful, use words that summarize your findings.

When you finish a satisfactory middle draft, make a clean copy. Go on to the next section, where you'll get help on the proofreading stages of your writing.

PROOFREADING

What Are the Three Additional Tenses?

We know that verbs indicate action and time, and we have looked at the three simple tenses of verbs: past tense, present tense, and future tense. Verbs have three additional tenses: *present perfect tense, past perfect tense,* and *future perfect tense.* Unlike the simple tenses that are set in one period of time, the perfect tenses either cut across the time periods (start in one and extend into another) or indicate an occurrence in time relative to some other occurrence in time.

How Are They Different from the Simple Tenses?

PERFECT TENSES

Present Perfect Tense

The present perfect tense tells us about an action or event that started in the past and is continuing into the present. For example,

What Is the Present Perfect Tense?

Johnny Carson has hosted the "Tonight Show" for a long time.

This sentence indicates that Johnny Carson started hosting the "Tonight Show" in the past and is still hosting it today. The present perfect tense represents two time periods: past and present. On a time line for the past, present, and future, the present perfect tense would be on line x, which starts in the past and extends into the present:

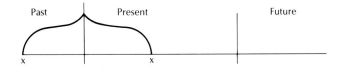

What differences do you notice between these sentences?

1. She has waited for hours for her brother to return from school.
2. She waited for hours for her brother to return from school.

In which of these sentences is she still waiting? To which of these sentences can we add "and left before he arrived"? Why? We can add this phrase to sentence 2 because in this sentence the simple past tense verb *waited* tells us that the action or event has been completed. We use the present perfect when an action starts in the past and continues into the present.

To form the present perfect tense, we use the helping verbs *have* or *has* plus the *past participle*. The past participle is the form of the main verb used with the helpers *has, have,* and *had.* In sentence 1 the past participle is *waited.*

How Do We Form the Present Perfect?

We form the past participle of many verbs by adding *ed* to the base form of the verb:

help—helped
talk—talked

There are many exceptions to this rule:

speak—spoken
sit—sit
ring—rung

Check the verb chart in Appendix 9 for various irregular forms.
The following verb chart is like the one on page 431. We've added two new columns for the past participle and the present participle.

Base form	Present tense	Past tense	Past participle	Present participle
(to) look	look/looks	looked	looked	looking
(to) ridicule	ridicule/ridicules	ridiculed	ridiculed	ridiculing
(to) write	write/writes	wrote	written	writing

Remember that in standard English, we use the past tense form, not the past participle, to form the simple past tense:

Write: She did enough.   Rather than: She done enough.
        She saw that movie.   She seen that movie.

The past participle is used with the helping verb *have* or *has*.

Practice with the Present Perfect Tense

1. Answer the question that follows each pair of sentences.
   a. Evan Hunter wrote over fifty mystery novels under three different names.
   b. Evan Hunter has written over fifty mystery novels under three different names.
   Which sentence indicates that Hunter still writes mystery fiction? _____

   a. The old farmhouse stood in the valley for one hundred years.
   b. The old farmhouse has stood in the valley for one hundred years.
   Which sentence indicates that the house has been torn down? _____

   a. The computer has revolutionized office procedure.
   b. The computer revolutionized office procedure.
   Which sentence implies the computer is still revolutionizing the office? _____

   a. Photography has been considered a new art form.
   b. Photography was considered a new art form.
   Which sentence implies that photography is no longer considered art? _____

2. Based on the information in brackets, change the verb forms in this paragraph to the present perfect or past tense if necessary.

I waited a long time to learn to swim [I still do not know how], but I decided to learn [I'm still thinking about it, but I'm pretty sure]. As a child, I was not afraid of the water [I am now], but when I was ten, a camp counselor had thrown me into the pool [it happened one day in July 1970], and I never recovered from my fear and shock [I'm still not over it]. As the years went by [these years are gone now], I sat on the shore [many years ago] and watched my friends bobbing and swimming in the water. I have been very envious [back then] of their skill and of the fun they had. I decided [I started making this decision last month and I am still toying with the idea] to conquer my fear. I wanted to learn to swim all these years but I was too afraid [these feelings have continued to this day]. Now I am ready. I have called a local health club [last week] and made an appointment with the swimming teacher. I hope it works out.

3. Write a draft of a paragraph about a skill you did or did not acquire in childhood that is still important to you. You might consider sewing, cooking, playing basketball, riding a bike, ice skating, or something else. Tell your audience how you felt about the skill years ago, why and how you learned or didn't learn it, and what it means to you today. When you proofread your paragraph, make sure you have used the present perfect tense only where necessary. Use your own paper.

Past Perfect Tense

The past perfect tense tells us about an action or event that occurred in the past *before* some other action or event. For example,

What Is the Past Perfect Tense?

When the bell rang for the fire drill, the class had finished the ten-minute quiz.

This sentence reports two events: (1) the bell that rang for the fire drill and (2) the quiz completed by the class. Which event occurred first? We can find the answer by finding the event that is reported in the past perfect tense. In this case, it's the second event, the completion of the quiz.

HINT: TROUBLESOME VERBS

We mentioned earlier that regular verbs simply add an *ed* ending to form the past participle (that is, *help* becomes *helped*). Some irregular verbs are troublesome because you may not recognize their past participle forms:

Base	Present	Past	Past Participle
[to] be	am/is/are	was/were	been
[to] go	go/goes	went	gone
[to] do	do/does	did	done
[to] write	write/writes	wrote	written
[to] take	take/takes	took	taken
_____	_____	_____	_____
_____	_____	_____	_____
_____	_____	_____	_____

Notice that all of these verbs have different forms for the present, past, and past participle. Can you think of other verbs that have different forms for each? List them on the blank lines. Then write them in your verb chart on page 431.

Sometimes people use the past tense form when they need the past participle:

> For several years, the Smiths have went to visit their relatives at Christmas.

> How long have you did this?

They should write

> For several years, the Smiths **have gone** to visit their relatives at Christmas.

> How long **have** you **done** this?

People also confuse the past and present participles:

> Eric is written his research report tonight.

> Gerard is taken his mother to a play.

They should write

> Eric **is writing** his research report tonight.

> Gerard **is taking** his mother to a play.

We form the past perfect tense with the helping verb *had* and the past participle. In the example sentence, the verb phrase *had completed* is the past perfect tense, formed by the helping verb *had* plus the past participle *finished.* The verb phrase tells us that the quiz took place before the bell rang for the fire drill.

How Do We Form the Past Perfect?

What difference do you notice between these sentences:

1. The band was finishing the song when the audience started clapping.
2. The band had finished the song when the audience started clapping.

In which sentence did the song end before the clapping began? What difference in verb tense do you notice?

Practice with the Past Perfect Tense

1. Answer the question that follows each pair of sentences.
   a. Mary had eaten breakfast when her mother called her to the phone.
   b. Mary was eating breakfast when her mother called her to the phone.
   Which sentence indicates that Mary was finished with breakfast when she was called to the phone? _____

   a. The soldiers had left for battle when the general changed his mind and ordered a cease-fire.
   b. The soldiers were leaving for battle when the general changed his mind and ordered a cease-fire.
   Which sentence indicates that the soldiers had left before the general's decision? _____

   a. God was creating the world when he created man and woman.
   b. God had created the world when he created man and woman.
   In which sentence did God finish the world before creating man and woman? _____

   a. The Shakers, because of their belief in celibacy, had become extinct by the beginning of the twentieth century.
   b. The Shakers, because of their belief in celibacy, were becoming extinct by the beginning of the twentieth century.
   Which sentence indicates that there were no Shakers by 1900? _____

2. Underline all the verb forms in this paragraph. Where you think the context requires it, change the verb forms to the past perfect tense.

   Between 1933 and 1949, Fred Astaire and Ginger Rogers made ten

   movies together. They appeared on stage or in films before they worked to-

   gether, but they achieved stardom only in their famous partnership. Before he teamed up with Rogers, Astaire danced with his sister, Adele, in vaudeville. Critics called him the lesser of the two Astaires, and when Adele retired in 1932, Fred's attempts to "go it alone" were largely unsuccessful. Rogers appeared in four movies before she joined Astaire, but she was far from famous. Together they were greater than either was separately. Their sixteen-year romance-through-dance excited audiences who were tired of war and economic depression. Advances in the technology of movie making allowed their dancing to jump out at audiences from coast to coast.

Future Perfect Tense

What Is the Future Perfect Tense?

The future perfect tense tells us about an action or event that started in the past (or is starting in the present) and will be completed some time in the future. For example,

By nightfall the bicycle racers will have traveled more than one thousand miles on their three thousand–mile journey across the United States.

In this sentence it is unclear when the race started, but it appears to be under way; it will be completed in the future. On a time line, we represent the future perfect tense by:

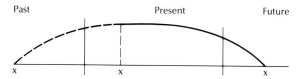

The dotted lines indicate that the action can begin in the past or present.

How Do We Form the Future Perfect?

To form the future perfect tense, we use a verb phrase that contains two helping verbs, *will* and *have*, plus a past participle.

Practice with the Future Perfect Tense

1. Answer the question that follows each pair of sentences.
   a. The rebels will have shot the ruling family by dawn.
   b. The rebels shot the ruling family at dawn.
   Which sentence indicates that the family is already dead? ____

   a. The marriage will have ended before the couple's first anniversary.
   b. The marriage ended before the couple's first anniversary.
   Which sentence suggests that the couple is still married? ____

a. The appeals court will have overturned the verdict when the reporters arrive at the courthouse.

b. The appeals court overturned the verdict when the reporters arrived at the courthouse.

Which sentence indicates that the verdict was overturned before the reporters arrived? ____

PARTICIPLES AS ADJECTIVES ▬▬▬▬▬▬

Sometimes we use the participle forms of verbs as *adjectives*. An adjective is a word that describes a noun. For example:

the *long* word   the *tender* word
the *brown* paper   the *bushy* eyebrow

Participles can function in the same way:

the *spoken* word   the *written* word
the *recycled* paper   the *raised* eyebrow
the *defeated* army   the *dedicated* soldier

What other adjectives fit these phrases?

the _____ word   the _____ word

the _____ paper   the _____ eyebrow

What other participles fit these phrases?

the _____ word   the _____ word

the _____ paper   the _____ eyebrow

the _____ army   the _____ soldier

Add any new verbs to your verb chart on page 431.

Using participles as adjectives can add detail and spice to your writing; one fresh word can create a new picture. When you use a past participle as an adjective, you need to use the *ed* ending if it is a regular verb (like *recycled, defeated,* or *dedicated*) or the appropriate form if it is an irregular verb (like *spoken* or *written*).

The present participle (*ing* form) also may function as an adjective:

the *conquering* army   the *aching* back
the *throbbing* headache   the *setting* sun
the *rising* moon   the *rolling* waves

What other present participles fit these phrases?

the _____ army   the _____ back

the _____ headache   the _____ sun

the _____ moon   the _____ waves

HINT: PARTICIPLES WITH VERBS

We often use past participles with the verbs *get*, *feel*, and *become*:

get married	feel tired
get divorced	feel refreshed
get involved	feel depressed
get suspended	become engaged
get driven	become annoyed

Remember that these phrases include a past participle form. Use the *ed* ending for regular verbs or the appropriate ending or word form for irregular verbs.

Practice with Participles As Adjectives

1. Read this paragraph about advertising, and circle all the nouns. (a) Where you see a caret in sentences 1 through 4, insert one of the participles-as-adjectives at the left. (b) In sentences 5 through 9, insert any participle-as-adjective that you think is appropriate.

concealed
hidden
unseen
unwanted
liberated
unattached

¹Advertising appeals to our ∧ desires. ²Ads really sell ∧ sex when they purport to sell ∧ products as diverse as toothpaste, cigarettes, and underwear. ³In the *Close-Up* toothpaste ad, a ∧ woman smiles seductively at a young ∧ man. ⁴They move closer and closer as the ∧ announcer says, "Brush your teeth with Close-Up." ⁵We buy the kiss, not the toothpaste. ⁶In the now-defunct Marlboro ads, a cowboy stared out at the horizon while he inhaled his cigarette. ⁷Any man

who fantasized about being this man, or any woman who

wanted to find him, was supposed to run off to buy Marlboros.

[8]Then there is Calvin Klein underwear, whose ads feature a

man and a woman in intimate embrace. [9]I'm not sure what

we're buying, but I know we purchase something else besides

underwear based on this ad.

2. Write a paragraph in which you make some judgment about advertising. Is it good or bad for the economy or society, helpful, or merely annoying? When you have finished writing, find three or four places where you can insert a participle-as-adjective and do so, indicating your insertion with a caret. Use your own paper.

PASSIVE VOICE

What Is the Passive Voice?

The word *passive* means inactive, letting someone else do the work. Being passive can be positive, as in Martin Luther King, Jr.'s passive resistance to gain civil rights for American blacks, or it can be negative, as in a person's letting someone else make the major decisions affecting his or her life. The passive voice in grammar is much the same. Subjects of sentences are waiting for something to happen to them. Sometimes the passive voice is the most effective way to express something you want to say, but more often, it is not. For example,

1. Robert B. Parker wrote *Early Autumn.*
2. *Early Autumn* was written by Robert B. Parker.

In sentence 1, the subject—Robert B. Parker—"performs" the action—writing *Early Autumn*—expressed by the verb. We call this *active voice.* In sentence 2, the subject—*Early Autumn*—"receives" the action—being written by Robert B. Parker—expressed by the verb.

How Do We Form the Passive Voice?

We form the passive voice by making a verb phrase out of a helping verb (*am, is, are, was, were*) and adding the past participle. *Was written* is the verb phrase in sentence 2.

We can also use the passive voice in the perfect tenses:

It **has been determined** that high blood cholesterol contributes to heart disease.

To form the passive voice in the perfect tenses, we use the helping verbs *has, have,* or *had* plus *been* (the past participle of *to be*) and the past participle of the main verb:

$$\left.\begin{matrix} have \\ have \end{matrix}\right\} + been + past\ participle\ (main\ verb)$$

We can also use the passive voice with other helping verbs:

The complaint *will be* investigated tomorrow.
The typewriter *cannot be fixed.*
This incident *should be reported* to the police.

We use

$$\left.\begin{matrix} would \\ could \\ should \\ may \\ might \\ must \\ shall \\ will \\ can \end{matrix}\right\} + be + past\ participle\ (main\ verb)$$

Why Do We Use the Passive Voice?

Sometimes we need the passive voice because we do not know who performed the action we are discussing:

The Bible was written thousands of years ago.
The dice have been cast and we now await our fate.

We are not certain who wrote the Bible, nor do we know who cast the dice of fate. In these cases, we may use the passive voice. However, often we can figure out who is "performing" the task if we think about it:

Prehistoric civilizations were found in Africa.

Who found them? American tourists, African tribespeople, archeologists? Whenever you can figure out who is performing the action, do so and use the active rather than the passive voice.

Use the passive voice as little as possible. It sounds fancy, but it takes the life out of writing. Compare the following two paragraphs:

Passive	Active
Early Autumn was written by Robert B. Parker. In the novel, a son is used by his parents in a bitter divorce. The youngster is kidnapped by thugs. The detective, Spenser, is hired to get him back. Paul, a puny, whining fifteen year old, is hidden by Spenser	Robert B. Parker wrote *Early Autumn*. In the novel, parents use their son in a bitter divorce. Thugs kidnap the youngster. The mother hires Spenser to get him back. Spenser hides Paul, a puny,

in the woods of Maine, where a house is built by the two, and Paul's spirit and character are built as well. The past indiscretions of the mother are revealed; the mob connections of the father are discovered also by Spenser. Life can then be attacked by a newly independent young man.

whining fifteen-year-old, in the woods of Maine, where they build a house together, and Paul builds his spirit and character as well. Spenser reveals the mother's past indiscretions; he also discovers the father's mob connections. Then this newly independent young man can live his life.

In general, the active voice holds the reader's attention better than the passive voice does. Imagine you are an editor choosing one of the preceding paragraphs to appear on the back cover of the Parker book. Which one do you think would sell the book better to prospective readers?

Practice with the Passive Voice

1. Read this paragraph, and underline all the verbs and verb phrases. As you proofread it, check to see that you have used the right ending in the passive voice and for other past participle forms.

Drugs should be use only as directed. If drug dosages are abuse, the patient may be harmed more than he or she is helped. Even abusing a simple substance like aspirin has been know to cause serious ill effects. Aspirin was prescribed by my mother's doctor for her arthritis symptoms. She dutifully took two aspirins every four hours, not more than five times a day. She must have build up a tolerance for them, because after a while she stopped getting relief. Two hours after a dose, when she was still in pain, the aspirin bottle was taked up hastily and another dose was consumed. Pretty soon thirty aspirins a day were being gobble. Then one day, while supper was being made, the blade of the food processor slash her hand. No tourniquet, no amount of pressure could stop the bleeding. I knew she should be took to the hospital, which she was. There, the emergency room doctor, who had been apprise of her medical history, explained that aspirin is an anticoagulant, that it will prevent blood from

clotting. Too much of her prescribe dosage was nearly fatal.

2. Several sentences in Exercise 1 are written in the passive voice and would be much more effective in the active voice. Rewrite the paragraph, changing verbs in the passive to the active voice. If you find a sentence you like in the passive voice, leave it. Use your own paper.

3. Write a paragraph explaining why

  a. the death penalty should be legalized (in your state), OR
  b. the writing of premarital agreements should be encouraged.

When you are finished writing, proofread your paragraph to see whether you have used the right endings for participle forms. Check also to see whether you have used the passive voice. If so, change the passive to the active voice. Use your own paper.

━━━━━━━━━━━━━━━━━━━━━ **SPELLING**

Spelling Demons

Spelling demons are words that confuse almost everyone almost all the time. Here are fifty demons, but there are many more. The parts of each word that cause the most trouble are in italics. Add the words that cause you trouble to your spelling list on page 31.

ab*se*nce	emba*rr*ass	knowledg*e*able
acc*i*dentally	envi*ro*nment	*lei*sure
a*cc*o*mm*odate	e*specially*	leng*th*
a*c*ross	equi*p*ment	li*c*ense
admi*ss*ion	exa*gg*erate	o*pp*ortunity
a*pp*roximately	exer*c*ise	paral*y*ze
beco*m*ing	exist*e*nce	posse*ss*ion
busi*n*ess	fas*c*inating	pro*f*essor
cigare*tt*e	fin*all*y	restau*r*ant
con*sc*ience	govern*m*ent	r*hyth*m
con*sc*ious	gua*r*ant*ee*	ridi*c*ulous
contin*uous*	gu*i*dance	sch*e*dule
dile*mm*a	hop*i*ng	simultan*eous*
disa*pp*oint	idi*o*syncrasy	su*r*prise
dis*c*ipline	int*e*resting	tru*ly*
	inte*rr*upt	*un*nece*ss*ary
	jud*g*ment	

482

Practice with Spelling Demons

This passage is about how our minds work. Proofread it for the correct spelling of the demons.

Our consciense (sometimes called the *superego*) constantly dissapoints our unconscious mind (sometimes called the *id*) with its reasoned judgments, whereas our unconsius mind embarasses us with surprising—but facinating—thoughts that seem quite ridiculus. While the two sides of the self go about the biusness of trying to accommodate one another, we cope with the dilemma of which side's existance to acknowledge.

Our conscience is our moral equipment. It makes disciplined choices about how we act in our enviornment, giving us giudance about what is right or wrong. Simultaneusly, however, our unconscious self is all ideosyncrasy. It is the absense of reason that paralyses our conscience with "unecesary" thoughts. We've stopped smoking because our consciense knows it's bad for our health, but the unconscious continues to crave a cigarete at the end of a hearty restaraunt meal and exagerates the pleasures of smoking as a liesure activity.

If the unconscious takes posession of our minds, the rythm of our lives is interupted and sound judgment is suspended. We may even start to smoke again. As the same time, we should admit that we could not live without these two sides, our "self" slipping back and forth accross the thin unconcious-conscience line, guaranteing the full human range of choices.

Now you are ready to proofread the middle draft of the essay you began earlier in this chapter. Read your essay again slowly, and aloud. Remember what you learned about word order and sense in Chapter 1 and about the conventions of writing in Chapter 2. You may need to look back at these chapters. Check to see that each sentence you've written contains a subject and a verb.

Make sure you can answer yes to the questions below as you proofread:

1. Are most of your verbs written in the past tense?
2. If you used the present perfect, are you certain that the action began in the past and continues into the present?
3. If you used the past perfect, are you certain that the action took place before another action did?
4. If you used the future perfect, are you certain that the action started in the past (or present) and continues into the future?
5. Are all your past participle forms correct?
6. When you used the passive voice, was it the best way to express yourself, or would it be better to tell the audience who is doing the action?
7. Have you spelled all your "demons" correctly?

Proofread slowly and carefully. When you've made all the changes you want to make, write out a clean copy of your essay.

ADDITIONAL WRITING ASSIGNMENTS

Your writer's journal may have some issues or ideas for you to develop into essays. Focus on your opinions of the issues. You may want to imagine that you are the editor of your school paper or of a major metropolitan newspaper, in charge of the editorial section. Speak out on issues of concern to the community.

Here are some topics that students have found interesting to debate. Remember to follow the writing process we are developing: Do focused writing first. Then look it over. You may want to review the Writing and Rewriting section of each chapter before you start your middle drafts. When you finish them, proofread them and write a clean copy.

Topic Suggestions

1. Do you agree or disagree with each of the statements below?
   a. Couples should live together before they get married.
   b. The United States should support revolutionary governments in Central and Latin America.

c. Students should have the right to sue their high schools for not teaching them to read, do math, and understand computers.

d. Children who are abused by their parents should immediately be removed from their parents' home.

e. The sale and use of marijuana, cocaine, and heroin should be legal.

f. Workers should be forced to retire at age sixty-five to make room for younger people in the work force.

g. A career is the most important thing in a woman's life.

h. Winter is a better season than summer is.

i. The acquisition of wealth is the most important life goal.

j. A good education can be had only in an integrated school.

2. You may also want to consider these topic areas and form your own statement of preference, judgment, or attitude:

a. studying foreign languages in school.

b. corporations being free to dump toxic wastes.

c. free tuition for public colleges.

d. the right to die.

e. influence of TV on youngsters.

f. need for adolescents to have privacy.

g. compulsory public service for people aged eighteen to twenty.

APPENDICES

APPENDIX 1:
DIRECT AND INDIRECT QUESTIONS

Direct questions are questions that request an answer, signaled by the question mark that comes at the end. There are two types of direct questions:

A. Questions that require a simple yes or no response:

> Question: Can we build more reliable satellites?
> Response: Yes, we can.
> Question: Are the ratings for CBS News rising?
> Response: No, they aren't.

In standard English, yes or no questions are formed by shifting the verb or helping verb to the beginning of the sentence:

> Statement: We *can* build more reliable satellites.
> Question Shift: *Can* we build more reliable satellites?

In nonstandard dialects, yes or no questions can be formed without a shift in word order:

> Statement: The plumber is here.
> Question: The plumber is here?[1]

In speech, a question is signaled by a rising intonation at the end of the sentence. Sometimes the verb is omitted:

> Statement: The plumber here.
> Question: The plumber here?

Exercises

1. Identify the standard English direct questions by circling the S and the nonstandard questions by circling the N.

a. All of you got jobs at the post office?	S	N
b. Did you check all your luggage at the airport?	S	N
c. The road was wet and slippery?	S	N
d. Are the hotels in New York expensive?	S	N

---

[1] Standard English uses questions of this form also in informal conversation, but the questions show a strong feeling of disbelief associated with them, as in "I don't believe the plumber is actually here."

2. Change the questions you circled N into standard English:

_____

_____

_____

B. Questions that are introduced with words like *who, what, when, where* and *how:*

> *What is the name of the plumber?*
> *When did the plumber arrive?*

In standard English the verb or helping verb moves ahead of the subject. What are the verbs and helping verbs in the example sentences?

In nonstandard dialects, the verb or helping verb is sometimes omitted:

> *What the name of the plumber?*

Exercises

1. Identify the standard English questions by circling the S and the nonstandard questions by circling the N.

a. When does our summer vacation begin?	S	N
b. Why you want to buy such an expensive car?	S	N
c. When you plan to finish studying for that exam?	S	N
d. What are the planets around the sun?	S	N

2. Change the questions you circled N into standard English.

_____

_____

_____

An indirect question is a question that does not request an answer. It is part of a larger sentence. If the larger sentence is a statement, then the sentence will end with a period, not a question mark:

> Question: When will the plumber arrive?
> Larger Sentence: We wondered when the plumber would arrive.
> Question: Do you like doughnuts with your coffee?
> Larger Sentence: He asked me if I like doughnuts with my coffee.

Notice that the direct questions have been made part of the larger sentences. When a direct question is reported as an indirect question, the verb tense and pronouns may have to be changed. What changes do you notice in the example sentences? Why are these changes necessary? In standard English the verb or helping verb in the indirect question does not move ahead of the subject. Look again at the questions in the example sentences. What is the subject and verb of each?

In nonstandard English there is a shift in word order:

He wondered when would the plumber come.

The words *if* and *whether* are omitted and replaced by the helping verb:

He asked me did I like doughnuts with my coffee?

What word replaced *if* in this sentence?

Exercises

1. Identify the standard English indirect questions by circling the S and the nonstandard ones by circling the N.

a. He asked me would I want to go with him to the Super Bowl game.		S	N
b. My brother called and asked could I lend him five dollars.		S	N
c. I don't remember when did he leave for the airport.		S	N
d. The repairman ask if the television was a portable model.		S	N
e. I wonder does he still have the flu.		S	N

2. Change the indirect questions you circled N into standard English.

_____

_____

_____

_____

_____

APPENDIX 2:
REFLEXIVE PRONOUNS

In standard English the reflexive pronouns are *myself, ourselves, herself, himself, itself, yourself, yourselves,* and *themselves.* As pronouns they have antecedents, and they substitute for nouns and other pronouns.

*Harold didn't want a part-time job for **himself**; he wanted it for his wife.*

Can you find the antecedent for *himself?*
    In nonstandard dialects and in informal and conversational speech, reflexive pronouns are frequently used as two words instead of one (for example, *her self* instead of *herself*). These reflexives often occur with an intervening word or phrase:

*Since Susan lost weight, she doesn't look like **her** former **self**.*

What word comes between the reflexive pronoun?
    There are also differences in the forms of reflexive pronouns in nonstandard dialects:

Nonstandard	Standard
his self	himself
our self	ourselves
your self	yourselves
their self	themselves
they self	themselves

Notice the nonstandard use of *his* for *him* and *their* and *they* for *them,* as well as the use of the singular form *self* for the plural form *selves.*

Exercises

Circle N if the sentence is nonstandard and S if it is standard. Then change the nonstandard sentence to standard English in the space provided.

1. Sam hasn't been his old self since his wife died.   N   S
2. At camp the scouts made breakfast for themselves.   N   S
3. Maxine taught her own self how to drive a car.   N   S
4. After the game the coach let the players watch they self on
   television.   N   S
5. Eric told Kim to take one of the concert tickets for herself
   and give the rest to her sisters.   N   S
6. Whenever we bought tickets to a rock concert, we always tried
   to get ourself seats in the front row.   N   S

491

7. I want to work for my own self, not for anybody else.   N   S

_____

_____

_____

_____

_____

APPENDIX 3:
MULTIPLE NEGATIVES

In standard English you make a sentence negative by adding a negative word like *no, not, neither, nor, never,* or *none.*

Positive: *The nurses will hold their convention in New Orleans.*

Negative: *The nurses will **not** hold their convention in New Orleans.*

Sometimes the negative word is a word like *barely, scarcely,* or *hardly:*

She ***barely*** survived the automobile accident.

She ***hardly*** moved when the paramedic told her to get up.

Sometimes the negative words are formed with a negative prefix or suffix:

Positive: *He is happy.*

Negative: *He is **un**happy.*

Positive: *She is lively.*

Negative: *She is life**less.***

Usually there is only one negative word in a sentence. If you use two, one will cancel out the other:

Positive: *He is happy.*

Negative: *He is unhappy.*

Positive: *He is **not un**happy.* (*Note:* This does not mean that "he is happy." It merely means that "he is not unhappy." In this case, two negative words cancel out the negative without asserting the positive.)

In nonstandard dialects two or more negative words can be used to make a sentence negative, especially when the negative aspect is emphasized:

Positive: *Somebody always remembers to lock the garage door.*

Negative: ***Nobody never*** *remembers to lock the garage door.*

In nonstandard dialects a negative statement can also be formed by shifting a negative helping verb to the beginning of the sentence:

Negative: ***Don't nobody never*** *remember to lock the garage door.*

Exercises

All of the following statements are negative. Identify the standard English negative statements by circling the S and the nonstandard English statements by circling the N.

493

1. Nobody locked the bank vault at the end of the day.   S   N
2. Didn't nobody know the words of that song?   S   N
3. Young people don't barely remember anything about the assas-
   sination of Robert Kennedy.   S   N
4. There are not more than two bank officials that know the combination to the vault of the bank.   S   N
5. The manager spoke unkindly to the customer.   S   N
6. Don't throw no garbage in the street.   S   N

Change the statements you circled N to standard English.

_____

_____

_____

_____

_____

_____

APPENDIX 4:
USE OF *WHICH*

The word *which* has three functions. It can be used as an adjective:

Which *motorcycle do you want to buy?*

Patricia couldn't decide **which** *motorcycle to buy.*

In these sentences the adjective *which* modifies *motorcycle.*

    Which also is used as an interrogative pronoun (that is, as a pronoun that asks a question). As a pronoun it has an antecedent, and it substitutes for a noun or another pronoun:

"All of these motorcycles are on sale, but **which** *cost less than $800?" Patricia asked.*

In this sentence the antecedent of *which* is *motorcycles.*

    Which also is used as a relative pronoun that introduces a relative clause. In the following sentence *which* begins the relative clause "which is on display in the window":

The Kawasaki 175, **which** *is on display in the window, costs $750.*

The antecedent of *which* is *Kawasaki 175.*

    In nonstandard dialects *which* can be used as a conjunction like *and.*

Patricia was interested in buying the Kawasaki 175 **which** *I thought it was a great bargain.*

Notice that *which* joins two independent clauses "Patricia was interested in buying the Kawasaki 175" and "I thought it was a great bargain." In standard English these clauses would be joined with a conjunction:

Patricia was interested in buying the Kawasaki 175, **and** *I thought it was a great bargain.*

Another way to join these clauses would be to make one of them a dependent clause by using *which* as a relative pronoun:

Patricia was interested in buying the Kawasaki 175, which I thought was a great bargain.

Notice that the pronoun *it* has been deleted from the relative clause "which I thought was a great bargain" and that the antecedent of *which* is *Kawasaki 175.*

    In nonstandard dialects the conjunction *which* is sometimes preceded by the preposition *in:*

Patricia was interested in buying the Kawasaki 175 in which I thought it was a great bargain.

Exercises

Circle the N if the sentence is nonstandard and the S if it is standard. Then change the nonstandard sentences into standard English.

1. Which bridge in San Francisco has the longest span?   N   S
2. The Statue of Liberty, which has recently been restored, stands tall in New York harbor.   N   S
3. New York Air has been waging a price war with Eastern Airlines which now passengers have decided to take advantage of the low fares.   N   S
4. I couldn't decide which airline to fly.   N   S
5. They decided to go on a picnic which I decided it was a good idea.   N   S
6. Several cars were parked in my driveway in which that made it difficult for my sister to park her car.   N   S

_____

_____

_____

_____

_____

_____

_____

APPENDIX 5:
FORMING PLURALS

Overgeneralization of Pluralization Rule

The standard English pluralization rule of adding an *s* or *es* ending to a noun has many exceptions:

Singular	*Plural*
freshman	freshmen
ox	oxen
deer	deer
foot	feet

In nonstandard dialects these words are not always treated as exceptions. They are pluralized by adding an *s* or *es* ending, as follows: *freshmans, oxes, deers,* and *foots.* The pluralization rule is overgeneralized to apply in places where standard English does not require the *s* or *es* ending.

Hypercorrection

In nonstandard dialects sometimes a word is pluralized twice: *freshmens, childrens,* and *feets.* These are hypercorrect forms that result from adding *s* or *es* to the exceptional plural forms.

Pronunciation Differences

Some nonstandard plural forms of nouns are the results of differences in speech patterns. The nonstandard plural forms *knifes* and *wolfs* are examples. In standard English the "f" sound changes to a "v" sound when *knife* and *wolf* are pluralized:

Standard English		*Nonstandard English*	
Singular	*Plural*	*Singular*	*Plural*
knife	knives	knife	knifes
wolf	wolves	wolf	wolfs

Exercise

Some of the words in the following list illustrate these dialect plural noun forms. Put a check in front of each plural word that is nonstandard. Then change it to standard English.

497

_____ **1.** womens _____   _____ **6.** wifes _____

_____ **2.** cavities _____   _____ **7.** sheeps _____

_____ **3.** contributions _____   _____ **8.** mices _____

_____ **4.** fishes _____   _____ **9.** yourselfs _____

_____ **5.** leafs _____   _____**10.** thiefs _____

Plural Nouns with Quantifiers

A _quantifier_ is a word that indicates an amount or number. Words like _two, all, many, few,_ and _several_ are quantifiers that indicate plurality when they are added to nouns:

> two boys   many exceptions
> all the hats   several computers
> few opportunities

When these quantifiers are added to nouns in standard English, the nouns must be pluralized. But in nonstandard dialects the plural endings are often not used with nouns that have quantifiers:

> _Standard English_   _Nonstandard English_
> fifty cents   fifty cent
> many exceptions   many exception
> several ideas   several idea

In the nonstandard dialect the _s_ or _es_ plural ending is not needed because the quantifier alone is sufficient to indicate that the noun is plural. But in standard English we need to indicate plurality twice, in, for example, the phrase _fifty_ cents (with the quantifier _fifty_ and with the _s_ ending on _cent_).

Joining Plural Nouns

In nonstandard dialects when plural nouns are joined by a conjunction, both nouns do not have to be pluralized:

The boys _and_ girl _are saving to take a trip to New Mexico._

Notice the noun _girl_ has no _s_ ending, even though it is meant to be plural. The _s_ ending is not used because _girl_ is joined to _boys_ by the conjunction _and._ Standard English, however, requires both plural nouns to have _s_ endings:

The boys _and_ girls _are saving to take a trip to New Mexico._

How does the meaning of this sentence change in standard English when the _s_ ending on _girls_ is omitted?

498

Exercise

In the following passage underline all nonstandard English examples of quantifiers, nouns, and joined plural nouns. Then rewrite the entire passage in standard English.

There are three advertisement posted on the bulletin board outside my classroom. One is an advertisement for boys and girl to work at the restaurant on Broadway and Spring Street. Another is an advertisement asking people to send two dollar and twenty-five cent for a Coca-Cola T-shirt. The third advertisement is about college entrance requirements. It explains the step and procedures a student must take to gain admission to Duke University.

_____

_____

_____

_____

_____

_____

APPENDIX 6:
SHOWING POSSESSION

Standard English uses the possessive form of the noun to express possession:

Duke's mother works in a bakery on Saturdays.

Susan's husband's foot was injured when he leaped from the burning building.

Each of the possessive forms, *Duke's, Susan's,* and *husband's,* has an apostrophe and an *s* ending.

In nonstandard dialects the possessive forms of the nouns are not marked with an ending:

Duke mother works in a bakery on Saturdays.

Susan husband foot was injured when he leaped from the burning building.

Exercise

Circle the N for the sentences that are nonstandard and the S for those that are standard. Change the nonstandard sentences to standard English.

1. Sam's mother's watch always runs fast.   N   S
2. Susan's diamond bracelet fell from her wrist when she stumbled down the stairs.   N   S
3. The chef's white apron was stained with food.   N   S
4. Maxine wasn't certain that Vickie blouse would fit her.   N   S
5. Susan naughty baby wouldn't keep quiet during the movie.   N   S
6. Harold red and blue tie didn't match his green shirt.   N   S
7. No one told Harry that his brother car was in the repair shop.   N   S
8. The zipper in the lining of Eric's coat was broken.   N   S

There are also some differences in the standard English and nonstandard English use of pronouns to show possession. One difference is the use of possessive adjectives. In standard English the possessive forms of pronouns that are used as adjectives are *my, our, his, her, its, your* and *their.* In nonstandard English some of these possessive adjective forms are different. For example, *they* and *it* are used instead of *their* and *its*:

> Nonstandard
> *All the passengers fastened **they** safety belts when the pilot announced that the plane was about to land.*
> *My dog always wags **it** tail when it is hungry.*

Standard
*All the passengers fastened **their** safety belts when the pilot announced that the plane was about to land.*
*My dog always wags **its** tail when it is hungry.*

Another difference between standard English and nonstandard English is in the use of possessive pronouns. The standard English possessive pronouns are *mine, ours, his, hers, yours,* and *theirs.* Notice that *mine* is the only one that does not end with an *s* sound. In nonstandard dialects *mines* occurs.

Nonstandard
*That glass of wine on the kitchen table is **mines.***

Standard
*That glass of wine on the kitchen table is **mine.***

Exercise

Circle the N for those sentences that are nonstandard and the S for those that are standard. Then change the nonstandard ones to standard English.

1. When a banana is too ripe, it loses it bright yellow color.   N   S
2. All the pennies in that jar on the shelf are mines.   N   S
3. The soldiers were required to polish their shoes every day.   N   S
4. The explosion shook the door loose from its hinges.   N   S
5. Only a few of the students brought they textbooks to school.   N   S
6. I couldn't tell which of the baseball caps was mine.   N   S
7. All the runners had to wipe the mud off they shoes.   N   S

_____

_____

_____

_____

_____

_____

The verb *do* can be the main verb in the sentence, as in

*When Rori dances, she **does** it well.*

The verb *do* can also be a helping verb, as in

*Rori **does** dance well.*

The helping verb *does* forms a verb phrase with the main verb *dance*. When *do* is used as a helping verb, it indicates the tense for the verb phrase. Notice the difference in meaning for the following sentences:

*Vickie and Tracey **do** have the flu.*

*Vickie and Tracey **did** have the flu.*

Which sentence indicates that Vickie and Tracey still have the flu? That sentence is in the present tense. Which sentence indicates that Vickie and Tracey had the flu? That sentence is in the past tense. The present tense and the past tense are indicated by the helping verbs *does* and *did*, respectively. The main verb *have*, however, does not change when the helping verb changes but remains the same in both of the sentences.

In nonstandard dialects the main verb of a verb phrase sometimes changes when the helping verb is in the past tense:

> Present: *Vickie and Tracey **do have** the flu.*
> Past: *Vickie and Tracey **did had** the flu.*

Notice that the main verb changed from *have* to *had* in the past tense.

This kind of change also occurs with the helping verb phrase *used to* (usually written *use to* in nonstandard dialects).

> Nonstandard: *Vickie and Tracey **use to had** the flu.*
> Standard: *Vickie and Tracey **used to have** the flu.*

Exercises

Circle N for the nonstandard English sentences and S for the standard. Change the nonstandard sentences to standard English.

1. Harold does walk well with a cane.   N   S
2. Eric did visited several colleges before he chose this one.   N   S
3. My father use to worked on the railroad.   N   S

4. Did you remember to bring money for lunch? N S

5. When did you said that you would be able to visit Henry? N S

6. When Eric smoked, he did it in the bathroom so that the fumes would not annoy anyone. N S

_____

_____

_____

_____

_____

_____

In standard English verbs in the present tense have an *s* (or *es*) ending when the subject is *he, she,* or *it* (or any antecedent for these three pronouns).

*He **knows** how to use the software for this computer.*

*She **wishes** to be an astronaut.*

*When it **rains**, it **pours.***

If the verb is irregular, the form changes for *he, she,* or *it.*

*She **does** have the talent and interest to be an astronaut.*

*Warren **has** to work late tonight.*

In nonstandard dialects the *s* (or *es*) ending is often not used with the subjects *he, she,* and *it.*

*He **know** how to use the software for this computer.*

*She **wish** to be an astronaut.*

*When it **rain**, it **pour.***

The irregular verbs *have* and *do* also do not change their forms.

*She **do** have the talent and interest to be an astronaut.*

*Warren **have** to work late tonight.*

Exercises

Circle N for the nonstandard English sentences and S for the standard. Change the nonstandard sentences to standard English.

1. My new stove have two ovens.	N	S
2. When the carpenter come, he will repair the cracks in the staircase.	N	S
3. When I am working on my homework, the phone never stops ringing.	N	S
4. My boss do have to pay me this Friday.	N	S
5. In the early morning the bright sun shine through my window and always wake me up.	N	S

6. The baby always yell and screams when we take her to the doctor's office.   N   S

_____

_____

_____

_____

_____

_____

Base	Present	Past	Past Participle	Present Participle
act	act/acts	acted	acted	acting
admit	admit/admits	admitted	admitted	admitting
bar	bar/bars	barred	barred	barred
be	am/is/are	was/were	been	being
bear	bear/bears	bore	borne	bearing
begin	begin/begins	began	begun	beginning
bend	bend/bends	bent	bent	bending
benefit	benefit/benefits	benefited	benefited	benefiting
bet	bet/bets	bet	bet	betting
bind	bind/binds	bound	bound	binding
bite	bite/bites	bit	bit	bitten
bleed	bleed/bleeds	bled	bled	bleeding
blow	blow/blows	blew	blown	blowing
break	break/breaks	broke	broken	breaking
bring	bring/brings	brought	brought	bringing
build	build/builds	built	built	building
buy	buy/buys	bought	bought	buying
cast	cast/casts	cast	cast	casting
catch	catch/catches	caught	caught	catching
choose	choose/chooses	chose	chosen	choosing
clean	clean/cleans	cleaned	cleaned	cleaning
cling	cling/clings	clung	clung	clinging
come	come/comes	came	come	coming
control	control/controls	controlled	controlled	controlling
cost	cost/costs	cost	cost	costing
creep	creep/creeps	crept	crept	creeping
cut	cut/cuts	cut	cut	cutting
deal	deal/deals	dealt	dealt	dealing
deny	deny/denies	denied	denied	denying
dig	dig/digs	dug	dug	digging
dive	dive/dives	dived/dove	dived	diving
do	do/does	did	done	doing
draw	draw/draws	drew	drawn	drawing
drink	drink/drinks	drank	drunk	drinking
drive	drive/drives	drove	driven	driving
eat	eat/eats	ate	eaten	eating
fall	fall/falls	fell	fallen	falling
fear	fear/fears	feared	feared	fearing
feed	feed/feeds	fed	fed	feeding
fight	fight/fights	fought	fought	fighting
find	find/finds	found	found	finding
focus	focus/focuses	focused	focused	focusing
forget	forget/forgets	forgot	forgotten	forgetting
free	free/frees	freed	freed	freeing

Base	Present	Past	Past Participle	Present Participle
freeze	freeze/freezes	froze	frozen	freezing
fry	fry/fries	fried	fried	frying
get	get/gets	got	gotten	getting
give	give/gives	gave	given	giving
go	go/goes	went	gone	going
grind	grind/grinds	ground	ground	grinding
grow	grow/grows	grew	grown	growing
have	have/has	had	had	having
hear	hear/hears	heard	heard	hearing
hide	hide/hides	hid	hidden/hid	hiding
hit	hit/hits	hit	hit	hitting
hold	hold/holds	held	held	holding
hurt	hurt/hurts	hurt	hurt	hurting
keep	keep/keeps	kept	kept	keeping
know	know/knows	knew	known	knowing
lay	lay/lays	laid	laid	laying
lead	lead/leads	led	léd	leading
leave	leave/leaves	left	left	leaving
lend	lend/lends	lent	lent	lending
let	let/lets	let	let	letting
lie	lie/lies	lied	lied	lying
lie	lie/lies	lay	lain	lying
lose	lose/loses	lost	lost	losing
love	love/loves	loved	loved	loving
make	make/makes	made	made	making
mean	mean/means	meant	meant	meaning
meet	meet/meets	met	met	meeting
occur	occur/occurs	occurred	occurred	occurring
pay	pay/pays	paid	paid	paying
put	put/puts	put	put	putting
quit	quit/quits	quit	quit	quitting
read	read/read	read	read	reading
rely	rely/relies	relied	relied	relying
refer	refer/refers	referred	referred	referring
ride	ride/rides	rode	ridden	riding
rise	rise/rises	rose	risen	rising
rob	rob/robs	robbed	robbed	robbing
run	run/runs	ran	run	running
say	say/says	said	said	saying
see	see/sees	saw	seen	seeing
seek	seek/seeks	sought	sought	seeking
sell	sell/sells	sold	sold	selling
send	send/sends	sent	sent	sending
set	set/sets	set	set	setting
shake	shake/shakes	shook	shaken	shaking
shed	shed/sheds	shed	shed	shedding
shoot	shoot/shoots	shot	shot	shooting

Base	Present	Past	Past Participle	Present Participle
shut	shut/shuts	shut	shut	shutting
sing	sing/sings	sang	sung	singing
sink	sink/sinks	sank	sunk	sinking
sit	sit/sits	sat	sat	sitting
slam	slam/slams	slammed	slammed	slamming
sleep	sleep/sleeps	slept	slept	sleeping
slit	slit/slits	slit	slit	slitting
slug	slug/slugs	slugged	slugged	slugging
speak	speak/speaks	spoke	spoken	speaking
speed	speed/speeds	sped/ speeded	sped	speeding
spend	spend/spends	spent	spent	spending
spin	spin/spins	spun	spun	spinning
spring	spring/springs	sprang	sprung	springing
split	split/splits	split	split	splitting
spy	spy/spies	spied	spied	spying
stand	stand/stands	stood	stood	standing
steal	steal/steals	stole	stolen	stealing
stink	stink/stinks	stank	stank	stinking
stop	stop/stops	stopped	stopped	stopping
swear	swear/swears	swore	sworn	swearing
sweat	sweat/sweats	sweat/ sweated	sweat	sweating
sweep	sweep/sweeps	swept	swept	sweeping
swim	swim/swims	swam	swum	swimming
swing	swing/swing	swung	swung	swinging
take	take/takes	took	taken	taking
teach	teach/teaches	taught	taught	teaching
tear	tear/tears	tore	torn	tearing
tell	tell/tells	told	told	telling
think	think/thinks	thought	thought	thinking
throw	throw/throws	threw	thrown	throwing
transmit	transmit/transmits	transmitted	transmitted	transmitting
waste	waste/wastes	wasted	wasted	wasting
wear	wear/wears	wore	worn	wearing
weep	weep/weeps	wept	wept	weeping
whine	whine/whines	whined	whined	whining
win	win/wins	won	won	winning
wring	wring/wrings	wrung	wrung	wringing
write	write/writes	wrote	written	writing

INDEX

B

Bad, worse, worst, 400
Baldwin, James, "A Kitchen," 181–82;
    189, 195
"The Bear Who Let It Alone," James
    Thurber, 128
Been, being, 272
Being, been, 272
Berth, birth, 170
Best, good, better, 400
Better, good, best, 400
Birth, berth, 170
"Blessings of Emptiness," Elizabeth
    Hanson, 381–83
Brainstorming, 352, 392, 458

C

Capital, capitol, 120
Capitalization, 69
    defined, 72–75
Capitol, capital, 120
Caret, carrot, karat (carat), 170
Carrot, caret, karat (carat), 170
Categorization
    of details, 395–96
Clause, 151
    defined, 256
    dependent, 256–57
    independent, 151, 256–57
    relative, 260–64
Cliche, avoiding, 196, 238
Clustering, 392, 458
Collective nouns, 111, 425
Combining ideas in sentences, 205–16
Comma
    with conjunctions, 208–11
    defined, 372
    with dependent clauses, 256–60
    in relative clauses, 263–64
    rules for use, 372–73
Comma splice
    correcting, 217, 269
    defined, 216–17
Commands, 165
Comparative forms 398–401
Comparing and contrasting words, list
    of, 399
Complement, of verb, 114

Conclusion, 462–63
Conclusion words, list of, 463
Conjunctions, 205–208
    adverbial, list of, 212
    defined, 206
    subordinating, list of, 206
    use of commas with, 208
    (see also *joining words*)
Consonants, 329
Consultant staff of dictionary, 50
Contractions, 78–80
Conventions, 27, 69–82
    abbreviations and numbers, 69, 75–77
    apostrophes, 69, 78–80
    capitalization, 69, 72–75
    hyphenation, 69, 71–72
    manuscript form, 69–70
    word boundaries, 69, 81–82
Could have, not *could of*, 78
Council, counsel, 170
Counsel, council, 170
Critical thinking, defined, 7

D

Dates, use of commas in, 372
Decent, descent, dissent, 272–73
Definition, in dictionary, 47
    common, 98
    special context for, 98
    specialized, 98
Definition in an essay
    extended, 354–55
    group, 354
    synonym, 354
Dell, Floyd, "When I Discovered I Was
    Poor," 130–32; 136–37, 141, 142
Dependence, dependents, 122
Dependent clauses, 256–57
Dependents, dependence, 122
Descent, decent, dissent, 272–73
Describe-a-Person Worksheet, 239–40
Desert, dessert, 220
Dessert, desert, 220
Details, 22, 26
    in argument, 460–61
    in comparison and contrast, 395–96
    in definition, 356
    in description, 192–94, 241–42
    in directions (process), 297

Fragments, 164–69
   defined, 165
   dependent clauses and, 268
Free writing, 17–20
   function in writing process, 21
   (see also *focused writing*)
"Fried Chicken," Jim Villas, 281–85
Future perfect tense, 470, 476
Future tense, 437

G

Galarza, Ernesto, "A Mexican House,"
   177–78; 192, 194, 195, 242
General statements, 356, 395
Goetz, Bernhard, 436
Good, best, better, 400
Grammar, defined, 27

H

Hanson, Elizabeth, "Blessings of
   Emptiness," 381–83
has, had, have, as helping verbs, 471
Hear, here, 82
Helping verbs, lists of, 414–15, 432
Here, hear, 82
Homonyms, 81–85, 120–24
Hughes, Langston, "Salvation," 93–94;
   103, 142
Hyperbole, 294–95
Hyphen, defined, 71
Hyphenation, 69, 71–72

I

Idea wheel, 191
Illusion, allusion, 272
Indefinite pronouns, 321, 426–27
Indentation, 70, 242
Indirect quotation (report), 91–92
Inference, defined, 6
Introduction, 356, 394–95
   in argument, 462
Irony, 142, 350
Irregular verbs, 418, 474
It's, its, 82
Its, it's, 82
Joining words (conjunctions), 206
   (see also *combining*)

Journal, defined, 32
   and Additional Writing Assignments,
     32, 86, 124–25, 173–76, 223–24,
     278, 336–37, 376, 440, 484–85

K

Karat (carat), caret, carrot, 170
"A Kitchen," James Baldwin, 181–82
Knew, new, 121
Know, no, 121
Know, now, 273

L

Language
   appropriate, 22, 57, 142–43 (see also
     tone, voice)
   creole, 56
   dialect, 56
   even-handed, 463
   figurative, 195–96
   levels of, 56–57
   native, 51
   official, 51
   patois, 56
   slang, 57–58
"Language," Malcolm X, 34–36
Least, little, less, 400
Less, fewer, 400
Less, least, little, 400
Letters, use of commas in, 373
Lexicographer, 49
Linguists, 49
Linking words (adverbial conjunctions),
   211–13
   list of, 211
Lists, 296
Little, least, less, 400
Locating words, list of, 195
Loose, lose, 273
Lose, loose, 273

M

Main point, of story, 142
main-point statement, 142
   of argument, 457
   (see also *lead sentence, statement of
     purpose, topic sentence*)

Malcolm X, "Language," 34–36, 44, 45
Manuscript form, 69–70
Margins, 70
Metaphor, 136–37, 195–96
"A Mexican House," Ernesto Galarza, 177–78
Middle drafts, 22, 309
Modals, 432

N

Names, use of commas in, 373
Native language, 51
Naval, navel, 170
Navel, naval, 170
Near-homonyms, 218–23, 272–77
New, knew, 121
No, know, 273
Nonessential elements, use of commas in, 373
Nor, 207
Nouns
    as adjectives, 310–11
    attributive, 310–11
    collective, 111, 425
    defined, 28, 111, 309–15
    how they function in sentences, 309
    how to identify, 309
    plurals of, 309–15
    possessive forms of, 365–67
    proper, 28, 309
Now, know, 273
Numbers and abbreviations, 69
    defined, 75–77

O

Official language, 51
Opening and closing phrases in letters, commas in, 373
Order, 22, 26
    in argument, 461–63
    in comparison and contrast, 396–98
    in definition, 356–58
    in description, 194–95, 241–42
    in directions (process), 297–98
    of the essay, 398
    in narration, 105, 109

P

Pantomime, 88
Paragraph, 243
    conclusion, 462–63
    indentation of, 70, 242–43
    introductory, 356, 394–95, 462
    lead sentence in, 242
    topic sentence and, 356–57
    unified, 242
Participles as adjectives, 477–78
Participles with verbs, 478
Parts of speech
    adjectives as, 28
    adverbs as, 28
    articles as, 29
        definite, 29
        indefinite, 29
    conjunctions as, 29
        coordinating, 29
        subordinating, 29
    defined, 27
    nouns as, 28
        proper, 28
    prepositions as, 28
    pronouns as, 28
    verbs, 28
Passed, past, 82–83
Passive voice, 479–82
    defined, 479
    perfect tense, 479
Past, passed, 82
Past participles, 471–72
    as adjectives, 477–78
    irregular verbs as, 474
Past tenses, 429–37
    continuous, 430
    simple, 429–30
Patience, patients, 122
Patients, patience, 122
Peace, piece, 83
Pedal, peddle, 170
Peddle, pedal, 170
Peer, pier, 170
Perfect tenses, 471–77
    future, 470, 476
    past, 470, 473–76
    present, 470–73
Period, 164
    in quotations, 91

R

Regionalisms, 54
Relative clauses, 260–68
Relative pronouns, 260–62
Rewriting, defined, 21–22
Roots, defined, 9
Rough draft, 21
Run-ons, 216–17
   correcting, 269

S

Safire, William, 436
"Salvation," Langston Hughes, 93–94
Semicolon, 211–16
Semantics, defined, 49
Sentence
   combining (joining) ideas in, 205–16
   defined, 151
   expanding, 151–64
   linking ideas with semicolon in,
      211–16
   subordinate conjunctions in, 256–57
Series, use of commas in, 373
Setting, 104, 142
Should have, not *should of*, 78
Simile, 237–38
   defined, 195–96
   in analogy, 456
Slang, 57–58
"Smokers Have Rights, Too," Ernest van
   den Haag, 444–45
Special context, of a word, 98
Spelling
   demons, 481–83
   homonyms, 82–85, 120–24, 169–73
   near-homonyms, 218–23, 272–77
   making your own list, 29–31
   rules
      ie, ei, 332
      for past tense verbs and *ing* forms,
         438–39
      pluralization, 329–32
      q-u, 332
      sede, ceed, cede, 332
Standard English, defined, 56
Statement of purpose, 241
   (see also *lead sentence, main-point
      statement, topic sentence*)

Statue, Stature, Statute, 274
Stature, Statue, Statute, 274
Statute, Statue, Stature, 274
Subject
   expansion of, 155–57
   of sentence, 27, 110, 112
Subject–verb agreement, 155, 417–28
Subordinating conjunctions, 255–56
   list of, 255
Subordination, 254–68
   defined, 254
Suffixes, 13
   defined, 9
   word classes and, 452
Superlative forms, 399–401
S-ending verbs, 417–19
Syfers, Judy, "Why I Want a Wife,"
   341–42; 356, 357
Synonyms, defined, 55, 244–45

T

Tense, 114, 413–38, 470–76
   continuous past, 430
   continuous present, 414–15
   future, 437–38
   future perfect, 476–77
   past perfect, 473–76
   present perfect, 471–73
   simple past, 429–30
   simple present, 414
Than, then, 220–21
That, in relative clause, 260–61
Their, there, they're, 83
Themes, 141
Then, than, 220–21
There, their, they're, 83
Thesis statement, 142
They're, their, there, 83
Thorough, though, through, 221
Though, thorough, through, 221
Threw, through, 121
Through, though, thorough, 221
Through, threw, 121
Thurber, James, "The Bear Who Let It
   Alone," 128
Time line, 109, 141
Time words and phrases, 413–14
Titles, placement of in composition, 69
To, too, two, 83

515